AmV

GERMAN ART IN THE 20TH CENTURY

GERMAN ART
IN THE 20TH CENTURY

by *Franz Roh*

with additions by Juliane Roh

NEW YORK GRAPHIC SOCIETY LTD.

GREENWICH, CONNECTICUT

FOR JULIANE ROH

The original German edition of this book was created and
published in 1958 by F. Bruckmann Verlag, Munich, Germany,
under the title *Geschichte der Deutschen Kunst von 1900 bis zur
Gegenwart*. For this English language edition, Juliane Roh has
contributed additional material covering the period from 1955
to 1968.
Translated from the German by Catherine Hutter and edited
by Julia Phelps.

Library of Congress Card Catalogue No. 68–12367.

© in Germany by F. Bruckmann KG, Munich
Reproduction rights for text and illustrations reserved for all countries.

Printed in Germany

CONTENTS

By "German Art" we mean here "Art in Germany," the art that developed on German soil, even if it was created by a Swiss (Obrist), an Austrian (Kokoschka), a Russian (Kandinsky) or a Hungarian (Moholy). This definition should not be interpreted as nationalistic presumption, for cultural environment is more significant than the birth certificate. Justifiably the French consider the Spaniard Picasso and the Russian Chagall as members of the School of Paris.

Moreover, we will sometimes pursue the further development of artists forced to leave Germany, so that we may present a full picture of their personalities.

We do not share the sceptical view that it is impossible to survey and evaluate one's own time. There is some subjectivity in all philosophical judgments. Even epochs distant in time have undergone extreme fluctuations in assessment–one has only to think of how much opinions have changed in the course of the last century on the late antique Laocoön or on the aesthetic value of Ottonian miniatures. The advantage of a period closer in time lies in our ability to interpret its works more intensively out of the spirit of the era. For our study we have had at our disposal a virtually unbroken documentation. I have known most of these artists personally.

The two-dimensional arts, Painting and Graphics, will be discussed first, then the three-dimensional expression of Sculpture, and finally Architecture, the structure within which everything is linked.

INTRODUCTION

Art Movements

Expressionism, Constructivism, New Realism, Surrealism, Nonobjectivism, Tachism – all these "isms" are cited as characteristic of our century. And there will certainly be further variations, for styles in art sweep over us like the stars in the sky. From 1900 to approximately 1940, however, we experienced such diverse world events and modes of creation that we may assume we face an era in which this variety of form and expression will be fused. Periods of synthesis tend to follow revolutionary phases; they should not be cursorily dismissed as signs of exhaustion.

Impressionism was followed in Germany by a group consciousness that was promoted at first by the artists themselves and subsequently was supported by the critics. In contrast, the next stage was characterized by the proliferation of completely individual modes of expression. Since then it has become evident that the recent emergence of Tachism as the dominant movement has led us virtually back to the point of our departure–Impressionism–for this latest method is actually a nonobjective form of Impressionism.

In our century, the development of expression and of the arts has been quick to change. Still, we must be cautious about attaching too much importance to this unstable tempo, for every era's judgment of itself seems to be distorted by lack of perspective. Conversely, we tend to ascribe too much uniformity to eras long past and to be unaware of their actual tensions. Seen from a greater distance in time, the many "isms" of our century may one day be recognized as the various nuances of one and the same antirealism. For all of them have one thing in common: gone is the artist's desire to mirror objects in a prescribed world; instead he wants to depict the forces that may lie behind them. In Impressionism it was the life-stream of light and air, in Expressionism the power of color, in Surrealism the fantasy of the dream. Each time a different style led far beyond objective reality, until the latter disappeared absolutely in abstract painting. This four-part development could be seen as a unity, as a gradual crescendo impelling the work of art to become increasingly the organization of inner expression. We may understand the finale of this development better if we refer cautiously to the analogy of absolute music; as in absolute music, the means of painting–that is to say line, structure, color and space–have become an end in themselves; their importance lies in their intrinsic value.

Inner Poverty ?

To look upon this consistent devaluation of the objects of the outside world as a dehumanizing force is, I believe, mistaken. If this were so, we would have to see something inhuman in other art forms, such as architecture and music, that shun a relationship to the world around them. Controversies of this nature bring to mind an academic question that once played an important role in post-medieval culture: was a representation of landscape or still life of equal value to a composition with human figures ? In our day and age, questions about the character of an object–we could go so far as to say questions about the object per se–have become irrelevant. Some interpret this as a *Verlust der Mitte*, a departure from the middle way; others see it as a purification process through which the arts have become more specific.

In the development of man, art first served magic, then religion; later it furthered the discovery and reproduction of external nature, however strongly the emotions of the artist may have been mirrored in his work. By casting off the straitjacket of these dominions through titanic processes of transformation, the artist has probably penetrated to the very core of all artistic endeavor.

There are many who believe that the painting of symbols alone must be monotonous, but I believe we can demonstrate that in abstract art the greatest contrasts are again possible. A concentric or eccentric perception of life, a harmonious or demonic world outlook, an optimistic or pessimistic display of color, a surface or spatial arrangement, a linear or a painterly form of expression, an open or closed organization of form–all may be realized in abstract art.

Germany's Exceptional Position

In Paris, which may still be considered the decisive art center, it has often been said that Germany's contribution to twentieth-century art was belated, or even a coarse variation of French developments. In the meantime, however, a fairer view has been accepted, and we can now determine accurately in which cases modern art emerged later in Germany than in France, in which it developed simultaneously in the two countries, and which are the occasions when German art should be given priority.

In architecture and industrial design, with the activity of Van de Velde at the turn of the century and of the Bauhaus in the twenties, we have instances where the decisive stimulus originated in Germany. Similarly, in the plastic arts Hermann Obrist developed abstract sculpture in Munich shortly after 1900 when it had not even been thought of in other countries, France included. As for painting, we have Kandinsky: in Germany around 1910 he created one of the first forms of purely abstract painting; its particular quality was not developed further elsewhere until much later, after his emigration to Paris in 1933. Paul Klee discovered his sublime dream world in Germany, and is recognized as a precursor of related styles. In other categories, different countries led the way.

On the whole, temporal discrepancies in the artistic development of nations seem to shrink as the delight in exchange intensifies. The numerous exhibitions circulated throughout the world and the color reproductions distributed to all four corners of the earth gradually produce simultaneity of progress. Such a joint development that does away with the isolation of former cultures could be considered regrettable without that prevailing diversity which is guaranteed by outstanding artistic personalities, or if typological schisms of stubbornly conflicting styles did not arise periodically. For many countries the cultural stability that was determined solely by isolation has been lost, but regional characteristics of style undoubtedly remain, thanks to such characteristics as the variety of landscape, local traditions and mores, and special rhythms of the local idiom.

German Impressionism, for instance, was completely different from French. Liebermann's paintings were sandier gray in tone and more severe in form. Corinth's pictures were more sensually aggressive, rougher in texture than the late works of Manet. Nolde's pictures and those of the *Brücke* group were coarser, more barbaric, more massive in effect than those of the French Fauves of almost the same period. Nolde may remind us of Rouault, but the color contrasts of the latter seem more harmonious. And when one compares paintings of the German *Blaue Reiter* group with various works of the French Cubists, one sees that the French works are more systematic and formal in effect, due to the Latin rationale, even when the object is fragmented. In Germany form became less an end in itself. Kandinsky (in his early works) lashed out furiously and improvised; Franz Marc used cubic refractions only as counterpoint for his color harmonics. In France, even with Picasso, the bizarre remains somehow under the control of rationale and taste, whereas the German masters often strove for a freer, more primitive expression. In the most recent abstract art, such regional contrasts also play a part.

Artistic Decentralization in Germany

The development of the arts in France in the twentieth century took place mainly in Paris, traditionally the great art center dominating the entire country; in Germany the development occurred in various places as a result of the absence of political centralization and consequent emergence of cultural centers in Germany's many principalities and small states.

Berlin was the focal point for the late German Impressionists because Liebermann, Corinth and Slevogt spent the most important years of their lives there, and the metropolis, as is usually the case, also sheltered the leading art dealers and collectors. Berlin remained important for later periods as well, but German Expressionism originated in Dresden where the Brücke group was founded, even though the artists later moved to the German capital.

Munich had already gained prominence at the turn of the century with the *Jugendstil* and became important subsequently through the Blaue Reiter group. Art in Frankfurt was transformed by the personality of Max Beckmann. A bold artistic life burgeoned in Cologne with Dadaism and the originality of Max Ernst and his disciples. Stuttgart received its artistic character from Adolf Hölzel, Oscar Schlemmer and Willi Baumeister. The little town of Weimar became the center of a new art form through Van de Velde, and after him, through the Bauhaus, which later moved to Dessau.

The art academies scattered across the country only partially served these new movements, but they periodically became centers of attraction for the aspiring young student by appointing interesting personalities, as was done in Düsseldorf, Breslau and Hamburg.

Although all special fields within a culture exhibit specific structural characteristics so that they diverge when one tries to compare their development, a certain mutual *Zeitgeist* may be said to prevail. In our epoch it seems that all fields of activity have thrown off some alien element or other in order to become more specific. Painting seeks independence from earlier representational forms. A new emotional lyricism evocatively shakes off many syntactic limitations. Modern physics, concentrating ever more intensely on mathematics, indulges in obscure abstractions. In art as in science, the end-effect is also supposed to illuminate, perhaps even lay bare, the method used to bring about the result. In both disciplines the formula dominates rather than the object, and instead of being evaluated rationally and technically, everything is conceived as hermetic. Einstein admitted that the most exciting thing we can experience is acquaintance with the mystical.

The growing interest in inner expression, which in painting and the plastic arts became more and more an end in itself, at first brought with it an increasing alienation from the objects of the outside world which had been mirrored in earlier art, no matter how subjectively. Painting next proceeded to abandon also the illusionistic space created by perspective, for which art had had no need prior to the Renaissance. With Impressionism perspective began to lose importance once again. The painters of the twentieth century speak constantly of "*die Heilige Fläche*", the sacred plane; since they wish to avoid imitation of external nature, they confine the representation of objects to a single visual plane. In the history of art such procedures have been introduced whenever there has been a desire to pass from mere reproduction to symbolic presentation, and nature becomes simply a starting point for the projection of inner expression. At any rate, the result is a complete amalgamation of outer and inner experience, through which life is conceived more and more as a single, gigantic process.

For the same reason, German poetry, from the late Rilke through Trakl to Gottfried Benn, tends more and more to abandon all description in order to give expression to mysterious perceptions through a system of sounds. In the novel many authors refuse to use an objectified plot, chronologically devised. Their efforts are bent toward mirroring reality through the opinions of their characters, through fluctuations of memory, flashbacks and projections, or, as in Joyce, by a flood of simultaneous associations. Drama often abandons the traditional boxlike stage separated from the audience, and the old unity of time and place as well, in order to join poet, poem and listeners in unique fashion. Music rises out of the close confines of fixed tonality and passes from one key to another. Often the conception of key is abandoned completely. Dissonance is accepted as an insoluble end in itself and at the same time as the symbol of a life that remains painful.

Today only the more conservative creators, who also continue to do valuable work, cling to perspective in painting, tonality in music and chronological sequence in narrative. In the visual arts also dissonance is often an end in itself, and extreme liberties are permitted in color and form. But the observer who is not wholly attuned tends to look upon every true union of creativity and life as "barbarism" whenever it becomes discordant.

Modern architecture has also expanded its conceptions of unity. The architect felt constricted by the closed, boxed-in room; now he plans interiors with as many rooms as possible opening out and encroaching on one another; the whole is held together by glass walls in order to make another link with free space, that of the exterior. The dividing supports are drawn inward so as to be hidden from the outside, giving the floors an effect of floating in space.

Science has discovered that a too-facile conception of basic principles has prevailed. Greater caution is observed in the formulation of exact forecasts. Psychologists no longer place as much value as they once did on human consciousness and refer more and more to the powers of the subconscious, which drives us all. Freud influenced Surrealism and its *expression automatique*; here the object world seems as two-faced as the soul of man in psychoanalysis. Biology tells us of the capricious mutation of genes; atomic research introduces an irregularity coefficient into the motion of the most minute particles; the theoreticians of physics draw space and time together. In modern politics, whatever trend is followed, ever closer attention is being paid to undercurrents of collectivism (mass psychology, etc.). The relativity of power has been exposed, but so has that of our social structure. Many doctrines, materialistic interpretations of history included, now deal with a destabilizing coefficient which formerly was often overlooked. In today's philosophy we find the idea of *Grenzsituationen* (limit-situations, Jaspers) and *Angst* (anxiety, Sartre) playing an ever greater role.

All such attitudes reveal not only uncertainty, but also a productive broadening of our approach to life. And as always, the various fields lie in mysterious connection with one another, producing a universal *Zeitgeist*. That the procedure itself sometimes seems more interesting than the final result could be interpreted as a refinement of our thought processes.

Today we realize that the so-called laws of nature which we lay down are always replies to the questions we ask of the universe. In this sense all experience, scientific experience included, is today seen "subjectively." In our exploration of nature we fashion it "thoughtfully." But that is just what the modern artist is constantly stressing. Faced with this attitude it seems senseless to deplore subjectivity of expression in abstract art only. Even in the representational works of our time the artist has been aware of the tension between his model in nature and the pictorial structure he is creating, and he has often had to struggle to resolve this relationship.

At the same time many creative artists see a secret union between themselves and earlier phases of mankind in which a form of calligraphy, equally unrealistic, predominated. Kandinsky and Klee reverted to a cryptography of inner communication, but like all expression of this type, theirs differs from those of earlier cultures in its lack of the compulsory overtones of magic and religion through which every work of art was then approachable. Today's calligraphy speaks primarily to kindred spirits.

But we should not reproach the artist of today with this reservation, for it lies in the nature of all modern culture, in which the value judgments of the individual prevail over those of society. The abstract artist will no longer be so lonely when the public, still attuned to the realism of past centuries, has divested itself of the idea that it must find repeated everywhere the objects of our external world. In absolute music, which is met for the most part with appropriate understanding, these cultural, prefixed symbols are lacking.

German Impressionism

The first major movement we must examine is Impressionism. It had developed in France over the last thirty years of the nineteenth century but was transplanted to Germany only around 1900–and then in a very general way. Liebermann, Slevogt, Corinth, Uhde, Trübner, Zügel, all of whom belonged more or less to the movement, proceeded from the momentary appearance of objects and sought to achieve a sketchlike, unstudied effect by dissolving their plasticity. They achieved only partially that luminous division of color in complementary stages so much stressed by the French.

Max Liebermann (1847–1935) started with a dark-toned, highly objective realism which places him somewhere between Millet, Courbet, and the seventeenth-century Dutch painters. But from the beginning he shunned all the anecdotal aspects that had dominated the genre painting of the nineteenth century. "The fascination of the naked truth" was his goal early in life. "If it is already beyond my powers to paint a goat as rich in form, color and motion as I see in the animal standing before me, how could I possibly paint Wallenstein's Death?" Liebermann's development as a painter falls between the muted "objective" realism of a Courbet and the "subjective" realism of a Manet. Not until shortly before 1900 did his style become more relaxed and begin to absorb color and light. Objects became the conveyers of atmosphere. Humans, animals and plants suddenly seemed to be woven of the same substance. "Drawing is omission," he now declared.

Bergson's philosophy of a general *élan vital* had stirred many Germans. Objects were to appear only as the emanations of a general life force. But the impatient strokes which now appear on Liebermann's canvases are still united by the same cool discipline that always dominated his paintings, even when the subject was rearing horses or excited polo players.

In his portraits, to which he devoted himself increasingly after 1900, we sense a strong psychological approach. The person portrayed is sharply individualized. Every portrait should include a nuance of caricature, he declared in true Berlin style. This statement was directed against the "refined", dark glamorizing style which Lenbach, for one, had cultivated before Liebermann. And with his psychological approach, Liebermann was a step ahead of the French Impressionists.

In his landscapes he favored ash-gray tones. His dry, grainy color seems to contain some of the sand of Brandenburg or the asphalt of Berlin. But no one can say that he was not truly a gifted painter. His Prussian, puritanical spirit, evident in his caustic Berlin humor, consciously sought to express what was temperate, even dry. And he deviated from the French Impressionists in that his later garden landscapes recede in depth and are dominated by a latent geometry. In his paintings that include several figures, this is again evident in the handling of the foreground. The French Impressionists would have none of this geometry; instead they developed a glowing sense of color. But just as it would be unfair to underestimate the gray coolness of Franz Hals–a favorite of Liebermann's–as compared with the mysterious warmth of Rembrandt, one should not measure Liebermann's austere color against the brilliant scale of Monet or Renoir, both painters Liebermann admired.

This Berlin master, son of a well-to-do manufacturer, showed great independence of opinion in his writings as well as his paintings, and he played a decisive role in the founding of the Berlin Secession. With ready wit he spoke up against the reactionary influences of the time, as personified by the court

Max Liebermann
Polo, 1902

Max Liebermann
Huis ter Duin,
1913

painter Anton von Werner, the art historian Henry Thode, and the Emperor Wilhelm II himself. He fought at first for a vital realism, but later for freedom of color as understood by the Impressionists. He wrote about Israels, Degas, and the woodcuts of Manet. His work, *Die Phantasie in der Malerei (Fantasy in the Art of Painting)*, is a belated German acknowledgment of impressionistic realism. He differentiated between literary and pictorial fantasy, yet he made a statement that should not be forgotten today: every *good* realistic painting always includes a hidden act of transformation. In Impressionism, the seed was already planted that was to lead to the emancipation of the media of painting which broadened in such extraordinary fashion in our century. Liebermann already declared that it was a matter of indifference whether one was painting a Madonna or a head of cabbage; he went so far as to quote a sentence by Schiller which was later to become very appropriate: "There lies the real artistic secret of the master–he effaces the original material through the form."

Liebermann's work as a graphic artist also had an effect on the evolution of German art. In 1887, when his steady activity as an etcher began, we first see dusky depths on which the stylus "paints" a blending of light and shade. Around 1897 the forms stand out more sharply against the white paper; using drypoint, he sought clearer contrasts. A third stage begins in 1906. The lines are even more freely separated from their white background, producing intense light areas against fewer, deeper shadows. The individual is stressed and, by the same token, the continuously varied self-portraits are increasingly important. From this period, too, date Liebermann's rolling landscapes with riders on the white sand. He now turned more and more to lithography as a quick form of communication. Whenever he undertook book illustration, he translated everything into contemporary terms–whether illustrating Kleist's short tales or the novellas of Goethe. As Liebermann lived for eighty-eight years, his work, typically, underwent three stages of evaluation: first, one in which his realism was violently attacked; second, one in which it was viewed with the highest regard; and finally, a stage in which he himself was unable to recognize a style which was in the ascendancy.

Max Slevogt (1868–1932), born a generation after Liebermann, studied at the Academy of Fine Arts in Munich. He left south Germany at the turn of the century and after a short stay in Frankfurt settled in Berlin. There he was exposed to Impressionism and he became a disciple. "I admired Manet so much because through him I could sense what made the world so beautiful." Slevogt brought German painting into the great European current. "Such a joyful, thunderous stream of strength, health and beauty issues forth from the culture of France that we must not fail to honor this enormous bounty, especially since we are so prone to recognize the fact that Germany gave the world an incredible abundance of music in the same century."

If Liebermann's Impressionism is austere, the effect of Slevogt's is lighter and above all richer in color. Here bold inspiration won over solid construction. No muted gray hues, but instead autumnal splendor in his landscapes. His palette was certainly influenced by Tiepolo's paintings in Würzburg, where he went to school, and perhaps also by the landscape of the western Palatinate to which he returned every summer. Light greens, gleaming yellows, gay blues, vibrate in his paintings. Whereas Monet's sparkling color seems in time to become more subdued, with Slevogt the particles of color remain surprisingly lively. In his portraits, which are not all of the same high quality, he stresses psychological elements more than the French painters, who translated everything into the realm of great painting in a more impersonal way. Slevogt's spirited portrait of the Portuguese singer D'Andrade gives one a sense of the musical-dramatic vitality of the painter, who himself wanted to be a singer. Slevogt painted individual portraits and pictures with many figures (sometimes in rather jumbled compositions), but above all pure landscapes. He started off with a dark palette which he gradually lightened. Slevogt was curiously attracted to murals. In 1912 he painted some quite impudent scenes on the walls of a pavilion on the Gadow estate. Pompeii, Tiepolo and Slevogt are combined here in a singular fashion. The compositions give the effect of having been improvised in the lightest calligraphy, as if fleetingly sketched water-colors were all the painter intended. Other commissions for this type of work followed.

Among his most lively work is the series of Egyptian subjects in the Dresden Museum, painted after a trip with friends to Egypt. Sometimes series of smaller paintings, such as those he executed for the Bavarian court, turn out to be more rewarding than his larger, overly diffuse works.

As a graphic artist, Slevogt displayed a delight in inventing fables that we find rarely in his paintings: peculiar inventions appear, strange capers, some with an epigrammatical twist which are reminiscent of the nineteenth century. But he does not penetrate the full content of what he wants to illustrate, as Menzel might have done; rather, he lets his message dart at you from an incidental point of the story as his strokes flash out in an improvised fashion across the surface. While Liebermann's illustrations confine themselves to more or less normal subject matter, Slevogt seeks the eccentric. His "black scenes," a series of etchings, appear in 1905. In lithography he attempts to go beyond the achievements of Goya and Daumier, but the effect is more playful. Yet he certainly enriched the black and white scale by his virtuosity. His lithograph *Sinbad* (1906) no longer appears on a page by itself but wavers into the text, and in his illustrations for *Lederstrumpf* (Cooper's *Leatherstocking Tales*), everything he does defies

Max Slevogt
Village
near Höhenreit,
1913

Lovis Corinth. In the Slaughterhouse, 1893 • Stuttgart, Staatsgalerie

bibliophilic custom. Whether we are dealing with the Arabian Nights, Indian lore or the Homeric hero Achilles, his figures are always twirling around like little furies devoured by light. His *tusch* (ink wash) lithographs for *Cellini* play around the text like rococo vignettes. In his etchings for *The Magic Flute*, he lets the liveliest scenes surge around parts of the score in an impressionistic interpretation of Mozart's more serious musical world. He so inspired the admiring craftsmen who executed the woodcuts for his illustrations for a book of fairytales that they reproduced completely his most temperamental little strokes, even in the much less tractable medium of the woodcut.

Lovis Corinth (1858–1925) stands between a sensuous, substantial kind of realism (which at first horrified people because of its coarse point of view), and a free flowing, impressionistic and colorful style (Plate I).

When dealing with sensual women, boldly interpreted Greek or Christian mythology, or landscapes bursting with life, he was more forceful than Liebermann or Slevogt. He attended the Academy of Fine Arts in Munich and the Academie Julian in Paris, and lived nine years in Munich; then in 1900 he moved to Berlin, married the painter Charlotte Behrend, and became president of the Berlin Secession. His powerful naturalism was such a drastic protest against the idealistic German classicism of Anselm Feuerbach and Hans von Marées, and also against the pseudo-vital pictorial rhythms of the Jugendstil, that he was called the butcher of painting. Although he turned his back on the art gallery tone of the nineteenth century, he favored a scattering of dull grays; everything is created out of the wet paint in an absolute furor. He threw himself into the force of life and wanted to make the work of art visible *in statu nascendi*. His close friend, the poet Eulenberg, said of him, "The strong smell of hides in his father's tannery evidently overpowered the boy at an early age." He painted in slaughter houses, "amid stiff cadavers, steaming stomachs and glistening entrails." He even saw the growth of plants in an animalistic fashion. The forcefulness of the brush was more important to him than impressionistic luminosity. He continued to struggle tenaciously with old-fashioned mythological compositions, although they did not suit his sensual approach to realism. In his subject matter we find Golgotha, St. Anthony,

Lovis Corinth. Storm on Cap Ampeglio, 1912 · Dresden, Staatliche Gemäldegalerie

Samson, Odysseus, Mars and Zeus. Great projects (*Perseus and Andromeda*, 1900) stand beside overwhelming and labored compositions (*The Temptation of St. Anthony*, 1908). The French Impressionists had wisely renounced this dated content, but Corinth was un-French, like his great pupil, Max Beckmann: two demonic masters, the first a product of Realism, the second of Expressionism.

Corinth's goddesses behave like bouncing wenches; his hard drinking heroes speak a cab-driver's German. Today he touches us most when he approaches life without any literary circumlocution, in his landscapes, in his abundant still lifes, in his animal pictures. His friend Max Halbe assures us that "he painted without first drawing, straight onto the canvas, and worked in the wet paint. With a portrait he often began by setting a nose or a pair of eyebrows or a mouth on the canvas, and let the rest emanate from them, executing what followed with a very quick hand."

He began with a massive, dull display of color which clung powerfully to the objects portrayed, until his technique became increasingly free. Gradually Corinth achieved the broad color style that paved the way to his later period. A stroke left him with a chronically shaking hand which influenced his style rather movingly. The effect of the involuntary vibrato of his brushstrokes is not that of the feebleness of age, but of a deeper vitality. In his late self-portraits he sometimes captured his robust, yet already failing individuality, with demonic grandeur. The Walchensee landscapes of his last years are filled with convulsive torrents of color and look as if they had been whipped up by a storm. They abandon completely the realistic pictorial legacy of the nineteenth century and pass to the freest forms of expression. The next generation could use them as a starting point. Kirchner, speaking as an Expressionist, stated, "At first he was mediocre, but in the end he was truly great."

The oeuvre of *Fritz von Uhde* (1848–1911) takes us a short way into the twentieth century. We need touch on him only briefly, but he was one the first Germans who accepted the wave of French Impressionism. In this he was a step ahead of Liebermann, and therefore for some time many eyes were turned on him and his ever brighter palette and lighter style which contradicted academic methods. He painted people in blossoming landscapes or brightly lit rooms. His early works, with their clear colors, remain his best. Later, driven by compassion and social consciousness, he turned to painting the poor. In this subject matter a straight line leads from Millet through Courbet, Daumier, and Lepage; then it passes into a twilit sentimentality with Israels, a feeble interpreter of Rembrandt's tradition. Uhde followed this sentimental vein in a more colorful way, but like Israels, was rarely convincing. After this Uhde turned to religious themes, transferring sacred events to a modern proletarian milieu in which Christ appears like a wandering vegetarian of our day. Only rarely did Uhde succeed in uniting the lingering sentimentality of the nineteenth century with the vital demands of Impressionism, as he saw them. Thus, in his work genre painting enjoyed a dubious renaissance. Here is an example of the unfortunate German tradition of trying to encompass too many aspects at once, instead of deciding wholeheartedly for one of the available possibilities. Uhde's paintings never attained the convincing power of Van Gogh, who belonged to the same generation.

Uhde's friend *Hugo von Habermann* (1849–1929) brought something very different to the art of southern Germany around 1900. A vigorous, billowing force swept across his canvases. The effect was not the result of impressionistic color divisionism but of the influence of late Baroque art. He employed its surging movement in his portraits and diagonally placed nudes. Unlike Wilhelm Leibl, he did not build

Fritz von Uhde. Daughters in the Garden, 1906 · Munich, Collection von Ritter

on realistically solid substance but proceeded from the undulating rhythm of the painting. Habermann became president of the Munich Secession which sponsored so many of the early advanced movements of the twentieth century.

Heinrich Zügel (1850–1941) also worked in Munich. His oeuvre lies somewhere between objective realism and the new conceptions of light in plein-air painting. In Paris the young man was more impressed by the realism of Constant Troyon than by the Impressionists. The bodies of Zügel's animals were not meant to merge flatly into the atmosphere but to emerge as heavy, blocklike forms from accentuated depths. He went out into the country with huge canvases that had to be anchored against the wind. When the Munich Secession was founded in 1892, he fought energetically with that group against the twilit hues and weak colors of the studio promoted by the conservatives of Lenbach's circle. "You have to create form with color," Zügel would tell his pupils. But he was not as gifted nor as capable of development as Liebermann or Corinth. This stouthearted son of a shepherd was attuned to cattle and

Hugo von Habermann. Portrait of a Lady, circa 1900

Heinrich Zügel. Semi-shadow, 1905

flocks of sheep, themes that he painted over and over again, gradually using lighter and lighter colors. However, Zügel's treatment of sheep was much shallower than Millet's or Giovanni Segantini's; actually the only effect Zügel strove for was the robust outer appearance of the animal. Court circles in Munich, which repeatedly honored him, could easily accept this painter and his conservative position; the south German aristocracy was more flexible than the Kaiser's court in the north, where Liebermann's more advanced interpretations had been anything but well received. A chronological parallel throws light on how conservatively Zügel interpreted animals in spite of the wide, free sweep of his brush: when he was

Wilhelm Trübner
Hemsbach Castle,
1906

at the height of his realistic style, another Munich painter of animals, Franz Marc, was already conjuring up on his canvases dreamlike abstractions of everything animalistic. Along these lines, as we shall see, a totally new era in south German painting was to arise.

In west Germany, *Wilhelm Trübner* (1851–1917) was painting on much the same level as Zügel. A man of means, he owned paintings by Franz Hals, Leibl and Schuch, a collection that is indicative of the man. His friendship with Schuch is evident in his paintings. Leibl falls outside our scope; he died at the turn of the century, which may be considered symbolic, for he produced only objective realism; subjective Impressionism was a style he had avoided. Unlike Leibl, Trübner gradually developed into a landscape painter. We are concerned briefly with his last period. He began with a dark tonality, with almost sculptural overtones; then his brushstrokes became more colorful and began to glow as if liberated. Yet his style remains weighty; some of his paintings give an effect of masonry. With their large firm squares of color they sometimes seem to have been spaded up, as if Trübner were seeking the way of Van Gogh (who had died in 1890). But Trübner never achieved Van Gogh's visionary dynamism. While the latter accepted the experience of French Impressionism, Trübner considered the corresponding French artists frivolous. Gradually, though, he began to use their chlorophyll-green impasto, which gave a colorful strength to his robust, sometimes too-thickly-painted planes. Juicy green fields and meadows, blue seascapes that seem almost lacquered, off-white buildings stand energetically in their frames. If Slevogt sometimes improvised too spiritedly, then Trübner certainly constructed his pictures too statically and heavily. Nevertheless, his virile, straightforward talent was drawn from our horizon too soon.

DIVISIONISM

Impressionism was followed by Divisionism, a kind of Pointillism which was developed more consistently in France by Seurat, Signac, Cross and Cousturier. These artists continued to develop earlier methodr, in bright, unblended color, but whereas the Impressionists seemed to have dashed paint onto the canvas so that the picture looked improvised, the Divisionists sought a more serene approach. Instead of swirling, irregular, color *commatica*, they now constructed a systematic color mosaic. In the history of art static modes of expression appear repeatedly beside the dynamic. Poussin's followers protested against Rubens, Ingres against Delacroix; in Germany, the disciples of Marées contested those of Menzel, and later Constructivists opposed the Expressionists.

Chromo-luminarisme, as it was called, was initiated in France, not Germany. Seurat died in 1891, and the theories relevant to his work had already developed in the 1880's, but the work of the German Divisionists does not appear until the twentieth century. In France, as early as 1880 when Impressionism was still very much alive, David Sutter announced a neo-impressionistic program; it was then formulated by Félix Fénéon in 1887, and also by Signac and Cross. It proclaimed the alliance of the artist with science, an alliance which would allow the artist to act autonomously. The breaking down of all colors into the elements in the spectrum was decisive in order to allow their blending in the observer's eye; this procedure was the only one which could assure a pure radiance. Black and brown were to be eliminated

Curt Herrmann
Pheasant,
1917

entirely. But the "stones of color" were to be arranged with a feeling for the plane surface, for the underlying format, which Seurat, especially, consistently preserved.

Although the introduction of this style, with its classical effect, into the world of impressionistic color seems especially characteristic of the Latin world, it was also introduced and adopted in Germany. *Curt Herrmann* (1854–1929) painted delicately colored pictures whose peculiar structure rested solely on their color. Liebermann, the realist, might have said, "Where talent ends, style begins," but Herrmann took another view. In 1911 he wrote a book, *Der Kampf um den Stil (The Struggle over Style)*, in which he advocated "the organization of the three-dimensional on the plane surface instead of stereoscopic illusion." This theory was to become one of the chief goals of our time, and with good reason.

Herrmann did not find his way to Pointillism until he was about forty years old, at the beginning of the twentieth century. He was the director of a private art school in Berlin which was oriented toward this method and he fought energetically for the new directions. Signac, Bonnard, Matisse, and in Germany, Van de Velde, were his friends. Later he developed a rather strange rhythm without, however, joining the Expressionists. Yet at that time he wrote, prophetically indeed, "Not only the form but also the color that fills the form is subject to rhythm, and the real obligation of modern painting is to achieve thereby an absolute balance between contrasts, complexes and complementary appearances and values."

Paul Baum
Seascape,
1906

Paul Baum (1859–1932) advocated similar ideas. He came from the Weimar school of intimate landscape painting and at the turn of the century was fascinated by Neo-Impressionism. The simplifying luminosity of neo-impressionist pictures brought a storm of protest from the conservative devotees of the art-gallery tone, for instance Menzel, who rejected this new, lighter world of color as inartistic and brutal. With pointillist color dots whose size was supposed to be proportional to the picture's format, the essential aim of the artist was to give the new painting a surface stability. Baum allied himself with Herrmann and the contemporary Belgian painter, Rysselberghe, but the group had only a small following. Baum became more and more isolated after he began teaching at the Cassel Art Academy in 1918. He reverted to an earlier style of detailed drawing, long a characteristic method of German art, just as Expressionism was beginning to make headway with the younger generation. Their viewpoint was represented by Nolde when he rejected Baum as "too sweet," although he handed down a legacy of solid and beautiful landscapes.

Neo-Impressionism had meanwhile infected the Italians (Segantini) and the Belgians (Rysselberghe and Van de Velde) whom we shall not pursue here. It also made its influence felt in the decorative murals of that era, which were, however, more affected by the Jugendstil, as we shall see in the work of Ludwig von Hofmann. Neo-Impressionism may be considered one of the steps that led away from representational painting. Through Impressionism, the flow of color, and through Neo-Impressionism, the mosaic handling of color, had become practically ends in themselves.

Ludwig von Hofmann (1861–1945), more than any other painter in Germany, brought a light color key to large-scale decorative painting. In 1889 he was in Paris and saw the work of Puvis de Chavannes and Maurice Denis. He turned away from the somber twilit depths of Marées, yet it was that painter's solemn compositions which he really wanted to develop further. Thus blond Arcadian landscapes, peopled by young, innocent figures, now blossomed under his brush. This direction was called New Idealism, and Hölderlin and Marées became its spiritual ideals. Stefan George, central figure of this new estheticism, wrote sonnets to Ludwig von Hofmann.

In Hofmann's paintings there was a Utopian, eurythmic feeling for life, a lyricism which found an outlet in decorative form. Hofmann painted murals for the Weimar Museum (1905–1906), for the Weimar theatre (1906), for Jena University (1909), and for Van de Velde's theatre at the Cologne *Werkbundschau* (Trade Union Fair) in 1914. Beside these large-scale assignments there are small, gentle, harmonious pastels that give no evidence of Pointillism, and lithographs, woodcuts and drawings. One of his early paintings should be mentioned because it is a unique example of this lyric style; it shows only the calm silent sea reflecting the light of a rising but still invisible moon–no coastline, no sign of a ship. But a broad frame encloses this void, and the frame is carved with large beseeching heads, plants, and the face of Beethoven: the painting depicts the adagio of the *Moonlight Sonata*. Hofmann's later paintings included figures, but still adhered too rigidly to this lyric mood. The effort to unite the diffuse accents in which the genre painters of the nineteenth century had dissipated their efforts into one unified arrangement of color and line carried away with it too much true expression. Not until the energetic

Ludwig von Hofmann. Mural, 1906

Swiss painter Hodler appeared on the scene were these various tendencies brought into harmony with each other, but he cannot be treated here. Hofmann, however, did help, albeit vaguely, to unite the fine arts with each other, and above all with architecture. With that rapprochement, the historical approach that had plagued not only architecture but nineteenth-century art as a whole, was overcome.

Decorative Nature-Lyricism and Jugendstil

Among the nature-lyricists we must first mention the Worpswede painters. As early as 1889 they formed a group, seeking to express their devotion to a gentle, quiet profundity in contrast to the immediacy of the Impressionists. Red-brick houses, green and blue ironwork and heavy-hanging thatched roofs stand reverently in their pictures. Trees, human figures, animals, detach themselves from the North German plain, quietly articulating the space. The paintings of the peat-digger village of Worpswede, near Bremen, with black-sailed skiffs lying in its canals, with its pines and birches, evoke a dreamy feeling for life. *Fritz Mackensen* (1866–1953) declared solemnly that he could develop "only in contemplating the wonder of nature;" the emphasis here, as in poetry, is on the quality of wonder. One of his most outstanding works is called *Die Scholle (Native Soil)*: two towering peasant women draw a harrow behind which strides the father. When Mackensen painted a church service, he represented the peasants in their Sunday dignity, sitting or standing outdoors, touched by a breath of monumentality.

Otto Modersohn (1865–1943), the Westphalian landscape painter, married Paula Becker in Worpswede. She was, in her own right, an even stronger artistic personality and we shall return to her later. Modersohn and *Fritz Overbeck* (1869–1909) sought to imbue their landscapes with an imperceptible rhythm, but they lacked the courage to do this as thoroughly as did their contemporary, Ludwig von Hofmann, who, as we have seen, was already a kind of counterpart to the French Nabis. *Heinrich Vogeler* (1872–1942), a friend of Rilke, treated his slightly affected pictures as mood poems. One is called *Homecoming*: an exaggeratedly slender couple are joined in an ethereal kiss; they are standing in a landscape of attenuated birches whose foliage has been virtually transformed into crowns of pearls. This fairy-tale atmosphere is echoed in the frame, which is ornamented with flat filigree scrolls. Vogeler later became a Communist and lived in Russia, where he painted scenes of the people and countryside in an eclectic style.

In 1895, these painters exhibited at the Crystal Palace in Munich, and scored a huge success with their rather artificial interpretations. Colors were rendered with delicacy, all shapes were slightly elongated. The youthful poet Rilke expressed his admiration of this craftsmanlike Worpswede approach in an elegiac whisper: "One is so fearfully alone among the blossoming trees and the brooks that flow by" – but this is hardly one of his more enduring insights.

Like the gentle souls just described, *Hans am Ende* (1864–1918) and *Karl Vinnen* (1863–1922) were ruled by a longing to escape, but it was not that more powerful, creative need which had driven Gauguin from Europe seeking strength from concentration on exotic forms. The Worpswede painters were also in revolt against an earthbound Impressionism, but they never achieved the freedom of pictorial structure that Gauguin had discovered. For this reason they had already lost all importance when the Brücke artists introduced their powerful colors and forms in 1904.

Meanwhile, however, the painter *Walter Leistikow* (1865–1908), living in Berlin, also represented a similar muted reaction against the Realists and the Impressionists. This cultivated, well-to-do man, who was also active as a novelist and art critic prior to his premature death at forty-three, was a close friend of Liebermann and Corinth, the representatives of the more forceful counter-trend. With them he founded the Berlin Secession in 1898, and subsequently the Deutsche Künstlerbund (German Federation of Artists) in Weimar. Both institutions were opposed to the conventional ideas of the German middle classes. Looking at Leistikow's pictures of the *Grunewald*, the Kaiser remarked that he knew that forest area better from hunting! The Impressionists, Liebermann, Slevogt and Corinth, as well as the decorative painters, from Leistikow to Franz von Stuck and Ludwig von Hofmann, were unpopular. Although the two groups had quite different approaches, both were trying to overcome the traditional painting methods of the nineteenth century.

In oppressive twilit colors, Leistikow depicted the melancholy surroundings of Berlin, not the lively suburban areas which remained a theme of the Impressionists. He painted the pine woods of the Havelsee with a wide, softly stylized shoreline, the sun shining rust-brown on the trunks of trees with dark green crowns, standing beside the secretive, dark blue water. Figures were banished from these tranquil canvases. A new romanticism reigned, but unfortunately it rarely went beyond the decorative. Sometimes Viking ships appear amid this Nordic monotony, their wakes, lit by the setting sun, undulating over the picture plane in the curvilinear style of the

Otto Modersohn. The Moors

Fritz Overbeck. The Moors

Heinrich Vogeler. Homecoming

Jugendstil. Broad frames with flamboyant patterns echo the elegiac mood of the painting. Occasionally Leistikow would transform all this into a decorative wall hanging.

Mild protests against realism could also be heard in German literature. Gerhardt Hauptmann turned away from his proletarian drama, *Die Weber*, to the dream poetry of *Hanneles Himmelfahrt*. Poetry, music, painting, architecture again sought unity. The men who maintained the momentum of contemporary art met in the studio of Leistikow, the leader: Liebermann, Munch, Corinth (who wrote a biography of Leistikow), the art historian Tschudi, the poets Carl and Gerhardt Hauptmann, the writers Max Halbe, Otto Hartleben and Peter Hille, the famous stage director Brahm, and the leading publisher of the day, S. Fischer.

Why, then, did a landscape painter like Leistikow leave so little of lasting value? During this opening phase of twentieth-century art, too great a value was still placed on a balanced approach to life. Granted, in 1892, when the Edvard Munch Exhibition in Berlin created such a scandal, Leistikow had defended this bold painter, who actually had influenced him somewhat. But Munch's rejection of realism was of a quite different calibre; it went deeper and sought radical change of form. As in the case of Cézanne, Van Gogh, Gauguin, and Hodler, there could be no question of classifying his work as merely a more or less decorative and transitional form of development. That these foreign painters were considered extremists by their German contemporaries was a sure sign that they were true innovators, the masters of tomorrow. Almost all of them had also passed through the Jugendstil, or Art Nouveau phase, but in a fashion very different from the nature-lyricists, who were totally unable to contribute any rejuvenating force to the twentieth century.

The Dachau Group

The Dachau group joined forces in 1893, somewhat later than the Worpswede painters. A more cohesive group than the latter, they were against all genre painting, more reserved in perception and statement and somewhat flatter in their color effects. But they too were unable to escape entirely a certain decorative weakness. Their influence on German painting was also brief. The Worpswede school had devoted itself to the landscape of the north German heath, while the Dachauers were attracted to the south German moors that run along the Amper River. Here too one could represent tall trees rising out of a sustained horizontal ground such as the Impressionists would have obliterated, in an arrangement that still betrayed the influence of the gentle curves of the Jugendstil. Muted colors amid thin, rolling mists, trees with flecked silver-gray trunks and crowns that seemed to hover in the sky like small clouds, were all organized into tasteful compositions by painters such as *Ludwig Dill* (1848–1940), who mixed watercolor and tempera on shag paper, or *A. Langhammer* (1854–1901). Today it seems incomprehensible that these paint

Fritz Erler. Fisherman's Idyll, circa 1920

ings should have aroused in many people a fervent sense of closeness to nature. *Adolf Hölzel* (1853–1934) is the only Dachauer who was important for the further development of German art as it began to turn toward abstract painting; this influence, however, was felt through his teaching in Stuttgart, after his Dachau period. We shall return to him.

Leo Putz. Nude, 1905
Formerly Vienna,
Collection Eissler

The Scholle

The painters of the *Scholle* (Native Soil) school were also devotees of a decorative picture form. The Scholle had flourished in Munich since 1899, and was represented by the art journal *Jugend*, founded in 1896. Japanism, Jugendstil, and the influence of the Nabis were here united in favoring a lighter and more broadly conceived tonality. The contrast between Munich and Berlin at that time was also reflected in their leading art periodicals. The Berlin *Kunst und Künstler (Art and Artist)*, was interested only in the fine arts and reported very factually on Realism and Impressionism; the *Jugend* stood for the merging of the fine arts with literature and humor, all under the heading of the *Jugendstil*, absorbing, notably in its illustrations, the already passé influences of Toulouse-Lautrec and Beardsley. For many of these painters the Paris World's Fair of 1900 was an important event.

In *Fritz Erler* (1868–1940) we find this ornamental style represented most purely. He decorated books for the publishing house Pan, stylizing the world of German legend, and painted huge festive triptychs, some religious, some mythological, that spread out endlessly like tapestries. The surface was intended to dominate; on it, decoratively simplified figures in subdued blond tones were interwoven in a rather hieratic manner. Erler worked always for the effect from a distance. He was called in to decorate the interior of the Kurhaus in Wiesbaden and the town hall in Hannover; he also received commissions to

32

decorate passenger vessels. His new, esoteric choice of colors was intended to overcome at last the dingy brown art-gallery tone of the masters of the nineteenth century. For a time his immaculate formal structure was valued in Germany as a new world of art.

Erler's brother, *Erich Erler-Samaden* (1870–1946) preferred stylized snowscapes in which he tried to unite Segantini's Neo-Impressionism with Jugendstil forms. The Silesian *Adolf Münzer* (1870–1952) also did richly ornamental work, without however, attaining the pictorial finesse or the melodious *haut gout* that poured forth from Gustave Klimt in Vienna. The Munich painter, *Angelo Jank* (1868–1940) painted an army of warriors in archaic armor, but no longer in historic guise as in the nineteenth century; Jank's painting is called *Die Eiserne Wehr (The Iron Defence)*. He also painted horses and race-track scenes with a momentary, almost impressionistic effect of life, but in a decorative ensemble. The Tirolean *Leo Putz* (1869–1940) achieved the same effect with nude ladies wearing enormous sunhats, painted in a mosaic of pasty color. Other *Scholle* painters were the three Saxons: *Max Eichler* (b. 1872), *Walter Georgi* (1871–1924), and *Walter Püttner* (1872–1953). Today their only historic value lies in their determined rejection of all genre painting. Most of them were preoccupied with the idea of incorporating the picture in wall space or room, but in doing so all of them succumbed somewhat to a summary poster style, devoid of any profound message–and this at a time when the quality of genuine poster art was at a very high level, especially in Munich. The liveliest of the lot was probably the Palatinate painter *Max Feldbauer* (1869–1948), who depicted heavyweight horses and soldiers in glittering uniforms, undeniably with a certain power. "When there were horses dragging a beer-cart … *that* was Feldbauer."

Franz von Stuck. Pan, 1909
Munich, Stuck Villa

Max Klinger. Brahms Fantasy

An artist with a unique position was the problematic *Franz von Stuck* (1863–1928), who chose to treat everything demonically. Like Lenbach before him, he was born a Bavarian peasant and lived to become owner of a palace. He painted *Sin* voluptuously, a woman with full breasts and glowing eyes, with glistening snakes wound round her. In an enormous painting he pictures *War:* Death rides, as if in a drama, over decaying bodies that cover the ground cadaver-white as far as the eye can see. The themes of Böcklin 1827–1901 are enlarged upon, and the ashen flesh of the figures of Albert von Keller 1845–1920 (a painter of interiors) is combined skillfully with decorative horror figures inspired by Munch. With a curvilinear structure and intensely glowing color, Stuck was striving for a shocking monumentality. Like other artists of the Jugendstil period, he was also a gifted sculptor and interior decorator. If one compares his paintings with the works of Max Klinger, who was just as theatrical and also worked in every kind of medium, then Stuck's work seems less overcast by the aestheticism that was dominant in Munich at the time. In any case, he must have been a stimulating teacher of new forms and expressions, for Marc and Kandinsky were among his pupils and always thought of him with gratitude.

Max Klinger (1857–1920) is of interest here because of his efforts to synthesize all the possibilities of his time, an attempt in which he sometimes succeeded through quite ingenious means. Today he is an underrated artist. A Brahms enthusiast and disciple of Nietzsche, Klinger was a link between the genre painting of the nineteenth century and the freely roving fantasy which followed. Late classicism, a few impressionistic features, veristic psychology and the symbolism of the Jugendstil are united in him, sometimes mysteriously, as in *The Blue Hour* and the *Brahms Fantasy*. In *The Cycle of the Glove* he anticipates some aspects of Objective Surrealism, whose followers later admired his prescience. In the graphic arts he initiated many extraordinary technical refinements, some of which influenced Käthe Kollwitz's early works; and in sculpture, where we shall come across him again, he experimented with new combinations of materials, sometimes with overly ornate results, as in his *Beethoven*.

THE DRAFTSMEN

The nineteenth century was an era of political satire. In 1830 it found expression in the magazine *Caricature*, which from 1832 was called *Charivari*, and in 1841 in *Punch*. These journals were inspired partly by English tradition from Hogarth to Gillray, Rowlandson and Cruikshank. In Munich the *Fliegende Blätter* was founded (1844) and the *Münchener Punsch* (1848–1875). All these periodicals attracted both mediocre and good draftsmen, but in 1896, the weekly *Simplizissimus* began publication in Munich,

Olaf Gulbransson
A Way To Prevent Submarine Warfare, 1918

Th. Th. Heine
Heavy-weight Patriots, 1915

bringing to satire and caricature a completely new and far more biting style. Most full-page reproductions were no longer carried out in woodcut, but by the new zinc-etching method which came much closer to the original. Here Germany's best draftsmen found a common meeting ground. All of them were highly original, even when influenced by the linearism of Toroop, Beardsley and Valloton, and by the French journal, *La Revue Blanche*. The revival of strong linear rhythms which the Jugendstil had brought with it was combined with a deliciously grim, realistic world view. The contributors threw themselves enthusiastically into the field of social criticism, while the distinguished and esoteric magazine *Pan* (1895) cultivated the more serious aspects of art. In Munich in 1892 the Secession had dissociated itself from the old guard and there was a ferment in more ways than one. *Jugend* was first published in the same year as *Simplizissimus*, 1896, but it was a much less aggressive publication. *Simplizissimus* ran for forty-eight years but was truly productive only during the first decades, as long as it continued to astonish its readers with the original ideas and caricatures of its draftsmen.

The most important contributor to *Simplizissimus*, from an artistic viewpoint, was *Olaf Gulbransson* (1873–1958), who came to Munich from Norway in 1902. He raised the art of German satire to new levels by originating comic types and situations with sinuous but dynamic contours, very simple yet newly exciting as linear expressions. It is still impressive today to see how he could illustrate a drastic situation with a minimum of delineation. His dignified economy of expression made him an impressive painter of idylls and a fine portraitist. He wrote and illustrated biographies and books of aphorisms, and taught at the Munich Academy of Fine Arts from 1929.

Th. Th. Heine (1867–1948) worked with a relaxed calligraphy. His humor lay more in the penetrating content of his imagination than in his line, although he too practiced a variety of styles from the bristly to the slippery-smooth. He collected Biedermeier *kitsch* and china pugdogs as if he were one of the Philistines he was fighting, and passed merciless judgment on men and their works. No one ever knew whether or not he meant it seriously.

Karl Arnold (1883–1953) made variations of the sort of thing that brought Gulbransson success, but in sketchier fashion and with greater emphasis on content. After moving to Munich at the age of seventeen and producing an altar painting as his first work, he became co-founder of the New Secession. His best caricatures are in the volume *Schwabing und Kurfürstendamm*, a striking comparison between the peculiarities of Munich and Berlin; also in a volume of collected works, *Der Mensch ist gut aber die Leut' san a Gsindel* (translated from its untranslatable Bavarian dialect: "The human being is good, but people are rabble").

Karl Arnold
Mei Ruh möcht i ham un a Revolution
(Peace and quiet, that's what I want,
and a revolution), 1923

Eduard Thöny. Fantastic, 1915

and true that once the police were able to identify a gentleman thief from them.

Rudolf Wilke (1873–1908), Thöny's friend, was color-blind. His first ambition was to become a carpenter, but later he developed into a very capable black and white draftsman. Ludwig Thoma sang the praises of his friend Wilke, who died very young: "A keen observer, with a profound sense of humor and a gift for reproducing all things comic with the greatest economy."

Bruno Paul (b. 1874) worked for *Simplizissimus* before devoting himself to the applied arts and architecture. Later, when recalling the Munich years from 1893 to 1907, he spoke of "a wonderful time and activity." But only the early editions of *Simpel* and *Jugend* published his imaginative work, in which a new surface rhythm circulates with a minimum of color. Paul was cofounder of the *Vereinigte Werkstätten*

Eduard Thöny (1886–1950), working with the brush on a white surface, painted rather than drew, which is why one should see his work in its original colors. His parents were Austrians, a provincial sculptor from Brixen and a peasant girl from the province of Vintschgau. Asymmetrically and with great power, he caught the look of strange bands of soldiers, insolent cooks, dubious cavaliers and coarse peasant lads. In 1904, with no passport or identification papers, he went off on a bicycle trip with Ludwig Thoma and his friend Wilke... to the Sahara desert. Later he resided quietly on the Ammersee. His drawings were so alive

Rudolf Wilke. Gymnasium Teachers, 1907

38

(United Workshops), and became director of the Berlin state schools for the liberal and applied arts.

A number of draftsmen were active in Berlin also, but they were not fortunate enough to have such a publication as *Simplizissimus. Heinrich Zille* (1858–1929) portrayed the Berlin proletariat in simple but accusing sketches. He was concerned mainly with the needy and pitiful creatures to be found in the backyards of dilapidated apartment houses. He treated this milieu in part realistically, sometimes in a style reminiscent of folk-singing.

Käthe Kollwitz (1867–1945) was of a quite different calibre. She too was consistently absorbed in proletarian subjects, but in her graphic series she endowed them with a sturdy gravity. She was more successful in etching than in lithography or woodcut. As Millet had treated his peasants and Van Gogh his farmhands, she monumentalized the pro-

Heinrich Zille. Innkeeper

Bruno Paul. Charity Concert, 1901

letariat with such plastic force that one already senses in her graphic art the impressive sculptor she was to become. Somewhat later Dix and Grosz would fight for the same cause in a quite different way, at times questioning *all* human values. They portrayed their contemporaries as wretched and hideous, whereas Käthe Kollwitz gave her working man a somber aura of nobility. At times, it is true, she lapsed into that stylized pathos which was to affect the value of Egger-Lienz's peasants, the "heroes" of Metzner's *People's War Memorial* in Leipzig, and even a few of

39

Käthe Kollwitz. Self-Portrait, 1910

Barlach's figures. Kollwitz found her first inspiration in Stauffer-Bern and Max Klinger, whose graphic teaching she admired. Her early works remained her best: the *Weaver Revolt* series, executed before1900, and *The Peasant War* (1903–1908). These were followed by single, more monotone sheets on the toil, sickness and death of the working man, and by forty self-portraits. Her form of expression became highly popular, because in these works her pathos remained pre-Expressionistic and she was not yet involved in the revolutionary methods that were to influence her later style. In spite of the monumental forms for which she strove, Käthe Kollwitz actually remained closer to the older Liebermann than to Emil Nolde, for example, who was born the same year as she, in 1867.

Emil Orlik (1870–1932) belongs to this generation. While Zille and Kollwitz confronted the social aspects of life accusingly, Orlik devoted himself to an aesthetic stylization in his efforts to overcome realistic Impressionism. Here we have an adjustment of decorative effects of the kind suggested at the turn of the century by the Jugendstil and East Asiatic rhythms, into which Orlik occasionally introduced the simplified concepts of late fifteenth-century Italian prints. His main achievement was in the woodcut, which he studied during a trip to Japan (1900–1901). He was widely traveled (Egypt, Nubia, China, Korea, Japan) and he fused the kindred stimuli from these areas with the decorative tendencies that had developed in Vienna around Gustave Klimt, and in Berlin around Otto Eckmann. From 1905 he was

Lovis Corinth. The Painter Bernt Grönvold, 1923

I

Christian Rohlfs. Magnolia, San Materno, 1937   *Emil Nolde. Fishing Boat, 1916*   III

Ernst Ludwig Kirchner. Sertig weg, circa 1936/1937

Käthe Kollwitz
Mother and Child, 1910

professor at the school attached to the Berlin Arts and Crafts Museum. All this helped him to develop a well-balanced artistic formula into which he incorporated the kind of mixed graphic techniques developed by Klinger. He also created stage sets for Max Reinhardt.

Marcus Behmer (1879–1958), succumbing entirely to a subtle aestheticism dominated by Beardsley and the particular finesse of Japanese graphic art, developed a decadent, sharply linear style. He illustrated Oscar Wilde's *Salome* in 1903, designed trademarks, bookplates and bookbindings, and in 1921 published the Behmer *Antiqua*.

Emil Orlik. Ernst Haeckel, 1901

Marcus Behmer. Salome, 1902

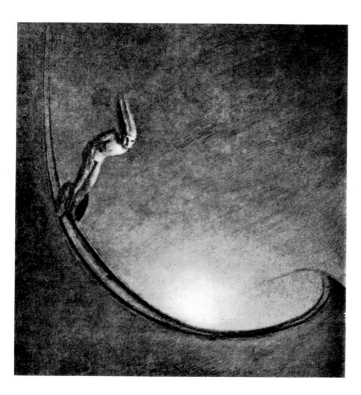

Alfred Kubin. Man, 1902

42

Alfred Kubin. The Fates, 1929

Alfred Kubin (1877–1959), more original than Behmer, is also to be considered exclusively as a graphic artist. The pale hues he favored appear to be color superimposed on his scratchy drawings. His illustrative bent closely allied him to literature, most significantly probably in his only novel, *Die andere Seite (The Other Side*, 1908). Beside producing innumerable single drawings, he illustrated approximately a hundred books and albums, among them many works of world literature. A sickly child and the subject of many disasters and much pain in his lifetime, he was influenced by Schopenhauer's dark philosophy, met Werfel and Kafka in Prague, and suffered hallucinations. Yet in spite of all vicissitudes he was able to buy the small estate, Zwickeldt, in the upper Austrian Inn Valley. There he became a brooding, fantasy-creating recluse who turned to the teachings of Buddha and the Upanishad. His work is in the tradition of such masters of phantasmagoria as Bosch, Callot, Goya and Daumier. In his youth he saw the Brueghel paintings in the Vienna museum and said, "My admiration was so great that my own efforts seemed to me superfluous." Of his contemporaries, he was influenced by Klinger, but also by Redon and Ensor. Kubin's early drawings are sharply realistic. Huge, weird creatures tower over barren space. Today these drawings make a more vivid impression than the later works, for they seem to anticipate some of that strange silent Surrealism which was later created by Max Ernst. But the later works often become overpopulated, in a purely anecdotal style. Nineteenth-century genre themes seem to reappear, even if only in a dusky twilight. In his pen drawings, Kubin grew very prolix; the unruly bundle of lines sometimes violates the laws of economy. Whereas Klee, whose early etchings remind one of Kubin, experienced the discipline of the Bauhaus and achieved a true pictorial transformation, Kubin gained broader popularity by developing an illustrative horror-realism.

In his nocturnal fairyland all things have aged, everything is torn and cracked, transformations occur amid a welter of decay. Trees turn into animals, houses become eerily alive, birds nest in broken-down machines. Yet often Kubin meant to convey no more than a black-comic travesty, a description, pure and simple, of the sadness and forlornness of the lonely footpaths he used to sketch in the Bohemian woods. Or sometimes he gives us ghostly folklore–the devil as companion, a vampire with the features of an old crone. It is not the "magic of line" that is forceful here, as some have claimed; over the multiplicity of nature he spreads a rustling twilight and from it emanates the miasma of swamp or forest thicket.

Kubin gave this interpretation of himself: "My creatures cannot be defined by any aesthetic canons, nor are they caricatures... Dream drawing... that gives the general direction, but it isn't exact enough... The chaotic abyss... it is our own, in its never ceasing transmutations... it gorges eternally on the world and the hallucinatory grandeur of our ego." Humor must reign supreme "in dealing with the grandiose marvelous fraud... And I consider it a matter of indifference whether one covers over the entrance and exit of this life with the mask of a kindly spirit or, like myself, uses a question mark."

EXPRESSIONISM AND RELATED TRENDS

Paula Modersohn-Becker (1876–1907) was a serene forerunner of Expressionism. She painted the peasant women and flaxen-haired children of Worpswede, but differently from the artists active there. "Mothers, breasts, the human body, children... how strange her heavy hand on flesh, humans, the earth," her friend Hoetger said of this painter who died so young. From 1899 she was a member of the Worpswede colony and married the painter Modersohn. But she soon outgrew the lyricism practiced there. Heavier colors appear in which the brushstroke is visible, and large, constructed forms within containing outlines. Her paintings give an effect of having been cemented. One must keep in mind that the Brücke painters had not yet appeared on the scene and the German students of Matisse were still far away in France.

She was an admirer of Rilke's symbolism, and the poet saw in her "solace and the future." For her decor she hung reproductions of Egyptian portraits, of Van Gogh and Gauguin. She was devoted to the Gothic style and to the archaic antique. Several trips to Paris nourished these attitudes. The qualities that in France set Gauguin apart from Manet, in Germany distinguished her from the mature Liebermann. But the developments appearing in France in 1880 first occurred in Germany shortly after 1900. Modersohn-Becker avoided all emotional expression and conceived humanity as blocklike and quiescent, but she did not attain in her figures the exotic sensitivity of Gauguin. Sometimes her peasant children have big potato heads, inexpressive and apathetic. Already in 1900 she wrote from Paris that construction was the order of the day, and in 1902, "I believe that when painting one should not always think of nature." At the same time she longed for the themes of her homeland.

Gradually she abandoned earth colors and achieved a more expressive and brighter tonality. She succeeded in creating freely only between the ages of twenty-five and thirty-one, for she died after the birth of her first child. As in the case of Van Gogh, a generation before her, deeply felt letters and

Paula Modersohn-Becker. Birch Trees, circa 1902

Paula Modersohn-Becker. Girl with Green Necklace, circa 1904 · Mannheim, Kunsthalle

diaries helped bring a quicker understanding of her style, which was new to the Germany of her day. Dr. Roselius of Bremen made an important collection of her works.

Rarely do the various trends in art succeed one another in an orderly fashion. Thus, in the period between 1900 and 1910, we find simultaneous directions: in France, Impressionism, the Nabi movement and Fauvism; in Germany, Impressionism, Jugendstil and related styles, and early Expressionism. The latter ran parallel to French Fauvism and originated in north and east Germany, whereas half a decade later the activity of the Blaue Reiter group is centered in south Germany.

A painter who worked towards Expressionism but without identifying himself with it was *Christian Rohlfs* (1849–1938) (Plate II). His birth-date places him in the generation of Liebermann, Uhde, Trübner. It is therefore all the more astonishing that after painting for a long time in the traditions of the nineteenth century, he should have adopted an entirely new style at the age of fifty. Certainly he is the only member of his generation who did not shut himself off from the revolution of Expressionism after 1900.

Christian Rohlfs. Soest, 1921

Rohlfs was the son of a Holstein peasant. When still young, he fell from a tree and was so seriously injured that he was bedridden for years and became an introvert. It was the aging writer Theodor Storm who advised him to take up painting. Young Rohlfs moved to Weimar, where for thirty years he lived as a recluse and painted in a traditional manner. But even before 1900 the influence of French Impressionism caused his color to blossom. In 1901 the collector Ernst Osthaus, on the advice of Van de Velde, persuaded Rohlfs to move to Hagen; there, in the Folkwang Collection then being assembled, he could study choice examples of the western painting that would eventually prevail over

Erich Heckel. Woodland Lake, 1910

Karl Schmidt-Rottluff. Forest Picture, 1921

Impressionism. At this point Rohlfs might have found his way to the cruder style of the Brücke, which was just emerging, but he was forestalled by his strong lyrical sensibilities, which sought a more malleable form of expression. A dreamlike quality and a beautiful sense of balance remain typical of his color when one compares him with his friend Nolde, for instance, with whom he worked in Soest from 1905 to 1906.

Gently flowing landscapes, churches, still lifes and religious themes were his domain. He used veiled, batiklike colors, and discriminating, though somewhat unexciting harmonies, very occasionally introducing a kind of lyrical-grotesque quality. He favored the color chords of cadmium yellow, rose madder, burnt sienna and delicate green lake. Working with a binding agent which he mixed himself, he brushed his colors on gently, or used a coarsely woven cloth instead of a brush, with the weave itself playing an effective part, as did also the texture of canvas or Japan paper ground. In spite of a similarity in style, he may be counted only conditionally among the Expressionists because of his more evanescent tones. In his town pictures of central Germany he reminds one vaguely of Feininger, but the forms of the latter are more sharply counterpointed. In the last two decades of his life Rohlfs painted mainly on paper in water-tempera. In 1926 he executed his last prints. The following year he moved to Ascona, Switzerland, where he saw flowers and landscapes as if through a light veil laid tenderly over simplified forms. But he had no intention of ignoring external reality. "Nature," he said, "should be drunk like fine wine, not like water, and one should be happy that it exists." Although Picasso said of him, "*pas de tout boche*," his lyric style was still too crude for the Nazis. Unreasonably neglected and disgraced, Rohlfs died in 1938, in his Hagen studio, alone, at the venerable age of eighty-nine.

Emil Nolde (1867–1956) may be considered the founder of German Expressionism. He was a hard-living, introverted peasant from the coast, born in Nolde (North Schleswig) of Frisian-Danish descent;

Emil Nolde. Prophet, woodcut, 1912

Emil Nolde. Brother and Sister, 1918 · Seebüll, Nolde-Stiftung

Emil Nolde. Sunflowers, 1943 · Seebüll, Nolde-Stiftung

his real name was Hansen. While the oxen bellowed for food, the boy was painting or drawing on carts or stable doors, using chalk he found in marl, or he was kneading figures out of clay. "I tried to paint with elderberry and beet juice, I liked red-violet so much." At fifteen he was "reserved, religious and shy." At times he would throw himself down in the cornfields to embrace the earth. Nolde served his apprenticeship at the Flensburg woodcarving school, and in 1889, a roving artisan, he came to Berlin, "a manure pit out of which grew lilies and roses." In 1894 he was painting in the Swiss mountains, interpreting them as trolls and demons. Next he proceeded to Munich, where he became acquainted with the nature-lyricism of the descriptive Dachau school. He met Adolf Hölzel, who was already feeling his way toward new color harmonies. But Nolde's color remained muted and indefinite.

"I painted landscapes with clouds in clusters or reaching convulsively across the sky like big dark fingers casting shadows far ahead of them." In 1900 in Paris he was impressed at first by the subtle color distinctions of Manet and by the dramatic mobility of Daumier. Then in 1905 stimulating new sources of power were revealed to him by the German collector Osthaus: Van Gogh's dynamics, Gauguin's feeling for forms in space and the abstract power of the exotic. Yet he was also haunted by Munch and Ensor.

It is not surprising that from 1905 to 1907 he joined forces with the Dresden Brücke, where a passionate give and take now developed on German soil. From this the powerful structure of German Expressionism was to arise, primordial amid conventions grown flaccid, and therefore shocking to the general public. Instead of the scattered, fleeting tonality of the Impressionists (in Nolde's early garden subjects one could already sense subterranean rumblings of things more substantial), we now find powerfully combined thrusts of color planted sturdily in a broad black framework. Instead of small, separate brushstrokes, masses in a "barbaric" color key roar at us; instead of Impressionism's transient image from the outside, we find in Expressionism the urge to attain a powerful statement from within, made by a creator who reforms and opposes the pressures of nature. As a result, we find those deformations which were at first so bitterly contested but were later accepted as new expressions in depth from an interior world. But the Expressionists, unlike Kandinsky, never wanted to blot out utterly the beloved objective world, however freely they treated it.

Nolde did not in any way stress the contours that were to become of such paramount importance to his colleagues. The powerful organization of his pictures is based entirely on intense glowing colors, which pour over the surface like lava, sometimes fiery, sometimes in a dark mass. In his pictures we are not concerned with the constructive linearity of Hodler, nor with the clearly defined and ornamental forms of Gauguin, nor with the emotionally directed impact which we find in Van Gogh; with Nolde everything depended on the substance of color itself, which glows willfully, at first with savage power, later with tropical transparency. Nolde's Expressionism flowed like an energizing bloodstream through all German feeling for color. (Plate III.) His short affiliation with the Brücke was soon dissolved because he remained an unsociable individual.

From 1909 religious compositions dominate Nolde's oeuvre, raw as in his earliest days, ecstatic, with a fierce solemnity: in 1909, *Whitsuntide* and *The Last Supper*; in 1911, a nine-panel altarpiece, *The Life of Christ;* in 1912, *Maria Aegyptica;* in 1915, *The Burial of Christ;* in 1929, *"So That Ye Shall Not Become As Little Children."* He fell upon this ancient sacred territory with such fervor, and interpreted its themes so drastically, that howls of rage went up from his viewers. Both Protestants and Catholics protested when Nolde's *Crucifixion* was hung at the Brussels World Fair in 1912. But Nolde, unperturbed, wrote, "The fact that during the Renaissance the Apostles and Christ were painted to look like Italian scholars may have given the clergy the idea that this traditional treatment had to remain constant." In his secular paintings he amalgamated exotic masks, primitive sculpture, elfin creatures and colored material, using them to find his way back to the expressive force of earlier cultures. It is indicative that in 1913 he joined an ethnological expedition that led him via Russia, China and Japan to Polynesia. He was receptive to primitive art, just as Picasso had been to African sculpture in 1907. "My interest in things foreign, in the primordial and primitively racial, was very strong... W. von Bode

(Director of the Berlin Museum) was still vehemently opposed to primitive art... clearly and frankly I expressed my opinion of Liebermann and his all-powerful position." (1910.) Not surprisingly, Nolde was debarred from the Berlin Secession. French Cubism, which had begun to make its influence felt a little while before and was to become very important to the Blaue Reiter group, made no impression on Nolde. "I think highly of Franz Marc's efforts toward a grandiose form, and I love his animals, but the things prismatic are foreign to me."

Nolde's unpretentious flowers and landscapes, in which his tendency to deform is less noticeable, gradually became popular. Here one feels the natural breath of life. Rampant, glowing plants, damp, reclaimed land with windmills; spring-green meadows with cattle and paddocked horses; the dark blue North Sea under rain-swollen clouds–everything swings wildly in space. At the same time he had no intention of abandoning his principles. "The farther one can remove oneself from nature, yet remain natural, the greater one's art." One must compare such theorizing with the opposite viewpoints of Liebermann and the nineteenth century to understand the giant step that had been taken. At the same time, impressionistic principles remained valid. "I avoided all blending of cold and warm, which has to result in muddiness and the death of all luminosity." Nolde's late watercolors remained for the most part airy and fluid, and his form consistently immanent.

Nolde's graphic art is also significant. Here he developed a discriminating tonality. In his etchings we find astonishing moods and nuances in spite of their abbreviated language. As early as 1904 the *Fantasies* appear, a combination of etching on a toned ground and drypoint; these were followed by aquatints that were permeated with ghostly burlesques and peasant humor. After this his forms became more massive, with the chance results of acid corrosion playing an attractive role. The year 1911 alone produced thirty-five etchings. Whereas the earlier etchings often look as if they had been squeezed out of a paintbrush, the later ones show a sparse, spectral linearity. In his woodcuts, large magical forms gradually take over, supported by the monumental tracery of the wood graining.

Lithography became an important medium of expression for Nolde since, unlike Kirchner and Schmidt-Rottluff, he always favored what was obviously painterly. After beginning with one-color lithographs, he felt the urge, in 1913, to set surging colors on the plate. Some of his sheets are based on as many as five different color plates. His earlier lithographs were perhaps influenced by Munch, but Nolde had less desire to describe and individualize. In his drawings a restless jerkiness gradually disappears and a quiet luminosity suffuses some of his later work. Early in Nolde's career, Gustave Schiefler of Hamburg became his friend and patron and published a compilation of his graphic work.

In today's world of artistic individuality, we rarely come across antipodes greeting each other with respect from afar, but Nolde saw in Paul Klee "a butterfly fluttering in celestial spheres," and Klee wrote farsightedly, "The abstractionist, earth-withdrawn or earth-fleeing, sometimes forgets that Nolde exists... in him the hand of man creates, not without weight, in a calligraphy not without blemish ... it is the mysterious full-blooded hand of the netherworld."

"DIE BRÜCKE"

In June 1905, four students of architecture at the Dresden Polytechnic Institute formed a group: Ernst Ludwig Kirchner, Fritz Bleyl, Erich Heckel and Karl Schmidt-Rottluff. Their purpose was to give the visual arts a strong, fresh impetus, to free themselves of Realism, Jugendstil and Impressionism. They were enthusiastic disciples of Van Gogh and Munch, the Germanic elements of the new style of painting. Simultaneously with the French rebels, the *Fauves*, they found a source of strength in the barbaric figures of primitive art. Their first shows were held in a lamp factory in Löptau, near Dresden. They went unnoticed or were reviled. The name, *"Die Brücke"* (The Bridge), expressed the desire to link all those who, like its members, opposed the individualism of the nineteenth century. The name originated with Schmidt-Rottluff, but it was Kirchner who drew up the program. The alliance was of short duration and unintellectual, being based actually on nothing much more than an exchange of intuitive and practical ideas. In the invitation to join, however, it was stated quite comprehensively that its members were out to "attract all revolutionary and fermenting powers." In 1906 they were joined by Nolde, "the wild visionary," as Kirchner called him. Other artists who became members were the Saxon Max Pechstein, the Finnish Symbolist Axel Gallén, the Swiss Cuno Amiet, and the Hollander Van Dongen, who came from Paris and acted as a connecting link with the Fauves. The last to join in 1910 was the Breslau painter Otto Mueller, who came from a group surrounding the writers Carl and Gerhardt Hauptmann.

The artistic aims of Die Brücke were: an abstracting, primitive style, the use of unbroken color, the dissolution of impressionistic aerial perspective and a dynamic blocking-in of form. Theses new ideas were inscribed in a book entitled *Odi profanum.* Graphic albums were published annually. They were completely unpretentious; here too the group started from essentials. Similarly, in the studios, home-made stools stood against walls painted in lurid colors. What Gauguin had achieved by emigrating to the primitive world of the South Seas, these painters arrived at at home: an attitude toward life that was again primitive yet at the same time forceful, that rejected the shallow life of big city civilization. Certain concepts of the medieval guilds were once more crying out for revival. It was similar to the yearnings of Ruskin and William Morris in the nineteenth century–in their case, a renaissance of the crafts, combined with a pallid revival of the Gothic. But the Brücke artists chose to join goals that were just as romantic with robust peasant and exotic art forms. Only the Bauhaus was to succeed in collectively influencing daily life and in a less sectarian way, attaining its goals through a rationalized approach and through its influence on industry.

The Brücke experienced the fate typical of small groups composed of exceptionally strong individuals. In the beginning, just as it was possible for a time to confuse the Cubism of Picasso and Braque, so too the work of the Brücke painters was sometimes difficult to differentiate; soon, however, the masters developed their own individual styles. The Brücke renewed painting and the graphic arts, but it was not significant in the development of new styles in architecture or design. In 1913 when Kirchner wrote a retrospective chronicle, the group was already breaking up, although a loose association was still effective between its members until 1920.

For a long time the Brücke style was attacked by art academies and the more conservative public,

Ernst L. Kirchner. Girls Bathing, 1913 · Feldafing, Collection Buchheim

Ernst L. Kirchner
Mountain Firs in Fog,
woodcut, 1917

and also by the lyricist Munch, who declared it augured ill for the future. The disciples of French Cubism also disapproved, perhaps because they were more oriented towards form, whereas the Expressionists emphasized expression, of course, and gesture. Cubism had undertaken to develop a plural vision deriving from exotic art, while German Expressionism, drawing a fresh feeling for nature from the same source, remained rooted in a reality which it wanted only to simplify expressively. That is one reason why the modern French art critics and Carl Einstein (in 1926) at first saw in the Brücke nothing more than a crude, drastic, poster-type rebellion. Kirchner expressed the group's aims in his chronicle of 1913 as follows: "Uninfluenced by today's currents of Cubism, Futurism, etc., the Brücke fights for the humane culture that is the foundation of true art." And in 1917 he wrote, "The great mystery that lies behind all events and things sometimes becomes spectrally visible ... we can never express it formally, all we can do is present it symbolically in form or word." A painting "is the circumscribing of a great mystery, and in the last analysis does not depict the individual personality, but a fragment of the spirit or emotion afloat in our world."

What a contrast to Dürer, who years before had confidently proclaimed an objective realism: "Abandon not Nature in thy estimation that it may be found better within thyself, for thou art being misled. In truth, art lies *in* Nature. He who can extract it, possesses it." Nowhere are the opposing epochs more sharply mirrored than in these avowals of two extremely masculine German artists.

The most mercurial and headstrong member of the group was *E. L. Kirchner* (1880–1938, Plate IV), from Brandenburg. He worked first, self-taught, in a Neo-Impressionist style. While studying architecture he was inspired by early German graphic art to try his hand at woodcutting. In Munich he attended the art school of Debschütz and Hermann Obrist. He was exposed to various currents in that city–he saw an important Neo-Impressionist exhibition, the drawings of Toulouse-Lautrec in the magazine *Pan*, and color plates by Vuillard and Bonnard in the journal *Insel*. But the northern world of Munch and German late-Gothic graphic art excited him more, and modern French art actually remained alien to him. "For the Latins", he said in one of his exaggerations, "beauty lies in appearances, others seek it *behind* things." In 1904 he returned to his architectural studies in Dresden, along with Erich Heckel. Both were strongly influenced by the Ethnological Museum there and by South Sea Island carvings,

Ernst L. Kirchner
Henry van de Velde,
woodcut, 1917

more strongly than by the more delicate Japanese woodcuts. Together they set up a primitive studio in a former butcher shop; then, in 1905, their friendship with Schmidt-Rottluff and Nolde led to the formation of the Brücke. They painted in an exotic manner circus subjects and suburban life, or summer scenes on the Moritzburg lakes in which human figures and nature were pantheistically interwoven. "The painter loves the tree as much as the human gesture. For him both are intangible mystery."

Kirchner may be distinguished from his friends by his energetic draftsmanship, his more angular, one might almost say Gothic, construction, his curves that converge or radiate. In spite of the passionate color, the graphic scaffolding of his work gives a dense effect until gradually the painting is dominated by a coniferlike arrangement. All perspective seems tilted, as if one were looking up.

In 1911, when the Brücke painters had moved to Berlin to take up life in the more cultured metropolis, Kirchner and Pechstein founded a school, the Muim-Institut, and *Der Sturm*, the radical magazine, became interested in Kirchner especially. In this second phase of his work his forms grow even more narrowly angular, his colors cooler and more transparent. Now his tonality is dominated by light blue, purple, black, a choice shade of salmon pink, green and yellow. But his psychological demon seems to grow more exaggerated. Mercilessly, treating his subjects like puppets, he captures the eternal schism between man and woman–even the Berlin prostitute–in all their roused sensuality, jammed between animalism and the machinery of a big city. Yet he does not accuse, as did Dix and Grosz later. While the latter, as social realists, eventually underwent a crisis in their art, Kirchner avoided this because his problems of color and form remained alive. In 1912, he participated in the graphic exhibition of the Blaue Reiter group in Munich. Kirchner and Heckel then painted the chapel at the Cologne Sonderbund Fair. In 1913, Kirchner wrote the chronicle of the Brücke; it was so subjective an account that it was instrumental in the group's breakup.

At the start of the First World War Kirchner fell ill, and in 1917 he settled in Davos, broken in health. Gradually there appeared in his paintings a sturdy peasant and mountain world: his colors became stronger and healthier, his forms were resolved more rectangularly, his structural organization was firmer. The distraught city dweller now lived like a peasant in an isolated mountain hut, dedicated wholly to his work. It was there that I met him, sometimes willing to talk, sometimes sunk in gloom. From 1922 Lise Gujer, a weaver of tapestries, used designs he created. In 1923 a comprehensive exhibit of his work was held in Switzerland which made such an impression that a Kirchner "school" developed in Switzerland.

In 1926, probably under the influence of the post-Cubist Picasso, Kirchner's symbolic period began. Bold linear loops and broad contours now form an abstract, highly individual rhythm. Divided objects are pulled together, the unity of others is broken up, figures and heads are shown from several angles in Janus-like double vision. But in the end Kirchner reversed himself, perhaps because he suspected a certain senselessness in these oversimplified symmetries. In 1936 he wrote, "My work grows richer in detail ... I think. The older man loves details. To shape them from the greater thing is delight and joy." Although he now became interested in Picasso and Klee, he found the former too intellectual, the latter too frivolous. His illness grew serious. Chronic pain and the German political and cultural catastrophe plunged him into a despair that ended in suicide.

He left behind an enormous graphic oeuvre of approximately 1500 sheets, among them bold drawings

Erich Heckel. Dunes on Sylt, 1932

in pencil, pen, crayon, charcoal and wash. Some were expressive sketches from nature, others were drawn from memory, still others were finished compositions. The high point of Kirchner's graphic art, unlike Nolde's, was reached in the woodcut. By combining woodcut with wood engraving, he achieved a singular dynamism distinguished for its grainy, linear quality. Noteworthy are his illustrations for Chamisso's *Peter Schlemihl* and for *Umbra Vitae*, by the expressionistic poet Georg Heym.

Erich Heckel (b. 1883), a Saxon like Schmidt-Rottluff and Pechstein, was also one of the great masters of German Expressionism, but he had a much gentler approach to life. He knew Schmidt-Rottluff from his youth; Kirchner he met in 1904 while studying architecture at the Dresden Polytechnic Institute.

A number of Expressionist painters were drawn from the study of architecture to this kind of painting, which was becoming more firmly established.

Heckel's early themes included the twilight world of variety artists and clowns, also primitive foresters, seafarers, peasants and gypsy-like girls, in strange contrast to the realistic scenes of city life that the public expected. He rejected all commissions for portraits, preferring to paint only close friends in the new language. He laid out his canvases with powerful wedges of color, but the forms thus hewn were concerned more with the things of this world and with realistic space than were Kirchner's. Consequently Heckel was able to bring atmosphere and light to his landscapes. In some of his paintings we find solidified a strong, almost crystalline luminosity. Sky, clouds and distance dominate to a greater extent than in the paintings of his friends in the group. At times he preserves the vanishing point and allows the horizon to arch imperceptibly, thereby developing a definite feeling for space between his exotic figures and green-laden treetops. Often in his summer landscapes, in which nudes on sunbathed shores lie waiting, a luminous life force prevails over the dark powers of nature. Above all, tension and order were balanced in his paintings.

After this period of demonic expression, intense color and angular forms (Plate V), a gentler benevolence toward all creatures becomes evident. From 1920 his colors grew softer and less stirring in effect. In 1940, decorative elements even began to appear in his work. Such a development may be found quite often in sensitive natures who have been carried along at first by stronger colleagues—in Heckel's case, probably by Kirchner and Schmidt-Rottluff. But other associations also play an intervening role in Heckel's relationships with the Brücke group, whose eccentricity and exclusiveness has long been

Erich Heckel. Self-Portrait, woodcut, 1917

Karl Schmidt-Rottluff. Rising Moon, 1956

overestimated. In 1910 he met Franz Marc in Munich; in 1912 he worked with Macke, and on the island of Hiddensee with Feininger. That same year, with Kirchner, Heckel painted the chapel at the Cologne Sonderbund Fair, where the entire art world was assembled. The First World War brought him in contact with Ensor and Beckmann in Belgium. There he painted his *Madonna of Ostend*. In 1927 and 1928 he traveled on the Rhine and in Provence, went to England and Scandinavia, and finally to Paris. In 1931 and 1936 he went to Italy, where he was excited above all by Etruscan art. The most important years of his life, however, were spent in Berlin. When his studio was destroyed by bombs in 1944, he moved to Hammenhofen, on Lake Constance, where the gentle landscape may have been dangerous for the strength of his art. In 1949 he was given a professorship at the Karlsruhe Art Academy.

In the graphic arts Heckel's woodcuts are especially noteworthy, but he also practiced etching, drypoint and lithography. Each of these artists from northeastern Germany spoke in universal terms, especially in their graphic work. But nearly all of them were also sculptors, strongly influenced by the austere rhythms of exotic art forms. Heckel's brother had introduced the group to African sculpture, which was quite similar to their own. Their acceptance of primitive art, which was to fortify decisively the expressive yearnings of European artists, was unequivocal. As the imitative nineteenth-century styles faded away, the basic laws of plastic structure again fascinated the artist.

The youngest member of the Brücke was the Saxon *Karl Schmidt-Rottluff* (b. 1884). According to Kirchner he started off with "a monumental Impressionism." Until about 1910 he worked with thick, exciting

Karl Schmidt-Rottluff
Head of a Laborer, woodcut, 1923

gobs of color flowing freely from the tube. In 1906 he painted with his friend Nolde on the island of Alsen, and in 1907 with Heckel in Dangast on the Oldenburg coast. In 1911 he went to Berlin, which enchanted him. Military service followed, after which he saw Italy, Paris, Rome. Under the Nazi regime he was removed from the Prussian Academy and forbidden to paint, but after the Second World War he was given a professorship at the Berlin Academy.

He was never one of those painters who are swayed by outside influences. The themes are constant: powerfully mobile landscapes (Plate VI), primitive figures, robustly conceived portraits and still lifes which are heavily weighted in the foreground. His paintings are never experimental in form, as are Klee's. Compared with Klee's almost feminine calligraphy and play of color, Schmidt-Rottluff's attack seems harsh. His forms fill the space block-like, as if hewn with an axe. His colors gradually attained a barbaric power through complementary contrasts, surpassing anything undertaken by other members of the Brücke. His painting, unlike Kirchner's, was not articulated by vertical graphic lines within the form. Because of this approach, Carl Einstein, in 1926, commented insolently: "He monumentalizes like a clod."

An unbroken architectonic power lies in his pictures, a forceful tonality with an almost symbolic color structure. Often his expression seems Cyclopean. "I realize that as far as I am concerned, I have no new art program, only the inexplicable longing to grasp what I see and feel, and to find for it the purest expression."

Nevertheless, latent struggles underlie his development. His brilliant colors often clash with the weight of his construction. After his thickly flowing early Impressionist style had disappeared, he began to work with larger, flatter pictorial elements, although by 1912 Cubist forms also strive for recognition. Schmidt-Rottluff, however, never analyzed form as did the French Cubists. His pendulum swings back and forth between such possibilities until, in 1920, his "zone painting" appears: color blocks and space areas are separated no longer by the simple, single stroke of a color-laden brush, but by means of complementary color halos which frame the object and create color zones around them.

In his watercolors, largely landscapes, Schmidt-Rottluff's color is subdued, sometimes almost flaccid. But in his late period the pictures glow once more with bold and luminous colors.

In view of his style, it is easy to understand that he was also a sculptor, like Kirchner and Heckel. At that time everyone was collecting African sculpture with its severely cut, barbaric juxtaposition of positive and negative forms. Since 1950, Schmidt-Rottluff has been cutting heads and figures from small pieces of limestone which he himself picked up.

In his graphic work, the woodcut was most significant, dominated by salient edges and deep-cut furrows, executed in powerful crosshatchings and contrasting light effects, which resulted in a geometric surface tension that is extremely effective from a distance and would have filled the Constructivists with

Otto Mueller · Nudes, 1926

enthusiasm. The older, gentler artist, Munch, however, was startled by these prints, and the director of the Kupferstichkabinett in Dresden called them "inchoate caricatures"–critical disagreement could reach the boiling point over such a painter as Schmidt-Rottluff.

The Silesian, *Otto Mueller* (1874–1930), was the least passionate of the Brücke group. Though older than his friends, he was admitted to their circle only in 1910. He painted slim or woodenly angular adolescent girls who daydreamed under dull green trees placed diagonally in his compositions, their crowns bending lyrically over the figures. Mueller's paintings are flat, limited in plasticity, devoid of rounded forms. The mild nature-lyricism of Ludwig von Hofmann, with whom Mueller had studied in Dresden when he was young, still echoes through his work. But under the influence of the Brücke he adopted stronger outlines and a more angular figure composition. The life of the east European gypsy was to him what the South Sea islands had been to Gauguin.

He should have been a muralist, so great was his command of large flat surfaces, as is evident from the cycle of figures he painted covering the walls of his studio. In the deliberate parallelism of attitudes and simplified contours, Mueller felt himself, in some strange way, to be on the track of Egyptian painting. But his colors lacked the necessary luminosity. In their close correspondence and limited contrasts they suggested the last light of day, according better with his personal elegiac view of life (Plate VII). Often we find a composition of nothing more than pallid green, ocher or sulphur yellow, brown or gray interwoven with black. Occasionally there is a matte red. Because he painted on coarse sackcloth–in the beginning with oil paint, and after 1911 with pigments mixed with lime–his pictures give the impression of Gobelin tapestries. They express the muted, bucolic expectancy of all creatures. Nothing for them will ever change. The result is a far cry from the analysis of form or the shifting viewpoint of the Cubists.

In the graphic arts, Mueller (who had been a lithographer's apprentice for years in his youth) favored the gentle colors that conformed with his reserved approach to life.

Mueller was a small man, taciturn, with a sallow complexion, blue-black hair and melancholy eyes. He always wore an amulet, and he believed in ghosts. His mother is said to have been an abandoned gypsy child. Spiritually he stood between the melancholy of Lehmbruck and the thorniness of Kirchner, both of whom were his friends. He was also close to Erich Heckel. In 1907 Mueller moved to Berlin; in 1910 he traveled in Bohemia with Kirchner, and in 1919 he was offered a professorship at the Breslau Art Academy. He was always frail and died in 1930, not living to see his work destroyed by the Nazis.

Max Pechstein (1881–1955) was the least difficult and most carefree of the Brücke painters. His nature was boyish and fresh, but for all that, he was less experimental, less inventive and sensitive to the new visual signs of the times. He differed from Kirchner just as Macke, in the Blaue Reiter group, differed from Franz Marc. Pechstein's themes were similar to those of his fellow painters: dancers and music hall artists, bathers on the beach, the sea with its fishermen–especially the fishermen of the Kurische Nehrung, the spit of land on the Baltic Sea where he spent his summers. He began as a housepainter, then studied at the Dresden Art Academy.

Max Pechstein. Head of a Worker, 1912

Franz Marc. Landscape with Horses, 1913

A. von Jawlensky. Lady with Red Shawl, 1909

Max Pechstein
Canoe, 1917

In 1906 he joined the Brücke, but disappeared again in 1907 into the relaxed atmosphere of Italy; then in 1908 he settled in Berlin. He was the first German Expressionist to become generally accepted and successful. His forms remained more representational, his figures more tactile, his composition more conventional, thus providing the viewer with a less antagonizing form of Modernism. Pechstein was not really in step with the radical innovations of this group; with him, the Brücke opened out into the general stream of modern art. In fact, his departure from the group was felt to be a betrayal of its specific quality. Nevertheless it was also Pechstein who confronted the "old" Secessionists in Berlin

Conrad Felixmüller
The Artist and his Wife,
woodcut, 1915

with a "New Secession," and he became its president. He did not completely abandon exotically forceful form and color. Around 1910 he produced his most vital paintings and drawings, and in 1911 he protested in the name of modern art against the slanderous publications of Karl Vinnen. [In 1911 the Worpswede painter Vinnen (cf. p. 28) published *Protest Deutscher Künstler (Protest of German Artists)* in which he attacked modern French influences].

In the wake of Gauguin's flight to Tahiti, Nolde had gone to Polynesia, and Picasso, Kirchner and Heckel had come under the influence of African sculpture; in 1913–1914 Pechstein visited the Palau Islands in the western Pacific Ocean. The exoticism we have mentioned frequently should not be interpreted as a flight from Europe or as a sign of degeneracy, as it was by the conservatives who frowned on it. It resulted in recharging European art with fresh blood. Such a development seems always to take place when art forms lose aesthetic distance or have been consumed by the mere reproduction of nature. The First World War surprised Pechstein in Palau. The Japanese took him prisoner, but after a breathtaking escape as a stoker, he managed to get back to Germany. He was at once drafted into the army and shortly after was wounded. A letter written in the summer of 1919 shows how well he survived these ordeals. "I am working and absorbing strength like the moss that swells in the rain and transforms the forest into something miraculous. I am living in a state of ecstasy; I eat the air and could break my brush in the rapture of creation." He considered himself less esoteric than the friends of his former group. "Art is not frivolity but a duty to the people." He was inundated with commissions, including orders for the design of mosaics and stained-glass windows, and in 1926 he designed the stained-glass windows for the Labor Exchange building in Geneva. He was also prolific as a graphic artist.

As in the case of Heckel and Schmidt-Rottluff, Pechstein's later style was softer, the colors lighter but at the same time less exciting, and balance was stressed, but the quality of the work was still high. Today the later work painted at the beginning of a long illness, is not given the recognition it deserves. After Pechstein's appointment to the Art Academy, the Nazis, insatiable in their desire to destroy all modern art, also banned this popular Expressionist as degenerate; in 1941 he was forbidden to paint and was put under police surveillance. In 1945 he was given a professorship at the Hochschule für Bildende Künste in Berlin where he died in 1955, his vitality consumed by his long illness.

The Saxon *Conrad Felixmüller* (b. 1897), the son of a Dresden blacksmith, may also be counted among the Expressionists. He became interested in the new art forms in 1914, and his work was published by Herwarth Walden in his magazine *Der Sturm*. Felixmüller painted somewhat in the manner of the Brücke masters, but more wildly. Then he turned to "action painting" and a politically-oriented Expressionism. The development of his style was extremely mixed in aim and form. At one time he toyed with both Cubist and Futurist vocabulary; he was drawn also to popular realism. Eventually, he adopted an eclectic manner. Basically his art suffered from the influence of the class struggle, sociological realism pulling him—and others—away from aesthetic problems of form, with inevitable dualistic results. The poet Carl Sternheim, who felt a kinship with Felixmüller's robust Expressionism, wrote rather exaggeratedly in 1923, "He tore the aesthetic mask from every landscape... and from the face of his contemporaries; in his pictures the proletarian who, until now, had been overlooked by the bourgeoisie, appeared for the first time."

The Silesian *Ludwig Meidner* (1884–1966) brought so much pathos to German Expressionism that the Brücke painters, who were certainly filled with urgency and passion, seem disciplined in comparison. Meidner's paintings and graphic art were so convulsive that one understands the virtual inevitability of a reaction against this emotionalism, a reaction that took the form of the New Objectivity. His was "cosmic outcry," even before the First World War. From 1912 he exhibited in the Sturm Gallery. From 1925 to 1932 he devoted himself to literary work, for words moved him no less powerfully than the visual. In 1936 he was forced to emigrate, but he eventually returned to Germany, living, after 1953, in the Taunus Mountains. He turned toward realism gradually. Of his writings, *Hymnische Prosa (Hymnic Prose)* and *Gang in die Stille (Walk in Silence)* are worth mentioning.

Ludwig Meidner
The City and I, 1913

Heinrich Nauen. Bathers, 1913 · Krefeld, Kaiser Wilhelm Museum

With *Heinrich Nauen* (1880–1940) Expressionism veered westward to absorb Lower Rhenish influences, becoming almost mournfully elegant. Nauen placed flat, leaflike, elongated figures diagonally across a wide canvas, partly in curvilinear and partly in triangular patterns. His color was light in key and extremely varied. He planned wall decorations whose effect depended on distance, and from 1912 to 1913 he was able to realize such a series at Drove Castle near Düren. However, because of the subjectivity of this approach he was incapable of devising a simple, adequate theme for such a major assignment. As a result we find juxtaposed in one room a classical Amazon battle, a modern harvest picture, an almost medieval Pietà, and a scene from the life of a contemporary lady–all done in the same style!

Between 1904 and 1910 Nauen worked wholly under the influence of Van Gogh, then developed, via Matisse, a broad but rather feminine sinuousity in his figures. The promise in his early work of a spacious style that was sensitively dynamic in composition was never altogether fulfilled. From 1921 to 1936 Nauen taught at the Düsseldorf Art Academy.

The life of *Wilhelm Morgner* (1891–1917) underwent many transformations. He painted foresters in their native habitat, herdsmen, strange self-portraits and above all, religious themes. He was one of those men of genius in whom strange contradictions murmur, yet who seek withal to form a unity. Profound agitation and harmony, the medieval mysticism of his native Soest with its seven church towers, Kandinsky's modern art—all these things he wished to unite harmoniously. The Expressionist phase through which he passed (Nolde and Rohlfs also worked in Soest for a while) lent his work a rhythmical order. His languid colors gave the effect of a heavy woven texture and in these years his originally objective art comes close to absolute painting. In his later pictures we find the green that clings to old garden walls, a beautiful brick red, a burnt-clay yellow; blue, on the other hand, he tended to avoid. In his best pictures the color is applied in long broad stripes, drawing foreground and background together into a single plane. At the time he was searching for a quiet little house with a few arable acres, he was already in touch with the Blaue Reiter group and influenced by Italian futurism. His *Entry into Jerusalem* is not altogether dissimilar in style to the medieval paintings in the churches of Soest. Making a critical selection from his varied works (235 paintings and almost 2000 sheets of graphic art), one could assemble an oeuvre that is much too little known. Had Morgner lived longer, he would in all probability have developed a more lavish color dynamic. More than forty years ago he wrote, "Now I want to capture in color the God who made the world, the strength that bears the earth... to transform this life into a color-form symphony." But in 1917, when he was only twenty-six, we read the bleak words, "missing at Langemarck."

Wilhelm Morgner. The Entry into Jerusalem, 1912

THE BLAUE REITER AND RELATED TRENDS

While the Expressionists of the Brücke group were still clinging passionately to the forms of the world around them, a second movement was experimenting even more freely with color and form. But before we discuss the circle of the Blaue Reiter, one other independent figure should be mentioned.

Johann Thorn-Prikker (1868–1932) came from Holland, but he developed his potentialities on north German soil. In 1904 he was called to Krefeld, where he revived mosaics, stained glass and murals. His work was based on the anti-realistic tendencies of the Jugendstil, but gradually he abandoned its soft curvilinear contours and stiffened his figures, which grew constantly more abstract. With his clear, penetrating mind, he had a stimulating effect on north German art circles. He dematerialized monumental art by a consistent renunciation of spatial illusion, at the same time finding attractive formulas for his figures which occasionally brought him quite close to a nonobjective art. He favored a taut dynamic linear expression rather than a wealth of color; in structuring contour and space he was somewhat too rational and decorative.

A more fruitful impetus for the further development of painting came, however, from Munich after the reforms of the Secession and Jugendstil had outlived their day. It was decisive for the artistic climate that the following painters were working in Munich, all of them less interested in an intensification of expression than in giving a many-sided spiritual meaning to form and color: Kandinsky, who had moved to Munich as early as 1896, Jawlensky and Marianne von Werefkin (all three Russians); and Franz Marc and Paul Klee, both of whom also arrived in Munich before 1900. At first they were strictly disciples of Cézanne, Van Gogh and Gauguin, but soon they became receptive to the simplifications of the Fauves. Kubin and Klee brought their surrealistic graphic imagination to the group. Kandinsky founded the Phalanx, a school of painting which in 1904 was exhibiting Neo-Impressionist work.

In 1909 the *Neue Künstlervereinigung* (New Artist's Federation) was formed, with Kandinsky, Jawlensky, Kanoldt, Kubin, Erbslöh, and the two women, Werefkin and Gabriele Münter. They brought in the Russians Bechtejeff, Kogan, and Sacharoff, the dancer; the French painters Girieud and le Fauconnier; and the Germans, above all Marc, Hofer, and the art historian Otto Fischer. Paintings by Picasso, Braque, Derain, Rouault and Vlaminck were shown, which gives an indication of the European radius of the group. Otto Fischer formulated what they had in common with the Brücke, which had preceded them: "Color is a means of expression that speaks directly to the soul. Color is a means of composition. The true nature of things is not captured by correct drawing but by a powerful and mobile, penetrating and permeating outline." Unfortunately he added, "A picture without an object is senseless." But controversy raged more over the goal of the greatest possible freedom for art than over nonobjective art. In this historic hour a schism developed among the artists themselves just as a new exhibition was being planned. The more fainthearted gathered around Erbslöh and Kanoldt; the more aggressive sided with Kandinsky and Marc. The quarrel was mainly about a painting of Kandinsky's, a *Last Judgment*, which was rejected as too big and bold. Kandinsky, Marc, Kubin and Gabriele Münter left the New Artists' Federation. In December 1911, they organized at the Thannhauser Gallery the now historic exhibition, *Der Blaue Reiter*. From Munich the exhibition traveled to Cologne, Berlin, Hagen and Frankfurt. In

Munich it included, among other works, paintings by Henri Rousseau, Delaunay, Macke, Kandinsky, Marc, Campendonk and Münter; Arnold Schönberg was represented as an amateur painter. Three months later an exhibition of graphic art was held at the Goltz Gallery, also in Munich, in which artists from the Berlin New Secession and the Brücke took part as well. Feininger did not join until later. In 1913 the more important members of the Blaue Reiter group exhibited at the first German Salon d'Automne in Berlin. This lively international interplay broke off in 1914, however, because of the war Kandinsky and the other Russians had to leave Germany; Macke was killed in action in 1914, Marc in 1916. Kandinsky, Klee and Feininger were not to meet again until the Bauhaus years.

The name *Der Blaue Reiter* (The Blue Rider) came from the *Almanac* compiled by Marc and Kandinsky in 1911 and published by Piper the following year. On the title page was Kandinsky's little figure on horseback. "We intend to publish an almanac that shall voice all the new and true ideas of our day. Painting, music, the stage... much will be clarified above all through comparative material... we shall bring old glass painting, French and Russian folk drawing, side by side with material of our own and of others." Kandinsky argued "the question of form," Marc wrote about the Fauves, Burliuk discussed related tendencies in Russia. Allard reported on Cubism and Busse on Delaunay, Schönberg wrote on modern music. Thus as early as 1911, almost all phases of anti-naturalistic expression were being examined collectively, and this may be considered the philosophical import of the manifesto. "The great success of the publication," Kandinsky said later, "was proof to us that it was born at

Wladimir von Bechtejeff. Diana Hunting, circa 1910
Munich, Bayerische Staatsgemäldesammlungen

Marianne von Werefkin. The Boat, circa 1910

Adolf Erbslöh. Mountains, Upper-Bavaria, 1911
Karlsruhe, Staatl. Kunsthalle

the right time. Encouraged, we made plans for the next issue, which was to unite the powers of artist and scientist."

All in all, this group was less fierce, less violent in expression than the Brücke. The latter included far more urban realism in its themes. In the Blaue Reiter group there was a great thirst for beauty and the romantic, although we must differentiate between two separate currents. Some members of the group inclined more strongly to Expressionism and French Fauvism, others bowed to the experimental form of analysis which Marc called "the mystic inner construction." He himself went through both phases and brought them to a harmonious conclusion.

In accord with the historic law of inertia, this new form of Expressionism at first provoked intense opposition. The *Münchner Neueste Nachrichten* wrote: "One either comes to the conclusion that the majority of its members... are incurably insane, or that we are dealing here with shameless bluffers who are well versed in the sensationalism of our times and intend to make the most of a favorable opportunity." Marc replied furiously, "Our sensibilities have become so blunted, our eyes so banal, that they see the most superficial comparisons with nature as useful criteria of art; our minds have become so lethargic that they can no longer tell the imitative impulse from the driving force of art."

Franz Marc (1880–1917) was a profoundly peace-loving nature-mystic; a revolutionary creator of form but with a Franciscan spirit; a rich colorist yet an abstract thinker. He was blessed with precise knowledge of the shapes of nature (as is proved by the drawings made in a veterinary school in his student days), yet at the same time he developed melodic rhythms, sometimes lyrical, sometimes

Franz Marc. The Red Deer, 1912 · Munich, Bayerische Staatsgemäldesammlungen

Franz Marc. Horses. 1913

dramatic (Plate IX). The supple unity binding his forms and their rounded beauty of shape and color
have led some critics to call his art decorative. But whoever knew him personally remembers the quiet
dominance that radiated from this dark-eyed man of Latin appearance.

Marc's rapid development reminds one of Raphael. Both men lived at a turning point in time, acting to
reconcile its contradictions; both died in their thirties; both in a few short years passed effortlessly
through multiple phases of growth. Raphael gradually developed and perfected an all-encompassing
system of wall decoration by proceeding from the stately groups of his teacher, Perugino, to a centralized
grouping, and then added to this the contrapunto of Michelangelo. Similarly, Marc passed through many
different stages before achieving his final solutions. He began with simple, lyrical impressions of nature,

and moved to an intense expression of the hidden inner spirit of animal life; from here he undertook Cubist-like analyses of form, adding to them Futurist variations, arriving at the very end at an abstract art. For each one of these steps any other painter would have required a decade; Franz Marc explored all these possibilities in eight years.

From representing people he turned to painting animals, for he saw in them a less isolated form of existence. He represented them in embryonic positions, as if resting in the sheltering mother-body of the earth. He drew the limbs of deer or cats so that they look like snail shells, thus joining aspects of nature that actually are widely separate. He thought he saw the animal to some extent as it sees itself. With all this he achieved a magical effect that went far beyond artistic questions, and he gradually became the first painter of his generation to achieve genuine popularity. Marc raised our perception of the animal to completely new heights. In 1912 he went so far as to hope "to create symbols that shall belong on the altar of a future religion of the mind, behind which the technical creator shall disappear... The art of the future shall be the form of our scientific convictions."

As he sought an ever more unified composition, he said, "Our minds already sense that the fabric of natural law hides something behind it, a greater unity." He also grasped intuitively the mutations going on in other art forms. In 1911 he wrote to Macke, after an evening of Schönberg's chamber music, "Can you imagine music in which tonality has been completely abandoned? I was reminded constantly of Kandinsky's large compositions which are written, as it were, in no single key... when listening to this music which lets every tone stand by itself... so that the conceptions consonance and dissonance don't even exist. A dissonance is simply a consonance that is more widely spaced... an idea that today absorbs me constantly in my painting."

Toward the war which was to end his life he had a strange relationship, characteristic of his almost-too-harmonious feeling for life. Although the horror of battle moved him deeply, he saw war exaggeratedly as a cosmic event which had to be accepted affirmatively (an attitude that no serious person could continue to hold when faced with World War II).

Marc was the son of a mediocre Munich painter. In 1900 he studied at the art academy in that city and visited Paris and Brittany in 1903. His pallid early paintings are interwoven with surging Jugendstil curves combined with impressionistic handling. In 1907, during another short stay in Paris, he was impressed by the intensities of Van Gogh. After this trip he moved to a rural section of Upper Bavaria and until 1908 painted chiefly single animal figures; then he turned to rhythmic compositions of animal groups. When Macke and Kandinsky became his friends, the former led him to a more luminous color key, the latter to a certain abstraction. During this time he painted large compositions of horses in which he let the colors rise to a crescendo. In 1910 he said, "I am constantly mulling over my system of complementary colors, the only way out of my insipid color scheme." (Macke had commented that the Germans unfortunately had a tendency to use light for color.) In 1911 Marc painted his *Three Red Horses*, which he based on the three complementary contrasts: red-green, blue-orange, yellow-violet... "their forms monstrously strong and clear so that they can take the color." *The Blue Horse* is also of 1911. From 1912 elements of Cubism enter, chiefly in the prismatic color scale of Delaunay, whom Marc, together with Macke and Klee, visited that year. After he had been dazzled by the Italian Futurists at a Berlin exhibition, his forms began to splinter dynamically across the canvas. "One is no longer attached to nature but destroys it in order to reveal the mighty laws beneath the beautiful appearance of things." At early as 1912 he said clairvoyantly, "In the twentieth century we shall live among strange faces, new pictures and unheard-of sounds." In his *Tower of Blue Horses* (1913) the expression of form was no longer dependent on the bulging animal bodies but manifested a demanding life of its own. Marc considered *Animal Destinies*, painted in the same year, his masterpiece. He wrote in a letter to Macke, "the trees bared their rings, the animals their veins," and on the back, "and all being is flaming sorrow." He was thirty-six years old when he was killed at Verdun. Marc's death was a great loss to German art because he had succeeded in extracting syntheses from almost all the progressive directions in the European painting of his day. Toward the end he experimented more and more often in purely abstract painting, in which he wanted to reveal only the radiance and motion of the cosmos.

August Macke (1887–1914) was born in Westphalia and grew up on the Rhine. He brought simple tone, fresh in color, into the melodics of the Blaue Reiter group. (Plate VIII.) Franz Marc's complicated emotionalism and the revolutionary intellect of Kandinsky, who was twenty years older, were foreign to him. "He was broad and tall, with a healthy, laughing face," his friend Schmidtbonn wrote, and Macke said, "For me, work is a joyous encompassing of nature."

First came the Düsseldorf Academy, trips to Italy and the Netherlands, and after 1907, increasingly often to Paris. The Berlin collector Bernhard Köhler soon made a carefree life possible. From 1910 on, he became friendly with Marc and lived with him on the Tegernsee for a year. In an abbreviated manner Macke experienced the stages of development that were usual in those days: from 1907 to 1909, a form of Impressionism, but even so in 1907 he wrote that he had tried "to assemble colors on a board without any objects in mind... what makes music so enigmatically beautiful, also has a magical effect in painting." He was still inspired by Cézanne's rejection of apparent form. In 1910 he saw a comprehensive Matisse exhibition in Munich which enflamed his color without, however, inducing him to break up forms. From 1912 he worked, like Marc, with a Cubist division of color. In 1913 Delaunay and Apollinaire visited him in Bonn.

His *Mitteilungen (Intimations)* provide confirmation of this development. At first he lauds the mere scattering of the purest colors possible, after which he praises the intensities of the Fauves and Expressionists. Then he stresses the point that in all good painting one finds "contrasting groups, either in color–a clash of red-green-yellow–or in a more formal conflict of space and lines." In Delaunay he admires the way in which the painter works without chiaroscuro, yet achieves a strong forward and backward motion in spite of it. "All the Futurists do is *illustrate* motion." While Marc was experiencing Cubism metaphysically, as "inner construction," Macke employed Cubism to attain a transparent, simultaneous and sensuously strong pictorial architecture. In Macke's prismatic color division there lies something juicy and worldly. While Marc was absorbed by animal symbolism, Macke remained true to the city dwellers; he painted people in ordinary parks or looking at shop windows, although he used a tropical color scheme.

From 1913 to 1914 he lived on the Thunsee and became friendly with Klee. Early in 1914 the two of them undertook a successful trip to Kairouan, the old Tunisian Berber capital, where Macke produced thirty-seven radiant, clearly constructed watercolors and hundreds of drawings. But later in 1914 Macke entered the army and was killed in action almost immediately. Marc wrote mournfully from the front,

August Macke. Red House in the Park, 1914

shortly before his own death, "With the elimination of his harmonies, all color in German painting will diminish by many degrees and will be duller, and drier in tone."

Alexej von Jawlensky (1864–1941) emerged from Russian folk art and blended a true fervor for color with the aspirations of German Expressionism and the French Fauves. (Plate X.) He painted gigantic heads with huge eyes; their firm scaffolding, which is so effective seen from afar, reminds one of icons, but his colors burn. Macke's colors had a noonday glow; Jawlensky painted with the fire of evening. Spread between dark outlines, red, blue, orange, cadmium yellow and chromium-oxide green press forward, often with ecstatic power. While his younger countryman Chagall was moving gradually toward dreamlike, ephemeral themes, Jawlensky adhered to a static, decidedly monumental form of expression. A severe, oversimplified canon of form was repeated again and again. The square format suited his tendency toward the compact. From 1917 he painted a series of mystical heads and also *The History of the Savior*. "In my latest works I have rejected the magic of color in order to concentrate on a spiritual profundity." Gradually these faces were filled with nothing more than silvery light areas, until, in a short final phase, we find only the muted colors of night.

76

Before these mystical heads he had painted heavy half-length figures, landscapes and still lifes. Following an old family tradition he was destined, as the son of a Russian colonel, to be an officer; at the age of eighteen he entered the Moscow military academy and was soon made lieutenant of a grenadier regiment. But he turned out to be a lieutenant who burst into uncontrollable tears when listening to Beethoven's *Pastorale* Symphony. During vacations on the estate of the young painter Marianne von Werefkin he painted the Tartar steppes. He served his regiment as captain, but in 1896 emigrated to Munich with Marianne von Werefkin and entered the art academy of which Kandinsky soon became director. Thus two Russian aristocrats fought through to the creation of a revolutionary art form. They were soon followed by another Russian officer, Bechtejeff (with whom we shall deal under the heading of sculpture). The impresario Diaghileff, whom Jawlensky had known in St. Petersburg, made it possible for him to exhibit in the Paris *Salon d'Automne*. All in all, the Russian contribution during this opening phase of modern art is noteworthy.

When he was painting in Brittany in 1905, Jawlensky at last felt that he was "painting what he felt, not merely what he saw." In Munich, his studio and the salon of Marianne von Werefkin became gathering places for the revolutionary artists. Here an international atmosphere prevailed, seething with new ideas. The dominant spokesman was Kandinsky, with whom Jawlensky painted summer-filled landscapes in Murnau. To Kandinsky's friend, Gabriele Münter, Jawlensky said, "A portrait does not have

August Macke
Promenade, 1913
Munich,
Städtische Galerie
im Lenbachhaus

Alexei von Jawlensky. Head, 1913
Winterthur, Volkart-Stiftung

Alexei von Jawlensky. Abstract Head,
circa 1926/1928

to be a likeness. A hundred years from now, no one will know what the sitter looked like." This is the group that formed the Neue Münchner Künstlervereinigung in 1909. Their shows were received by the public with scorn and ridicule. Jawlensky did not join the Blaue Reiter until 1912.

With the outbreak of the First World War, Jawlensky had to leave Germany. He lived rather wretchedly on the Lake of Geneva where he painted small, reduced landscapes from his modest window. "Variations" were now his chief concern. In 1921 he moved to Wiesbaden and immersed himself again in his abstract heads. In 1924, with Kandinsky, Klee and Feininger, he formed *Die Blauen Vier* (The Blue Four), a group which enjoyed its greatest success in the United States. But in 1929 he began to exhibit symptoms of paralysis and was able to paint only small heads, which he called *Meditations*, faces and visions that gave the effect of a double cross which at first glowed magically only to darken later. In 1938 total paralysis put an end to his last most serious efforts. The Nazis forbade the showing of his paintings, and he died a broken man in 1941.

Wassily Kandinsky (1866–1944) was soon recognized by his friends as the true leader of the group. Elsbeth Macke, who was close to him, wrote, "There was about him a peculiar and fantastic aura, combined with a strange pathos and dogmatism. His art was like a doctrine, a world viewpoint." Paul Klee, from a different viewpoint, declared he had "developed an increasingly deep confidence in him," and Marc, in spite of occasional doubts as to Kandinsky's humaneness, declared "Kandinsky's art is as prophetic as his word; he is the only seer in our group."

He was born in Moscow in 1866, thus belonging to the generation of the Impressionist Max Slevogt. Seemingly this contradicts the art historian Wilhelm Pinder's theories concerning the similarities of style among artists of the same generation. Kandinsky, however, was definitely a pioneer of the next generation, though late in terms of his own personal development. "Until I was thirty, I longed to be a painter... at the time it seemed to me that art was a forbidden luxury in Russia... but six years later I noticed that my belief in the therapeutic value of social science had vanished... so I proceeded to Munich, whose art schools were highly thought of in the Russia of those days." He failed the entrance examination for a drawing class at the Munich Academy, but Franz Stuck accepted him in his class. In 1900 he began to create independently and in 1903 was already teaching at the private art school, Phalanx. He traveled to Paris, Tunis, Rapallo. From 1908 he lived with Gabriele Münter in Murnau or in Munich. In 1910 he wrote his manifesto, *Über das Geistige in der Kunst (On the Spiritual in Art)*, which was published two years later by Piper, a total program for the nonobjective aims of the new painting. In 1913, *Der Sturm* edited a Kandinsky album, and Piper published *Klänge (Sounds)*, which included woodcuts and related short poems.

He began by painting figures objectively, in the decorative Jugendstil, sometimes even in a mosaic of color. He was in full control of conventional forms, contrary to the assumptions of some of the naive opponents of his later abstractions. He abandoned Stuck's pallid colors for a restless, forceful tonality that already seemed inclined to go beyond the controls of the object. Kandinsky explained what had been decisive for his nonobjective painting: Moscow under the setting sun had created in him an enthusiasm for the value of color per se, but the abstract folk art of Russia had played its part too. "There I saw peasant houses, their interiors covered with paintings, nonobjective ornamentation without theme, furniture, dishes, all painted. I had the impression of stepping into a painting that told no story." Finally he became excited by Monet's *Haystacks*, and by Matisse, who had almost completely transformed the object into pure color. Three currents, therefore, coalesced in producing the great turning-point: nature itself, an old folk art tradition, and the pioneering in color of the moderns. (Plate XII.)

Kandinsky's nonobjective painting may be best understood as a form of dynamic expressionism, a movement of inner feeling that fought to escape the limiting effect of the fixed object. In 1937 he wrote, "I went from Expressionism to abstract painting slowly, through endless trial, despair, hope and discovery. You can see that I never had anything to do with Cubism." In him the separation of art and nature was gradually completed, "until I was able to contemplate each by itself as entirely different from the other." "When in a picture," he goes on to say, "a line is freed from objective description and functions as a thing in itself, its inner tone is not weakened by the obligation to play a secondary role; rather it recaptures its full inner strength" (1912). And with all this he knew, in 1941, "the object by itself has a pervasive spiritual note that is art for art." Since his experiments were rejected everywhere as too intellectual, a further confession is important in which he says he never used a form "that had developed from logical rather than emotional perception."

The second phase of his development, between 1910 and 1920, he called his dramatic period, for now his colors and unreal forms force their way out and beyond the memory of the object, as if a volcanic power had been released. In this phase the pictorial elements separate, lines thrust beyond the color mass, transparent color is detached from the color of the ground. Yet the paintings preserve an irrational unity. But in 1913 he wrote, "Every work is created technically like the cosmos, through catastrophes which in the end form a symphony out of the chaotic roar of the instruments – a statement he would scarcely have made in later, more serene times. In his theories he constantly introduces analogies

Wassily Kandinsky. Landscape with Tower, 1908 · Paris, Collection Nina Kandinsky

to absolute music. But he did not rob painting of its unique nature, for he never rejected the specific properties which do not belong to music—line, color and space. His first completely nonobjective painting is dated 1910; he was already forty-four. "A frightening abyss, a wealth of significant questions worth an answer came to me. And the most important one: what is to take the place of the missing object? The danger of becoming decorative stood clearly before me." The problem of perspective also troubled him. The intrinsic weight of colors varied, and for this reason they produced different spatial effects, resulting in a pictorial depth "that brilliantly replaced the former depth-through-perspective."

It is deeply moving to witness his inner hesitation in constant struggle with instinctive confidence. "In those days I stood alone, because my painting was being passionately rejected. What I had to endure in the way of abuse was fantastic. 'An untalented swindler' was the favorite phrase." In 1914 the declaration of war drove him to Switzerland and from there he returned to his homeland and Moscow. After the Russian revolution he was offered professorships at home, but under Communism the opportunities for

Paul Klee. Villa "R", 1919

Wassily Kandinsky. Big and Tiny, 1937

Wassily Kandinsky
Dreamlike Improvisation, 1913
Munich, Collection J. Bienerl

modern art were short-lived. Therefore he returned to Germany in 1921. Gropius called him to the Weimar Bauhaus in 1922 (his work there will be discussed later). At the Bauhaus he joined Klee and Feininger again, and was able to develop a full career as a teacher while consolidating the foundations of his theories. The interaction of Kandinsky and Klee at Weimar reminds one of the friendship that once flourished in this same place between Schiller and Goethe: a dualistic, extremely rational and controlled vital empathy (Kandinsky) opposed to a monistic, irrational sensibility (Klee). Again antipodes joined forces and interacted.

Wassily Kandinsky. Composition IV, 1911 · Düsseldorf, Kunstsammlung Nordrhein-Westfalen

Of the women painters associated with the Blaue Reiter, *Gabriele Münter* (1877–1962) was the most prominent, through her friendship with Kandinsky. From her landscapes in a bright chromatic key, still lifes in forceful colors, flower pieces and portraits, radiates a tone which is sometimes dark, sometimes luminous, expressive yet always harmonious. "It was a time of great artistic renewal when I came to Munich to study in 1901." A year later Kandinsky was her teacher, and soon after that she lived with him in Murnau until the First World War. While he was developing his method of nonobjective painting, she remained faithful to an objective world which she embraced in a friendly fashion, except for brief efforts in other directions. She loved Bavarian folk art and the old *Hinterglasmalerei* (paintings on the reverse side of glass). Her south German form of Expressionism, very rich in color, therefore developed into something less massive and glowing than Jawlensky's. Her paintings remained serene, even when she used warm and cold reds, ultramarine and Prussian blue, together with black and white, also used as colors. Münter was born only a year after Paula Modersohn-Becker. The latter developed from the climate of solid formal values of Gauguin, whereas Gabriele Münter passed through the more mobile world of the Blaue Reiter. But we sense nothing revolutionary or radical in her long life, in the course of which her colors gradually become somewhat more transparent and lighter.

She spent the First World War in Scandinavia and Lapland. In 1931 she moved back to Murnau. Here, in the country, she was able to pursue her work, never spectacularly, yet never quite forgotten. Pleasant outline drawings with which she captured friends on paper give evidence of her ability as a portraitist. "More often than not I draw my picture with a brush, in black, on board or canvas, before I use color."

Often she painted in the evening because the effect of such painting was more powerful when seen later in the daylight. But her art, too, which no one could have called extreme, excited the fury of the National Socialists. Although only her more harmless paintings were to be shown at a certain exhibition in the Munich Art Academy, the Gauleiter in charge at the time had every picture taken down at the last moment and threatened to have them burned. In her later years, made sedentary by age, she tried her hand again at abstract art, as if she felt that her cycle was about to close and she wanted once more to recall her former mentor.

Heinrich Campendonk (1889–1957) was also a member of the Blaue Reiter. The style of his paintings and graphic art lies between Marc and Chagall. Strange animals and human forms are depicted in primeval coexistence amid willful vegetation, with a primordial connection to each other. But his compositions are not as melodically symmetrical nor as resplendently improvised in color as Chagall's. Campendonk's animals are unfamiliar creatures that belong to a rather gloomy, amphibian world. His colors are heavy with chthonian moisture. Whereas Marc seemed to be reaching harmoniously and ethereally upward, Campendonk gives an impression of groping downward. Later, however, his leaning toward the fantastic conflicted with his tendency towards decorative space composition. After a trip to Italy in 1920, during which Giotto and the mosaics of Ravenna made a profound impression on him, he developed an affection for static or monumental form. He was able to give it expression in decorative commissions: he designed stained-glass windows, primarily for churches in Wesel, Hamburg, Bonn and Fochen, but also for public buildings in Amsterdam, and after the Second World War he executed commissions for churches in Münster and Düsseldorf.

Gabriele Münter. Snowburden, 1943 · Munich, Städtische Galerie im Lenbachhaus

Gabriele Münter. Pensive Woman, 1917 · Munich, Städtische Galerie im Lenbachhaus

Heinrich Campendonk.
Interior, woodcut, 1918

Heinrich Campendonk
Cow Stable, 1917
Düsseldorf
Collection Fischer

As a young man in his hometown, Krefeld, Campendonk was led through the teachings of Thorn-Prikker to work in a rhythmical, decorative style. In 1911, through Marc and Kandinsky, who invited him to join them in Upper Bavaria, he was inspired to create fantasies in which he used cubist forms. *Der Sturm* published his woodcuts. In Bavaria the colorful fire of *Hinterglasmalerei* excited him. Although he did not succeed in reviving this folk art among people, he remained faithful to it. But even here he worked less with outline and more in color areas into which he subsequently scratched the drawing, thus achieving varied graphic effects. Later he turned again to glass painting and in 1937 created a huge painting on glass, several yards square, for the passenger ship Nieuw Amsterdam. In 1926 he was appointed to the Düsseldorf Academy of Arts; in 1933 he was dismissed as "degenerate," and the National Socialists removed eighty-seven of his works from German museums–simultaneously, he received the Grand Prix at the Paris World's Fair. Campendonk emigrated first to Belgium and then to Holland where he taught at the Academy of Fine Arts in Amsterdam. He became more and more introverted, never again took part in German exhibitions and disappeared prematurely from the consciousness of his country.

The Bauhaus and its Successors

We owe the foundation of the Bauhaus primarily to Walter Gropius whose innate qualities fitted him exceptionally for the task. Gropius quickly grasped new possibilities, and at the same time possessed the intellectual capacity to develop a unified program; furthermore, he was a gifted organizer, equally capable of translating his ideas into reality. Although he gave the impression of absolute determination, he was so broad-minded that he could combine under one roof opposing personalities of such stature as the humanist Schlemmer, the innovator of form Kandinsky, the dreamer Klee, and the geometrist Moholy-Nagy.

The Bauhaus was founded in 1919 in Weimar and in 1925 moved to Dessau. It may be considered the fourth effort made in this century to form a working community of artists in individualistic Germany. The first was associated with the Jugendstil movement and led (in Munich, for instance) only transiently to those "craft workshops" which added refinement to the aesthetic surface. This was followed by the Brücke, which injected new strength into the life stream of modern art through form and color, but which lasted only as long as the friendships of the group were maintained. The same applies to the Blaue Reiter. But the Bauhaus was based on architecture on the one hand and on a connection with industry on the other, with the result that much of the romanticism and introverted aspects of earlier attempts at unity were overcome. The idea of the medieval workshop took on a new shape: sculpture, furnishings, lighting, weaving, dance and other forms were brought under the encompassing aegis of modern architecture. But most important, at the Bauhaus a new method of teaching was evolved which enabled the further development of much that had already been achieved. No other country had ever succeeded in uniting so many highly individualistic masters under one roof. Now, for a few years at

Wassily Kandinsky. Yellow, Red, Blue, 1925 · Paris, Collection Nina Kandinsky

least, a constructive union was achieved in Germany that was able to overcome all individual eccentricities.

The concept of the Bauhaus was based on the combination of planning, handwork and the machine, putting aside all projects conceived on paper. Toward this end it was decided to proceed from one general basic course which should include, beside the study of nature, a demonstration of methods of composition with the most varied materials and designs. But the Bauhaus met with vehement opposition. The conservatives suspected too much "machine culture;" the moderns were against the inclusion of the crafts. Then came the National Socialists who considered Bolshevik the entire form world of the Bauhaus, at the same time as the Bolsheviks themselves had forbidden Bauhaus ideals and were propagating an art which was identical with that of National Socialism.

The Bauhaus sought a connection between its workshops and industry; as many students as possible should be able to earn their living. The experimental was encouraged, partly to shake off all imitative styles, partly to further the development of forms representative of the spirit of the times, but above all to give the student the opportunity to discover his own specific talents, which could evolve only in actual contact with the material required. The dangerous separation of fine and applied art had disappeared. The Bauhaus included cabinetmaking, pottery, metal shops, weaving, mural painting, work in glass, typography and architecture, and all were interrelated. At first each department was under the direction of a master-craftsman and an artist; this scheme was abandoned in Dessau, where architecture was more heavily stressed after Gropius had constructed buildings for the school. Today these buildings count as the most important examples of architecture of the energetic twenties. To the department of architecture were now added teachers of construction, statics and descriptive geometry.

When the Weimar administration switched from the left to a "nationalistically oriented" policy, the school, which on the whole had been unpolitical, was considered dangerous and was liquidated. Through the farsightedness of the Dessau mayor they were able to settle immediately in that city (in 1925), and on an enlarged scale. Nearly the entire staff of masters moved to Dessau with Gropius: Feininger, Kandinsky, Klee, Schlemmer, Moholy, Muche; former students such as Josef Albers, Herbert Bayer, Marcel Breuer, Hinnerk Scheper, Jost Schmidt and Gunda Stölzl became teachers. Since they now had a stage, Schlemmer was able to broaden his ideas on pantomime and the geometrical human figure, which later was to be re-expressed in "unliterary speech." Moholy brought freer, more modern possibilities of expression and communication to subjective photography. Dance and pageantry were also drawn into the curriculum.

As closer cooperation developed, an increasing number of outsiders spoke lightly of a "Bauhaus style," but Gropius rejected this formulation. "The aim of the Bauhaus is not a style or system, not a dogma or

Wassily Kandinsky. Reciprocal Conformity, 1942 · Paris, Collection Nina Kandinsky

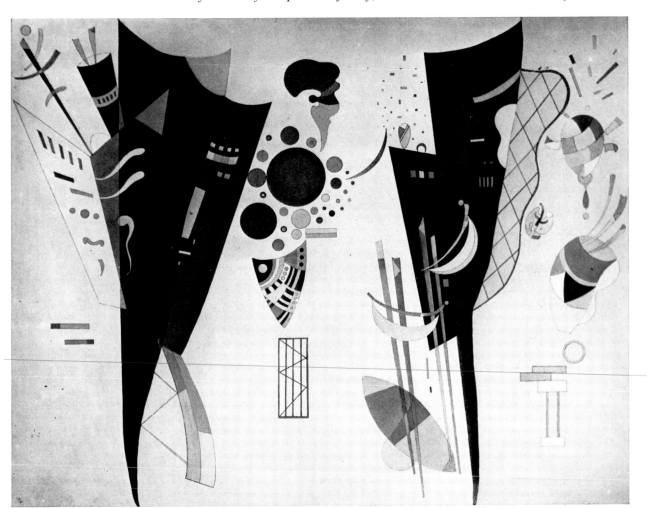

canon, not a prescription or fashion. It will be alive as long as it does not cling to form but seeks the fluidity of life behind all mutable form." Marcel Breuer wrote at the time that "every good and purposeful object should fit into any room, just like any living object, a flower or a person." Many of the varied curriculums conducted by Kandinsky and Klee have been published: beginning with the elements of painting, they taught a new way of thinking about plastic form.

Wassily Kandinsky (1866–1944) became a decisive influence in the Bauhaus. He had arrived at a differentiation between three aspects of his work: he called *Impressions* works which had evolved from objective motifs; his *Improvisations* were the result of feeling or sensitivity, of "inner movement;" the *Compositions* were thoroughly thought-out and organized works, on a monumental scale. In his Bauhaus period, his third phase, he consolidated his pictorial creativity. Exact forms of plane geometry appear, dots, segments of circles, triangles, conglomerations of straight lines. Instead of an irrationally flowing dynamism, we have strict regulation. Clear colors confront each other additively, apparently aiming at a constructivist statement wherein highly individualized visual tensions are achieved. In *Punkt, Linie zu Fläche (Point and Line to Plane)*, a Bauhaus publication (1923–1926), he pursued his theoretical experimentations, systematically analyzing his pictorial organization. Here the stress is on the meaningful purity of the elements as opposed to "just painting," which he deplored in his classes. Of course, in the writings of an artist, one should not always expect art historical logic, but rather one must feel the creative direction that is sought.

From the beginning Kandinsky strove for a synthesis of all the arts, including the dance, music and architecture, as the foundation for a rebirth of human society. For this reason he was a decisive influence on the Bauhaus. In 1928 he said, "I would be satisfied if the viewer sensed the inner life and relationships of the powers utilized." He found Constructivism too intellectual, saying, "An unfeeling mind is worse than mindless feelings." He denounced the practical *art engagé*, with its socialist content; it was an attempt, he wrote in 1935, to "salvage art by forcing it into the service of daily living. In it I see the only artistic crisis of our dismal times." The protest was aimed at the sociologically critical verism of Dix and Grosz, but above all at the "political realism" which grew so powerfully under dictatorships. But Kandinsky knew very well wherein the old and the new remained joined. "The basic law that governs the working method and energies of the objective and nonobjective painter is absolutely the same" (1931). And he had no intention of creating a conflict between the nature surrounding us and his radical transformation. "The abstract painter gets his inspiration not from any random piece of nature but from nature as a whole, and from its diverse manifestations which are summed up in his work" (1935).

When the National Socialists closed the Bauhaus in 1933, Kandinsky emigrated to Paris where exhibitions of his work made him internationally famous. His paintings fetched high prices and he was recognized as one of the most important painters of the day. In France he contributed significantly to the development of every aspect of abstract painting and furthered its continuous enrichment until it gained world acceptance. In 1944, at the age of seventy-eight, he died in Paris, working undiminished until his last breath. In his final period we see large, irrationally playful forms, bold color contrasts and radiant symbols that seem to stand on an infinite plane. Once more the echoes of the folklore of his west Siberian homeland may be heard, as if telling a story, but caught now in glasslike clarity. We see constructed and organic shapes; subtle and elementary colors meet in an ambience of purity. His last painting, like the swansong of a very old man, he called *"L'élan temporé" (Tempered Elan)*.

The art of *Paul Klee* (1879–1940) developed entirely on German soil until the year the National Socialists banished him and he withdrew to his native Switzerland. "My art lacks a passionate kind of humanity. I dearly love animals and many nonearthly creatures." He spun a dreamlike web, gathering his threads from the most remote sources. He began with subtle, extremely representational drawings and somewhat satirical prints. But this was followed, under the influence of the ideals of the Blaue Reiter, by a visionary transposition of form. After his journey to Tunis in 1914 his work became more colorful. This development was followed in the Bauhaus period by the introduction of an abstract play of forms, leading to a subtle and systematic dissection of the structure of his paintings through flat spatial areas, linear concentration and a kind of pointillist technique. At the end of his life, during his final illness in Switzerland, a somber symbolic sign language emerged.

In a mysterious way he managed somehow to reconcile all contradictions, to juxtapose unrelated, grotesque forms in pleasing harmony, to transform anxiety into reverence. "Investing Creation with permanence," as he himself put it. His importance lies less in his having given content to symbolic forms than in his transformation of them into pure signs (Plate XI). Whereas Surrealism aims at alienating us from the world we know, Klee makes us feel at home in an unknown, perhaps traumatic world. He writes, "The visual, in its relationship to the world as a whole, is but one isolated example, outnumbered by other latent truths." With this statement he comes mysteriously close to the sphere of nonobjective painting, although he rarely entered it. Again and again he hovers over the line between the expression of organic life and abstract art, holding both fields in magnetic conjunction. A special magic lies in his titles, which we should read while viewing the picture. The letters seem to twitter mysteriously, like little birds on a telephone wire. They indicate a mood: *Unstable Equilibrium, Fugue in Blue and Red, Three Notes Squared, Active Line Circumscribing Itself, Limits of the Intellect;* or they signalize remote constellations: *Laughing Gothic, Latticework Fence and its Enemy, Exit of Three Freaks, Growth of Night Plants, Pessimistic Allegory of Mountains, Countercurrent by Full Moon, Revolution of a Viaduct, Dance, Thou Monster, to my Gentle Song.*

Klee was born in Bern, Switzerland, in a household that cultivated music and cats. His mother's family came from the south of France; from her he may have inherited his dark hair and large Bedouin eyes. As a schoolboy he was already painting landscapes with a graphic feeling, and in 1898 he began his studies at the Munich Art Academy. On a journey to Italy he was excited by early Christian mosaics and Gothic art; in Naples by the life of the aquarium. In the Munich Kupferstichkabinett he discovered Beardsley, Blake and Goya, and his ironic-realistic, early graphic style was formed. But already he wrote, "Bound only very indirectly by the impressions of nature, I dare to give shape to whatever burdens my soul." Moving away from Kubin, he wrote that the latter "could not extricate himself from the tough slime of the world of appearances." Klee's pen drawings for Voltaire's *Candide* (1911–1912), with their spidery strokes and extended, spectral bodies, already wave and dart freely beyond the bounds of reality. Soon the drawings of children inspired him: they should be "taken more seriously than all the picture galleries put together when it comes to a question of today's reforms." His second period began in 1911, when he joined the Blaue Reiter group. A brief visit to Paris in 1912 was of minor importance for him, but through the Berlin *Sturm* he became acquainted with Delaunay and the Futurists, who led him to use more intense colors. After the short trip to Tunis with Macke, he was suddenly jubilant: "Color and I are one." In 1912 many of his works were exhibited at the Goltz Gallery in Munich. In 1920 Gropius brought him to the Weimar Bauhaus. At the same time short monographs on Klee by Zahn (1920), Wedderkopp (1920) and Hausenstein (1921) appeared.

At the Bauhaus Klee's third period began. All imitation was expunged; his intimate communications

Paul Klee
Variety Artist,
1924
Stuttgart
Private Collection

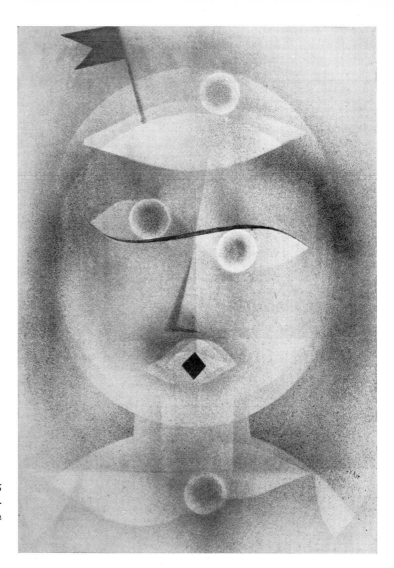

Paul Klee. Mask with Little Flag, 1925
Munich, Bayerische Staatsgemälde-
Sammlungen

now became exquisite color miniatures. A subtle order pervades his pictures, the effect partly of his teaching glass painting and weaving, and partly of Kandinsky's influence. For at this time these anti-podes were united through their work–Klee's pantheism was joined with Kandinsky's ordered dualism. Their teaching methods differed correspondingly. Kandinsky emphasized construction, Klee fostered his pupils' inner growth, although he too racked his brains over formal problems, as we know from his diaries, his *Pädagogische Skizzenbuch*, his essays and lectures. But reason, as in Leonardo's case, could never obliterate the mystic in him. "Evil," he acknowledged darkly, "should be allowed neither to conquer nor to confound us, yet it must be recognized as part of the whole creative process."

After Gropius left the Bauhaus, Klee accepted a professorship at the Düsseldorf Academy (1931–1933). Then he was summarily dismissed by the National Socialists, who saw this visionary artist as a "Siberian

Jew" and "a dangerous culture-Bolshevik." A series of drawings has been lost in which the banished artist articulated his fury, comparable to the *Songes et Mensonges (Dreams and Lies)* with which Picasso protested against the Franco regime in Spain at almost the same time.

With ever greater consistency, the world had been transformed for Klee from a frail correlated web into a delicately constructed scaffolding, without his colors having lost their intrinsic flexibility. Klee's gestures, forms, structures and parables had long since left behind any infantile aspects. The veins of his unfurling leaves, his loops, flowing lines, circles, the grillwork of his crystals were now clarified. For him, man had not been the measure of all things for a long time.

Soon after his flight to Switzerland in 1933 Klee's last period began. All aesthetic delicacy, precious transparency, miniaturization of the sublime disappear, and even the mocking quality in his personality. He worked with a broad brush and his symbols attained a sober grandeur; the format of his pictures became monumentalized. He preferred coarser materials; the crossthreads of the sacking cloth canvas show through and over it flow doughy, pasty colors. Often we see a leaden black grillwork that produces an effect of threat and obstruction; when the human body appears it is not infrequently dismembered and inert, as if its massive limbs were never to be rejoined. Forms overflow in a swollen effervescence; heavy

Paul Klee. Around the Fish, 1926 · New York, Museum of Modern Art

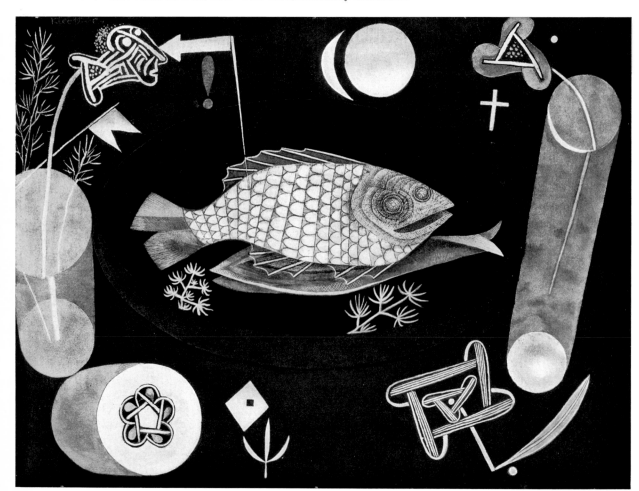

Paul Klee. Small Dune Landscape, 1926 · New York, Collection F. C. Schang

outlines dominate even his pastels. Sometimes he uses crayon on cotton or jute, or chalk is pressed down into a wet, heavy, absorbent surface.

It is not my intention to probe too deeply into the secrets of this last phase of his work before his death (in Muralto in 1940). Klee the magician was still not without hope and had not stopped creating pictures in joyous colors; in these, yellow and orange-to-terra cotta, or yellow-green and dark green are closely related, or certain dark symbols are outlined in lighter tones. But now we find oppressive titles: *Demonism, Outbreak of Fear, Monster in Waiting, Death and Fire.* Much of what he did in these last years of fatal illness and banishment now has the effect of a weighty *memento mori.* He died a lingering death, inexorably wasting away. On his grave is inscribed one of his profound confessions: "In this life I am no longer to be grasped. For I live with the dead as well as with those not yet born. A little nearer to the heart of creation than usual, yet not nearly near enough."

Lyonel Feininger
Church, 1936
New York
Metropolitan
Museum

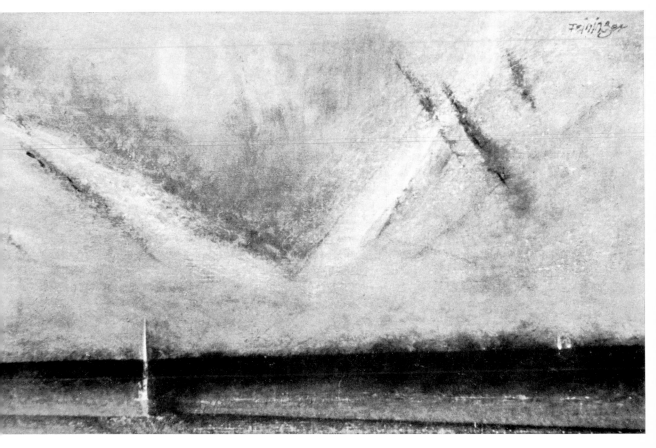

Lyonel Feininger. Baltic Landscape, 1946/47

Lyonel Feininger (1871–1955) joined the staff of the Bauhaus in 1919. (Plate XIII.) With his soundly constructed, spring-blond, gold-brown or delicate blue canvases, he turned Cubist principles towards a uniformly ordered transparency. He was easier to understand than Klee, who was more varied and jocose. Feininger's paintings are dominated by a smoothly polished elegance which does not always escape the pitfalls of virtuoso design. In his illuminated landscapes we find visionary edifices, their surfaces self-reflecting or faceted like crystal. A glassy stillness lies over everything. When Feininger places transparent vessels against the shimmering surface of the sea, he is able to condense the reflecting atmosphere so that it enters into every element of the encompassing fugal structure on which his composition is based. All growing things–trees, for instance–are assimilated to the architecture, yet his straight lines always remain dynamic. Reality and unreality are meant to permeate each other. One could call his seascape and architectural paintings polished dreams of light, from which he either eliminates the human figure or inserts it as punctuation.

As a child Feininger lived in New York, where he saw the crowded forms of that metropolis shoot up out of the ground. At the age of twelve he was already playing the violin at concerts; at sixteen he crossed the ocean to study music in his parents' native Germany, and also to become a student at the Academy of Applied Arts in Hamburg and at the Berlin Academy. At twenty-one he saw Paris for the first time, after which he settled down in Berlin and made a living by contributing drawings to German, French and American comic magazines. In 1907, with the advent of Cubism, he turned to more abstract forms, and in Paris in 1911 he met Delaunay, whose transparent-color Cubism, "Orphism," had also made a great impression on Marc and Macke. Macke invited Feininger to join the Blaue Reiter and to exhibit at the first Berlin Salon d'Automne, in 1913. In 1919 Gropius asked him to come to the Weimar Bauhaus. With Kandinsky, Klee and Jawlensky, he founded the *Blauen Vier* group. Feininger was also unable to escape National Socialist enmity; even his noble works, which never evoke the demonic aspects of Expressionism, were considered "degenerate." In 1936 he was offered a professorship at Mills College in California and after that settled in New York. The circle was closed. The little boy, born among the skyscrapers of New York, had traveled half way around the world only to return there in the end.

Some of Feininger's statements characterize his position as an artist: "For years I have wanted to present too much of nature, and for this reason have become increasingly popular with those who see a progression in my painting corresponding to their idea of closeness to nature." But everything had to pass "through a process of transformation, through a crystallization" (1907). About his feeling for color he writes, "It could be that in this respect I am poor when compared with others." And in 1950 he speaks of "the will for law and order and the elimination of all traditional accessories."

Oscar Schlemmer (1888–1943) stood a little apart from the Bauhaus because basically he carried on the tradition of monumental figure painting of Runge, Marées, Puvis de Chavannes and Hodler. His subject was the same, but his figures were more abstractly handled and presented at unusually close range. While Marées painted lonely humans interwoven in a twilit haze, Schlemmer, who was after all a contemporary of the Constructivists, turned his figures into columns rising up in imaginary spaces as if to achieve a system of coordinated forms. (Plate XIV.) He rejected improvisation and subordinated everything to strict laws of geometry. His color areas were severely composed; only later did he give them a more abrasive and warmer character. Important to him was a rhythmic parallelism in terms of towering verticals or extended horizontals which corresponded to one another; at most he admitted an occasional diagonal thrust. Any effect of motion in his paintings was harnessed in a way that congealed its living quality. He stated, "Runge's sentence has always appealed to me: 'Severe regularity is indispensable above all in those works that spring from the imagination and out of the mysticism of our souls, without external matter or content.'" Most rarely did Schlemmer resort to abstract paintings; even when he employed chiaroscuro, his figures did not soften, but seemed to stand out more independently than ever. All techniques were subservient to his intentions, whether oils on canvas, watercolors, pastels, *Hinterglasmalerei* or lacquer.

Schlemmer admired and wrote a monograph on his friend Meyer-Amden, who had studied painting in Stuttgart (1909–1912) and who died prematurely. In a muted and smaller format, Meyer-Amden had realized that tense stillness which Schlemmer heightens to monumental proportions. Schlemmer was

96

Oscar Schlemmer
Boy with Red Vest, 1928
Munich,
Bayerische Staatsgemäldesammlungen

also a sculptor, and it is in his sculpture that the human figure is abruptly reduced to a mere construction of limbs and signs. He executed reliefs on the stairwell of the Art Academy in Weimar, but Schulze-Naumburg, Gropius' successor, had these reliefs brutally obliterated. In his final years Schlemmer painted a cycle of small "window pictures" in which the human figure is magically captured on the cross of the window frame. At one time during the last years I commented to him that his whole life would be devoted to the human figure; he denied this and pointed out that now he also wanted to subject pure

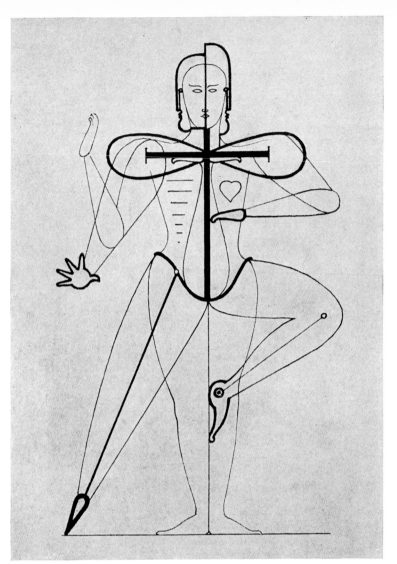

landscape to the mysterious order that he had in mind. His death prevented this dream from being realized. His idea of the human body was founded, so he said, on the Apollo of Tenea. His favorite colors were, "in the earlier years, black, gray, silver, pink; later—orange, blue, pink, gentian blue, semper vivum." At the Bauhaus he directed the workshops for murals, for wood and stone, and for the stage. In this last he had androgynous human and machine creatures perform, sometimes majestically, sometimes in a burlesque style. The geometrical masked bodies he created were supposed to move as mutely as possible—mime, therefore—and on no account were they to lapse into verbal expression. Varied spatial tensions were his aim. His *Triadic Ballet* made use of completely new, anti-realistic means. His ideas on the dance were the exact contrary of the expressionistic style which Duncan, Wigman and Laban had developed. What he had in mind was motion governed by laws, almost akin to those of classical ballet.

In 1928 Schlemmer painted large murals for the Folkwang Museum in Essen. He left the Bauhaus shortly after Gropius and taught first at the Breslau, later at the Berlin Art Academy. After he had been dismissed from his teaching post as "degenerate," he spent the last years of his life in the country, isolated and broken by the regulations that had outlawed him and forbidden him to paint.

For a time *Johannes Itten* (b. 1888) brought his own individual method of teaching to the Bauhaus. He was a versatile artist, a Swiss country boy who became an elementary school teacher, then a painter and art pedagogue. Most of his work was done in Germany and therefore he is treated here. His art is uneven, but sometimes a healthy, plastic vitality breaks through his structure and color. His teaching, however, seems to have been more effective than his painting, from which he was often distracted. As pedagogue he sought irrationally to combine the ancient Persian religion, Mazdaism, the wisdom of Zen and a futuristic mystique of motion. In his youth he was impressed by the newly born abstract painting of Kandinsky in Munich, and in Cologne by the important Sonderbund Exhibition of 1912, where he came

Oscar Schlemmer
Dancer in Mask and Costume, 1926

Oscar Schlemmer
Linear Metal Figure in Living Room.
1931

in contact with the masters of Neo-Impressionism. In Stuttgart, where Itten painted his first pictures in 1915, he was influenced by Hölzel's color theories. In 1919 Gropius invited him to the Bauhaus at Weimar where he gathered around him the disciples of anthroposophy, and the basic teaching he offered was interspersed with hygiene studies concerned with nutrition, breathing exercises and psychic concentration. Such aberrations led to conflict because the Bauhaus was also under the influence of the Dutch *Stijl* group, and its leaders wished to devote it to more rational and severe activity in the world of modern industry. After Itten's departure from the Bauhaus in 1926 he founded his own school in Berlin which existed until 1934. In the large facsimile edition of his diary one finds, with many examples, his ideas on the various types of mankind and their structure. At this time he was also director of the Krefeld Textile School. Then he disappeared from view until, in 1938, he took over the Zurich School for Applied Arts and the Applied Arts Museum in that city, and devoted himself to the Swiss *Werkbund* while the German unions were being liquidated by National Socialism. Itten then organized the Rietberg Museum (Zurich) which was largely devoted to the Oriental art that had always fascinated him.

His own art developed typically. At first he absorbed the representational world in the spirit of Cézanne, then color and mechanistic abstractionism became increasingly important to him, following which he returned occasionally to objective representation. But in the end he devoted himself to geometric abstractions and worked in "variations" that tried to fix rhythmically the "logical" sequence of related forms and contrasting colors.

Johannes Itten. Relief, 1919

Of the Bauhaus masters, *Josef Albers* (b. 1888) was the one who devoted himself most rigorously to the teaching of color and form. While Moholy, in his book *Vision in Motion*, dealt for the most part with the changing functions of art in life as a whole, Albers was working out a kind of physiology and psychology of the picture itself. He made a study, for instance, of optical illusions, of how, by changing the disposition of lines, surface and color, an illusion in depth could be created. Since Constructivism had made a strong impression on him, his pictures of the Bauhaus period consist mainly of straight rodlike forms which are intended to have an impersonal effect through the arrangement of varied materials or of unmixed, structureless, warm or cold color areas. In his "glass painting" we find a Venetian-blind effect. In his purest works he shuns all romantic flourishes. But when one takes a closer look at his dispassionate drawings or paintings, one finds irregular relationships between ground and figure, even spatial and temporal attractions that seem to contradict the outward appearance, so that the work does not become boring. In spite of this, Marcel Breuer called him "a frustrated architect." In Albers we find no trace of the cult of the subconscious which the Surrealists and the Tachists favored. In such pursuits he saw only "sick individualism and wild confusion," as he wrote to me in 1956. "Let us face clearly the fact that no hand, no tool or medium could possibly be quick enough to follow the bare currents of the subconscious." In his teaching his attitude was like an engineer's, in that he tried to solve visual problems with a minimum of material outlay.

Albers came from the Ruhr, was first a schoolteacher, and then studied at art academies in Essen, Berlin and Munich. In 1920 he came to the Bauhaus where he stayed until its dissolution. He went from there to Black Mountain College in North Carolina, and from 1950 until his retirement in 1960 taught at Yale University. He has written quite extensively on art education, on the teaching of form and abstract painting, and for a time he lectured at the Ulm Hochschule für Gestaltung. In recent years his color studies of the square in both painting and lithograph have been his major original contribution.

Josef Albers. City, 1928

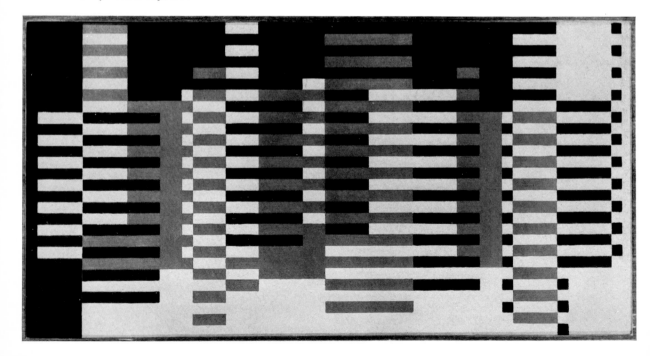

Ladislaus Moholy-Nagy (1895–1946) was
a richer "purist," a source of inspiration
in many different ways of our visual
attitudes during the second quarter of
this century. Like Van de Velde in 1900,
Moholy wanted to influence our life as
a totality, through an essentially visual
cultural education. He was active as
painter, graphic artist, sculptor, typographer, photographer, stage director,
theoretician, teacher and organizer of
exhibitions. With astounding agility of
mind he grasped every idea that was in
the air and systematized it. At the end
of his much-too-short life he compiled his
thought in the abundantly illustrated
work, *Vision in Motion* (Chicago, 1947),
a book that should form the basis for
every school of fine or applied arts.

His life was dedicated ceaselessly to work
until he died of leukemia at the age of
fifty-two. He came from Hungary, where
he had studied law until it occurred to
him that one might lead mankind out
of the chaos of empty conventions
through a new sense of vision–and the
first step toward it would be to wipe the
slate clean. While he was still in Hungary

Ladislaus Moholy-Nagy. Woodcut, 1924

he founded the group *Ma*. He seems to have been inspired by the master of the black square, Malevich,
and by the organizer of the simplest rectangular forms, Mondrian. After he left his country because
of the Communist revolution there, Moholy lived in Berlin, in poverty. However, he was able to exhibit
his early abstract works–which did not go beyond an elementary organization of space–in the Sturm
Gallery. From 1921 foreshortened lines appear in his work, as in the Constructivist Lissitsky's,
introducing spatial problems. Moholy wanted to arouse awareness of the surrounding space while
limiting himself strictly to plane geometry. From 1923 he experimented with transparent materials
such as rhodite and plexiglass. He created reliefs in which the light from the exterior casts delicate
shadows within. From this he later developed the space modulator. All this was abandoned for irrational,
curving forms at the end of his life.

In 1923 Moholy took over the metal workshop at the Weimar Bauhaus. As a propagandist he was the
most active member of the Bauhaus, and for this reason Gropius published with him a series of fourteen

Bauhaus books. Moholy's *Malerei, Photographie, Film* (1927) was one of these. Not in painting but in photography was the hunger for objective reality finally to be stilled. But it was also in photography, to which he devoted himself almost exclusively from 1923 to 1927, that he conquered new visual territory. Here, too, by changing accents or viewpoints, by photomontage or photogram, he departed from the mere reproduction of nature to a free construction with light.

His first pictures had shown only a few contrasting, smooth color areas. From this stage he turned to spraying paint in thinner, more iridescent chromatic effects, or he introduced greater differentiation of the surface. In abstract sculpture he coupled artificial materials with polished elements, with the intention of dissolving matter drastically by reflections from the work's surroundings. Finally he wanted to

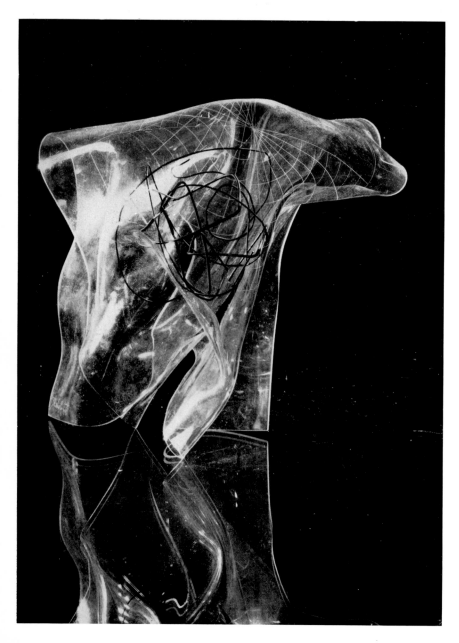

Ladislaus Moholy-Nagy
Space modulator, 1946

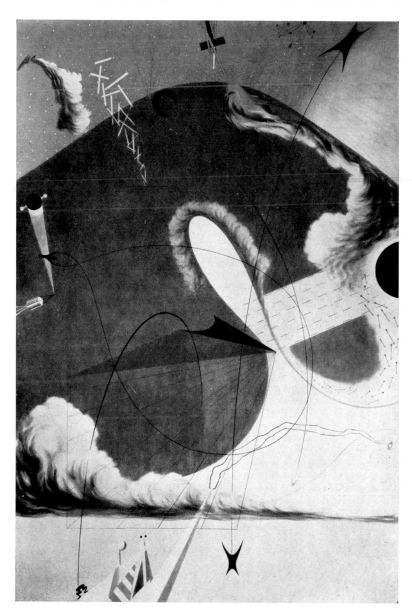

Herbert Bayer
Events in Atmosphere, 1941
Hollywood, Collection Stendahl

"paint" almost exclusively with light from a reflecting agent, that is to say, with the screen. Painting might be replaced by a transparent play of light that would either radiate statically, in which case the painter's original would be a slide, or it would set everything in motion, as in an abstract rhythmic film. In 1929 appeared his Bauhaus book *Von Material zur Architektur*, an excerpt from his Basic Teachings lectures given there. In 1928 he left the Bauhaus with Gropius, and lived in Berlin where he worked for the State Opera, for the Piscator Theater and in advertising. It was here that he created the rotating "light requisite" for an abstract play of colors. National Socialism drove him from Germany, first to

Amsterdam, then to London. In 1937 he founded the New Bauhaus in Chicago, and after that his own School of Design, in which he was active until his death. In 1946 *The New Vision* was published in Chicago, a revision of one of his earlier works. *Vision in Motion*, which he was not able to complete, he called his last will and testament. In it he related the study of optics to life, always envisioning a universal rejuvenation. In the last two years of his life, already partially bedridden, he yielded to the trends of a new era, drawing with crayons in more colorful and irrational forms.

He summarized his aims with the following theses: "An emotional education must go with an intellectual one." "A passionate preference for transparency is one of the most characteristic signs of our time." "Not a life founded on metaphysical miasma, but on a fair balance... culminating in justice and the capacity to express oneself, is the best security for social harmony."

Herbert Bayer (b. 1900) must be included among the Bauhaus masters. In 1921 he came to the Weimar Bauhaus as a student; four years later he was a master in Dessau, where he took over publicity and typography. These were to remain his fields of activity. In 1928 he was working in Berlin for the advertising agency Dorland and for *Vogue*, designing brilliant, evocative covers. Exhibitions organized by him were artistic achievements, as for instance his contribution to the Pressa Exhibition in Cologne (1929), the Paris Trade Unions Fair (1930), on which he collaborated with Moholy and Breuer, and the Architects Fair in Berlin. In 1938 he came to New York; he moved from there to Aspen, Colorado, where he acted as advisor on questions of design for the Container Corporation's Aspen development. There was little time for the creative art of painting, but just because of his work in the service of the more pedestrian aspects of life, he was able to contribute much to the cultivation of the new vision.

Herbert Bayer
Convex-Concave, 1945

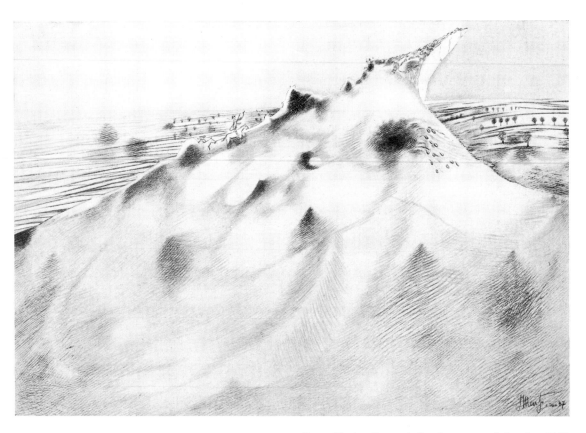

Georg Muche. Fantastic Landscape, pencil drawing, 1947

Those in Germany who were narrow partisans of Expressionism called him "the dandy of design," but he has created melodious and luminous works. The special attraction of his work lies just in those sustained, sleek, melodic qualities which are so often lacking in Germany.

Georg Muche (b. 1895) was teaching at the Bauhaus at the age of twenty-five, but he was not really suited to the constructive ideas favored there, at least not in painting. His first paintings were abstract, and as early as 1916 to 1919 he was exhibiting works in this vein at the Sturm Gallery in Berlin. But then he turned to swelling forms and a turgid color key. Some paintings and drawings from this period, in pleasant delicate tones, succeed very well, but every now and then he lowered the value of his work with an overlyrical sweep and too feminine colors. No other master of the Bauhaus has been carried so far from the original program. Morning mists, as if filtered through Venetian blinds, wide-open calyxes, delicate spider webs amid leaves, are some of themes of the his recent pictures. A pinkish-red, a curious yellow modified by muted black, remain characteristic of his tonality. Brownish nuances, lilac, leaf-green, delicate smoky tones and a dusty mortar gray float over many of his pictures. His subjects and palette are surprising in view of the fact that as a teacher of the Sturm Art School he had assimilated an

Georg Muche
Flower Thirsting, 1954

abundance of invigorating modern methods which he passed on to his students–at the Bauhaus, later at Itten's Berlin Art School, and after that at the Breslau Academy and the Krefeld Textile School. In 1939 he wrote a beautiful book from a vast store of experience, *Buon Fresco*, and in 1950 *Bilder, Fresken, Zeichnungen*, which included illustrations of his own work. In 1954 he wrote a bold article confuting the feeble notion that the advance of technical science would destroy art. Muche's father was the amateur painter Ramholz, a witty, satirical eccentric and an early collector of avant-garde art.

Max Bill (b. 1908) was a Swiss pupil of the Bauhaus, of a younger generation. He is discussed here because he spent decisive years of his life in Germany, where he carried on the Bauhaus traditions and to some extent tried to reform them. In 1951 he was made director of the Ulm Hochschule für Gestaltung (School of Design), which he built up and organized; in 1957 he was dismissed and he returned to Zurich. Early in his career as painter, sculptor, architect and theorist he was won over by the constructivist principles he hoped to apply in every field. He belongs to the category of those who like to explain as rationally as possible exactly what they are doing and how they manage to do it. Like Moholy, he has always viewed our visual habits as a totality, and sought to lift us from our habitual inertia and guide us toward a disciplined and rational order. His austere paintings consist of simple cellular forms repeated over and over again, the color of a single one accentuated to bring tension into the arrangement. Or he creates sweeping curves in a sublimely blended, transparent polychromy. His sculpture tends to be large in format; his smaller works often have a decorative effect, in spite of the precise realization of surfaces. Sometimes his rationalized lyricism achieves a degree of grandeur, for instance in his *Continuity* of 1947, the now-famous "bow" that turns in upon itself, which has been installed on the shores of the Lake of Zurich. Bill and a few others have demonstrated the fact that some mathematical models may also strike the layman as beautiful and harmonious—for instance those in the Paris Salon Poincaré, which are symbols of mere equations and were certainly invented and installed there for rational purposes only. Here we touch upon the "prestabilized harmony" between intellect and emotion, and experience a new sphere of artistic enjoyment. To call such creations unhuman would be as foolish as to describe as inhumane our astonishment when faced with celestial equations.

Bill's activities should be judged like those of Moholy, in the context of a whole vision with which he seeks to expunge our preconceptions of form. Whereas the individual arts constantly display tendencies to diverge, Bill tries to find the significant and beautiful form of our time for everything, and to shape it as rationally and non-egocentrically as possible. This idea corresponds to his "understatement," by which he declared he no longer intended to educate anyone to "art." Here certainly lie healthy anti-elements

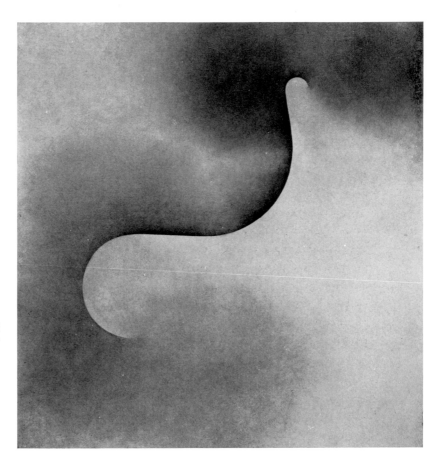

Max Bill
Defined and Undefined, 1947

against the highly subjective thinking-in-depth with which so many pompous abstract neo-romanticists like to work. Bill's publications have also been effective. He wrote studies on the bridge builder Maillart, on Swiss architecture, on Mies van der Rohe and Kandinsky. His dogmatic article "Zur mathematischen Denkweise in der Kunst unserer Zeit" ("On Mathematical Thought in the Art of our Time") is characteristic.

Bill was responsible for bringing to the Ulm School of Design *Friedrich Vordemberge-Gildewart* (1899–1964), who had been living in retirement in Amsterdam since the advent of the Third Reich. This painter had remained faithful to the unswerving, ascetically severe form of expression the Constructivists had made prominent in the twenties. He worked with strictly defined surface tensions and pure color contrasts more consistently than the Russian Constructivist Lissitzky. Vordemberge called himself an "elementarist," and was more radical in his reduction of all pictorial methods to a puristic minimum, but he knew how to put his "nothing" into the picture in a manner that immediately gave a delicate, expansive effect. With a very few upright shapes, some highly original colors and a minimum of clean textural contrasts, he could conjure up a sure, asymmetrical equilibrium that went beyond the mere decorative effect, even when it was intended to give an impression of beauty. In the beginning, like his friend Schwitters (whom we shall treat under Dadaism), Vordemberge would sometimes mount a plastic form on his painting. In such cases Schwitters would have toyed with the decadent beauty of aged material, but Vordemberge always sought precise accents that one might say had preserved their youth. He placed his few lines and immaculate colors on the picture surface cautiously, as if he feared some disaster might enter the field of action if these elements were to touch each other too soon. One must keep in mind all the things that such purely constructive painting denies because from the constructivist standpoint they would have a garrulous effect: improvisation, profusion, gushing color, vital-dynamism, personal calligraphy, density of structure, any suggestion of real space. In 1948 Vordemberge wrote, "Wherever one seeks bravura or virtuosity, one comes up with deception." For Vordemberge, any system that could produce a rich effect with a minimum of means was superior to a system that required more complex means to get the same effect. He wanted to transfer this thesis from theoretical and economic spheres into the realm of beauty.

He divided the picture as simply as possible, never, however, arranging it in a banal way. For instance, he avoided a centralized composition, undeviating symmetry or static progression, as they might prevail in merely ornamental work. If two straight lines converge, they do not meet at the edge of the picture. When he grouped several panels together to form a unity, he was not in any way aiming at a straightforward equilibrium. Although in some respects related to the Dutch *Stijl* group, he does not belong with them; yet he was a founding member of the geometrically oriented group, *Abstraction-Création* (1932). During the Nazi regime he lived first in Switzerland, later in Amsterdam. In 1952 the Rotterdam Art Academy appointed him to teach "color as a space-forming element in architecture." He wrote programmatical essays and a volume of poetry with the characteristic title, *Millimeter und Gerade (Millimeters and Straight Lines)*. Arp praised his work, somewhat extravagantly, as "a withdrawal from confusion, from frenzy, from the love of filth."

Hans Richter (b. 1888), who was a decade older, is introduced only now because his inclinations and experiments led in the direction of the modern film. But he came to the film from painting. In 1915 he was

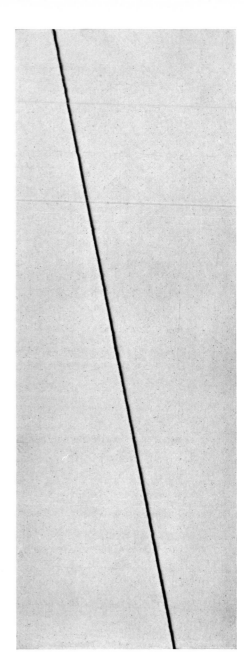

already working cubistically. After this he developed his *Rollbilder* (scroll pictures) long horizontal strips on which abstract motifs were painted and diversified in stages. Here he created a new type of picture which unfortunately, in his opinion, functioned only as an intermediary development toward the abstract film. In fact it actually possessed a special faculty, allowing the single picture to remain static and the eye to jump forward and backward. Within these works he shifted with great precision from the

111

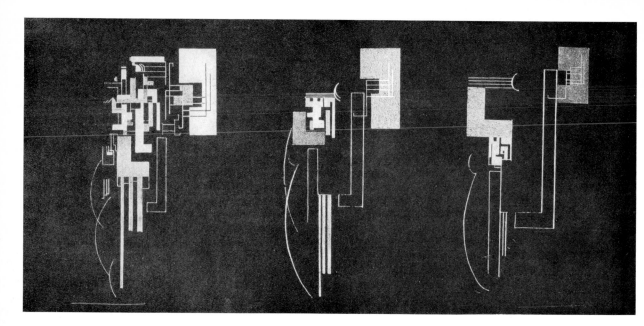

Hans Richter. Part of "Prelude," 1919

vehement to the delicate. While still in Germany he published with Mies van der Rohe and Werner Graeff the periodical *G* (*Gestaltung*, Formation), which was the foremost German publication on abstract art from 1923 to 1926.

In 1918 the Swede Eggeling, the most important innovator of the abstract film, became his friend. Eggeling created his *Diagonal Symphony* in 1921, and Richter in the same year his *Rhythm 21*. Richter produced some thirty motion pictures, and in New York, to which he emigrated in 1941, he became director of the Film Institute and taught at City College.

THE NEW OBJECTIVITY

The development of the fine arts in the twentieth century was regarded in Germany and elsewhere as a progressive alienation from the object, as a crescendo in the transformation of forms and in the autonomous life of color. Nevertheless, as early as the First World War a countermovement developed, one of those retardations which history likes to throw in as a breathing spell when we have experienced too many innovations. The charm of the object was rediscovered. In opposition to Expressionism, the autonomy of the objective world around us was once more to be enjoyed; the wonder of matter that could crystallize into objects was to be seen anew. In an article written in 1924 I coined the phrase *Magischer Realismus* (magic realism)—magic of course *not* in the religious-psychological sense of ethnology. In 1925

112

Max Ernst. Grasshoppers' Song to the Moon, 1953

Oskar Kokoschka. Venice, 1924

the expression was attached as subtitle to my book, *Nach-expressionismus* (Post-Expressionism). The same year Hartlaub organized the important exhibition at his gallery in Mannheim with the title *Neue Sachlichkeit* (New Objectivity or New Realism)–a formulation I had avoided–to imply that we were not dealing here with a repetition of the more neutral realism of Courbet or Leibl. This New Objectivity was aimed in quite a different direction, seeking an approach to the autonomous sharpness of objects, as in the late Middle Ages, the quattrocento, or to the revolutionary form-hardening classicism of David or Ingres. Moreover, the emphasis in relation to the objective world implied abstraction, not empathy.

This new direction, however, included too many restorative components; too many expressive structural styles which had been successful were now thrown overboard. To succeed, restorations must include, transformed within themselves, almost the total wealth of the period being broken up–and thus of the preceding revolutions; otherwise, as soon happened in this case, they are swept away by the impact of new revolutions. At this time the usual efforts were made to build a bridge to science in self-defense: if all matter consisted of minute abstract particles intrinsically in motion, then it was declared to be astonishing, even miraculous, that given such fluctuations, matter should crystallize and solidify into what we can call things. Hence, the thing, the object, must be formed anew. In way of explanation, the static, anti-dynamic pictorial form was considered a coordinate of the "rigid fourth dimension" with which modern physics can reduce everything dynamic to states of being.

The original features of this new direction came from the Italian *arte metafisica* (metaphysical art) or from related aspects of Constructivism, which sometimes made use of the objective. However, as soon as these premises were abandoned, the banal realism that was soon to flourish in the Third Reich appeared. The New Objectivity is best understood in contrast to the Expressionism that preceded it.

EXPRESSIONISM:	*NEW OBJECTIVITY:*
Ecstatic subjects	Sober objects
Suppression of the object	The object clarified
Rhythmical	Representational
Extravagant	Puristically severe
Dynamic	Static
Loud	Quiet
Summary	Thorough
Close-up view	Close and far view
Monumental	Miniature
Warm	Cold
Thick color texture	Thin paint surface
Rough	Smooth
Emphasis on the visibility of the painting process	Effacement of the painting process
Centrifugal	Centripetal
Expressive deformation	External purification of the object

Alexander Kanoldt
Hoarfrost, 1921

The painters who stressed anew the objective approach fall into three groups. In north and east Germany, George Grosz, Otto Dix, and Kurt Günther were aggressive and socially critical. In their opinion the social order could also be changed by a new kind of painting: *art engagé*. But in the south, in Munich, the artists were more melancholy and were associated with the Italian *arte metafisica*, which, like the work of Germany's nineteenth century "Nazarenes," sought a link with Italian art of the early Renaissance. However, the new Italian style, in the early work of de Chirico, was permeated and enriched by surrealistic constructions, whereas the corresponding movement in Munich was simpler and more decorative. A third group, which included Georg Scholz and Walter Spiess, favored the detailed, fussily painted idyll, similar to some paintings of Henri Rousseau.

As a young man, *Alexander Kanoldt* (1881–1939) lived with the paintings of his father, who worked in the tradition of the heroic landscape style of the nineteenth century. But his son, influenced by French

114

Post-Impressionism, soon adopted a simplifying, stylized method with dark contours, not unlike that of Jawlensky. At first glance it could be called expressionistic if it were not so strikingly quiet and impregnated with such heavy, hypernaturalistic colors; his empty interiors and mute landscapes were painted accordingly. In 1909 Kanoldt was active in the founding of the revolutionary *Neue Künstlervereinigung* (see p. 70). Gradually, however, he developed a more graphic style, hardening all individual objects and covering them with a smooth metallic surface. In schematic modeling, houses, trees and figures were now severely "objectivized," as precisely rendered as if photographed. As in the quattrocento, all personal calligraphy disappeared. But the characteristic richness of the fifteenth century was never equalled because the later artists were too obviously bent on a decorative, closely knit, oversimplified composition and a smooth, lacquered surface. Ingres—misunderstood—became increasingly Ka-

Georg Schrimpf. Still Life, 1923

Georg Schrimpf. Sleeping Girls, 1929 · Hohenheim, Landwirtschaftliche Hochschule

noldt's standard of perfection, with the result that he produced frigid, lifeless portraits and still lifes (a characteristic ideal of his was the rubber plant). A few painted or lithographed landscapes give an inkling, at least, that Kanoldt possessed a certain stature. He was excessively bitter over Expressionism and made a "purifying" pact with the National Socialists, who gave him a professorship at the Berlin Art Academy. There his style became increasingly torpid.

Georg Schrimpf (1889–1938) also strove for a quiet, purified form. A former baker's apprentice who had wandered all over Italy on the proverbial shoestring, he started as an amateur painter and never entirely lost a certain naivety. A deliberate structural monumentality is found in his best paintings.

In Schrimpf's early works figures are distorted, but lack, however, any dynamism, so that it was immediately evident that he was actually striving for a calm solidity. This period was followed by some quite beautiful paintings of big peasant girls resting on the grass, of statuesque cattle and sheep. He gave a new direction to the old theme of the pastorale: passive color areas and solid close-up views with clear silhouettes. He succeeded once more in salvaging the old native German landscape for contemporary art. Some of his pictures exude simplicity and a silent grandeur; others are much too insipid, for something of the amateur painter remained in this sincere man. His naive insights often hit the nail on the head, and at the time he was particularly popular–surprisingly–with the complicated intellectual. His smooth-surface paintings held their own artistically as long as they were supported by his peculiar, ascetic colors; later they became more balanced and conventional. Some of his landscapes are too reminiscent of the minor painters of 1800.

Carl Mense (1886–1965) painted in this Munich style. He tried to combine the New Objectivity with a rather sultry Italian romanticism, less pure in color but with a certain decorative finesse. While Schrimpf preferred matinal tones, Mense's taste ran to the twilit colors, sometimes deeply glowing.

A shimmering palette and acute perspective foreshortening are characteristic of *Heinrich Davringhausen* (b. 1900). He placed his figures in seemingly airless hollow spaces, boxlike constructions in precise linear perspective of the kind developed by de Chirico in his early period. This type of space formation will recur with George Grosz in his earlier works, and with the Surrealists Edgar Ende and MacZimmermann. From 1936 Davringhausen lived in France, and following the trend of the times, painted in a calm, non-objective, surface style, while others of this group (and some still to be mentioned) remained true to the emphasis on representation.

Heinrich Davringhausen. In the Attic, circa 1922

Kay H. Nebel. Steer, 1921

Kay Nebel (1888–1954) and Franz Radziwill, both from the North Sea coast, were the northern representatives of the New Objectivity. In his animal paintings Nebel strove to emphasize objective delineation. His paintings look as if the color had been brushed on as an afterthought. But his understanding of animal life was not deep enough to counterbalance the beautiful, formal schematic arrangement which he gradually established for himself and consolidated in his north German murals and in his teaching at the Cassel Art Academy.

Franz Radziwill (b. 1895), who grew up in the harbor city of Bremen among wharfs, ships and railroad tracks, was a soldier in both World Wars. He discovered German romanticism in Dresden. Because he saw our humble human existence as something uncanny and experienced the world around him as eternally alien–although, like the nineteenth-century painter Caspar David Friedrich, he reproduced it with painstaking precision–the Nazis objected to him, in spite of the naturalistic definition of his paintings. Furthermore, he employed a rather unusual color key. The silence of the grave dominates his miniaturelike pictures, in which strange events are always taking place against a darkling sky.

Carl Grossberg (1894–1940) represented the more idyllic wing of the New Objectivity, sometimes with a slightly ironic undertone. He lived near Würzburg, in a tower of the old city wall, from which he kept a watchful eye on the historic cultural landscape. He combined the entangled wire structures of modern technology with small rural houses with their ells, ledges and eaves, as if everything had been forcibly arrested, immobilized, like a stopped clock beneath our astonished gaze.

An aggressive painter of the New Objectivity was *Otto Dix* (b. 1891), a Thuringian of proletarian origin. Just as Caravaggio had brought back to earth the transcendental proclivities of Mannerism in 1600, Otto Dix wanted to lead an overpathetic German Expressionism back to a mercilessly realistic conception of life. But for him reality was a gruesome thing, never to be glossed over idealistically. He exaggerated this almost timeless type of Expressionism with a pessimistic force and inflexibility never seen before. His horror over the murderousness of war was inextinguishable. He expressed it in flat, spaceless paintings of war cripples and match sellers. In one of the former, as in a Dada montage, four huge men with artificial limbs are pressed life-size onto the surface, like broken marionettes of death. A monstrous scorn exuded from these pictures, which have an effect somewhat akin to our macabre modern ballads, and they were more powerfully constructed than the famous painting of the trench which came later (in 1923), provoking controversy for years. In *Trench Warfare* terrifying figures appear in panoptikon style, but a too-detailed description of swollen foxhole corpses makes a comprehensive appeal, an overall effect of horror, impossible. A series of fifty etchings, *War*, forms a third grotesque manifesto. To express the most extreme of his grim statements, Dix employed the graphic arts, to which he remained passionately devoted. His youthful period in Dresden (1919–1922), and the fours years immediately following in Düsseldorf and Berlin, produced his strongest work as a painter. At the Dresden Art Academy, where he taught from 1926 to 1933, he painted religious subjects and very capable pure landscapes that are nevertheless not so convincing as his earlier works because they run counter to his

Franz Radziwill
Karl Buchstätter's
Dive to Death,
1928
Essen,
Museum Folkwang

Carl Grossberg. Dream, 1931

aggressive personality. Now he began to use too many old-master techniques. When he was outlawed by the Nazis, he settled down rather opulently, thanks to a wealthy marriage, on Lake Constance. There he made a forced peace with society and devoted himself to pure landscape painting in which influences of Cranach, Brueghel and the later Dutch painters may be felt, paintings in a clear-cut, mixed technique of oil and tempera, with a fine glaze.

After the Second World War Dix seemed to tire of this painstaking style and threw himself into a belated, superficial Expressionism which gave the effect of a repeater course, since he only rarely succeeded in letting his colors speak with primary force. The merciless verism of his early works remains his major contribution. In them he functioned as social critic, in spite of his bleak acknowledgement of all forms of life. Behind his milieu of profiteers and prostitutes, of night and bar life glowing in poisonous colors, a *memento mori* leers at us—not the traditional symbolic skull, but the visages and muscles of living people, whether the obese exploiters of the inflationary era, or rattling skeletal victims, dancing lewdly, tin robots in a vacuum. In 1928 he painted *Metropolis*, a kind of negative altarpiece of Satanism, a triptych of lascivious appetites. One shudders when he poses a gray, starving proletarian woman in front of a poisonous red factory, or when he places a rich widow—like a reverse image of an angel annunciate—in

119

front of a voluptuously padded wall. These moments are much more convincing than his purely symbolic efforts, as in the *Seven Deadly Sins*, which impress one as melodramatic. He lacked the symbolic imagination for themes of pathos, for, as he wrote to me once, he never dreamed. On the other hand, he was successful in preeminently naturalistic, if somewhat caricaturizing portraits; in 1921, he painted the portrait of his parents—an ironsmith and his wife seated on their proletarian sofa; the enormous hands of the laborer, the careworn faces, but above all, the iron-hard color scheme, are overwhelmingly expressive. In 1926 he depicted the art dealer Flechtheim, deliberately evoking the effect of a pantherlike animal; Silvia von Harden, with monocle, looking like a bloodshot snake; the writer Ivar von Lücken in his attic, consumed, a Don Quixote leaning against the wind. Dix painted the poet Theodor Däubler, obese, pompous, with the head of a lion; he is posed beside stout pillars under a ceiling of clouds. The painter gave children the animal-like quality and sharpness with which childhood charges into life. His early uncompromising verism was also recognized as something unique by the French, who had nowhere succeeded in so fearlessly nailing down the horrors of modern life. Their art was dominate dessentially by the form and color problems that were missing in this German draftsman; with his powerful, provocative subject matter he simply pushed them aside.

Dix and his friend *Kurt Günther*, both from Gera, were the chief Thuringian contributors to the aggressive verism of the twenties. They painted each other in a double portrait. At first Günther organized his

Otto Dix. Match-seller, 1920 · Stuttgart, Staatsgalerie

Otto Dix. Silvia von Harden, 1926 · Paris, Musée National d'Art Moderne

pictures in Dada style: in the background of an ironic painting of a young salesman telephoning, we see his whole world of screws, keys and gadgets, individual photographs simply pasted on. Günther went on to pure painting, and he too experienced the decrescendo that seems to go with this veristic style. His sharply characterized graphic portraits are his best works. At first carnal woman seems to be his favorite theme; a self-portrait revealing his subjugation to her powers remains a freak example of his painting.

Between Dix and Grosz stands *Karl Hubbuch* (b. 1891), a significant graphic artist, also full of accusations against our civilization, but with more expressive tension in his outlines and his unfolding perspectives. He could transform a twilit city scene into a primeval landscape. In 1931 his book *La France* was published. In it he lashed at the social misery there: gluttons, so-called patriots, evil women

Otto Dix. Little Match-seller, 1926
Mannheim, Kunsthalle

Kurt Günther
Petty Bourgeois at the Radio,
circa 1920

122

Karl Hubbuch. Aging Metropolis

and the plundered proletariat swarm in front of the voluted facades of nineteenth-century architecture. Later he switched to the woodcut and since 1951 paints in oils, sometimes coming very close to the style of Max Beckmann. During National Socialism he managed to keep alive by working as handyman, clock maker and painter of ceramics. In 1947 he returned to the Karlsruhe Art Academy where he had previously taught. Asked what his aim is, he will say that he wants to hold a mirror to the world.

While a somewhat idyllic form of the New Objectivity was expressed in Munich and a more aggressive version in other parts of Germany, a third tendency emerged among those painters who saw their world as if contained in a toy box. This trend was a reaction against the summary, monumentalizing aspect of expressionist painting, whose effect depended on distance from the observer. For the new style closeness to the picture was necessary, as if viewing an ant hill with a magnifying glass. On the other hand, some landscapes showed the use of aerial perspective.

Georg Scholz (b. 1890), from Baden, dealt ironically with small town life, in appropriately intimate paintings and lithographs–trim little houses, adults looking warlike yet going about their business like dolls. A village is laid out as if on the curvature of a globe, or the living room of a station master is depicted as a miniature idyll, satirizing the familiar joys of the petty bourgeois. Thus, from a pathetic expressionism, Biedermeier genre rose again, quite unintentionally, and now with a satiric sharpness.

Walter Spiess (1896–1947) gave this style a dainty exotic turn. His *Farewell* seems to be viewed from the nearby moon, and it has the tone of a music box of Mozart's time, of a silvery melody heard from afar. In his *Folk Festival*, Spiess shifted the dimensions of his miniscule description in such a fashion that something of Chagall's fantastic quality enters into the picture (Spiess loved this painter, by the way). Spiess was a musician and a supple dancer. He emigrated to Indonesia, collected its gamelan music, directed the orchestra of a prince and built himself a curious home in his tropical paradise. In 1938 he published *Dances and Dreams in Bali*, with B. de Zoete.

One could call this branch of the New Objectivity "the Rousseau complex," for many of its disciples had this strange "amateur painter" in mind. *Gyorgy Stefula* (b. 1913) repeatedly acknowledged the

Walter Spiess. Farewell, 1921

Gyorgy Stefula. Bathing Beach, 1948

association. Stefula, self-taught, also transforms the art of Rousseau into Biedermeier genre. He is an articulate painter who, with faint irony, is in love with the small happinesses of everyday life, which he describes meticulously. All the outdoors is turned into a trim park for our Sundays, and the people in it look like tiny toy figures. In storybook style he wants to show to us what life in the country and intimate family life can be, and all the time he is smiling at himself. Stefula comes from the cool north and lives on the Bavarian Chiemsee; his wife and all his children paint. Once, when he was called upon to design huge Mardi Gras decorations, people were astonished to see that this miniaturist could also command a larger format—certainly a sign that he can not only daub a picture but also knows how to construct one. There are a number of painters of this type. In north Germany, the graphic artist *Gustav Wimmer*, whose softly veiled landscapes again take up the tradition of C. D. Friedrich, and *Otto Wulk*, who, like Dürer, lifts a plant or a little moss from the earth to capture it faithfully. For south Germany we should mention the compact formalism of *Peter Dülberg* (b. 1911), who has also gained prominence as a writer, and *Paul Mildner* (1901–1957) from Rottach, who painted muted landscapes in the tradition of Edmund Steppes.

Karl Rössing. From Crete, 1952

Josef Wedewer, Rudolf Wacker, Franz Lenk and *Wilhelm Heise* practiced this precise objective style. The last specialized in miniature, detailed wood engravings of flowers. A few of these painters, however, also made the transition to the factual reportage of external matter which was the National Socialist idea of art; their artistic legacy was meagre for they were not connected in any way with the fruitful mainstream of our day.

Karl Rössing (b. 1897), who lives near Stuttgart, grew out of the New Objectivity of the twenties. In his calm portraits and landscapes of that period he already restricted his colors, so that one could sense the

126

draftsman he was to become. He concentrated on drawings, producing symbolic series, easily understood, often small in format, and with a slight admixture of surrealism, as for instance in *My Prejudice
against the Times*. Gradually he turned to making large single-sheet drawings until he had arrived at the
"graphic picture suitable for a wall." Technically his way led from the woodcut to the finer wood engraving, and then to the meticulously prepared three-plate print. The black plate carried the scaffolding
of the composition and the darks; the gray plate gave the middle tones and a third plate the nuances
between the two. This third plate, which one might say was the result of Rössing's basic gentleness, very
often concealed the graphic structure, to its disadvantage. On such sheets sculptural fragments, autumnal plants and abandoned shells lie waiting, sometimes piled in front of a quiet windowsill behind which

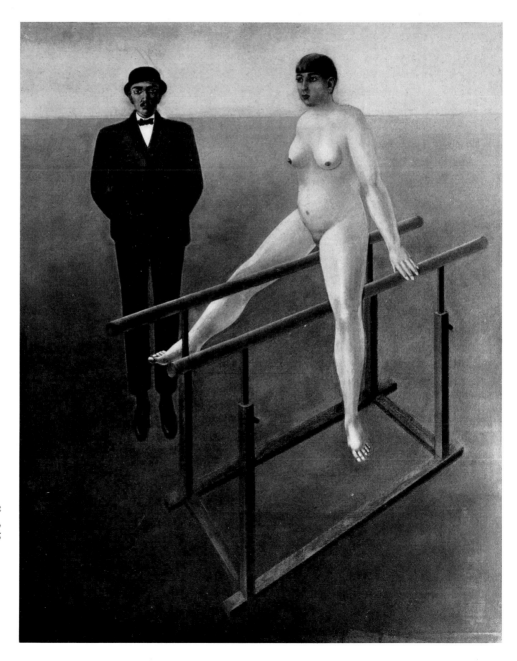

*Anton Räderscheidt
Nude on Parallel Bars,
1925*

lies a still, nocturnal landscape. Classical themes, a post-classical attitude and a grain of Surrealism taken from the early, more exciting works of de Chirico, are characteristic of Rössing's oeuvre.

Anton Räderscheidt (b. 1892), from Cologne, is a lonely figure. Since he possessed a lurking tendency toward Constructivism, he gave the New Objectivity of the twenties some relentlessly geometric features, so that even a man like Moholy could admire him. Räderscheidt portrayed the human body with a cold verism, subordinating it to a system of rectangular coordinates. He gave the ancient man-woman theme a provocative new turn. In *Nude on Parallel Bars* (p. 127) the woman is naked, with moonlit, shimmering flesh; next to her stands the man, dressed in raven black evening dress with a bowler hat on his gruesome head; both figures are placed as rigid parallels in hollow space. After Räderscheidt had turned his back on Magic Realism, something very strange took place: he tried his hand at practically every style and method of modern painting, one after the other without ever losing the peculiar Räderscheidt tone. From icy polished surfaces he switched to a furious brushstroke; from strikingly simple themes to complicated cityscapes (Rome, Naples, Cologne); then, after emigrating to France, he began painting heavy baroque abstract colossi, and went from there towards nonobjective art. He then announced that he was thinking of going back to the sharp objective painting of his youth. In his recent paintings, however, he develops a rearing-horse theme, strongly emphasizing vertical rhythms and, at the same time, a cyclical form.

W. Schulz-Matan
Sphere in Space,
1932

DADAISM

Dadaism came into prominence during the First World War in Switzerland, the United States, Paris and Germany, only to disappear a few years later. It was given many different evaluations. Some refused to take it seriously; others saw in it an important link between Italian Futurism, which had existed since 1909, and French Surrealism, which appeared in 1924. One can probably trace back to Futurism and its mystique of motion the Dadaists' pleasure in the tumultuous event, which they used to startle the bourgeois with their antics. From Futurism the Dadaists also adopted the break with all conventionality in favor of a new age, or *futurum*, and the vigorous activity that seeks to penetrate every phase of life, whereby art was no longer to be seen as art for art's sake.

The delight in fantasy, in the shock effect which must also be contained in art as explosive material, led eventually to Surrealism. The elementary, said the Dadaists, lives in us repressed, held down by rules and "style consciousness." While Futurism had a political aspect in its shameful glorification of war as "the most spontaneous form of life," Dada aimed at more playful effects. Schiller's thesis that art was a "game" was intensified by Dadaism into something more contemptuous, even grotesque, although they did not deny the existence of profound problems. A low humor lurked behind some of their projects, whereas Surrealism had a clearer program, felt life as a more mysterious entity. The museums were considered cultural graveyards, Expressionism sentimental, patriotism and the church mere apron strings, constraining all the spontaneous impulses of life.

In Hülsenbeck's manifesto of 1920 he said, "Dadaism symbolizes the most primitive relationship with the reality surrounding us... a new reality takes its rightful place. The simultaneous jumble of sounds, colors and rhythms of the intellect is imperturbably accepted as life by Dadaist art, along with all the sensational outcries and daily fevers brought forth from its distorted psyche and in all its brutal reality... The bruitic poem describes a streetcar as it is: the *essence* of the streetcar, with the yawning of bourgeois Mr. Schulze, and the screeching of its brakes. The simultaneous poem teaches the meaning behind the confusion of events: while Schulze reads, the Balkan express crosses the bridge near Nisch, a pig whines in the cellar of butcher Nuttke... The static poem turns words into individuals."

During the First World War, in 1916, when artists and writers of all countries assembled in the security of Zurich, Dadaism was directed against a union of art and life with politics. From Germany came young Dr. Hülsenbeck, poet and philosopher, the painter Hugo Ball, the film innovator Hans Richter and the Alsatian Hans Arp, who at the time was writing in German. But between 1918 and 1922 in Berlin, which was in turmoil from the deprivations caused by war and politics, Dadaism assumed a character that was partly political, leftist in its orientation. (The same schism was later to develop in Paris, to form two opposing camps among the Surrealists.) The Berlin Dadaists included, beside Hülsenbeck, the graphic artist George Grosz, the painter Raoul Hausmann, the brothers Herzfelde (one of whom changed his name and is known as Heartfield), famous for their political montages, the "nature philosopher" Baader, and the poet Mehring. But the Berlin Dadaists were not absorbed solely by political problems; they also fought constantly over questions of life and art in general. In 1918 Hülsenbeck held a Dadaist meeting with the New Secession and signed the aforementioned manifesto; Friedländer wrote about "creative indifference;" Grosz, Hausmann and the Herzfelde brothers started revolutionary attacks in *Der Dada*.

This was followed by tumultuous evenings in Dresden, Hamburg, Leipzig and Prague. In a 1920 Dada exhibition provocative works by Max Ernst, Schlichter, Citroen, Arp, Hausmann, Hanna Höch and Picabia were displayed. In 1922 George Grosz and the Herzfeldes defected to the Communist Party, into the circle of *Aktion* and the Malik publishing house; with this step the artistic freedom of the movement was buried.

The poet Baargeld, Hans Arp and Max Ernst, who called himself Dada Max, were active in Cologne. An extreme magazine, *Der Ventilator*, was banned by the British occupation forces. Max Ernst and Baar-

Raoul Hausmann
Photomontage,
1921–1924

Raoul Hausmann
Sign, 1956

geld projected ideas for mutual participation to counteract the too-bombastic individualism; *Fatigaga* was a witty abbreviation for *Fabrication des tableaux guarantis gazometriques*. But soon Hans Arp stopped coming to Cologne, Max Ernst moved to Paris and the Cologne Dada spoof disintegrated.

In Hannover, however, it lived on. There Paul Stegemann published books by Arp, Serner, Vagts and Kurt Schwitters, to whom we shall come later. The exuberant development of the movement in Paris and New York is outside our province.

In Germany the outstanding Dadaists are Raoul Hausmann, Kurt Schwitters and Max Ernst. *Raoul Hausmann* (b. 1886) was a painter, writer and photographer, whose inspiration and experimentation were influential immediately. It was probably he who first practiced photomontage with intellectual content, that graphic art with pasted fragments which became meaningful through the creation of plastic tension between its segments. It was an offshoot of French Cubism, but it employed Cubist idiom more formally and colorfully–that is to say, nonobjectively. Hausmann hit upon this procedure in a Pomeranian village in 1918, before George Grosz, Max Ernst and Hanna Höch took it up. It is not only an abbreviated method of composition, but an expression of the feeling that our existence is a contradictory assemblage of compartments forcibly joined together with the joints showing. Hausmann used similar possibilities in language: in his *Manifest von der Gesetzmäßigkeit des Lautes (Manifesto on the Rules of Sound*, 1918), he took language beyond its logical connotations, treating it with complete freedom as a structure of sounds and associations. Independently of Hugo Ball, who preceded him, Hausmann wrote poems consisting of sounds only, and read them at a Berlin Dada soirée as early as 1918; these inspired Schwitters to his *Sound Sonata*. Hausmann was full of optical tricks. He fled National Socialism from country to country, in the course of which, like the true fragmentist he was, he lost a number of original sketches. The stations of his unrest were Spain, Paris, Ibiza, Zurich, Prague, and again France. (I mention this only to indicate how far afield some of the spokesmen for the new values in Germany were driven in that period.) Since 1944 he has been living in Limoges, ailing and almost blind. He wrote an essay on the history of seeing, one about the optics of early cultures, another on Mediterranean peasant settlements. His novel, *Hyle*, is uneven in depth, but in it, like Joyce, Hausmann tries to grasp life simultaneously. He also invented something called "psychomorphology," in which he made efforts to modify psychoanalysis. Almost none of his work was ever published.

George Grosz (1893–1959), a true Berliner, was a Dadaist from 1918. In 1920 he produced some exceptionally terrifying collages consisting of slogans, which aroused furious opposition but could not be obliterated. His painting in these years was influenced by Futurism: in *Burial of the Poet Panizza*, *Germany, a Winter's Tale* and *Adventurer*, all completed before 1920, he succeeded in uniting through a kaleidoscopic frenzy of motion events that actually lay far apart. His gigantic "adventurer," armed with a revolver, storms through shattered skyscrapers. Soon Grosz was excelling in series of graphics that pitilessly unmasked the gluttonous, lewd petty bourgeois, brutal militarists and the inhabitants of a garish prostitute world. Compared with these drawings, Hogarth and Daumier produced comfortable genre, and Gulbransson is merely an aristocratic satirist. With them Grosz developed a new graphic style—an unsparing verism is carried out with cubist changes of viewpoint and splintered abbreviations, while elements of childlike drawing cut like a knife through the explicit meaning of his forms. Militarism and religious hypocrisy were the chief objects of his scorn, as exemplified in his graphic series *God with us, Tragic Grotesque of Night, Bloody Serious, Ecce Homo, Bankrupt*.

The Nazis would have hanged him if he had not already taken a position in 1932 at the Art Students League in New York. Later he established a private school there. His caricatures dealing with the life of that city are crowded and no longer as precise in their draftsmanship. Gradually he turned to an anecdotal and gruesome romanticism, which also characterized the fantastic landscapes which he painted on the east coast of the United States. In 1955 his biography was published in German, with the characteristic title *Ein Kleines Ja, Ein großes Nein (A Little Yes and a Big No)*.

George Grosz. Chamber of Horrors, 1920

Kurt Schwitters (1887–1948) "participated in the successful campaign of Dada against the armies of the Golden Section" (Arp). He drew his own drastic but sensitive conclusions from the phantasmagoria of Dada with the result that he produced true works of art valued today throughout the world. A resounding lyricism restrained the aggressive quality of his dreams, and the startling effect he intended to have on the petty bourgeois is now lost. But at first the public was enraged because he went beyond the accepted materials of art: "I simply could not see any reason why old streetcar tickets, driftwood, coat checks, wire and wheel parts, buttons, junk from the attic and heaps of refuse should not be used as material for paintings, any less than colors made in a factory." A work of art therefore came to pass when various substances, fragments of objects, structure and color were brought together in a relationship replete with expression. The visual meaning of the parts, used as whole or completed units, was transformed by their being placed in new and unexpected relationships. In these works, Schwitters often connected his diverse

George Grosz. Self-portrait, 1919

material by nothing more than a few dim passages of color. Under his hand the opposing sections seemed to respond to each other. In his combinations of materials he went far beyond French Cubism, for he sought a more aggressively plastic effect. The perishable aspect of broken-down, decrepit forms of being was the message of his pictures, through which he interjected what we might call a sense of historic time–the exact opposite in intent of the scientifically engineered, precise collages done by his friend Vordemberge-Gildewart. He mumbled a play on his own name and the word weathering, "Verwitterung, Verschwitterung"–one might say in English "Withered by Schwitters." In a typical Dada christening he called such works *Merz* pictures, inspired by a successful example of this type of painting which had been built up around the graphic symbol MERZ, part of the word KOMMERZ or commerce; moreover, he realized that these creations belonged to neither Expressionism nor Cubism, nor could they be called paintings, drawings or reliefs. Later he used this designation also for his poems. *I-Bild*, (I-picture), from *invenire*, was the name he gave to another category, in which a complete element of nature (like a "found object") played a decisive part. Consequently he occasionally ran

133

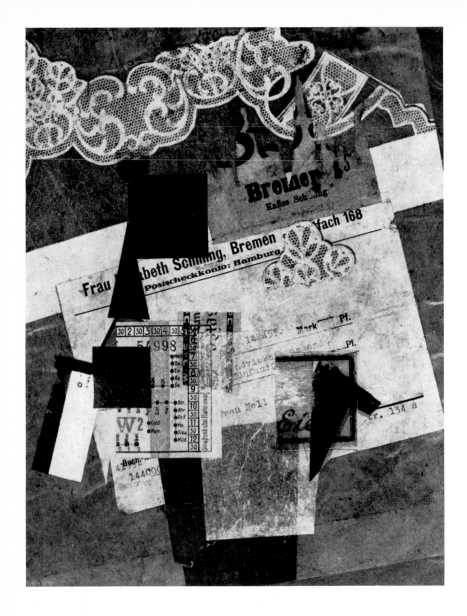

Kurt Schwitters. Picture, 1921
Basel, Collection Tschichold

around with a small empty frame through which he would focus on something specific in the sense of the "ready made," a concept which also interested the Dadaists and Surrealists. All one had to do was to alienate a symbolically attractive piece of nature from its surroundings and put it in a different context in order to give it "artistic" significance. The achievement lay in the correct detection. "Tell me what you stop and stand before and I'll tell you what you are."

Something of the sculptor was also active in Schwitters. In a gigantic cubist Merz-construction, *Cathedral of Erotic Misery*, an "open sculpture" which he gradually built up through the stories of his house in Hannover, all life was to be mirrored, as in Joyce's *Ulysses*. In it he puttered with and put together the strangest finds: Barbarossa's Kyffhäuser mountain, dog enclosures, Nibelung treasure, art exhibit, sex murderer's lair, Goethe relics, and "many almost-worn-out-by-writing-poetry pencils." In 1943 a bomb reduced it to ruins, along with many other works. Photographs give an inadequate idea of these compositions because the original identity of the objects is often blurred by an overlay of paint.

For a while Schwitters had a stimulating effect on typography and on the Bauhaus, whose architects he warned against the pitfalls of mere functionalism. Everywhere he went he fought for a new freedom in art. As poet, in accordance with his principles of montage, he used scraps of clichés and assembled them in new relationships. When Arp and Schwitters gave readings, Arp of his *Pyramidenrock*, Schwitters of his *Anna Blume*, Arp sounded like transposed Hölderlin, Schwitters like a transformed Wilhelm Busch. In his *Sound Sonata* Schwitters was experimenting with a nonobjective, i. e. wordless literature. Short or long sounds, staccato or legato, were produced, high or low, in gurgling or cutting tones, connected by

Kurt Schwitters. Picture, 1925
Brussels, Sammlung Janlet

vowels or consonants, but arranged in counterpoint. Here one was faced with a totally new art form which was neither speech nor music, nor song, nor mere noise, but included elements of them all. And this he presented with such perfection that it gave the effect of a thoroughly organized structure. (The typographer Jan Tschichold later printed a score of it.) In France experiments in a similar vein had been undertaken, but Schwitter's efforts may be traced back to Hausmann's *poème phonétique, fmsbw.* Arp said later, "Schwitters was as different from the cobblers of poetry as a songbird is from a pachyderm."

Hans Reichel
Death-blossom, 1924

136

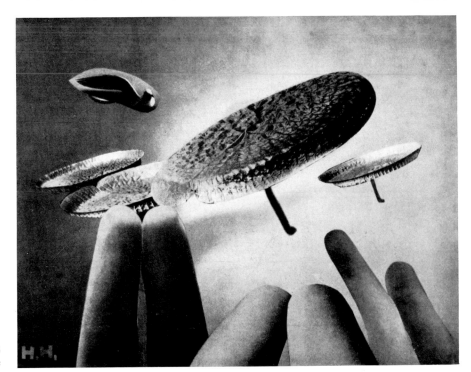

Hanna Höch
With Flying Leaves

In his paintings Schwitters developed an astonishing feeling for material and color contrasts. In the middle and late twenties they became simpler and a little more severe. He was always in touch with international trends. A few of his works appeared in *Esprit Nouveau, Transition* and *Cercle carré*. The last years of his life–typical of the fate of many exiled artists of those days–may be described briefly: 1935, emigration to Norway; 1940, after the German invasion, flight to England on an icebreaker; seventeen months in a internment camp; from 1941 in London, eking out a living by painting portraits; in 1945, in the English lake district, busy again with efforts to revive his great Merz structure; at times crippled and blind.

SURREALISM

While Magic Realism turned daily life into eerie form, Surrealism, which developed only a few years later, set out to smash our existing world completely, inspired by the extremism of Dadaism which had intervened. Surrealism shared with Magic Realism the urge to leave nothing veiled, to grasp all things as sharply as possible. But it went further to construct a new world, a world none of us had ever seen before, possibly not even in our fantastic dreams. The ordinary things of life were bewitched; constellations, ideas of space and the function of gravity were transformed. Without this transformation we are still in the realm of Magic Realism, and many artists shifted from one area to the other and back again,

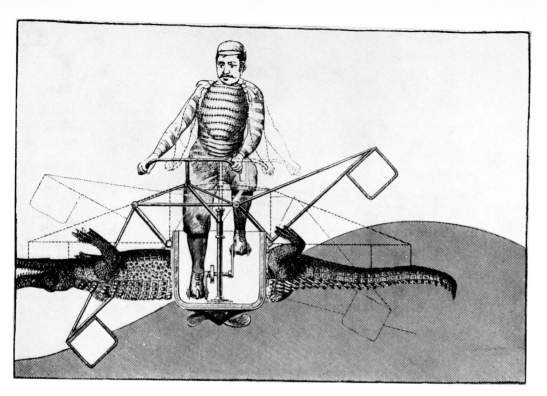

Max Ernst. From "Les malheurs des immortels," 1922

especially the Belgian painter Magritte. Typical surrealistic themes are a burning tree or a giraffe tumbling out of a window; a creaking ox-cart rumbling through a Louis XVI salon; the fastidious study of a scholar resting on the damp bottom of the sea; a slaughtered steer lying on an open grand piano. First, therefore, we are shocked, but to be effective the desired tension must rest on structural unity. Undreamed of images or combinations of experience beset the viewer, "like snow and thunderstorm, like cyclone and trembling of the earth," according to a Surrealist manifesto. They sought to emphasize in a sublimated fashion the mystery and insecurity of life as we know it really is if we think beyond the order we accept in everyday life. Their conception was a variation of the demonic vision with which one can at all times confront the harmonious view. Since comparable conceptions arise in our dreams, the Surrealists admired Freud and the subconscious, spoke of "trance" and the *expression pure*, and were against all "enlighteners."

It is not surprising that the genesis of German Surrealism occurred in the Lower Rhine regions, where it was developed mainly by Max Ernst, from Brühl. This was not far from the area–one of the most civilized in Europe–that had produced Bosch and Breughel, who had also lived in an epoch of social and religious upheaval. The result, then as now, was a pictorial form that no longer strove for a stable overall composition but indulged in a type of compartmentalization that was to make evident, even in its formal structure, the ambivalence of all appearances and values. But Bosch and Breughel had an easier time with their contemporaries because even in their most bizarre pictures they could rely for comprehension on their public's familiarity with the strange customs of the time, sectarian ideas of a

138

general nature, or the wisdom of traditional proverbs. The twentieth-century Surrealists had a harder task because they were driven by purely individualistic fantasy.

The art of *Max Ernst* (b. 1891) is extraordinary for many reasons. His unprecedented compositions make superb use of the latent possibilities of all nonobjective art. He has created new technical procedures which not only allow a shortening of the painting process but the creation of fantastic surface textures and effects (Plate XV). He has invented beings and objects never before seen or heard of. From all this he has produced a commensurate pictorial universe–literally out of this world. The result is a terrifying Utopia.

The harmony-seeking artist creates his Utopia by transcendentalizing his world. His demonic counterpart descends to the unfathomable depths of being. To condemn or reproach the latter as meaningless would be a failure to recognize the entire sequence of development from Bosch, Arcimboldi and Goya to Max Ernst. The historian of art must exert greater effort to penetrate the meaning for mankind of what we call "black humor."

Max Ernst gave modern Surrealism in painting its greatest range. Dali is also in command of objective fantasy and a refined technique, yet he remains caught in a bewildering dexterity and tends to be theatrical. Max Ernst appeals to us not only with his ludicrous themes but also through form. Phantoms appear in which organic life is captured. Hybrid creatures, part animal, part plant, gesticulate in front of nocturnal mountain shapes. A forest becomes a jumble of bough-like human limbs; creatures are ejected, creatures which remind us of ourselves but have insect eyes and bird feathers. In a night sky, where alien suns circle, a huge cosmic symbol glows. The most precise representational quality is interspersed with abstractions of which the object forms a part. Thus they seem ruled by a comprehensive order.

Like all the great painters of our century, Ernst was an experimenter. In his montages, to which he gave content, he revealed to us a strange world. (We find it also in his writings, *Répétitions*, *La Femme 100 Têtes*, *Rêve d'une petite fille*, *Semaine de bonté*, etc.) Concerning his montages, he wrote to me in 1926, "It meant less to me to construct new entities than to create electric and erotic tensions by relating elements which until now we have felt were alien and unconnected. This resulted in explosions and high voltage, and the more

Max Ernst. Equivocal Woman, 1923

Max Ernst. Phases of the Night, 1946 · Pittsburgh, W. Read Hovey Collection

unexpected the associations (for instance: gun-barrel, beetle mimicry, lace skirt) the more surprising was the flashing spark of poetry." In the course of these experiments he made two discoveries–first, that the sentimentality of nineteenth-century wood engravings, a material he made use of, could become expressive through a new combination of the parts; and second, that one could combine single sheets to form a whole series, thus creating a new type of consecutive pictorial narrative, with or without text.

Another technique he revived was *frottage* (rubbings) which he employed in 1925 in his *Histoire Naturelle*. At that time he wrote, "I shall be glad to give you the instructions. Take wood from the fir tree–but let it be quite dry–or any wood that has been exposed to sea air for years so that its veins stand out clearly. Cover it with a not-too-thick piece of paper and rub it with a soft pencil. Soon stripes and wavy lines will appear on the paper–the sea. These waves will seem to be coming toward the viewer or disappearing on the horizon, depending on how you regulate the pressure. Now lay the paper on the center of a gramophone record and rub it until the sun rises...Instead of fir wood or record you may use any material you like. Press one on top of the other, beside each other, mix them up. If at the same time you have the necessary quantum of fantasy, the world opens up before you. What a field of endless possibilities, my young painter! The procedure just described is as old as it is new. Our dear ancestors who practiced human sacrifice used to describe the lines that birds drew in the sky. In them they recognized–always with the necessary quantum of fantasy–future and truth."

In painting he employed related procedures, which he interpolated in his pictures in fascinating contrast to the parts that were freely painted. In 1953 he isolated these strange micro-effects in his *Sept Microbes*, which was composed of nothing but colored structures in miniature. His large picture, *Father Rhine*, displays the same qualities. Many small pieces are united in a large composition, yet remain separate from it. Both are meant to exist in a state of tension with one another. Microcosm and macrocosm are not intended to merge. In such later works Ernst moves away completely from objective Surrealism as practiced for instance by Dali, although we find early paintings by Ernst in a pure narrative style, transmitting a representative phantasmagoria.

The private life of this painter has been equally turbulent. As a child he was tormented by hallucinations and the unexplained death of a sister. He studied history of art, wrestled with philosophy, then, self-taught, groped his way to painting; he was harried through the First World War; in despair and scorn he became the leader of the *Dada W 3* group in Cologne; in 1920 he was already exhibiting his strange collages in Paris; he moved there, and in 1924 he and his friends founded the Surrealist movement. Already in 1922 he had painted the original group of Surrealists in the numbered portrait that

Max Ernst. Father Rhine, 1953

has since become a historical document. In it the artists are seated on the edge of a glacier, between Raphael and Dostoevsky. In 1941, amid the confusion of World War II, Ernst arrived in the United States, married Peggy Guggenheim, lived for a short time like a millionaire, collected exotic folk art; then, with a new wife, the painter Dorothy Tanning he fled to the desert ioslation of Arizona, only to return finally to Paris. In 1953 he returned to his birthplace in Brühl, where a truly surrealist "happening" was created to celebrate his sixtieth birthday: the trim little rococo castle of Brühl was filled with his terrifying paintings and drawings.

Ernst is also a sculptor and the author of poems and essays. His book, *Beyond Art,* is well known.

At the time Dadaism erupted in Cologne and Surrealism was already being heralded, *Heinrich Hoerle* (1895–1936) lived in that city. In his *Factory Worker* of 1921, he does not present us with a nature-picture, as Dix and the Magic Realists would have done, but offers us a ghostly robot composed of metal cylinders, crane-joints and hook-hands, standing ready to start any machine, a pressure meter in his limbs, on his head a metal boiler with a zero on it, and, where we would expect to find the face, a needle for reading pressure–a symbol of our frightening affiliation with the machine age. Later he developed similar themes in a more felicitous style.

Heinrich Hoerle. Factory Worker, 1921

Here we must mention *Franz W. Seiwert* (1894–1933) who, like Hoerle, died young. Seiwert felt close to the radical worker's movement, and with constructions similar to Hoerle's tried to express the meaning of solidarity and the masses in the turmoil of modern life. *Rudolf Schlichter* (1890–1955) fell between Surrealism and the New Objectivity. In 1922 he entered the highly spiced cultural climate of Berlin, where he moved in the politically inflamed circles of Berthold Brecht and George Grosz. In his drawings he ridiculed the times or elaborated on sex. He illustrated, among other works, the *Arabian Nights* and Bret Harte's *Tales of California.* In these he carried on the illustrative art of the nineteenth century, even planning, in his enthusiasm for all its manifestations, a revindication of the sensual viewpoint of Richard Wagner. In 1932, after having turned his back on the sin-ridden Tower of Babel that was Berlin, he withdrew to his home province of Swabia, and then in 1939 he moved to Munich. Under the influence of Theodor Hecker, Schlichter embraced Catholicism, as the Dadaist rebel Hugo Ball had done before him.

In his paintings, Schlichter increasingly stressed surrealistic inventiveness, but because his powers of artistic transformation were inadequate his work remained overly objective and for the most part unsatisfactory. At times his paintings seemed to depict nothing more than nightmarish dummies in a state of petrefaction. Fearful visions of childhood were consolidated in strange landscapes in which he erected abstruse symbols of brutishness or of cultural barbarism—"a materialized mélange of chthonian and daytime reality," as he put it. Characteristic of his sharp writing style are his books, *Das widerspenstige Fleisch (The Recalcitrant Flesh, 1932)*, and *Das Abenteuer in der Kunst (An Adventure in Art, 1949)*. The first includes astonishingly frank sex confessions, the second polemicizes against all abstract art, which had meanwhile gained prominence, and in which he saw cultural ruination, or at best a merely ornamental value. If Schlichter had at least experienced these possibilities of expression, his considerable talent might have achieved greater freedom. Certain landscape drawings remain gripping. In them—according to him—stone should call to mind muscles; the bark of the tree, the texture of animal hide, for instance—"all deformations and monstrosities included."

Mac Zimmermann (b. 1912) was renowned in Germany as a Surrealist. He came from the north; hence, no doubt, the emphasis on the lowlands and monotonous beaches in his pictures. Gesticulating dream figures are manipulated rhythmically; fantastic inventions give an intellectualized effect. Whereas his delicately tinted, transparent, enamellike style of painting is not always convincing because he does not give his color full play, as a draftsman he was completely successful. In his drawings, strange spectral women haunt a combed, striated, half-tone

Franz W. Seiwert. Machine Worker, 1927

world. Gigantic, but drawn with a net-like transparency, they fill the foreground, rising abruptly against the far-off horizon. His strokes trace delicate wood grain patterns, alternating in their density to create sharp contrasts of light and dark, legato versus staccato areas of linear activity. These figures remind one of voluptuous maenads, with wildly flowing hair, caged in wire and composed in a curious calligraphic counterpoint. Dead trees stand on a glowing earth as if they were receiving stations for distant radio announcements. Some of his human bodies look like gigantic insects on a dead star. A highly spirited *Skizzenbuch* by Zimmermann was published by Piper in 1955.

144

Edgar Ende. Quarrel, 1957

Edgar Ende (1901–1966) also came from the North German lowlands. Like his fellow Surrealists from this area–Zimmermann, Cremer, Battke and Lüdcke–he tended to emphasize the surface plane of his paintings, allowing his figures only to perch on the top, without spatial penetration. His perspective construction, in common with Ernst, Tanguy and Dali, was derived from the early work of de Chirico, and accentuated the emptiness of space. Dreamlike pavilions stand upon this surface, helpless cripples somehow emerging from them. Naked female forms rise up from decayed walls, holding slogans aloft, as if to present messages. A boat, pale as death and overloaded with frightened passengers, hovers in the sky. Ende's interiors, again reminiscent of de Chirico, are represented as separate sealed-off rooms, frames, as it were, for the inevitable loneliness of mankind. He presented neither the specific actions nor the fulfillment of erotic desires which are implicit in Ernst and wholly explicit in Schlichter. Ende was drawn to anthroposophy, which he interpreted in a passive form, from a sense of unavoidable destiny. The specific difference between man and woman disappears. We find none of Dix's social protest, none of the products of engineering which Ernst introduced as contrasts to organic life; hence no support for the pictorial structure. A discreet, sometimes dull, sometimes glowing color scheme prevails. Fear and longing cry out in harmonious stagnation. Some pictures reveal a schism between the source of the will and its bizarre results. It is as if a mystic order is to be founded, and is subsequently negated.

Edgar Ende
The Last Man, 1931

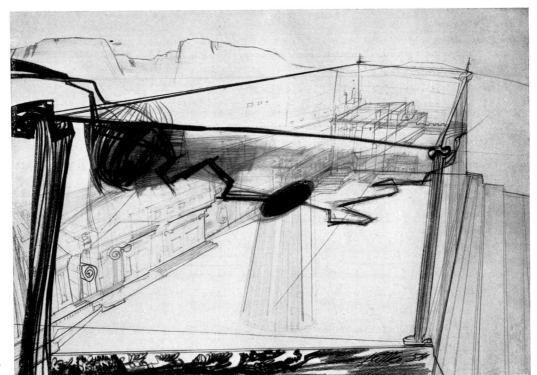

Heinz Battke
tage Thunderstorm,
1954

Heinz Battke
The Mathematician,
1952/53

149

Leo Cremer (b. 1911), restorer for the Bavarian Staatsgemäldesammlung (State Collection of Paintings), also gained prominence especially for his Surrealist drawings. He invented scenes with mythical or obsolete parts of ships or disintegrating articles of furniture, emphasizing more strongly than the other Surrealists these objects and figures in his work, and revealing an almost Baroque sense of composition. His wash drawings are also more lyrical, occasionally expressive of a gentle pathos. The shock effect of a tower of ruined objects is mitigated by the softness of his colors, allowing us to recognize not only a demonic type of Surrealism but a lyrically harmonious one—if, indeed, it can still be called Surrealist. Unlike others of his generation *Joachim Lüdcke* (b. 1922), another north German, proves that this movement lives on into the present generation, even if only rarely. Lüdcke lets his brushstroke disappear entirely. Enamellike compact surfaces are created in a type of oil-resin painting. With uncanny precision he depicts gruesome, dreamy landscape happenings.

Heinz Battke (1900–1966), a late convert to Surrealism, was also best known for his graphic achievement. Whereas the fashion of our time has dictated preservation of the surface, objective Surrealism, since the early de Chirico, surrendered to the magic of space. Battke worked with deep perspective thrusts which are cut off in the distance. It was his aim to orient the human figure, in fact all nature, toward mysteriously divergent *Augenpunkte*, or vanishing points, on the horizon. Perspective is introduced as magical construction, just as the important masters of the quattrocento used it, not solely for scientific pictorial construction but also as an element of expression. His spatial structure is based on a subtle linear order, apparently electrically charged, which encompasses the energy of all matter. Battke, who came from East Prussia, settled in Florence in 1935, wrote a history of his collection of rings as well as articles on numerous and diverse contemporary artistic questions.

Friedrich Schröder-Sonnenstern From "Creatures," 1953

150

The Regression of National Socialism

Many new artistic impulses were developing in Germany when the devastating storm of National Socialism broke, sweeping everything before it. In the most varied fields of development the clock was drastically turned back. Not only were democratic achievements of communal life destroyed, but freedom of the arts was lost in a way never before experienced by any culture in modern history. To be sure, earlier ages have sought to throttle new stirrings of expression, for an inertia of the soul, an intellectual sluggishness rules a majority of observers. In my book, *Zur Geschichte des künstlerischen Mißverstehens (The History of Artistic Misunderstanding)*, I have been able to show that the average educated man usually requires several decades before he is able to assimilate new intellectual creations.

To a certain degree, the National Socialists produced art of their own, but on close view one finds nothing but a repetition of the attitudes of the nineteenth century, a stereotype imitation of external nature interspersed with a declamatory pathos, either in the cause of heroism or for "Blood and Soil." Strange how similar in this respect were National Socialism and Bolshevism, however much they professed to hate each other. We are dealing here with the artistic ideals of the ever-culturally-retarded petty bourgeois, who are always opposed to the new and unwilling to respond to the intense cultivation of formal values. In 1945 German art could do nothing but pick up where it had left off in 1933. All in all, the art that was created on order by National Socialism is a foreign body; it would be a waste of time to illustrate it here. I shall therefore limit myself to summarizing the basic attitudes of that time and pointing out the results.

Even before the Nazis came to power, reactionary cultural forces had arisen which would have been incapable of following any of the progressive developments. One has only to recall the Werdandi Bund at the turn of the century, Theodor Alt's protest against Impressionism (1911), the "flaming protest" of the Munich representatives in the *Reichsverband* of Creative Artists against the acquisition at the time of paintings by Van Gogh, or the *Protest deutscher Künstler (Protest of German Artists)* by Karl Vinnen. But heretofore all such views had remained in the background, whereas now the obscurantists could surge to the fore and take over the leadership.

In 1923 Hans Günther published his *Rassenkunde des Deutschen Volkes (Racial Science of the German People)*, in which he mixed scientific information with pure superstition. The aggressive myth of the unique superiority of Nordic Man gained ascendance, a racial belief that was now to form a decisive foundation also for the arts. In 1925 *Die Drohung des Untermenschen (The Menace of the Underman)* was published;[1] in 1928 L. F. Clauss moved into the limelight with his work *Die nordische Seele (The Nordic Soul)*, founded on the grotesque polarity "Viking or Bedouin." Schultze-Naumburg, who wrote about "heroic man," seconded Clauss from the aesthetic side. Thus were assembled the various sources of National Socialist teaching of art.

Alfred Rosenberg's *Mythos des 20. Jahrhunderts* (1930) closed the cycle: according to him, one had arrived at "impressionistic and expressionistic impotence." What Van Gogh, Gauguin, Signac and

---

[1] A translation of selections from *The Revolt of Civilization, the Menace of the Underman,* by the American Theodore Lothrop Stoddard.

Picasso had created "emerged boldly and openly after the [First World] war: mestizoism [mongrelization] demanded the right to present, as expressions of the soul, its bastardized abortions, created by the syphilis of intellectualism and painted infantilism. The Kokoschkas, Chagalls, Pechsteins, etc., were worshipped by Jewish writers as leaders of the painting of the future... Lovis Corinth gave evidence of a certain robustness, but even this butcher of the brush descended to clayey, corpse-hued bastardizations in a Berlin gone Syrian." Rosenberg's *Kampfbund* was soon talking about art that was "cheap and degrading... a fist in the face of Germany, its heroic army and the Führer." Bauhaus methods, in Italy called *stilo tedesco*–German style–were considered foreign and were branded by their own countrymen as "cultural bolshevism." One could hear criticism of Paul Klee's "foolish scribblings" and Kokoschka's "daubing." "We see cultural bolshevism in the subhuman style of Kollwitz, Zille, Barlach, the technical bungler Nolde, Schmidt-Rottluff, Chagall, and in the ethical nihilism of Dix, Hofer and Grosz." In 1933, the Nazi news agency *Deutsche Korrespondenz* demanded that: 1) All work giving any indication of foreign influence should be removed from museums and collections. 2) All museum directors falling under the same heading should be dismissed. 3) The names of all Marxist and Bolshevist artists swept along by this tide should never be mentioned publicly again. A *Schandausstellung* (Abominations Exhibition) was organized under the heading of "Government Art from 1918 to 1933," in which Liebermann, Slevogt, Corinth, Marées and Munch were dispatched too. Karl Hofer in Berlin and Paul Klee in Düsseldorf had already been dismissed in the spring of 1933. At this time the *Deutsche Kulturwacht (German Cultural Sentinel)* wrote: "What we are being offered in the Berlin Kronprinzenpalais as young modern German art is Jews, nothing but Jews." Actually the Jewish contribution was two percent. Barlach, Nolde, Schmidt-Rottluff, Kandinsky and Klee were considered especially nefarious. Rosenberg attacked Nolde as "negroid, impious, crude, and lacking in any formal inner powers." The art historian Schardt was arrested when he delivered a speech on the twentieth anniversary of Franz Marc's death.

In 1934 Hitler spoke out on the subject for the first time, rendering the situation even more acute. When a few sensible people made efforts to save what they could, the *Völkische Beobachter* wrote, in 1935, "The rats are coming out of their hiding places and are trying to spread themselves out again in the sacred temple of German art." In the same year Hitler declared that art must be comprehensible to the people, although he had to admit that the nation's masses could not share in the achievements of science "or any of the other loftier expressions of life or philosophy." In 1936 Count Baudissin, the director who had been forced on the Folkwang Museum, wrote, "The most perfect form, the most glorious thing constructed in the course of the last epoch, did not originate in the studios of our artists; it was the steel helmet which our storming gray columns wore." The time had come "to ferret out the most important works from their private hiding places, to confiscate them and to arrange for their disposal, and to make their previous destruction punishable by law." The Racial Political Bureau brought to the attention of the Reich Cultural Chamber the fact that pictures were still cropping up which "regrettably depicted the German family with only one or two children." And in 1937, at the inauguration of the House of German Art in Munich, Hitler forbade painters to use colors that the normal eye could not apprehend. Whoever did so in spite of this edict was either sick, in which case a doctor should see to it that he left no heirs, or he was a fraud and should submit to the law.

152

At the same time the exhibition *"Entartete Kunst"* ("Degenerate Art") was opened in the House of German Art; twenty-five German museums were plundered for it. There one could see hanging, along-side their imitators and followers, the finest painters of the nation, all the masters who today enjoy international fame. One hundred and twelve artists were "disgraced" in this exhibition. The loss for the Berlin National Gallery alone ran into more than a million gold marks. In the plundering of the Berlin Kupferstichkabinett, the vandals went back as far as Van Gogh and Munch. In a Berlin lecture course in 1937, Matthias Grünewald was attacked as a psychopath and Rembrandt denounced as a portrayer of ghettos. The opportunist Franz Hofmann announced triumphantly at a "Cultural Convention" that approximately 12,000 drawings and 5,000 paintings had been confiscated. In 1939 the famous Lucerne auction of these precious German art treasures took place. Hofmann suggested that "the remainder be burned in a bonfire as a symbolic propaganda action." 1,004 paintings and 3,825 drawings were actually reduced to ashes in the courtyard of the Main Fire House in Berlin in 1939.

Germany's Loss in Artists

The position of National Socialism had catastrophic results. The most productive and courageous spirits either retired into a silent inner emigration or escaped to freedom abroad. That Germany had not bled to death artistically by 1945 is a miracle. We cannot touch here upon the effect on German literature caus-ed by the exile of writers and poets like Thomas and Heinrich Mann, Arnold and Stefan Zweig, Franz Werfel, Jacob Wassermann, Leonhard Frank, Hermann Kesten, Joachim Maass, or of a theatrical pro-ducer of the calibre of Max Reinhardt–men who were dependent on the German language in which they had thought, felt and created. For those who worked in an international idiom, banishment was less tragic: the language of the composers, architects, painters and sculptors was comprehensible in any country, even if it bore the impress of Germany. A few artists perished in concentration camps: the architect Paul Meller, for instance, an important associate of Oud and Bartning; and Friedel Dicker, an immensely gifted weaver and sculptress. The following artists fled: Kandinsky, Klee, Feininger, Moholy, Bayer, Molzahn, Itten and Albers–all the important masters of the Bauhaus–as well as Beckmann, Ko-koschka, Schwitters, Scharl, Adler, Reichel and Vordemberge-Gildewart. The highly original graphic artists T. Heine and George Grosz, were also among the exiles, and the sculptors Belling and Gabo (who lived in Berlin until 1933) and the typographer Jan Tschichold. Max Ernst had left Germany previously, a disappointed artist. Every one of these men enjoyed international fame at the time. Other masters such as Nolde, Schmidt-Rottluff, Heckel, Hofer, Baumeister, Nesch, Fuhr, the sculptors Marcks, Ma-taré, Knappe and Baum, just barely managed to survive total isolation in their own country. Barlach and Schlemmer perished, forlorn and in misery, broken by Germany's "new culture." German architec-ture was also robbed of its most productive forces. Gropius, Mies van der Rohe, Mendelsohn, Marcel Breuer, Hilberseimer, Ernst May, Bruno Taut, Rading, all managed to get out, in good time or at the last minute. How important these men were was appreciated by the uncomprehending only later, when most of these exiles became famous far away from their homeland. In Germany the architects Döcker, Häring, Korn, Mächler, Max Taut and Scharoun were prevented from working. One could also add the names of important art theoreticians and critics who were also lost to Germany. It was above all those German art historians who emigrated to the United States who were able to bring to fruition their comparatively new branch of scholarship.

Fundamental Errors

Now that we have given a brief résumé of the proclamations and measures of National Socialism, let us consider, *sine ira et studio*, the reasons which made it impossible for the National Socialists to accept the new formal methods of their day. Here we find two levels of prejudice which we should separate from each other. One is the result of the special demands of their political attitude, the other is of a more general nature and still exists in the attitude of the middle class today. We should discuss both of them if we want to understand the very core of modern creative methods.

The National Socialists demanded that art should conform to the values of the Nordic race; it must also include some sort of moral ideology, and, above all, it must be beautiful. Twentieth-century artists rejected all these criteria, although they have remained popular with the public of today.

Taking them briefly:

1. Today's creative artists seek to express their inmost feelings, without regard for either biological or historical normative demands. The study of races, still very obscure, has come up with certain hypotheses, but has drawn no compelling conclusions from them. It recognizes that Germany does *not* constitute a unified race, and that the relatively small area where the race is relatively pure happens also to be the least fruitful artistically. In addition one recognizes that modes of expression have changed radically in the course of history in order to give adequate form to the prevailing emotional needs of the time. Furthermore—and this is a sensible aspect of art today, in Germany too—there is a spontaneous search for elements that bring people together and do not stress national and consequently divisive idioms. The situation is in fact similar to the internationalism of artistic expression of the Middle Ages or Baroque period, and therefore in this respect hardly new.

2. It is a mistake to try to make the fine arts an instrument of political ideas. This has been proved in today's Russia, where such a bond has resulted in the atrophy of painting and sculpture. National and political bonds insofar as necessary at all, belong in a *civilization*, in which it is necessary to work through organization, rule and prescription. But they are not a part of a culture. On the contrary, twentieth-century art seeks to present a realm for the free-flowing of our inner being, and thus to counterbalance the political control—and this is one of its healthier aspects, opposing the innumerable pressures arising from today's collective life.

3. The precept that art must be generally understood is also highly dubious. The artist hopes, in due course, to become comprehensible to as many people as possible, but he wholly rejects any idea of working deliberately toward such an end or of making any concessions; in this such disparate painters as Hans Thoma and Picasso agreed. This attitude of the artists is also nothing new, for it accords with the trend in all recent intellectual history. All comparatively new, unexpected or truly original creations

154

were at first unpopular. Only later, like a stone dropped into water, did they leave behind them ever widening circles of effectiveness. Abstract painting, when it is good, may be expected to find a growing response among the public, after the usual delay.

4. Fidelity to nature may be demanded of realism, but not, however, of today's creative procedures, which aim to project the artists' spiritual condition with or without reference to a prescribed world; in this respect, therefore, contemporary art is akin to absolute music. According to Willi Baumeister, when "abstract" art no longer deals with the world of things in finished form, it turns its attention to and re-forms *other* manifestations of nature, such as rock or lava-like substances, the bark of trees, even microscopic structures whose individuality may be recognized as infinitely variable. It may well be impossible for the artist to find a form that does not already exist somewhere in nature.

5. There is no need for a work of art to illustrate an idea, much less a moral. Those who expect some kind of message (the eternal question: What does it mean?) are too rational in their approach to art, for its essential function is the manifold expression of feeling, not the transmission or illustration of thought. Such mistaken demands arose from the nineteenth-century conception which assumed an early convergence of the lines of development in art and science. The contemporary view relegates this moment of merging to some time in infinity.

6. The last demand is perhaps the most sensible one: every work of art should somehow or other be beautiful. But this makes sense only if one interprets it as the expectation that a formative process has occurred that of itself uplifts and carries us beyond the mere imitation of nature or any indiscriminate piling up of abstract elements. Behind this common demand, however, always lurks an antipathy to the enigmatic and profound, to the mysterious intensities that might shock us. The works of Bosch, Breughel, Goya, Daumier, Ensor, Picasso, and also comparable works of literature, were not beautiful, but they were profound. Beside the harmonious, there is a demonic world view and form of expression. To prove its exceptional importance in our life as a totality is one of the most difficult questions of aesthetics, still unanswered. Because the nineteenth century tended to be overly harmonious, it is not surprising that in the twentieth century the pendulum has swung the opposite way. Since time began such historic contrasts have taken place within the dialectic development of the human spirit.

A FEW INDIVIDUAL MASTERS

In twentieth-century art, Oskar Kokoschka (b. 1886) occupies a place all to himself (Plate XVI). This Austrian appears here because he spent decisive years of his life in Germany. Landscape, figure compositions and portraits were his special domain; the rarity of his still lifes is indicative of his inner restlessness. In landscape and human beings he felt fiery-fluid forces. His work is more nervous and improvisatory in effect than that of the masters of the Brücke, with their cumbersome and heavy combinations of form and color. Kokoschka did not seek a firm scaffolding for his pictures; one could say rather that he carried on the Slavic-Austrian tradition of the late Baroque painter Maulpertsch. One could also link him with Corinth, for both stress the quick, intuitive creative process: the painting should be experienced *in statu nascendi*. In his last years Kokoschka returned to a new Impressionism, and

Oskar Kokoschka. Professor Forel, 1908 · Mannheim, Kunsthalle

156

although his brushstrokes and color were livelier and more pulsating, one could say that finally he approached Slevogt.

His first style was developed in Vienna. Already in 1897 a strange, subliminally stimulated, decadently nervous atmosphere had been created there–first by the Secession under Klimt and Schiele, then by the publication in 1900 of Freud's dream theories, and by the intermingling in this atmosphere of waves of emotion of an echoing Jugendstil. In 1904 Kokoschka enrolled at the Vienna School of Applied Arts. In 1908 the *Wiener Werkstätte* published his color lithographs, *The Dreaming Youths*, in which something of Picasso's blue period work may be felt. In 1907 Kokoschka began painting portraits that give a trance-like effect. The Viennese critic Karl Kraus and the Swiss psychiatrist Professor Auguste Forel are depicted as if seen from within, made tensely transparent, in a few muted, faded, yet somehow phosphorescent colors. Beside such works even the mysterious personalities portrayed by Munch, his predecessor in this field, seem stable. Take Kokoschka's *Still Life with Dead Sheep* (1909), his *Dent du Midi* (1910) and the drawings that appeared in the Berlin *Sturm*: in all of them his exciting strokes whirl out from a vital sensitivity. Sometimes, though, he resorts to a wiry structure, especially in the illustrations for his drama, the first Expressionist play, *Murder, Hope of Women*.

Oskar Kokoschka. The Painter, 1924 · St. Louis, Missouri, Collection Morton D. May

Subsequently he painted with oilier pigments. The spots of color were more saturated, became heavier and blended more naturally with the object. But the pressures of life also increased constantly, producing Kokoschka's most intensely dramatic period. He totally disregarded the formal problems which the Cubists were working on at this time. Everything was wildly thrown together, sometimes in burlesque, sometimes in apocalyptic style, whether he was painting or drawing illustrations for Ehrenstein's *Tubutsch*, or for his own dramas, *The Fettered Columbus, Bach Cantata, Hiob*. His painting, *The Tempest*, is filled with a passionate unrest.

In 1917 Kokoschka moved to Dresden, and in 1920, when he was appointed to the Art Academy there, his work entered a third phase, taking on a lapidary quality. His color areas developed even more sweep and glowed more specifically in purer contrasts of green, red and blue. The spacious splendor of nature overwhelmed the psychology of the subconscious; neurasthenic traits, evident at the beginning, began to recede. The more expansive color areas with which Nolde and the Brücke masters were painting had probably made an impression. Powerfully burgeoning colors now appeared in the picture as constructive elements. In these years Kokoschka achieved his most enduring results.

In 1924 he left Dresden suddenly for Switzerland, Vienna and Paris. Now, ever more uninhibitedly, he mastered the infinite space of landscape. Then followed the series of cityscapes in which the handling is broadly spacious and at the same time is infinitely complex in that it presents a number of spaces. He painted Bordeaux, Rome, Marseilles, Toledo, Madrid, Paris, London, Venice, Constantinople—an *orbis*

Oskar Kokoschka. The Louvre, 1929 · Hamburg, Kunsthalle

Oskar Kokoschka. The Matterhorn, 1947 · Zürich-Küsnacht, Collection H. Lütjens

pictus was created. He brought back the old post-medieval theme of views of the world, with high horizons to permit the widest possible view, as had been customary since Patinier, Breughel, Merian, Canaletto and Guardi. But Kokoschka never resorted to historic methods, always remaining true to himself. These pictures should be brought together sometime as a cycle illustrating the great centers of man.

In 1934 Kokoschka moved to Prague and then to London because he had been declared "degenerate" and a warrant was out for his arrest. In a fourth phase his painting became even more strongly impressionistic. Beside fully realized works we find others that disintegrate in soapy colors. The parables that he turned to so often did not always come off. Today he lives on the Lake of Geneva and in the summer teaches in Salzburg. With a total lack of understanding he has polemicized against Picasso and against the progress of art, in the same manner in which voices were once raised against him.

Kokoschka also produced a rich graphic oeuvre. Here, characteristically, he did not resort to the difficult art of the woodcut but favored lithography, and also preferred the more painterly lithographic crayon to the etching needle. It is astonishing to see how a man who was specifically a painter could also express everything he felt in black and white.

Another great master, *Max Beckmann* (1884–1950), stands in isolation, not connected with the exuberant experimenters of the Blaue Reiter nor with the expansive Brücke painters. The virile Beckmann was the opposite of his contemporary, the more feminine Franz Marc. While the creations of the latter seem to rest in the lap of Mother Earth, Beckmann's are stubborn, lusty creatures that deny pictorial space. (Plate XVIII.) The same applies to his landscapes–whereas with Marc all seems to swing in spherical harmony, with Beckmann trees and rocks block each other in a threatening manner.

This broad-shouldered, sturdy man with the powerful head came from Leipzig, studied briefly at the Weimar Art Academy, and paid a fleeting visit to Paris, which made little impression on him. It was in Berlin, where he lived from 1907 to 1914, that he began to shape his world. The horrifying years of World War I were followed by a first period of affirmation in Frankfurt. From 1925 to 1933 he taught at the Art School there, and then he fled from National Socialism, never to set foot on German soil again. In 1938 he found refuge in Amsterdam, where he stayed until 1947, when he accepted a teaching position at Washington University in Saint Louis. Three years later he died suddenly while taking a walk in New York City.

He painted mysterious orgies, bold circus scenes, lewd women, but also Greek mythological themes in powerful triptychs. Already in his early period he dared to approach majestic symbolic themes: *The Bearing of the Cross, Rape, The Sinking of the Titanic, The Night, Resurrection.* Death and life seem interwoven in these pictures, but this applies also when he paints a lonely portrait, a compact still life or a vigorous landscape. Over and over again he outlines or cages his sensually turgid colors within dark tones. In his composition we find the contrast of figures pressing forward as if their vitality would burst the frame assunder, yet they are crowded together within the limits of the picture as if imprisoned. Characteristic was his tendency toward compact, oblique compositions, or narrow rectangles, vertically placed.

He emerged from the gloomy, flowing late Impressionism of the Corinth school, inevitably attracted by its bleak vitality. Then, from 1917 on, cohesive, almost stereometric forms appear in his pictures, most probably through the influence of German late Gothic masters. At the same time he touched upon themes of social criticism in paintings, akin to the Magic Realism of Dix at that time, distorted pictures of a sordid world, reminiscent of our more macabre modern ballads. The figures, with their over-lifesize heads, seem clamped together by some kind of bizarre mechanism. We see rigid forms, as if masked, pressed against the picture plane, often glassy and cold in color, sometimes looking almost like random daubs of paint. In this period Beckmann also produced many drawings.

During the twenties, in his third period, his innate color drive breaks through, inspired perhaps by renewed visits to Paris. His segments of reality are more natural and free; the graphic aspects of the picture have been sucked up by a new richness of color. A luminous yellow, a rich green and a deep blue

Carl Hofer. Man in the Ruins, 1943

Max Beckmann. Apache Dance, 1938

dominate, interrupted by night-black. Some figures give the effect of fruit, ripe to bursting, but everything is pictorially linked. The structural power of his painting gradually reaches a high point of effectiveness even if here and there occasional free-flowing areas of color are not ruled out. He created nine huge triptychs–almost like the nine symphonies of Beethoven, Schubert, Bruckner, Mahler–worldly altarpieces, yet fraught with meaning; among them are *Departure* (1932–1933), *Antonius* (1936–1937), *Perseus* (1941), *The Actors* (1942), *The Argonauts* (1950). The period in which he had ridiculed all structural approaches and had slandered the paintings of Franz Marc as primitive "Siberian-Bavarian *Marterlplakate* (votive tablets)" lay far behind him. Now he wrote, almost exaggerating the opposite viewpoint, of a necessary "mathematics of expression."

In lithography, in his woodcuts, etchings and drawings, Beckmann also expressed himself powerfully,

Max Beckmann
Self-Portrait, 1944
Munich, Bayerische Staatsgemälde-
Sammlungen

Max Beckmann
Winter Painting,
1930
Munich
Collection
G. Franke

stamping these techniques with his own world of feeling. In translating the three-dimensional space of the objective world into the two-dimensional space of the picture plane, he was moved above all by a passionate desire to compress the multiple substance of life. But he chose to steer clear of nonobjective art; it was enough for him to declare, "In principle every alteration of an object is permissible, provided the necessary capacity to create form is demonstrated." To the end he shaped things out of an inner demonic passion. "I would worm my way through all the sewers in the world, suffer every humiliation and disgrace, to paint."

162

Max Beckmann
opi and the Hindu,
1941
Essen
Museum Folkwang

Carl Hofer. Ticino Landscape, 1927

Carl Hofer. Sokrota, 1924

Carl Hofer (1878–1955), Beckmann's contemporary, started his career from more serene premises. In his southern landscapes he sought to construct an idyll, doubtless influenced by impressions of Rome–by the "relentless clarity of this city, which not many can withstand," as he put it. Favored by fortune in his early years, he was supported by a rich Swiss patron, Dr. Theodor Reinhardt, who made it possible for him to live in Rome, Paris and India. In the twenties and thirties he painted groups of young girls in which harmony of existence was bound up with monumentality of form. His landscapes of the Ticino combined melancholy loneliness with a conciliatory harmony of color planes: violet, pink, green and a curious shade of brown or gray. Despite the apparent placidity of his temperament, however, he was disturbed by the First World War and the revolution that followed it, and he gives us also a world of drummers, lemurs, nocturnal ruins (Plate XVII) or a dance of death –even an *Atomic Serenade*.

Gradually he included curious forms and abstractions in his paintings, which became flatter and chromatically duller. Partly as a result of the destruction of many of his paintings during the second World War he began to repeat himself, copying the lost compositions. In addition, as overworked Director of the Berlin Art Academy from 1945 he had little time for new works. And Picasso's deformations seem to have influenced him in a way that did not suit him. In Picasso he admired "that so rare *unio mystica* of form and color which determined his unique personality." But Hofer's figures increasingly resembled masks. Only Beckmann, with his richer powers of observation, was able to avoid a similar weakening–a hazard of age.

Anton Kerschbaumer (1895–1931), somewhat younger, came from the Alps. He developed a style of painting that was based on the broad rhythms of Expressionism, but he made them suit his own ends. In realizing his aim to clarify the structure of a painting, he stressed the continuity of lines and made harmonious use of colors, although he thereby lessened their tensile quality. Quiet

Anton Kerschbaumer. Street of the Red Rock, 1929

Anton Kerschbaumer. Self-portrait, 1919

Werner Scholz. King Saul, 1949

chords of dull green, matte red, blue, brown or yellow are united in his landscapes of city and harbor, with houses massed in cubic fashion. In his paintings the diagonal played an important part. He painted the corner of a room in a nondescript apartment, letting the angles of the walls diverge like fans; a feeling of ownership, pictorially expressed, is combined with a mood of dreamy lingering. "Now expression is the fashion, form is derided," he said in 1919. "Why can't we have both side by side?" In this connection he often stressed that he was "a southerner in Germany," a barb aimed probably at the northeastern Brücke group. He no longer painted from nature, but from memory. His pantheistic confession reads, "With a landscape one must sleep, with a river glide, with the clouds float, with bridges leap over the water."

Some painters chose only the superficial aspects of expressive painting; others however developed it further. *Werner Scholz* (b. 1898) paints close, threatening figures flowing over the picture surface. Frightened communicants, anxious nuns, strange animal creatures, gesticulate in colors that could denote life or death. Whenever his colors try to bloom, their effect is blunted by black barriers. All life is filled with affliction, even in his summer landscapes, whether painted in oils or pastels. The former seem heavy from overripeness and remind one of sleek mushrooms. The mystique of this painter is merged with a dark pathos: he does not seem quite sure whether he wants to reject life or surrender to it.

During the twenties in Berlin, Scholz developed a grayish Expressionism filled with sharply angular, flattened figures of beggars, cripples, orphaned children. In the thirties this style changed when he moved to the Tirolese mountain village of Alpbach and lived in an old wooden house among the peasants there. Now a little more color and feeling for space permeated his pictures, but he continued to throw in some black and white. He painted ponderous peasants, oversize flowers and butterflies, but above all biblical themes, some of them in large triptych form. "How should a genuine picture serve in any other way than as a symbol?" he asked.

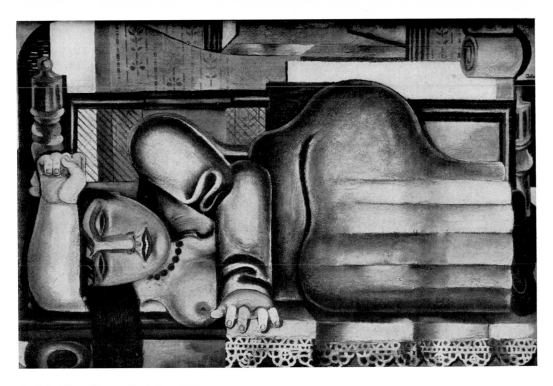

Jankel Adler. Woman Reclining, 1923

Jankel Adler. Old Man Reclining, 1925

An astonishing painter who has unfortunately been forgotten in Germany was *Jankel Adler* (1895–1949). A few of his paintings are in London's Tate Gallery or New York's Museum of Modern Art. He came from Poland and developed as a painter in the art circles of the Lower Rhine. His art lies somewhere between Léger and Chagall. The former influenced him to produce oversized figures, the latter, who was of the same faith, inspired him to paint Jewish types. At the international Hygiene Fair in Düsseldorf, the *Gesolei* of 1926, he established himself as a monumental painter in his decoration of the planetarium. His paintings from this period look as if they had been molded in viscidly flowing clay, yet his tonality remains varied. His figures seem imprisoned by their own weight. Everything is developed in a soft, hushed gray-brown. His later works were influenced by Picasso and are more radically abstract in the treatment of objects and excibit stronger color contrasts. But strong contrasts were not his forte, for his chromatic scale is less convincing than his tonal gradations. Today the pictures in which he employs the least pure color (an occasional late work included) are the most effective–those, therefore, where he concentrated on varying the tones.

Xaver Fuhr. Blue Bay, 1928

Adler's life was filled with oppressive unrest, which never succeeded, however, in deflecting him from his course. He was the seventh of ten children, son of a Jewish miller who lived near Lodz. Early in life he was trained to be an engraver. Then he moved to Barmen in west Germany, where five of his brothers and sisters made their living as artisans. During the First World War he was under police surveillance and his parents had to flee. Following this he lived precariously in Berlin, Düsseldorf and Spain. Klee had just created working quarters for him when he had to leave Germany. He vegetated in Paris, in Italy, the Balkans, Russia, finally again in France. He was drafted into a section of the Polish army that was moved in 1940 to Scotland, where he was discharged on account of illness. When at long last he had found somewhere to rest his head, he died in London of a heart attack.

Xaver Fuhr (b. 1898) was a unique figure, self-taught. He came from Mannheim and the impressions of his youth there affected his painting: reddish stones, bridges, tow barges on the river, and the harbor. Everything has an exotic air, although Fuhr never left Germany. When he paints mountain tops, graveyards, caravans, a laboratory or figure compositions, he seems to have a realistic point of departure, to be pinning down a fleeting observation of a banal event; but he proceeds simultaneously to spin it into a web of lines and color strands curiously inimical in their effect. His color scheme reminds us of a defoliated autumnal world in which flashes of color and pallid tones alternate, wherein fragments of nature crop up which he tries to overcome by transforming them into energetic lines. In all, a strong linear structure underlies his color. Painting and drawing are expressed in counterpoint, deliberately opposed to create tension. His forms are placed on a slant, as if everything were teetering on volcanic soil. It is often astonishing to see the way he is able to combine daubs of color and firm drawing with a certain realism. The small formal matrices are fragments between larger thrusts.

Fuhr is an enemy of abstract art. He is working on a polemical book of aphorisms in which he evidently intends to speak out against the present development. But his own work could not escape the trend of the time. The objects he paints look as if they had been melted; extension into depth by means of perspective is reduced, the scale of individual elements is larger and at the same time they are more abstractly rendered and stretched out over the surface of the canvas. What is actually represented loses its identity, hardly recognizable any longer (Plate XIX). The sharp, significant bits of reality, like thing-turned to stone, with which he interspersed his early pictures, have disappeared. Since 1946 he has been teaching at the Munich Art Academy.

In the work of *Rolf Nesch* (b. 1893), from Württemberg, a German Expressionist style was also shot through with a network of drawing, but Nesch went farther than Fuhr in abstraction. An innovator in the graphic arts, he drilled through etching plates and the holes thus formed left gleaming spaces on the print. He soldered wires onto the plate which pressed deep grooves into the paper; he also used wire netting of various sizes and tin cutouts that could be shifted around. Sometimes he prepared his plates with soldered tin, all of which, when he did the printing himself, resulted in remarkable graphic effects. Suddenly he saw in the plates themselves their intrinsic value as reliefs, whereupon he painted them

Rolf Nesch. Growth-forms, 1941

with oil or tempera. With the fantasy of a tinkerer he playfully produced attractive pictures with new materials and fresh structural techniques. The abstract tinkerer Schwitters would have enjoyed them. But Nesch, unlike Schwitters, continued to relate everything to particular objects, whose strange quality he sometimes used to create a mood of Oriental splendor and sometimes to develop toward caricature.

At one time he had been strongly inspired by Munch and Kirchner; in 1924 he worked with the latter, who split his color areas more vehemently than his friends in the Brücke. Nesch also produced gouaches, oil paintings and etchings; he was less interested in woodcuts and lithographs. Among his numerous print cycles are twenty-four etchings depicting Muck and his orchestra; *Sankt-Pauli*, on life in German sailor bars; and *Bridges*, which inaugurated a new method. These were executed before he left Germany in 1933 and emigrated to Norway. Other cycles followed: *Snow* (1933–1934), *Herring Catch* (1936), *The Lofoten Islands* (1936), *St. Sebastian* (1941), *Theatre in Alta* (1946–1948), *Night-bird* (1949), etc. Some of these were permeated with grotesque humor.

Werner Gilles (1894–1961), a Rhinelander, was a less flamboyant personality. In his Italian landscapes he had no intention of being merely imitative, but brought together diversely constructed color areas and enclosed them with a minimum of color outline. (Plate XX). Sometimes he came close to figurative symbols, especially when he was dealing with mythical Mediterranean themes. In these he fell somewhere between Klee's later period and Picasso, even if his abstract lyricism never attained the floating quality of the former or the vitality of the latter. Every now and then he produced something poetic in narrative cycles: *Rimbaud* (1933–1936), *Orpheus* (1947), *Tibetan Death Book*, etc. In such series he was at his best, since he sometimes tended to oversimplify his single sheets so that they resembled heraldic emblems. He somewhat underestimated his early works, which at times display a deeper sensitivity.

Rolf Nesch. Trumpeter, 1934/35

After a short period of study at the Bauhaus under Feininger, Gilles went to Paris and profited by exposure to the French formal heritage. Subsequently, his experience of the southern landscape in Italy was similarly enriching. Later he spent his winters in Munich, surrounded by a peaceful circle of friends who revered him as a prophet. His summers were spent in Ischia, completely lost in the beauties of this southern volcanic isle.

H. A. P. Grieshaber (b. 1909), somewhat younger, raised the color woodcut to the status of a mural. In the nineteenth century the graphic sheet had been used to communicate only the more intimate charm of things one wanted to see at close range. Expressionism had already passed beyond this, more by means of stronger graphic methods than through format. But Grieshaber raised both to such heights that his woodcuts may be hung as rhythmic articulation of the largest walls. While turning the colored woodcut into monumental painting, he in no way abandoned its graphic structure. Picasso's *Guernica*, which also gives the impression of a gigantic print, may have influenced him. Be that as it may, this mural composition deeply excited Grieshaber, and he traveled through Germany lecturing on it. He enlivened almost every graphic technique, making each serve his own proclivities, which swung between recollections of things seen and free formal rhythms. But unlike Picasso, he did not always succeed in preserving the object in its most extreme deformations. As a result one does well sometimes to read Grieshaber's oeuvre nonobjectively, even though it was always intended objectively. He is more successful in the primitive method used to construct his forms than in his handling of their color.

After leaving the Stuttgart Academy, Grieshaber lived in Africa and Asia Minor, dedicated always to prerealistic mythological forms. Between 1933 and 1940 he eked out a living as handyman and newspaper deliveryman, then as soldier and miner. Finally he found a place on the Achalm, where he led a

172

H. A. P. Grieshaber
Outlawed, Colored woodcut,
1953

173

frugal life in a lonesome village in the Swabian Alps. There he established a work community with students and friends, and the young people came to him in droves. In his *Bernsteinschule* ("Amber School"), near Sulz on the Neckar River, he demonstrated his ability to develop their feeling for form, and he was soon called to the Karlsruhe Art Academy.

The German Matisse School

Several German painters who went beyond the technique of Impressionism as early as the first decade of the twentieth century come under this comprehensive heading. Each in his own way came in contact with the new French feeling for form since all of them lived in Paris for some time, beginning around 1908. Here in the Café du Dôme they met other painters–from Vienna, Warsaw, St. Petersburg, Bucharest and the Scandinavian countries. Under the leadership of Matisse they raised color and form to autonomous pictorial values, thus, effecting a relatively smooth transition from pleinairism, unlike the contemporary Brücke painters. This absence of violent contrast with the recent past also explains their success with the general public which was achieved much earlier than was possible for their more primitive and radical colleagues in Dresden. But the latter produced a more profound caesura in the history of art. With our superstitious belief in the continuity of history, we would have to consider the Brücke–were we not familiar with the dates–a later radicalization of those tendencies which the Matisse disciples brought back to Germany.

Rudolf Levy (1875–1943) at first studied in Germany, then from 1903 to 1914 lived in Paris, where he studied with Matisse. Levy painted colorful landscapes, still lifes, human figures, and developed a pulsating color key. For the most part he carried on the tradition of opulent bodies and the pliant lyricism of his master; sometimes he reminds us of Derain. Since the plastic volume of his figures gradually became his chief concern, he tended to concentrate his colors on them, whereas Matisse let his colors sweep more freely across the canvas. Of the styles that followed, Levy admired Franz Marc, but shied away from the distortions of Klee and Kandinsky. Levy moved to Berlin, where the art dealer Flechtheim became interested in him because, in contrast to German Expressionism meanwhile grown so powerful, Levy's culture was more French. From Berlin he went to Düsseldorf, but made constant visits to Paris. In 1926 Matisse turned his school over to Levy. During the period of National Socialism Levy lived in Italy, painting harmonious Mediterranean landscapes, until he was captured, deported, and later put to death in a concentration camp.

Hans Purrmann (1880–1966) was also a Matisse pupil. Purmann's paintings are broken down into smaller parts than those of Matisse, with rust-red tones intervening between deep green and blue, as if all were glowing under a setting sun. (Plate XXI.) His landscapes and portraits are threaded with innerlinear drawing, as if old Germanic elements–from Dürer's time, for example–were trying to unite with the teachings of Matisse. After having served his apprenticeship as a housepainter, Purrmann studied at the Karlsruhe and Munich Art Academies and was subsequently inspired by Slevogt. But in 1906 he moved to Paris, and with Levy, Moll, Ahlers-Hestermann, Pascin, the writers Wilhelm Uhde

Rudolf Levy
Paesaggio di Procida,
1939

Hans Purrmann. Interior, 1937

Oskar Moll
Winter Window, 1935

and Theodor Heuss, became one of the Café du Dôme set. "In my personal contact with Matisse, I noticed how strictly he examined and judged the effect as a whole. He always seemed to ask himself how he should fill his canvases in order to create something expressive, clear and penetrating, without any superfluous ballast." In 1935 Purrmann became director of the Villa Romana in Florence. After World War II he lived in Montagnola, painting in pithy colors with a close feeling for nature. He was still very vital in his later years; at the age of seventy he took a positive view in the dispute over modern methods, pointing to the fact that the arts are constantly subject to change: "They are based neither on a yearning for destruction nor on sensationalism."

176

Right: Xaver Fuhr. Butterflies on a Blossom

Werner Gilles. Bird Cape, Ischia, 1952

The third painter in the Matisse group, who became a part of it in 1907, was the Silesian *Oscar Moll* (1875–1947). More delicate and lighter in tonality but more nervous in his composition, he was the only one in the circle who went beyond Matisse and squarely faced the problems of Cubism. "I fight against Nature, yet I try to construct something unified and new with her means." However, with his rather feminine sensitivity, he was unable to carry through the dialectics of Cubism. The inexhaustible theme "View from a Window" was his favorite; he repeated it over and over again. When the romanticists cultivated the same theme a hundred years ago, they caught an actual landscape view within the window frame. Moll, however, especially in his later, increasingly abstract paintings, imagined nothing much more in the picture square than a contrapuntal play of summerlike color areas. After his return to Germany he lived in Berlin and owned a choice collection of French paintings. In 1918 he was called to the Breslau Art Academy and eventually became its director. He rejuvenated the institution by bringing in the architects Scharoun and Rading, and the painters Kanoldt, Schlemmer, Molzahn and Muche. His academy was one of the three art schools

Rudolf Grossmann. The Poet, 1918

Friedrich Ahlers-Hestermann. The Painter at Twilight, 1936

Helmut Kolle. Large Still Life, circa 1920

in the border regions of Germany that at the time were offering good instruction and producing fine work: Dessau, Breslau and Düsseldorf. But everything he was striving for was eliminated by National Socialism as "degenerate." According to Moll, every effort should be encouraged "that moves away from the view offered by nature. One forms an equivalent for it by constructing a new visual experience with one's imagination."

Ahlers-Hestermann (b. 1883) was not actually a member of the Matisse group, but he was allied to the German circle in Paris. He devoted himself to a poetizing style in dreamily veiled colors, as if seeking a lyrical union with old romantic motifs. In *Pause vor dem dritten Akt (Pause before the Third Act)*, he told the story of his life in art historic terms, and in *Stilwende (Turning Point in Style)* conveyed the enduring importance of the Jugendstil.

One of the first artists to encounter the new art forms introduced by the Fauves and the Cubist painters

178

in France was *Rudolf Grossmann* (1882–1941), a casual, somewhat vacillating painter and graphic artist who was constantly improvising. But his landscapes give little evidence of any new methods, and in his drawings and etchings he is closest to Cézanne. With thinly drawn strokes, more often than not in a pointedly ironic tone, he takes aim at all the questionable aspects of cultured man and strangely enough manages somehow to convey the same type of message in his landscapes.

Helmut Kolle (1899–1931) was a member of this group. Self-taught, he moved to Paris in 1924 but died of a heart ailment there when he was only thirty-one. He painted in subdued gray values, contrasting them with black, brown and red areas, thereby bringing movement into his pictures which increased as time went on. Kolle's friend, Wilhelm Uhde, extolled his sovereign artistic attitude in a monograph on his work.

Albert Weisgerber (1878–1915) belonged to this Paris circle for a while, although he was not happy in it. After that, in Munich, he sought to develop a sweeping, more malleable variant of early Expressionism,

Albert Weisgerber
Saint Sebastian, 1910

but he died too soon. He seems to have been inspired by Cézanne and Greco. As a disciple of the new endeavor to overcome the realism of pedestrian painting, he made less use of the modern pictorial methods developed by Marc and Klee, or by Kandinsky (formerly his fellow student in Franz Stuck's classes), but seemed to feel more strongly drawn to the expression of emotional content. He won several important prizes for his posters and indulged in passionate but very representational effects, as, for example, in his many paintings of St. Sebastian, in *David and Goliath*, in a pathetic Absalom or in *Mother Earth*, a gigantic overscaled nude stretched out luxuriously in a typical German landscape. If he had not been killed in the First World War he probably would have adopted the style of New Objectivity since it laid stress on themes with content.

Special Traditions

Munich

Munich was a broad reservoir for the art of painting even after Jugendstil and the Scholle (see p. 32) had died out. But the art of the Blaue Reiter group, once its leading members had been killed in action or had scattered, left scarcely a trace worth mentioning on local artists. In the place of this stormy group more conservative painters now stepped forward, picking up a point in the development of style which the Blaue Reiter painters had bypassed. Variations of the possibilities implicit in the work of Cézanne and Van Gogh now appeared in more restained forms.

Richard Pietzsch (1872–1960), still bound to a more solid, older form of realism, depicted his native Isar valley in muted colors. *Otto Geigenberger* (1881–1946) painted his native city, Wasserburg, with its unusual encircling wall. He favored controlled colors and a loose, free style with which he captured felicitous motifs, and he became very popular with the general public. *Adolf Schinnerer* (1876–1949) produced, beside etchings, compositions with allegorically meaningful figures in which a varied and

Richard Pietzsch
River Landscape, circa 1930

180

Otto Geigenberger. Wasserburg, 1943

Adolf Schinnerer. The Boat, 1924

Hans Gött. Young Girl, 1931

Heinrich Brün
Landscape
with Goats, 192

Wilhelm Maly
Woodland Lake
with Horses,
circa 1930

almost blazing green dominates. *Hans Gött* (b. 1883), painting in a more subdued palette, still and somber in his expression, continued the romantic tradition in landscapes of his homeland. When he painted figures, he favored the female nude in the attitudes of Marées, but worked out in greater detail. Unlike the painters just mentioned, *Wilhelm Maly* (1884–1943) adopted the stronger colors which Macke introcuced in Germany, but he blended them more gently. He also created primitive wood carvings in a quasi-Brücke style. *Heinrich Brüne* (1869–1945) paints more lightly. His works are delicate in color and seem to be floating; they remind us of Renoir, whose portrait he painted when the French master went out of his way to visit him in the Bavarian highlands where Brüne was living.

In his landscapes, *Adolf Jutz* (1887–1945) favored tempera painting, when possible on blue-gray paper, to capture a peaceful, fallow, early-evening mood. *Hugo Troendle* (1882–1955) lived in Paris before the First World War. Very often his pictures are peopled with chubby figures, such as children waiting innocently in the landscape, all in pale colors that are often repeated and at times give one the feeling that he looked at life through milk glass. *Hans Lasser* (1891–1932) was a peculiar personality whose life was brief. In a strange, dusty-gray palette he created curiously plastic female bodies, using a formal canon that seemed like an attempt to endow Cubism with lyric Expressionism. *Joseph Eberz* (1880–1942) absorbed the color theories of Hölzel (see p. 243), but later sank into a sentimental, rather oppressive, one might almost say perfumed, mysticism. *Karl Caspar* (1879–1956), on the other hand, was an artist whose religious paintings could be taken seriously. At first the church rejected them, even though he had

Karl Caspar
ster Morning,
1930/1931

Maria Caspar-Filser
In the Park, 1926

given a south-German twist to Expressionism. He began with relatively dark colors, then adopted a more modern chromatic key, although his tonality remained rather chalky. His religious figures were conceived in blocks of color and worked in with the foreground. Only in his later years did he receive the important commission to decorate the apse of Bamberg Cathedral. He taught for many years at the Munich Academy and was a strong influence on the development of the south German school of painting. His wife, *Maria Caspar-Filser* (b. 1878), was influenced by him, but her work was lighter and remained closer to Impressionism. She moved her figures back towards the middleground, where they merged into colorful space or luxurious vegetation. She painted still lifes, richly articulated in color, and summery, flowing landscapes. *Julius Hess* (1878–1957) translated the forms of Cézanne into subdued, tapestrylike creations, while *Erich Glette* (b. 1896) turned nature into tonal values, with strandlike brushstrokes.

Willy Geiger (b. 1878) was a unique case– "a square peg in a round hole." His attraction to gruesome themes was totally uncharacteristic of Munich where he was working. He also frequently painted attacks on militarism and war, symbolizing their devastation in an intensely glowing palette. His form was expressionistic-Baroque, fantastically interwoven with surrealistic satire. Spain, where he lived for years, is a recurrent theme. Beside his individual graphic works, he created an abundance of book illustrations, including illustrations for Goethe, Kleist, Tolstoi and Dostojevski.

Max Unold (1885–1964) used the new expressive method of painting to bring out a restrained idyllic quality. He falls between various camps. He preferred to work on a small scale, portraying the ordinary

184

activities of harbor life and cities, now and then trying his hand at portraits. Everything is painted in strangely subdued, fuzzy, yet harmonious colors. As a writer he had a lot to tell, in an easygoing style, about the painter at work. If we may say that Unold's work is in a minor key, then that of *Richard Seewald* (b. 1889) is definitely in a major. His favorite subject was the clear Mediterranean landscape, which he tried to stylize in simple forms. In spite of the pagan-classical overtones in these works, he has been continuously drawn to religious themes, and he has painted church frescoes and illustrated many sacred legends. He has also written tracts, illustrated books, and during recent years has been teaching at the Munich Art Academy disputing current artistic trends.

Walter Teutsch (1883–1964) strove for stability of form and color with decorative effect. He created mythical happenings in imaginary landscapes, using strange color combinations. *Joseph Achmann* (1885–1958), on the other hand, devoted himself to uninhabited landscapes. His early work shows precise, detailed drawing, in a style somewhat akin to Schrimpf's handling of the same type of country-

Willy Geiger
Flower Vase by the Sea, 1953

Richard Seewald
Adieu, circa 1930

Max Unold. Evening on the Adriatic, 1947

Walter Teutsch
Herd on the Alm, circa 1925

side; later, however, Achmann stylized his landscapes with broad tracks of color. *Erwin von Kreibig* (1904–1961), in another variation on this theme, used landscape for storytelling purposes. Here, irony, colorful finesse and a popular-magazine style of illustration are combined. *Erwin Henning* (b. 1901) could be called the "Valentin" of painting, and he actually did portray the famous Munich comedian. In Henning's paintings, city youths and skinny girls fill the foreground, often spun in a web of luxuriant nature.

Josef Achmann
Early Spring, circa 1930

It is almost impossible to exhaust the abundance of greater and lesser talents active in Munich; every nuance could be found there, from the conservative but fresh style of *Anton Leidl* (b. 1900) to the sparse, abstract abbreviations of *Joseph Karl Nerud* (b. 1900). The paintings of *Oscar Coester* (1885–1955) were highly original. A gay pessimist, he liked to describe the singular forlornness of the human animal or some unlikely misfortune. In the beginning he favored dark, sibilant colors and a large format; later he painted small, light pictures with moss- or fresh-meadow-green landscapes stretching under a blue sky. He wanted to bring back Impressionism, but an Impressionism that was to contain the ambiguous life-feeling of the twentieth century.

Josef Scharl (1896–1954) achieves an impressive effect with monumental forms. He

188

Erwin Henning
Big City Juveniles, 1949

Josef Scharl. Sunrise, 1944

Josef Scharl. Albert Einstein, 1955

Oskar Coester
Peasant Garden,
1928

Carl Crodel
Café in Tunis,
1940

Adolf Hartmann. In the Mirror, 1948

Babs Englaender. Leopards, 1952

started, like the early Van Gogh, with dull heavy colors, but eventually developed a powerful style with surrealistic, grotesque forms. Everything remained representational, but exaggerated in size. In an extraordinarily simplified, strictly formal landscape with rising sun, threatening rays thunder through space.

In the twenties and thirties a strange Greek was working in Munich, *Jorgo Busianis* (1885–1959), whose primitive painting developed an eerie, barklike pigmentation. In later years, *Carl Crodel* (b. 1894), came to Munich from the east, bringing yet another style into the Bavarian field. He was a versatile, imaginative painter and graphic artist, always improvising, subdued in tonality, and versed in all techniques: woodcut, color lithography, glass painting, mosaic, wall hangings.

Adolf Hartmann (b. 1900), like his brother, the composer Karl Amadeus, took an energetic part in Munich's art life after the Second World War. He organized the avant-garde into "The New Group." He began by painting in the style of Corinth, in a grayed, muted tonality, after which his forms became more colorful and forceful. His later paintings are based on a more precise calligraphy and sometimes give the effect of monumental drawings that have been subsequently colored. His wife, *Babs Englaender* (b. 1922), at first painted lively animal sketches, then adopted the style of the New Objectivists. One might say that both tried to swim upstream against the current of European trends. *Max Hauschild* (1907–1960) also minimized color. He favored chiaroscuro in a beautiful gentle brown, stressing the

Hans Purrmann. Landscape, Southern Italy

Max Kaus. Volterra, 1945

Max Hauschild. Winter Sun on the High Moors, circa 1945

Hans Jürgen Kallmann
Elisabeth Flickenschildt,
1939

193

Emil Scheibe. Snow Shovelers, 1955

Christof Drexel. Mountain Massif, 1948

Hubert Distler. Trees in Winter, Glass print, 1956

loneliness of his landscapes. The paintings of *Jürgen Kallmann* (b. 1908), who has been living in Munich for years, are more pretentious. Some remote event or an unusual pictorial detail is effectively realized in broadly flowing colors. Lately, he too has been trying to paint abstractly, without, however, obliterating the object. He also gained prominence as portraitist, with his series of President Theodor Heuss. *Christof Drexel* (b. 1886) is at his best in his broadly rhythmic wash drawings. He developed a curious system of teaching called choric drawing. *Hubert Distler* (b. 1919) is best known for his bold, free, black and white printing on glass of fantastic landscapes. *Emil Scheibe* (b. 1914) went from sprawling to angular forms in the style of the French painter Bernard Buffet. *Arnold Balwé* (b. 1898) and his wife Elisabeth,

Arnold Balwé. Evening on the Harbor, 1953

Thomas Niederreuther. Mysterious Harbor, 1950

Remigius Netzer. Circus Wagon, 1952

influenced by the Expressionism of Karl Caspar, created glowing southern landscapes, while the country-side that *Thomas Niederreuther* (b. 1909) was painting attracted attention because of his plastic and energetic spatial organizations. *Remigius Netzer* (b. 1916) tried to find a balance between Expressionism and clarity, especially in his colored graphic work. He also became well known through his radio activities, an article on Kokoschka's lithography, and his translations of Mallarmé and the French poet, Francis Jammes.

Forms derived from reality are found in the work of *Ernst Weiers* (b. 1909) whose paintings and graphics are organized in swinging curves, far removed from any geometricizing *abstraction froide. Joseph Kien-lechner* and *Hugo von Habermann* carried on in Munich pictorial methods that had been developed under Cubism. *Carl Rabus* (b. 1898), a native of Munich who emigrated to Brussels, began by painting large abstract compositions with figures; then, in exile, he developed a nonobjective geometric style.

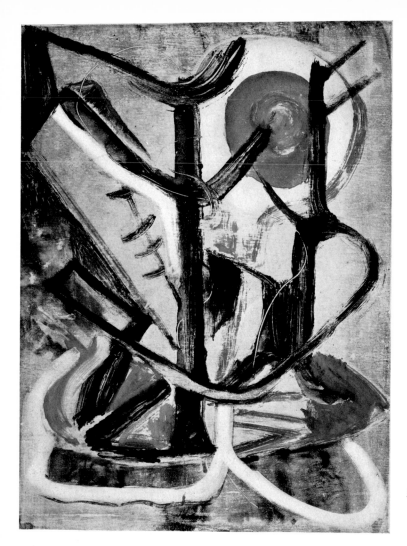

Ernst Weiers. *And the sun rises, 1952*

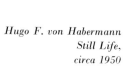

Hugo F. von Habermann
Still Life,
circa 1950

198

Josef Kienlechner. Before the Mirror, circa 1950

*Carl Rabus. Family
circa 1945*

Johanna Schütz-Wolff. Self-Portrait,
Colored woodcut, 1956

Ursula Rusche-Wolters. Orpheus, 1956

200

Paul Strecker. *Terrace, circa 1945*

Two women should be mentioned here, both working in Munich. *Johanna Schütz-Wolff* (1896–1965) was noted for her colorful graphic art but above all for her weaving, with its serenely flowing designs. "The monumental effect of my tapestries," she explained, "comes from the creation of a black area of wool fibers which absorbs all light, and thereby creates depth–in my abstract space the figures are confined to the surface…" *Ursula Rusche-Wolters* (b. 1914) started from the premises of graphic art, but uses a strongly colored surface as a foil for the interaction of her intense, linearly defined figures.

Other Sections of Germany

If one looks around South Germany beyond the radius of Munich as far, let us say, as the Main River, one finds no closely defined tendencies, only pleasant individualism, a variety of personalities. Let us select a few painters who present a number of contrasting points of view, and list them just as they appeared. First, only those who remained faithful to representational art:

Otto Dill (1884–1956) has continued the tradition of Impressionism but in truly cultivated colors, proof that a late flowering need not always be of inferior quality.

Paul Strecker (1898–1950) also had a very light hand, creating an overall effect of a mere impression. He belonged to a younger generation, yet approached the shorthand style of Dufy though without ever achieving the elder painter's rich color scale.

Walter Becker (b. 1893), who has been teaching at the Karlsruhe Art Academy since 1951, lived in

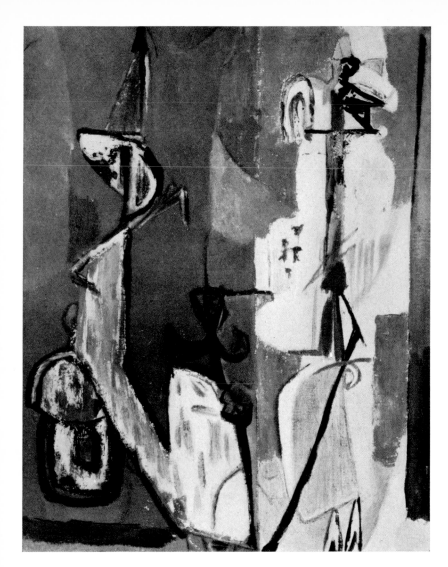

Walter Becker
Street Scene, circa 1950

Werner von Houwald. Thaw, 1948

202

*Will Sohl
Dwarf Pine in
Sand and Mud*

France for twelve years. In his early paintings and lithographs one first senses a smooth French tradition. Later he achieved bolder distortions and a less restricted color application, connected only loosely with the object.

The landscape painting of *Werner von Houwald* (b. 1901) now working in Stuttgart, is less problematic. Houwald loosens the tradition of Karl Caspar by alternating sketchlike color areas with denser ones, as if he sought to fuse Impressionism with Expressionism. He applied the same method to his flower pictures.

The work of *Will Sohl* (b. 1906) is curious, especially in his landscapes. Although his compositions are very smooth, something uncertain haunts his countryside. In Sohl's presentation of sea and dune world, Ernst Wichert saw "wild, immeasurable loneliness between sky and sea." A disturbing versatility and a unifying lyricism are at war with each other, but his flowing line is more effective than his gushing color.

In Freiburg, *Rudolf Rister* (b. 1904) is absorbed with the human figure. Introverted, tragic figures are grouped side by side, alien and silent. "Then space becomes a monstrous thing." In Nuremberg a different bleakness pervades the paintings of *Willi Cramer* (b. 1900). His work is no longer hesitant, but seems to be driven by divisive powers. He continues Expressionism in his still lifes, painted with a harshly flowing, weighty brushstroke, and in generalized landscapes which have a sinister glow.

203

Ernst Saemisch
Long Ago, 1957

Ida Kerkovius. Village in Brittany, 1953

Hannelore Busse. Fruit Harvest, 1953

Walter Wörn. Roof Garden, 1951

Karl Rödel. Zebu, 1953

Ferdinand Lammeyer. Fallen Tree

Only three Stuttgart artists must be mentioned here, since Oscar Schlemmer was discussed in the Bauhaus chapter, and Baumeister, his pupil, belongs to a later chapter. *Walter Wörn* (1911–1963) developed further Schlemmer's problem of figures aligned in parallel on the picture plane, and united them with a warm color scheme. *Ida Kerkovius* (b. 1879) studied at Adolf Hölzel's school, having followed him from Dachau to Stuttgart, but she was also active at the Weimar Bauhaus. She organizes her paintings and tapestries in wide sweeps of color, combining objective and nonobjective elements. *Hannelore Busse* (b. 1926) belongs to the young generation. Her paintings, also in Schlemmer's tradition, are peopled with voluptuous female bodies which she compresses, resulting in a crowded ebb and flow of curving forms in a baffling chiaroscuro. In her recent work she creates rays which gently penetrate space.

With *Ferdinand Lammeyer* (b. 1899) we come to the region of the Main. He creates very painterly landscapes, achieving a heavy balance with his tempera colors. A petrified form of nature is constructed, its emptiness relieved, if at all, by an occasional figure, symbolically interwoven. Somber colors dominate– heavy ocher, rich red, a darkening blue. Lately he has turned to painting pure signs in color. He

Kurt Weinhold
Night on the Mount of Olives, 1951

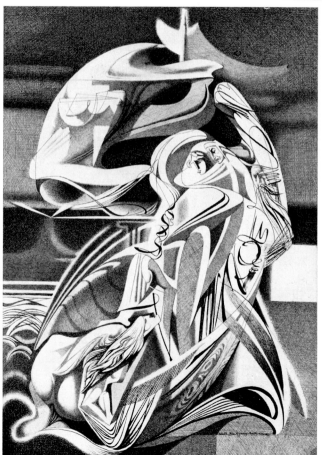

Karl Kunz
Dante's Inferno, Canto VIII, 1955

207

Rudi Baerwind. Mysterium from the Pictorial Cycle of Life, 1953

teaches at the Frankfurt Städel School, where he was once a student, and is author of *Maltechnik für Kunstfreunde (A Technique of Painting for Friends of Art)*.

Kurt Weinhold (1896–1965), from Calw, stood between Expressionism, New Objectivity and Surrealism, and we must add his Swabian humor to this mixture of influences. He had great difficulty in reconciling these contradictory styles. The parablelike content of his paintings and his graphically united forms are more effective than his colors.

Karl Kunz (b. 1905), originally from Augsburg, now active in the Main-Rhine region, is in a class by himself. He has painted huge, gloomy pictures on wood, in which structural form and tense colors are combined with fantastic surrealistic fragments. Gradually graphic forms have come to dominate his very full and increasingly precise compositions. In his Dante cycle he concentrates almost entirely on pure graphic effects with a mysterious internal linear articulation.

Rudi Baerwind (b. 1910) lived for a long time in France, and then in Mannheim. He has painted large-figure groups and demonstrated his capacity as a muralist with a number of wall paintings for his adopted city. "If possible, let us have once again large themes of universal significance," he demanded a few years ago, but he has since turned to nonobjective painting. His aim is warm, full-toned color,

208

undiluted by graphic elements. Lately he has been working on the problem of a chromatic, abstract wall relief. *Bernd Krimmel* (b. 1926), from Darmstadt, studied architecture, then turned, self-taught, to painting. Probably inspired by Picasso, he circles around the human body, entangling it in curious formal tensions.

Curth Georg Becker (b. 1904), not to be confused with Walter Becker, was a student of Nauen. A fluid movement of color and form flows through his pictures. Everything seems to have been improvised. Whether he is dealing with people, still lifes or landscapes in bucolic colors, there is always something to surprise or to delude us with a seeming gaiety that could turn into aggressiveness at any time. Becker eludes every "program." *Hermann Henry Gowa* (b. 1902) strives for a soothing pictorial organization, whether he is painting the human figure or a landscape or working in graphic media. Since 1954 he has been director of the *Werkkunstschule* (Art Workshop) in Offenbach.

Rolf Müller-Landau (1903–1956) used to live in the South Palatinate amid farmlands and vineyards, in approximately the same area where earlier Slevogt and Purrmann developed their palettes. At first he tried to adapt the achievements of the French Fauves and was influenced especially by Braque, but then he developed more abstract structures which he spread out on colorful ground areas. They were more convincing in composition than in color.

Arthur Fauser. Autumn Bouquet with Deer Skull

In Bopfingen (Württemberg), *Fritz Landwehr* (1897–1966) worked with wall hangings in suitable materials and created small paintings in a dense palette. His work is illustrated on page 291 in the chapter on Abstract Painting, to which he turned about 1956.

Arthur Fauser (b. 1911), living in Frankfurt, is an autodidact and has attracted attention with the strident construction of his post-Cubist still lifes and landscapes. These paintings, probably inspired by Picasso, are carried out in heavy, luscious colors and diagonally accentuated forms.

Among his generation, *Eberhard Schlotter* (b. 1921) is a representational painter of interest, for he seems somehow to succeed, paradoxically, in bringing back the ex-

Eberhard Schlotter. At the Silent Seashore, circa 1955

ternal world with the methods of nonobjective art. He paints southern landscapes in which the walls of the houses overlap like wings on a stage set, with abrupt views of monotonous shores or the lonely sea. Structural elements alternate in the composition with painterly surface areas. He never models anything, yet succeeds in producing depth, a perspective effect which remains strictly on the surface. Ambiguous wires or rods unite the lifeless architectural parts. Time seems to stand still; village squares and beaches are deserted, yet the whole has an almost ghostlike life since all the colors are so right.

Finally, an artist should be mentioned here who stands alone. For many years *Paul Kleinschmidt* (1883–1949) lived in Ulm, later in the wooded heights above the Bergstraße in the Odenwald. His paintings fall between Corinth and Beckmann. In them we find strange men wearing tight-fitting costumes with puffy, ruffled borders, monstrous creatures who both intoxicated and grieved their interpreter. Kleinschmidt was the son of a vaudeville-theater owner, and in many paintings he unfolded impressions of his youth. In these he used a heavy impasto technique with brushstrokes creating separate layers of paint, contrasting especially horizontal and diagonal surface movement. Had his colors not developed such a monotonous yellow-gray tonality, he might have become a master of the monstrous. But on this account we can not agree with Meier-Graefe's evaluation of him as the equal of Van Gogh, or with other favorable comparisons of his work with that of Corinth.

Paul Kleinschmidt
Circus Woman

Ernst Fritsch. Bathers, 1925

Berlin

Contrary to Munich, where with few exceptions the conservatives were in the majority, more progressive forces concentrated in the schools of West Berlin after the unfortunate division of that city. This made it possible after the Second World War to re-create an art center there that could play an important contemporary role in modern German painting. Since it is our intention to treat in this chapter only those artists who are still struggling with external reality, we must mention at this point that the painters of Berlin rarely lose themselves in the impressions of nature, certainly not with any passive feeling of delight. Most of them tackle reality as a competitor who should not be evaded, who must be overcome. In Berlin we find cutting straight across the various generations a tendency toward a translation of reality in graphic terms, with intellectual precision and ambiguous fantasy alternately expressed in

Dietmar Lemcke
Winter, circa 1952

equal proportions. The so-called *art informel* plays a less important role in Berlin than in other parts of Germany.

Ernst Fritsch (b. 1892), a typical Berliner, developed under Expressionism a dry but powerfully simple style, noteworthy for the plastic clarity of composition. Later he indulged in experimentation and invented fantastic themes. Impressed early in his development by Henri Rousseau, whose style he strongly modified, he seems to have been influenced later by Chagall. But since the Berliner lacked the dreamlike fantasy and light touch of the "Parisian" Chagall, his later works give a realistic impression. We shall have to see whether he succeeds with a new synthesis on which he is working, wherein a more serious feeling for life is crossed with a strain of Surrealism.

Dietmar Lemcke (b. 1930) is related in feeling and just as emphatic, although he is nearly forty years younger than Fritsch. His angular, plastic, cubically constructed landscapes or city scenes are worked

Hermann Teuber. Bird Island, circa 1955
Munich, Bayerische Staatsgemäldesammlungen

213

Werner Heldt. Stormy Afternoon on the Spree River, 1951 · Berlin, Collection Brandes

out in a naive, drastic stylization, with simple, dense, and thereby powerful volumes. Pictorial architectonics are here willfully crossed with distortion, color and spatial force.

Hermann Teuber (b. 1894), a Dresdener, is a more reserved painter. He comes from the Hofer School and since 1950 has been teaching at the Berlin Art Academy. He paints the still, peaceful ambience of a room or the serene view from a placid, sheltered spot; a lonely figure or a beckoning structure awaits us. Or he places in his pictures objects of equal size–birds, or tiny riders–letting them rest motionlessly as if on a chessboard, seeming to imply pictorially that all living things are alike, lonely yet dependent on each other.

Three Berlin landscape painters have mastered the architectural picture so that one may compare them: Werner Heldt, Rudolf Kügler and Otto Eglau.

Werner Heldt (1904–1954) made contact with all aspects of the life of his city–one might well call him the Utrillo of Berlin. But he was less concerned than Utrillo with the painterly quality of his mute, white-walled houses. Heldt belongs to another time, and he presents the monotony of a metropolis. Foreground planes dominate–bare, curving zones; rows of deserted streets, seen as if from a window, lead into depth, and where the lines of perspective end, houses bar the way, as on a stage. Trees and people scarcely enter the picture. The cityscape here becomes a dehumanized abstraction, utterly contrary to the Old Berlin tradition which began with Hummel, Krüger and Menzel, and continued

214

with Liebermann and Corinth. Surrealistic undertones are insinuated when Heldt paints *Berlin on the Sea*. Sometimes he makes things easy for himself by constant repetition of his architectural formulas. Details of still life turn up in the foreground of some of his pictures–a lonely fruit or a mandolin lies abandoned on a window sill, and the cool houses behind, painted with much white, have an allegorical effect as if they were merely spatial symbols. Shortly before his fiftieth birthday this strange man died on the island of Ischia, a more beautiful world.

Rudolf Kügler (b. 1921) has been active mainly as a graphic artist. His color prints–exotic cityscapes or harbor scenes–consist of a network of intersecting and cross-secting lines, between which are compressed towering architectural forms, people or plants that look as if they had only subsequently been touched by color. Paul Klee may have influenced him fleetingly; Kügler's generation finds an abundance of pictorial means which it adapts skillfully. His forms are reserved, and he surrounds them with clean contours. In his prints nearly every proof is a different color. Kügler gives a new, albeit unrealistic, charm to the old form of *vedute*. His color prints, easily appreciated, are much in demand.

In a colorful calligraphy, *Otto Eglau* (b. 1917) seeks to prove that space truly expands, sometimes sideways across the surface, sometimes in depth. After having mastered the illustration of nature, he tried to control it through a bare scaffolding of diminishing lines; this device increased the impact of his compositions, although it sometimes led to monotony.

Rudolf Kügler. Spanish City, 1948

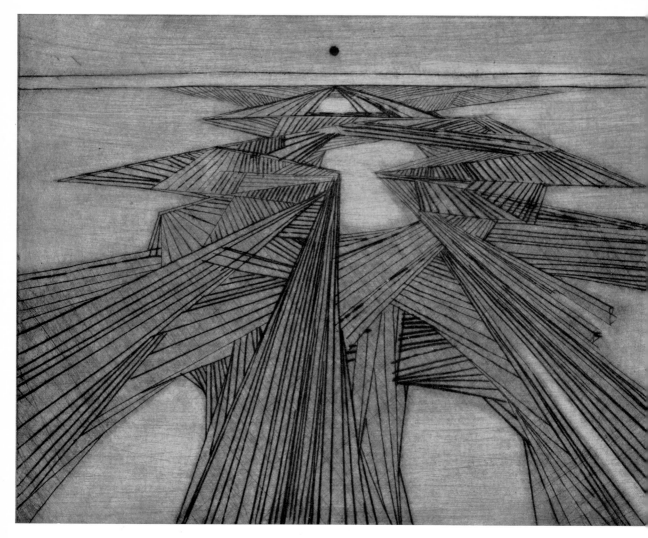

Otto Eglau. Floating Landscape, 1956

The landscapes of *Ernst Schumacher* (1905–1963), who also lived in Berlin, were quite different. From 1948 until his death he taught at the Berlin Hochschule (the Academy). Opulent, colorful nature is alive in his pictures, but the summery vegetation is painted in a few blocklike forms and colors. In the beginning he absorbed Parisian stimuli and was associated with the Fauves, though gradually his sense for pictorial order led him to greatly simplified contrasts of horizontal and vertical planes, with relatively few extended diagonals. Beside him an Expressionist like Schmidt-Rottluff is an extremist. With yellow, blue and rose facades and intensely green vegetation, Schumacher sometimes succeeded in achieving a mood all his own in very simplified compositions.

216

Ernst Schumacher
Rhine Landscape,
1950

Carl-Heinz Kliemann. The Wall, 1955

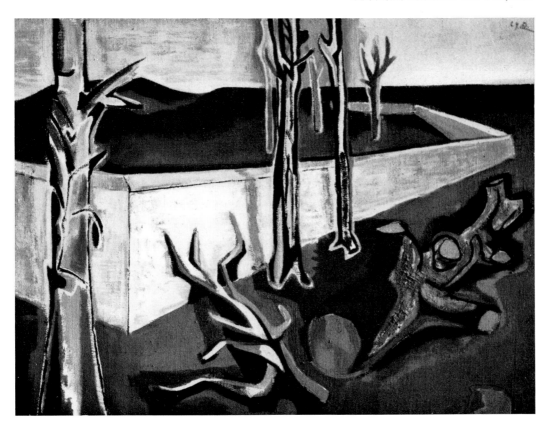

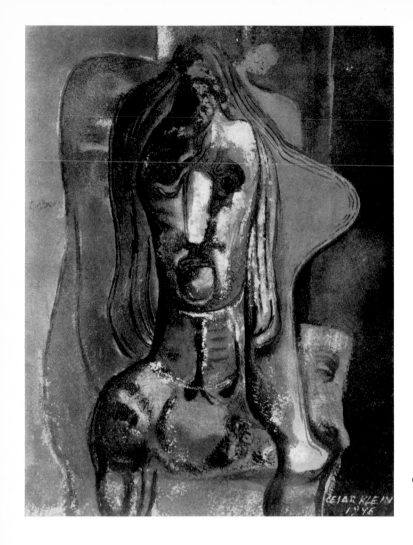

Cesar Klein. Mandrake Queen, 1946

We now come to the painters who "deformed" more freely and who aimed to put reality at a distance. First, *Cesar Klein* (1876–1954), who worked through all the trends of his time, passing through Expressionism, a severely objective phase, and the dream world of Surrealism. In his first works we are reminded of abstract surrealism, but his figurines in this style rarely succeed in arousing any profound emotion. Klein was in command of all the tricks of his trade, able to mix his own paints and to teach every technique. He lectured at the Berlin Art Academy from 1919 until his dismissal by the National Socialists, when he retired to the lonely forests near Lübeck. He was active also as a scene designer, with the result that the decorative element in his talent was too prominent. He favored especially frescolike color harmonies that were too strongly rooted in brown-yellow. In spite of his failings he succeeded in making a considerable impression. The poet Theodor Däubler wrote a lively monograph on him.

The Berliner *Max Kaus* (b. 1891) has been teaching since 1945 at the Academy in that city. He was a pupil of Erich Heckel, but abandoned the virile wood-block style of the Brücke painters, letting it dissolve into a colorful lyricism. Smooth curves converge in his paintings, forming no sharp contours, only amiable guidelines for the colors bedded in them. In the thirties he was still working with a certain degree of perspective, but he soon began to arrange his color forms over the surface in the fashion of enamel work. He has also been using this style since the forties in his portraits, landscapes and still lifes. (Plate XXII.) Slowly but steadily he arrived at a basic handling of his materials, achieving sweeping bands of color which trail in a subdued, tapestry-like fashion through his pictures. He does not work in contrasts of complementaries, but tends toward a homophonic color key, so that his paintings are carried out either all in gold-brown tones or in twilit blues. A contrasting color may turn up along the edges. His subject matter is frequently the weary, lyrical mournfulness of a convalescent, of a woman, or a landscape.

Max Kaus. Duet, 1955

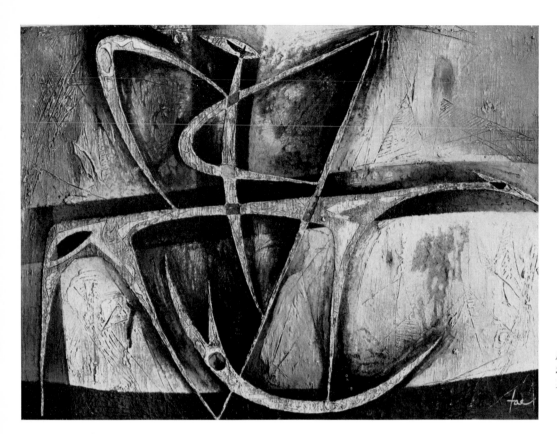

Hans Jaenisch (b. 1907) as a very young man went through the visual revolution achieved by the *Sturm* group. From the beginning his pictorial forms existed without any realistic space. Everything is spun onto the bare surface and held together by large simplified curves drawn through the whole picture. The result is rather like runic script scratched on a weathered wall. These strange graven, relieflike figures suggest dream-images of people or animals. Age-old colors are produced by a curious mixture of techniques. Flattened fossils and skeletonized bodies are covered with crackles or scabrously weathered material, as if to indicate that these creatures must remain at the bottom of this surface forever, and that their value is solely symbolic. A few of his landscapes look as if slices of huge tree trunks had been

Alexander Camaro. Autumn Angel, circa 1954

placed in rows across the surface, with their bark, edges, veins, knots and splits forming a consistent totality. Here the color is stifled, as if the picture were only a print. Lately, though, his tonality has become more glowing as his style becomes increasingly abstract. (Plate XXIII.)

In the work of *Alexander Camaro* (b. 1901) we find a similar attitude, yet his intention is something quite different. A village built on piles evaporates into a dream grating; a girl at a window into a pale ghost; the slope around a coal pit into a twilit tapestry. With him one never knows whether a recollection of reality has been extended into a dream, or whether a dream symbol has gently absorbed a piece of the real. Camaro is a disembodying poet; sometimes, though, he is little more than an insipid symbolist. Parables of modern technical civilization appear—the spectral flight of a bird may turn portentously into a kind of airplane.

More richly creative and versatile, *Curt Lahs* (1893–1958) wove a chain of signs across the surface,

Curt Lahs
Upper and Lower Field, 1951

Hans Orlowski. Meadow Flowers, circa 1950

Alfred Winter-Rust
Black Sun, 1950

Hans Thiemann
Nocturnal Shores,
1951

Harry Kögler. Machine Parts, 1954

Otto Herbig. Reclining Girl, 1928

switching willfully from painterly to linear areas. He too wandered off more and more into the world of abstraction. Self-taught, he lived in foreign countries for many years, was then an instructor at the Berlin Academy, was removed by the National Socialists but called back in 1948. His contemporary, *Hans Orlowski* (b. 1894), also teaches there. The quality of his painting is weakened by a lack of exciting color, and it is less impressive than his graphic work, especially his woodcuts. In these, curious figures and elements from nature, overlaid with parallel hatchings, rise in the foreground. *Hans Thiemann* (b. 1910) has developed a clear style that captures objects in a clean, still-life fashion; they are permeated with veins or parallel hatchings which gives a certain dogmatic uniformity of effect. From his early surrealistic pictures, when he was still working with perspective, he has progressed to an increasingly planimetric surface style.

A few Berlin artists who were born in the nineteen-twenties should be mentioned here. *Alfred Winter-Rust* (b. 1923) has painted expressive, pictorially rich landscapes which are at the same time puzzlingly simplified in form. He is moving more and more toward nonobjective art, although various mysterious

224

recollections of nature still echo in his work. *Harry Kögler* (b. 1921) constructs massive machine and architectural fragments in his pictures, as if to develop further the monumental style of Léger. The paintings of *Otto Herbig* (b. 1890) remain more conservative and are closely allied to the tactile, corporeal world. His themes are the child, the young mother, or rhythmically broken landscapes, depicted usually in pastel. For more than two decades he lived in Berlin, and he taught at the Weimar Art School. *Hermann Bachmann* (b. 1922) came from East Germany and began to paint in a style somewhere between Hofer and Beckmann. His eerily monotone seascape was a prize winner in the Davis Competition (at Munich's German art exhibition) of 1950. Always experiment-

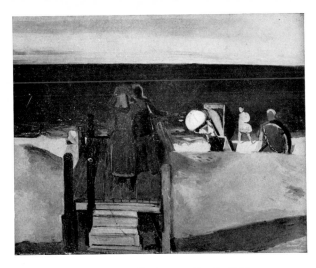

Hermann Bachmann. Beach, 1947

ing, he has probed almost every possibility so that it is virtually impossible to characterize his style. *Manfred Bluth* (b. 1926) paints like a C. D. Friedrich of the twentieth century. In his landscapes the dessicated countryside stretches out in clearly ordered planes from which all human life is banished. Everything is based on a horizontal structure, even where an occasional vertical projection seeks release. Here precise measurements and a geometric plan rule supreme. (Plate XXIII.) After he had almost achieved a totally nonobjective pictorial form, he "discovered" Claude Lorrain. "Lately I find myself seeking a greater simplicity in my painting, for to my mind the secret lies more in a realization of concrete images... than in an original or exaggerated treatment of the materials of painting."

Manfred Bluth. The Wall, 1954

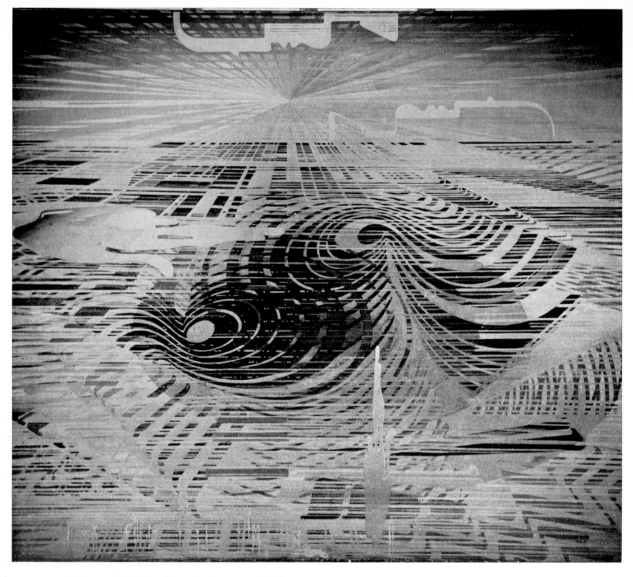

Johannes Molzahn. Memoria in aeterna, 1946

Johannes Molzahn (1892–1965) sought a precise, similarly geometric joining of objectivity and abstraction. (Plate XXIV.) We mention him here especially because he emigrated to the United States in 1938 and was totally forgotten in Germany. The architect Bruno Taut called him to the Magdeburg School of Applied Arts, after which he was given a chair at the Breslau Academy. Using the vocabulary of plane geometry, he created endless spatial compositions which give the effect of a grill-like network of repeated and flattened architectural units. One might describe it as a transcendentalized architectural metropolis; there is no above or below. Occasionally, classical and Christian symbols are interwoven. Molzahn's unpublished tract, "Ist die moderne Kunst ein Ausdruck unserer chaotischen Zeit ?" ("Is modern art an expression of our chaotic times ?"), is aimed at today's culture-pessimism.

226

As in south Germany, we find individual styles of painting that adhere to older traditions dispersed across all north Germany. Although the art we are about to discuss is not strong enough to form the basis for a school of painting, a few exponents have done work of high quality and refinement.

As an example of solid tradition we have *Tom Hops* (b. 1906), who paints harbors and the shallows around the North Sea island of Sylt. The objects depicted provide the strength of his composition, not just the emotional atmosphere. *Hans Hubertus von Merveldt* (b. 1901) creates harbor scenes with heavy forms in original color harmonies; boats and broad sails are prominent in the foreground.

The more fundamental painting of *Friedrich Karl Gotsch* (b. 1900) was influenced especially by Kokoschka, although Gotsch lives in the north. Dull, minor-keyed tones alternate with broadly glowing areas. The paint is thick, almost doughy. Figures, animals and landscapes are treated with the utmost freedom. He remains faithful to representational art, but declares. "God alone knows to what point you can drive

Hans Hubertus von Merveldt. Marignes, circa 1945

the object." His watercolors, pastels, drawings and prints also bear witness to his somber view of life. Almost his entire oeuvre was destroyed during the war.

A north German friend of Gotsch's student days, *Hans Meyboden* (1901–1965), was also first influenced by Kokoschka. With both Gotsch and Meyboden, the color does not flow, like Kokoschka's, but stands in the painting as if congealed, broad and stubborn. Meyboden's pictures give an effect of thickly woven carpets. Again like Gotsch, he speaks a rather clumsy language, as if he had long been isolated from human society. The transience of all earthly things, allusions to sickness and death, are themes in Meyboden's work, but he never dealt with religious subject matter. *At the Window* (Plate XXV) is a symphony in surface patterns, all in mossy green. In his etchings he tried to balance linearity and expressive sweeps in a more painterly style. *Curt Sohns* (b. 1907), who lives in Hannover, paints interiors in warm colors, inhabited by schematic human beings. His quiet compositions are extremely simplified and forms are distorted, but they never offend; instead they tend to have an appealing, almost helpless effect, amid pleasantly spread, astonishingly beautiful color areas. (Plate XXV.)

Max Pfeiffer-Watenphul (b. 1896), born in Brunswick, became known for his pictures of Venice, painted in a flaky style adopted from a late-Impressionistic technique. His is a strange Venice, wrapped in fallow light and a wooly atmosphere. Nobody would dream that this artist was a product of the Weimar Bauhaus; he seems to follow more in the footsteps of Bonnard. *Arnold Bode* (b. 1900), who teaches in

Friedrich Karl
Gotsch
Studio Interior,
1957

Arnold Bode
Landscape, 1958

Cassel, has no intention of breaking down the representational world but seems rather to want to condense it harmoniously in a few suggestive colors, endowing it with a degree of plasticity. He drew attention to himself through his extraordinary presentation of the international art exhibition in Cassel, *Documenta*, in 1955.

Finally, two women painters from north Germany must be mentioned. *Irmgard Wessel-Zumloh* (b. 1907), who lives in Iserlohn and is the wife of the painter Wilhelm Wessel (see p. 285), depicts groups of figures painted very freely in flat, interwoven color compartments and giving the effect of still life. *Sigrid Kopfermann* (b. 1923), from Hannover, constructs abstract landscapes with heavy spots of color in a more ponderous rhythm.

Hamburg, a city which is often considered indifferent to cultural activity, has produced several quite important objective painters. *Fritz Kronenberg* (1901–1960), a much traveled painter originally from Cologne, carried on in Hamburg the tradition of Cubism and painted still lifes or figures that derive from

Irmgard
Wessel-Zumloh
Spanish, 1958

the later work of Braque and Picasso. He never took a painting lesson in his life and developed a highly original tonality; sometimes he achieved a weblike effect, with the underpaint showing through; sometimes he used light tones, with much delicate gray; at others he used saturated colors in which the entire scale of red hues is dominant. A true painter, as Nolde called him.

In the landscapes and figure compositions of *Karl Kluth* (b. 1898) form and color as ends in themselves struggle with a more realistic viewpoint, lending unrealistic tension to the pictorial plane which becomes independent, crowded, and staccato in its color effect. His style of painting, inspired originally by Munch, wrestles wildly with the monumental. *Willem Grimm* (b. 1904) from Darmstadt, now living in Hamburg, sees man in a mask; a clamorous tumult of masqueraders erupts from his paints. His tonality is exciting, even when he is only painting still lifes. Kluth and Grimm are temperamental painters, carrying on the possibilities of Expressionism. *Herbert Spangenberg* (b. 1907) seeks a bridge between representational forms and geometric abstractions, working therefore in a borderline area that is very difficult to master.

Eduard Bargheer (b. 1901) of Hamburg moves back and forth between the fogbound lowlands of the German north and the radiance of Italy, which is perhaps the reason his inner conflicts are not always resolved. Large figures and suggestions of landscapes are linked with more geometrical forms and composition. On the other hand, he also seeks to capture, perhaps under the influence of Klee, a dreamlike

230

Fritz Kronenberg. Ana, 1950

Karl Kluth. *Singing Peasant II, circa 1950*

Willem Grimm
Carnival in Basel,
1949

Eduard Bargheer
Figuration,
1955

quality in a muted, almost evanescent tonality. He calls his pictures *Gewebe* (woven things). "It is a simple word, but I know no better. God knows, it does not mean a decorative problem, but actually a metaphysical one, because *Gewebe*—oneness—is everywhere."

In the Rhineland, when we look at the painting that has remained close to nature and avoided clearly defined movements, we find a lively concentration of old and new forces. Conservative artists, some of whom adhere to traditional Rhenish painting, still carry a good deal of weight. On the other hand, in just this region and in the nearby Ruhr area, we find a growing concentration of young talent pressing forward to new areas of expression. Some day when the freshness of their artistic conception has been accepted, people will speak of a typically Rhenish palette.

Among the conservative landscape painters, *Julius Bretz* (1870–1953) should be recalled. Some of his uniquely drawn segments of nature are still of interest today. The painter of idyllic landscapes, *Max Clarenbach* (1880–1952), and *Theo Champion* (b. 1887) should also be mentioned. *A. Buschmann* (b. 1895) introduces intimate surroundings in fragmented color, and brings shadows of objects to life. *Carl Barth* (b. 1896) tries to unite old painterly traditions with greater emphasis on structure, sometimes with

233

poetic inventiveness, as in *Birds at the Window*. *Robert Pudlich* (b. 1905) and *Josef Piper* (b. 1907) are popular for the pleasing sweep of their colors. *Carl Schneiders* (b. 1905), *Felicitas Auer* (b. 1902), *Willi Deutzmann* (b. 1897), and above all *Oswald Petersen* (b. 1903), press forward more in the direction of an expressive organization, each in a different way, of course. *Peter Janssen* (b. 1906), who was appointed to the Berlin Academy, favors multiple small details, mild in color, such as the facades of houses with innumerable windows, or a throng of human figures in a landscape, seen as silhouettes against a coarsely painted ground. In these paintings one senses that Janssen passed through abstractionism. In his monumental still lifes, *Friedrich Vordemberge* (b. 1897) stresses strange colors which are worked out in flat, immobile areas, existing eternally as expectant parallels of their objects.

Finally, we come to two more Rhinelanders who, in their serious concern with human beings as subject matter, hardly fit into our usual conception of Rhenish *joie de vivre*. *Peter Herkenrath* (b. 1900) paints emotionally oppressive interiors or uneasy portraits in which the person seems to be turned into stone

Carl Barth. Birds at the Window

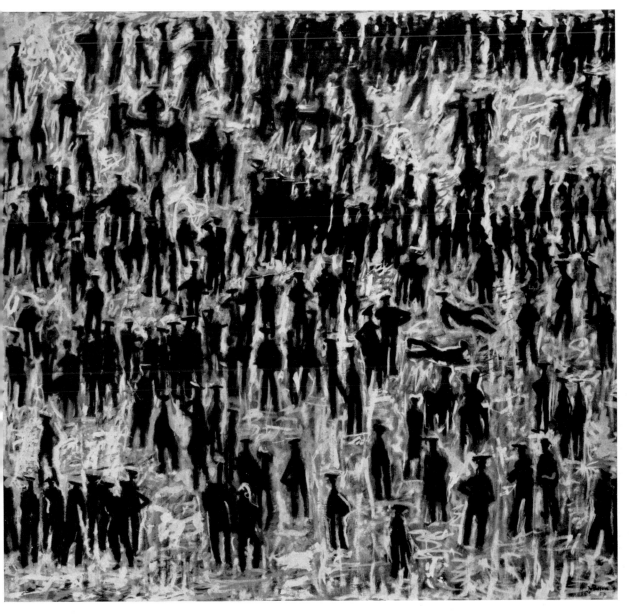

Peter Janssen. Figures after a Catastrophe, 1957

and pressed into the surface of the painting. The expression is uncanny, reminding us of monumental caricatures. *Bruno Goller* (b. 1901) does his best work in murals. He arranges his humans in checkerboard zones, using the meager hues of fresco but clearly delineating his figures. On occasion he chooses only a part of the human body, magnifying it to mythical proportions, as in *The Big Ear*.

Peter Herkenrath
Space I, 1958

Friedrich Vordemberge. Still Life with Blue Chair, 1951

Bruno Goller
The Big Ear, 1956

Draftsmen

Under this heading we must name several masters who were exceptionally active as graphic artists. *Otto Pankok* (1887–1966) may be viewed as a tardy descendant of Van Gogh. He transformed the latter's use of line and his conceptions of nature into a romantic, sometimes overexpressive variation. The clear, very deliberate compositions and the graphic methods of Van Gogh are changed to whimsical curlicues, suggesting an unusually lively work by a Sunday painter. Pankok was also an amateur writer and sculptor. Sometimes the rolling waves of his strokes are exaggerated until they become threatening. But in his "April Sermon" he said, "Art is never difficult to understand... for it is the joy that penetrates through our skins into the very heart of us, without any of man's famous intellect." He drew lonely

237

Otto Pankok, Water Wheel, 1955

landscapes with carts drawn by donkeys; fields of thistles stretching out before us; the moon rising over a tiny human figure–in a disheveled forest. Pankok roamed everywhere in the North Sea region, on the isle of Capri, on Riviera beaches, in Holland, in Sardinia. In fact, the gypsies, with their roving life, bewitched him. But he also gave us religious cycles such as his great *Passion of Our Lord*, in six parts. With ghetto and pogrom pictures he fought against man's inhumanity. This artist, who was color-blind, withdrew more and more into graphic work. He also dabbled in sculpture and writing.

Josef Hegenbarth (1884–1962) was another master of pure drawing. He became prominent only after the Second World War since even his completely traditional work was unpopular under National Socialism. With pen or brush he described on paper the most fleeting attitudes of men or animals, characterizing them actuely, with widely sweeping lines or dexterously inserted swirls of ink. He never lapsed into impressionistic or expressionistic formulae but remained true to a high-spirited, free, realistic statement.

Albert Schaefer-Ast (1890–1951), a one-eyed Eulenspiegel who reveled in fanciful conjecture, was especially adept at spinning a web of grotesque rhythms across the surface. "In my lithography, I magnified my comic drawings in order to give them new artistic form." He wanted to prevent caricature from sinking to the level of all-too-detailed journalism where "it would no longer be taken seriously as a work of art." He was in command of every graphic technique: pencil, reed pen, burin and brush. He worked for many periodicals. This childlike giant loved beetles and butterflies–and his thick sketchbook: this "Flower Bible," with its hundreds of nature studies, was the only thing he took with him into air raid shelters during the war.

Bele Bachem (b. 1916) reveals her true personality in her drawings. She too is a comic artist, giving us ironic idylls of city life, sometimes in an old-fashioned

Josef Hegenbarth. Portrait

Albert Schaefer-Ast. *Headless Dancers*

239

Bele Bachem. At the Fortune Teller's, 1956

W. Kramm
Santa Maria Soccorso in Forio d'Ischia, circa 1955

Gerhard Hintschich. In the South, 1955

style, sometimes with almost macabre effect, using bold outlines and curious intralinear details. Daring subject matter is presented in a childlike style. The drawings of *Willibald Kramm* (b. 1891) exist by means of the contrasts in their graphic structure. Long, drawnout strokes are laid against bare white planes, irregularly checkered areas or blotches of cloudy black. Landscape and people are turned into bearers of ornaments, and all things pass by in tragi-comic fashion.

As a transition to abstract drawing, let us examine the work of *Werner Schreib* (b. 1925). He creates a network of lines which form a compact wirelike structure of varied three-dimensional shapes, quasi-geometrical, quasi-organic, completely interpenetrating and inseparable–a secret writingso mehow suggesting meaning. For it he recommends "the use of a pleasure-magnifying glass." In 1958 he published a curious little book called *Die makabren Zeichnungen des merkwürdigen Herrn Schreib (The Macabre Drawings of the Peculiar Mr. Schreib)*.

Werner Schreib. Needle-Drawing, 1957

ABSTRACT PAINTING

The German "Old Masters"

Our investigation of abstract painting has been confined so far to the pioneering efforts of Kandinsky and the work of his Bauhaus colleagues. Its further evolution as a many-sided and far-reaching movement in the general history of twentieth-century art has occurred only since the second World War, and it is this phase with which we shall now deal. But first some basic principles must be made clear.

Abstract painting, as we understand it, is an approach that rejects any reproduction of the outside world of visual experience, even the freest interpretation. From the very beginning, however, virtually as soon as the public had become aware of the development, there was a quarrel over definitions. The expression "abstract" was at first used also for Cubism and the more radical aspects of Expressionism whenever objects had been transformed into an abstract scheme, but eventually only that which had relinquished every relationship with the object was termed abstract. Then, in an analogy to absolute music, the expression "absolute painting" came into use, a term meaning that line, color and form were now to be read and experienced for their own sake, without external reference. The expression "nonobjective art" *(ungegenständlich, art non-figurative)* was less popular, since it defined only negatively. The paradoxical expression "concrete art" *(konkrete Kunst)*, first used by the Dutch painter Theo van Doesburg, was intended to convey that in this style of painting, line and color were autonomous. That is to say, they were complete and independent concrete realities, in contrast to their status in a painting–in a still life, for example, where they would serve dependently to create something else. The expression "concrete" was not generally adopted, however, because Doesburg claimed it for his own constructivist style and consequently for only one aspect of nonobjective art.

The gradual disintegration of the object came about historically as a result of various conditioning factors. Impressionism, in its most radical phase–with Monet, for example–had already dissolved the world into ephemeral nuances of color, and it is significant that Kandinsky should have declared that one of his inspirations for the omission of the object had come from this direction. Then Cubism, radically modifying Cézanne, split the outer world into a system of surface fractures, and Expressionism ignored the confining outlines of its forms to express ecstatic gesture. All three of these currents were able to flow into the waters of absolute painting. When one takes a closer look, they may be followed further. One may speak today of an Impressionism that has become abstract whenever a riot of color predominates–Tachism; and one can recognize an abstract Expressionism when the expressive gesture is paramount and in nonobjective reference; and finally there is an abstract Cubism that works today with purely geometric forms – *abstraction froide*. But with this the possibilities of nonobjective art are by no means exhausted. Grown independent, it gives birth to children of its own. Here again are all those possibilities which Heinrich Wölfflin established as polarities for objective painting: centric or eccentric, unified or multiple composition, linear or painterly technique, flat or three-dimensional spaces, closed or open forms; to these must be added all the possible approaches to life, from gay to tragic.

The "grand old men" of German nonobjective painting are Kandinsky, with whom we have already dealt, Hölzel, Baumeister, Ritschl, Hans Hofmann and Theodor Werner. Each of these men struck out into this new territory in a different way, but the earliest point of departure lies with Kandinsky and Hölzel. Kandinsky's contribution was a spring which gushed forth; Hölzel's flowed in a more leisurely fashion.

Adolf Hölzel (1853–1934) was influential, although less directly than Kandinsky, through his teaching He was a member of the Dachau group, and as early as 1893 founded a school of painting in that city which for a time included the young Nolde among its students. Since Hölzel belongs to the generation of Klinger, Liebermann and Corinth, it is astonishing to realize that in 1904, when he published his first theoretical work, he was already introducing an emphasis on broad surface areas and colors in his paintings, thus stressing pictorial architecture rather than the object. The Jugendstil had prepared the way with its effective pictorial rhythms, and however strongly Hölzel tended toward compressed forms, his statement remained softly lyrical. In 1906 he was called to the Stuttgart Art Academy, and in 1910 he finally achieved nonobjective compositions. Yet he was devoted to religious themes and therefore only rarely excluded the representational world. With his friend Theodor Fischer, an architect interested in moderate reforms, Hölzel at first devoted himself to murals; then he became more radically abstract in colorfully composed glass windows and, after 1923, in pastels. In 1917 and 1918 he painted compositions on a new theme, *Farbige Klänge* (colored sounds). He was a firm believer in good comradeship and insisted on communal work, as for instance in the banqueting-hall of Pfullingen, where under his direction the Swiss Brühlmann and other students created as freely as possible. For the Ulm Garrison Church he painted a mural of a huge crucifix; for the Hannover firm of Bahlsen and for Stuttgart, cycles of glass paintings. In Stuttgart, Meyer-Amden (see p. 96), Schlemmer and Baumeister sat at his feet for a time.

But Hölzel's main contribution lay in his theories, in his teaching of the *Farbenschlüssel* (Color Keyboard). He was of the opinion that when a work of art "excites our feeling most, we are in the presence of order... Just as a *maestro di cembalo* has to have full knowledge of the chords for every given note, so must we know the triads, transitions and other sound effects, and how to use them." Characteristic of the anti-realism of the twentieth century was the fact that he had in mind a science of harmony such as had been developed in music long ago. As early as 1916 he knew that "there exist certain qualities that are justified in their own right and do not require representational supplementation, in fact suffer and atrophy under it." The following declaration was also something quite new: "If anyone believes that he must first thoroughly study nature in order to arrive at a picture, he is greatly mistaken... first we must grasp the idea-picture, in order to take from nature what we require." The artist should work with eight categories of color: the primary colors themselves, with light and dark, cold and warm, and with the complementaries; then with intensity, quantity, the non-colors (black, white and gray) and the simultaneous contrasts.

Under Hitler's dictatorship the eighty-year-old artist was cruelly relegated to the ranks of the disgraced. Hölzel's pupils were Brühlmann, Pelligrini, Eberz, Itten, Ackermann, Hildegard Kress, and also H. Stenner, who was killed in action at the age of twenty-three.

Willi Baumeister (1889–1955) also developed in Stuttgart, becoming Germany's foremost nonconstructive abstract painter. The richest contrasts and the greatest powers of transformation were innately present in this artist whose natural talent for painting was undiminished by strong tendencies toward

Adolf Hölzel. Composition

theory. He established a strange secret connection between the oldest cave drawings and the spiritual explorations of modern man. Artists such as he like to symbolize the mystery of life in opposition to the rationalized orders that control us, and to express it in an irrational sign language. (Plate XXVI.)

In the beginning Baumeister was impressed by the monumental forms of Léger and later he was inspired to some extent by the fantastic imaginings of Miró. But he transformed both approaches, even when he was at his most eccentric, into a more appealing play of material and color. When one tries to compare the two Swabian friends, Schlemmer and Baumeister, who for years lived side by side in Stuttgart, one finds a supratemporal contrast—the dualistic linear tensions of Schlemmer confront in Baumeister a revelation of the painterly abundance of nature, an organic germination and growth. An ethically normative spirit confronts a personality filled with a passionately open-minded relationship to life. It is

urt Sohns. At the Table

ans Meyboden. At the Window

Willy Baumeister. Gay Ensemble, 1949

indicative that after Baumeister had become an abstract painter he declared that this method of painting "is not abstract in the sense of being alienated from mankind and life. The perception of the artist is entirely natural. Certain manifestations of nature, such as the surface of water, waves in the sand, tree bark, geological formations in quarries, branches, everything structural or modulative that is visible in nature, stands very close to the painting of today."

In 1919 he began to paint "wall pictures" that sought their stability in the consolidating wall or were turned into wall-reliefs through an admixture of sand and putty. But soon his forms became less identifiable, more complicated and agitated, and his signs became whispering symbols. In 1938 he painted his *Eidos* pictures, in which appear amoebalike forms, single-cell creatures reminiscent of the mysterious early stages of organic life. These were followed in 1943 by his "African Pictures," which remind us of cryptographs of early cultures and whose puzzling forms attract us. Out of these developed, in 1945, his *Peruvian Walls;* here he again established a unity with the wall, but he now let punctured color forms haunt the surface ("Perforation Pictures"). These were followed by works he called "painted reliefs," in which colorful symbols seemed to float on a sustained surface. Finally he painted gigantic *Gelände* (territories), black and white continents that filled the entire picture in monotone, emitting glowing color or revealing close details at their outer edges only, delicate jags, specks, twisted lines.

Such forms interpenetrate in his work, at times in a subdued nocturnal light, at others in a matinal glory of color, sometimes spread flat over the picture plane, then again in high relief. "A predilection for

Adolf Hölzel
Composition, 1927

245

immobility is also evident," he declared, "and for perceptions of movement, for a state of floating, and for decompositions. The forms react to each other, create spheres of action or rhythmic chains, which color serves as music." Baumeister remained a man of surprising transformations—the pointed could become cloddish, combed effects are placed beside granular, smooth areas adjoin the lumpy, firmly drawn lines are next to jerky strokes. A gray murmuring, runic tone could appear beside unexpected signs in saturated color, dull material beside the most beautiful glaze. After sometimes suspecting the painter of a certain caprice, on close acquaintance with the work one realizes that everything is in its rightful place after all. In his book, *Das Unbekannte in der Kunst (The Unknown in Art*, 1947) he declares that "all great results are found casually, through coincidence or in uncontrolled ways." Although he could be quarrelsome, he was a hedonist, with a budding embonpoint and an earthy sense of humor. Once he wrote to me that he would have liked to be "a designer of fakir nail beds or a stenographer for the conversation of two grasshoppers." His favorite books were *Tristram Shandy* and *The Tibetan Death Book*. In 1928 he was called to the Frankfurt Art School, but was dismissed as "degenerate" in 1933. After the war, in 1946, he took over the direction of the Stuttgart Academy. In 1955 he was sitting in front of his easel, lost in a problem of painting, when he suddenly sank to the floor and died.

Hans Hofmann (1880–1966), who became a highly esteemed painter in the United States, was inspired originally by the Fauves. Before the First World War this Bavarian artist lived in Paris, in close relationship with Matisse, Delaunay, Braque and Picasso. In 1915 he founded a school of painting in the Schwabing section of Munich which flourished unnoticed, but taught already the possibilities of abstract painting. After the war Hofmann used to spend his summers in Ragusa, Capri or St. Tropez with his pupils. In 1930 a friend brought him to the Berkeley Campus of the University of California, and four years later he started his school of painting in New York City, with summer semesters in Provincetown. During the first half of his life Hofmann was a teacher; in the United States, however, he developed a chromatic tech-

Willi Baumeister. Ideogram, 1942

Willi Baumeister. Aru, 1955

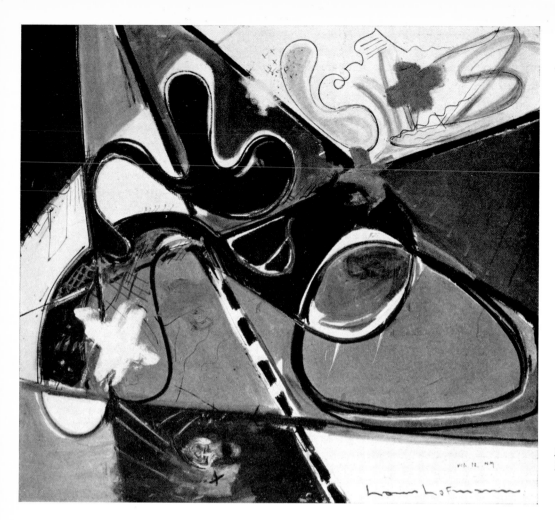

nique of considerable force. American critics have described his powerfully colored paintings as "controlled explosions." He was not dependent on nature–although he did not necessarily eliminate the object–or on the principles of Cubism. He looked upon his colored formations more as "complexes of pressure and forces," barely held in balance. Titles such as *Ecstasy* and *Burst into Life* are characteristic.

With his seemingly improvised, riotously colorful pictures in which life permeates all matter, he contributed the element of complete freedom of nonobjective expression which has become so decisive for the development of the most recent American painting. His teaching stressed the difference between tonal painting, with its emphasis on light and dark gradations, and pure painting (to which he assigned his own work) that established "open" elementary color contrasts, with the superabundant color serving also a formal function.

Theodor Werner (b. 1886), with Baumeister and Schlemmer the third Swabian to achieve international fame, was quite different–more the meditative painter-philosopher. He lived for a long time in Greece,

Theodor Werner. Mural (nineteen meters wide), Musikhochschule, Berlin, 1954

Paris and Berlin. Inspired originally by Cézanne, he moved gradually toward nonobjective painting of space-creating colors and interpretative rhythms. In the 1930's he was still using corporeal forms, shaped like elongated wedges or rising up like bundles of rays. In the 1940's he used ellipses and circles, and passages that give an effect of astronomical tracks. Since 1950 he has been filling his pictures with more limited forms, some plantlike, some crystalline. Between such "psychic signals" we now find pauses, connections are less direct, many possibilities remain open. Sometimes a circle or a staff-shaped form is placed in front of the more amorphous color areas, as if to measure symbolically a specific place in this semi-articulated realm. Even when he resorts to broken—one might even say splintered—rhythms, Werner's tonality remains original and definitely aesthetic.

In 1954 he successfully carried out the commission for a nineteen-meter-wide mural for the Berlin Academy of Music, one of the largest abstract murals in Germany. Here a symphony of forms is developed in three movements, clearly demonstrating—for the first time in Germany—that nonobjective painting,

Hilla von Rebay. Leggiero, 1946

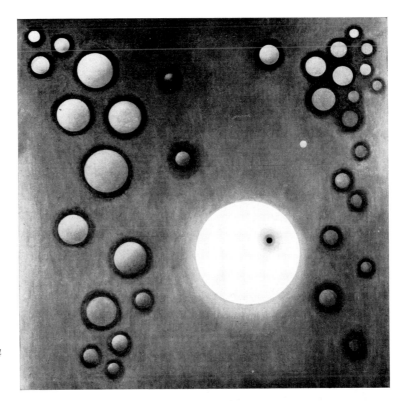

Rudolf Bauer. Blue Balls, 1934

going far beyond its improvisational features, can dominate gigantic surface areas. Werner is of the opinion that "paintings are not made of ideas or objects," but out of color.

Woty Werner, the painter's wife, gave the art of weaving a similarly new approach by working without preparatory drawing in order to develop out of the specialized technique itself, completely free, color-fully rhythmicizing forms.

For years *Otto Ritschl* (b. 1885) has represented the Constructivist-Purist wing of abstract painting, although his origins were wholly different. (Plate XXVII.) Self-taught, he is one of those artists who mature slowly and fulfill their potentialities in the work of their old age. For him painting is "neither a mirror of the soul nor a trampoline for subjective emotions, but a building up, a constructing." He presents us with stereometric, clearly defined forms designed for large surfaces, severely built color and line structures; they are devoid of all subjective effect and in the most harmonious order possible–a style which today is called much too disparagingly *abstraction froide*. "At present I am striving for a picture that shall be formed completely on the surface, without the dual effect of a ground on which the forms rest. I also no longer want anything more than form, neither expression, therefore, nor mood... To me it seems contradictory to use in an abstract painting a color that has been developed for a representational subject, that is to say, a color that possesses material, spatial or atmospheric qualities." If one compares such a "program" with the words of Baumeister, one senses the antithesis of commitment.

251

Otto Ritschl. Composition, 1956

In an earlier phase, between 1932 and 1938, he treated in a painterly manner symbols floating in illusory, almost atmospheric space. This phase was followed in 1945 by a brief figurative period in which he was trying out a new language of gesture, although here we find already a hardening of form. Ritschl, who lives in Wiesbaden, has been working in his current style since 1949. Painting imperturbably, and always with elegant color harmonies, he has gone his rather lonely way.

Hilla von Rebay (1890-1967), born five years after Ritschl, passed through Expressionism and Cubism to arrive earlier than he at abstract painting–in her case of a loosely rhythmicizing nature. She was a fanatic exponent of nonobjective art. She emigrated to the United States and in 1937 took a decisive part in founding The Museum of Non-Objective Art in New York City (now the Guggenheim Museum) which was focused chiefly on Kandinsky and Rudolf Bauer. In 1937 she wrote *Innovation*, and in 1939 *Art Tomorrow*. *Rudolf Bauer* (1889–1953) grew out of the Berlin Sturm group, where he met Hilla von Rebay. In 1929 in Berlin he founded Geistreich, a private museum for abstract art. In 1939 he emigrated to the United States. He painted monumental pictures with geometrically firm color forms.

Hans Hartung. Picture, 1948

Construction or Expression?

At this point I would like to remind the reader that as early as the second decade of our century, non-objective art had already split polarically into two major possibilities, even though many of the artists involved developed hybrid forms of the two approaches. Beside Kandinsky's vehemently expressive, irrationally affecting configurations, Malevich, Mondrian and Doesburg were stressing the strictest order of simple, undifferentiated painted surfaces which allowed no calligraphy with the brush. Beside flowing improvisation, therefore, stood the rationally restrained effort; beside a vital abundance of form and color, a purist, Platonic order. At the Bauhaus both possibilities existed side by side, Kandinsky and Klee beside Moholy and Albers. In the 1920's geometric clarity as propagated by the Dutch Stijl group was highly esteemed, especially since it conformed with the new, purely constructive, functional architecture of the time. After the Second World War, however, this geometric approach was forced definitely into a defensive position. As *abstraction froide* it was considered schematic and lifeless, as if in the arts only the intensely warm and intoxicating were of value. However many exciting events may have taken place in the meantime in the field of the new *élan vital*, one should not condemn the opposite principle. We must cease rejecting as old-fashioned the idea that there exists in art a masculine principle of control which is opposed to a feminine principle of dynamic expression, for this polar tension, this contrast in attitude, is necessary for the completeness of life. Anyone wandering through a representative exhibition of abstract art today will find that after the stimulating excitement of Tachist paintings, he will experience with pleasure the severe organization of works which represent the opposite point of view; he may even find that they have an enhancing effect on one another. They rest, after all, on two fundamental requirements of our souls which should not be too hastily blended.

Such a contrast develops in most periods rich in art. Beside the iron of Piero della Francesca appeared the vital motion of Pollaiuolo; beside the strict order of Poussin, the overflowing vitality of Rubens; next to the luminosity of Vermeer stood the "darker" Rembrandt; next to the reserve of Ingres, the exuberance of Delacroix. Beside an organizer like Seurat, Monet worked in his own evanescent style; and a figural, almost constructive, painter like Schlemmer worked side by side with a visionary, playful Klee. In poetry and music we find the same polarities. To some extent they are connected with the difference between the power of abstraction and the capacity for empathy (Worringer[1]), but also with the eternal archetypes–classicism and romanticism. However, such axes incline obliquely toward each other in the globe of possibilities. The contrasts in today's art, like everything else in a period devoted increasingly to the specific, seek to reach an extreme, an exceptional purity. Thus some put their faith in the stability of Vordemberge or Bill, others in the whirlpool of Pollock or Wols. In all cultural lands, not only in a divided Germany, this antithesis is logical.

Some of the German Constructivists who felt themselves bypassed by the critics joined together in Hamburg in 1948 as "The Group." Prominent among them was *Hildegard Stromberger* (b. 1904), who carried on and partially transformed the tradition of Vordemberge-Gildewart. *Max H. Mahlmann* (b. 1912) and

---

[1] Wilhelm Worringer (1881–1965). His *Abstraktion und Einfühlung, ein Beitrag zur Stilpsychologie (Abstraction and Empathy, a Contribution to Psychology of Style)* was published in 1908.

Max H. Mahlmann. Composition, 1956

Hildegard Stromberger. Composition, 1955

his wife *Gudrun Piper* (b. 1917) work in a similar vein. Mahlmann declares his goal is "to confront chaos with order. That is why the constructive formation should be represented by the most economic execution. The function of the elements of form is expressed by a renunciation of all bravura, and must demonstrate a crystal-clear transcendentalism."

Joachim Albrecht. Composition, 1957　　　　　　　　　　　　　　*Gudrun Piper. Composition, 1956*

254

Joachim Albrecht (b. 1916) strives constantly for clarity with large smooth surfaces and colorful tensions which are effective from a distance. *Hans Hermann Steffens* (b. 1911) constructs his pictures with straight and bent bars of color. *G. F. Ris* (b. 1928) and *Günter Frühtrunk* (b. 1923) also belong here. *Leo Breuer* (b. 1893), who lives in the Rhineland, also works in this style, proving that complicated forms and sharper contrasts of color may be successfully stretched to the corners of the canvas. But above all, Otto Ritschl, with whom we have already dealt, demonstrated in his oeuvre the mysterious transitions from organic to constructive form.

Günter Fruehtrunk. Composition, 1955

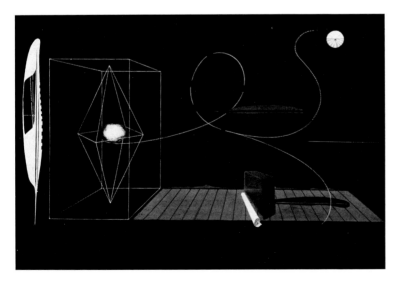

Martin Andersch
Dream of Flying

German Innovators in France

Hans Hartung and Wols developed two specific forms of nonobjective art that were destined to create schools of painting: Hartung with a rhythmic linearity, and Wols through an equally uncontrolled manner of expression which was termed *informel* or "tachistic." Both developed their art after they went to France. The Leipziger *Hans Hartung* was born in 1904, the year the Brücke was founded, which may be considered symbolic, for he was to become one of those who overthrew Expressionism. (Plate XXVIII.) Raised in eastern Germany, he at first accepted Expressionism–certain of his early drawings resemble those of Nolde–then he gradually turned away from anything that recalled reality. The semi-abstract quality of Marc's *Animal Destinies* excited him, but he found he preferred Kandinsky's total abstraction. His is a more austere sensitivity, however, and he was primarily concerned with the projection of broadly swinging forms in front of a shimmering, transparent ground plane, as if he were writing a message in the sky. Dark arcs floating in colorful space take on grotesque grill shapes, fine lines are overpowered by heavy crossbars, the elastic spring of linear dynamics is blocked by heavy beamlike forms, quick curves are braked by inert black passages. For a time Hartung was inspired by Miró and by the sculptor Julio Gonzales; he had married Gonzales' daughter and worked in his studio in France. But basically Hartung was not in the least interested in Miró's apparitions or grotesques. Ever more strongly he was developing into a master of rhythmic balances. Man's simple, psychomotor basic energies were

Hans Hartung. T-18, 1948

Hans Hartung. T 56–16, 1956 · Hannover, Collection Sprengel

Wols. Painting

his concern, and he proceeded from an entirely physical feeling to develop them in broad sweeping forms. He submitted his monumental, autonomous, expressive motion ever more intensely to harmonious pictorial controls. During the last years his paintings have become simpler. Individual sweeps of the brush rest on a greater harmony of form, even the shimmering ground from which the latter unfolds is becoming more monotone.

258

In the history of art one finds sometimes that a steady stylistic development is based on a highly unstable exterior life, as in Hartung's case. He studied philosophy and history of art in Leipzig, then abandoned it all and from 1932 to 1934 lived on the Balearic Island of Minorca; moved from there to Paris, where, as a passionate opponent of National Socialism, he joined the Foreign Legion in 1939 and fought in North Africa. In 1943 he fled to Spain, was interned, but joined the Foreign Legion again, fought in Alsace-Lorraine in 1944 and was severely wounded. Not until the war was over was he again able to resume the painting he had so long been deprived of. Then, in Paris, he began to work furiously, soon becoming internationally famous.

Wols (Alfred Otto Wolfgang Schulze, 1913–1951) brought something quite different to the art of abstract painting–the unpredictable whirlpools of totally irregular line and color motion which are to be experienced as symbolic of the unfathomable wealth of life. Within the realm of abstract painting it is impossible to conceive of a greater contrast than that which prevails between the Constructivists and Wols.

In his early surrealist watercolors, Wols came close to Klee, but only superficially. When he exhibited

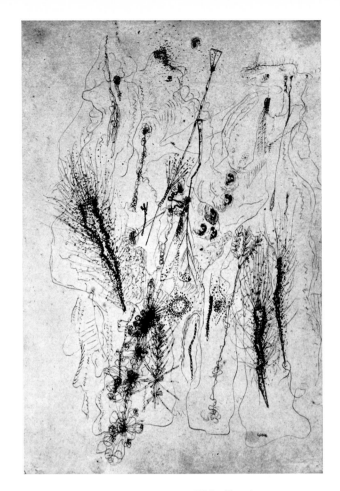

Wols. Drawing

for the first time at the Drouin Gallery in Paris in 1945, he was hailed by many, in Germany as well as France, as the prophet of *Tachism*. This vague name (blot-painting) meant in those days a turn toward an irrational, dynamic experience. In Wols' paintings an abundance of linear and color particles dart, whirl, and are knotted together. One might call it "Cosmic Impressionism." His work bespoke a renewed faith in the life force, the momentary inspiration which, without any planning, would burst into something significant, a complete picture. An ambiguous but comprehensive form of being was to be made perceptible–not, however, an existence that could be distinguished in stone, plant, animal or human being. And in all this the agony and the humor of this remarkable personality was captured.

His life, which ended all too soon, was even more of an odyssey than Hartung's. As a boy he played the violin so beautifully that Fritz Busch advised him to join an orchestra, but he took up photography instead; in no time he was creating strange pictures and montages which he exhibited in Paris. Suddenly he found himself working in Frobenius' Africa Institute; then, in Berlin, under Mies van der Rohe and Moholy. For a time he lived in Barcelona and in the Balearic Islands. The outbreak of war found him in France again, where he spent fourteen months in an internment camp. When he had to flee from the German troops, he left all his works behind to be destroyed but took with him a heavy sack of beloved shells and little stones. These were the things that let him forget "the meaning of man and the chaos of his actions. Eternity is demonstrated in these harbor trifles." After he was freed he remained in France, starving. Suddenly he found support in Sartre, and illustrated his works as well as those of Kafka, Artaud, Paulhan, and Solier. In the course of this detailed work his eyes began to suffer, all light became painful and he left his room only at night, wandering along the Seine accompanied by a faithful dog. He began to drink. Unable to buy an easel or paint, he resorted to the smallest format. After finding a modest place to live on the Marne, he died accidently of food-poisoning at the age of thirty-eight. In the end, he who had never wanted to exhibit found his way to a free, irrational painting that skyrocketed him to fame.

Munich

In 1949 a number of painters working in the vicinty of Munich formed a group that called itself ZEN. It was the first important association of mutually sympathetic artists to be created in the German post-war era, and in the following five years almost all the abstract painters of significance joined the group.

Fritz Winter (b. 1905) had studied at the Bauhaus under Klee and Kandinsky (from 1927 to 1930), but from the beginning he worked in a style all his own. His early paintings are dominated by dully glowing

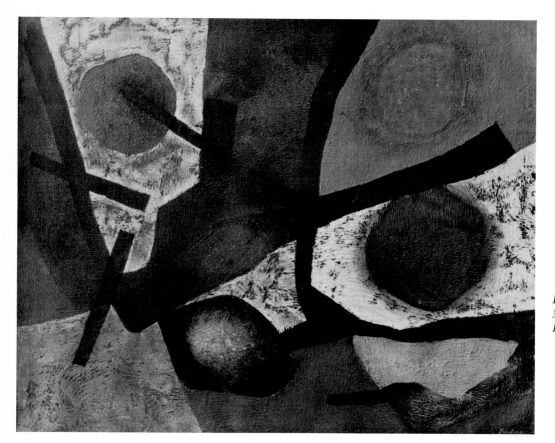

Fritz Winter
March,
1950–1951

Fritz Winter. Grey Shadows, 1953

and twilit colors. Other pictures remind one of crystal formations that have been raised out of the depths. Through the Second World War and the Russian captivity that followed (1939–1949) his creativity was largely interrupted, but after this period he worked in Diessen on the Ammersee, painting in richer colors and fuller forms. At one time he gave titles to his work—as in a series of oils painted in 1944, *Triebkräfte der Erde (Driving Forces of the Earth)*. It may well have been Hans Hartung who led him in the direction of a more energetic articulation. Hartung, however, elected a calligraphic rhythm, whereas Winter's dark forms are laid more somberly, like inert beams, over shimmering foundations in yellow, red or greenish tints, and are locked together with a certain grandeur. (Plate XXIX.) The two-layer effect sometimes achieved a maestoso quality. In 1955, at the Cassel Documenta exhibition, he showed a gigantic painting in rhythmic forms which extended across an entire transverse wall, dominating the whole room. Here was another proof that solely through color and form abstract painting could articulate and enhance a large-scale architectural assignment, and do it equally as well as any of Léger's representational compositions with comparable purpose. It is, in fact, just this kind of art that needs the opportunity to go beyond the movable easel picture.

Lately Winter has been incorporating more luminous color areas, without, however, abandoning the somberness of his forms. Since 1955 he has had a chance to develop his pedagogical capabilities at the Cassel Academy. "Greater faith and greater strength are needed," he says, "to make visible the invisible in a free formation than is required simply to confirm the visible and tangible as such."

Conrad Westpfahl (b. 1891) is one of those artists who have turned from objective painting and drawing to a passionate endorsement of the new art, rather as a poet might turn from narrative novel writing to a lyricism that has no aim but to project man's inner condition. Westpfahl has been living near Munich since 1940. At first he made a name for himself with paintings and drawings in which youthful female figures were spun across the surface in a lively shorthand, sometimes in a painterly fashion, sometimes with the stress on linearity. A line would take its course so willfully that one could already sense this artist's future development as an abstract painter. He began with a muted palette but with the most extreme freedom of rhythm, later using more intense colors in order to strengthen the pulse of life inherent in them. He has taken part frequently in philosophical discussions on modern art, has written articles, and in 1948 a brochure, *Zur Deutung des Bildhaften* ("Toward an Interpretation of the Pictorial"). Occasionally he returns to figural themes, based for the most part on classical mythology. "The visibility of the representational world is not arrived at through the visible world but by way of the surface that has been made to vibrate through color and form. We are not portraying the dead fruits of detached observation, we are rendering the event itself." He believes that "the use of perspective makes things rigid. Solely decisive for the essence of the picture is the tempo of the line determining the direction; the modulations of the transitions of haptic motion; the power of color, radiant or dull, bearing a transcendental message." But pessimistically he adds, "All this can be followed only by those who can feel music in form."

Rolf Cavael (b. 1898) came to Munich from the north German city of Königsberg, but he was able to develop his potentialities only belatedly because of the war and the National Socialist ban on his work. His aim is the freedom of motion and dynamics of color and line that result from a feeling of physical relaxation. His tonality is not based on striking contrasts of complementary colors but on a differentiation of cold and warm. Working with small formats, he began as a linearist whose forms, derived from handwriting, rarely went beyond a tinted calligraphy, remaining essentially self-contained. Later, however, everything became expansive and free. Yellow, red and green glimmer between a tracery of lines which are now more dynamically extended. The foundations are enhanced by a variation of transparent and opaque colors, and improvised lines dip and dart like the flight of a gull before an approaching

Conrad Westpfahl
B M 6, 1958

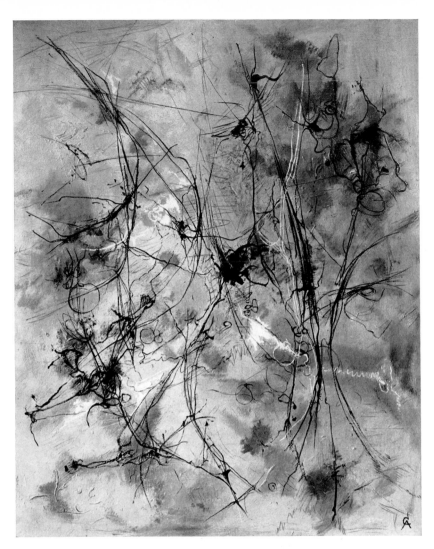

Rolf Cavael. F 9, 1958

thunderstorm. They seek to become increasingly unified with the picture ground, which in its turn also vibrates. The result is a fluid, sensitive, but also rather nervous style. It cannot be called Tachism because this concert of pictorial events is dominated by a few voices more developed than the rest, which remain calligraphic.

In courses at the Munich Volkshochschule, the pedagogue Cavael succeeded in implanting in simple working people the desire to express themselves abstractly by discovering their own inner rhythm and learning to project it with pencil and brush. It is encouraging that many people were willing to indulge in such a very private adventure.

Gerhard Fietz (b. 1910) came to Munich from eastern Germany. His paintings are quiet and fine-meshed, and avoid all gestures. They improve when seen close to, whereas those of Soulages or Schneider, to name two somewhat comparable French painters achieve their effect from a distance. Fietz worked first from

Gerhard Fietz. Picture, 1949

the external world around him and did not turn his back on it until he was thirty-five. Around 1949 he began to construct geometric pictures which gave evidence of a rational and spatial tendency in which color was nothing more than a delicately balanced afterthought. But in 1950 he seemed to find this type of organization constricting and began to seek more lapidary symbols. This resulted in vitally streaming forms out of which one can rarely wrest a single event. Line and color whorls now unfold a rich, free universal life and the most varied techniques are joined. In some of his paintings his earlier economy of color has been preserved, for instance when a swirl of motion is embedded in a monochrome ground, but at times he lets his color become overheated. His more austere compositions are more convincing because he is at heart a reserved personality.

He worked first at the Breslau Academy under Kanoldt and Schlemmer, then studied at the academies of Dusseldorf and Berlin, and settled down finally in Bavaria. The war years also handicapped his development. He lectured for a time at the Hamburg Art School and was then called to the Berlin Academy.

Karl F. Brust (1897–1960) lost all his early paintings in the war. He worked at many professions and only took up painting again much later. He too was a disciple of nonobjective art, and stressed a specific painterly style, but used fewer lattice-structures than Fritz Winter. A warm red, a richly modified blue and a deep green glow on his canvas, the colors running in broad tracks that travel diagonally through the picture, becoming more loosely organized as they approach the edges. The color is intended to flow, yet the dissolution of the pictorial organization in a tachistic sense is avoided.

Fred Thieler (b. 1916) is a second-generation abstractionist. Around 1950, after leaving the school of Karl Caspar and having applied himself mainly to expressive portraiture, he succeeded finally in creating nonobjective pictures. His colors do not ebb at the outer edges, and the effect is less painterly than that of Brust; also he leaves fewer interstices, since it is his intention to fill the entire surface with a hammerlike motion of color (Plate XXXIV). Here organic and mechanically rigid forces seem to

264

Karl F. Brust
Breakthrough, 1956

plough through each other. Some of his expressive paintings are called, indicatively, *Nature and Technology*. Often the colors are limited to a mere contrast of blue against yellow, or blue against red. Whereas Hartung or Winter would have let a black latticework emerge with something white shimmering through, Thieler explodes these contrasting non-colors within his mosaic of motion. His tonality denies the naturalistic implication that blue has a cosmic meaning or green a vegetative one; the colors react "abstractly" to each other, but some dominant note still rules, even within a situation that explodes. *Ernst Geitlinger* (b. 1895) was called to the Munich Art Academy in 1951, where he filled the position held in 1900 by Franz von Stuck, whose teaching had attracted the then unknown Kandinsky and Franz Marc. Similarly, Geitlinger succeeded in surrounding himself with young painters. In the import-

Ernst Geitlinger
Autumn Evening, 1954

Ernst Weil. Flower Picture, 1951

Armin Sandig
Visions, 1957

Rupprecht Geiger
Silence, 1955

ant yearly exhibition in Munich's Haus der Kunst, he made ever increasing room for the abstractionists. At Gallery 17, together with his highly intelligent student *Walter Gaudneck* and the society of "Freunde der jungen Kunst" (Friends of New Art), he introduced those young artists to whom too little attention had previously been paid because they had turned their backs on tradition. Before Geitlinger turned to abstract art he painted pictures with objective content. At that time I wrote of his work, "Pour Chagall into a bottle, add a little of Paul Klee and a shot of Adolf Oberländer[1], shake well, and Geitlinger will pop out of the bottle." In his case, numerous decorative commissions may have contributed to his shift from an intimate fantastic genre to comprehensive abstractions.

Armin Sandig (b. 1929) also developed his art in Munich, but today he lives in Hamburg. His compositions are sustained by a lyric feeling beyond which he experiments in a playful calligraphy or in tachist color whorls.

Ernst Weil (b. 1919) constructs heavy forms in his paintings. One senses that he studied architecture and has been influenced by Léger.

Rupprecht Geiger (b. 1909), son of the famous graphic artist and painter, Willy Geiger (see p. 184), began by painting large still lifes with a southern luminosity in a style similar to his father's, after which he turned to rectangular abstractions. Out of varied mobile forms he developed geometric compositions, until he finally arrived at constructivist painting. His style differs from that of Mondrian or Doesburg, which was continued in Germany by Vordemberge-Gildewart; Geiger does not place evenly colored planes against each other, but instead lets the color within each compartment swell, from the most delicate transparency to the bleakest glow. The introduction of drastic chromatic modulations produces imaginary distances and an appearance of space, without, however perforating the surface. An intangible stratospheric stillness is contained in these mute canvases. There is an effect of silent energy emanating from the tensions that arise between varied overlapping horizontal layers with a supporting framework of off-angled verticals.

Jürgen von Hündeberg works in less hardened, mysteriously harmonizing color structures (Plate XXXVI).

---

[1] Adolf Oberländer (1845–1923), a satirist, one of the first to make collages.

Hans Platschek. Picture, 1956

Heinz Trökes. *Crazy Machine, 1955*

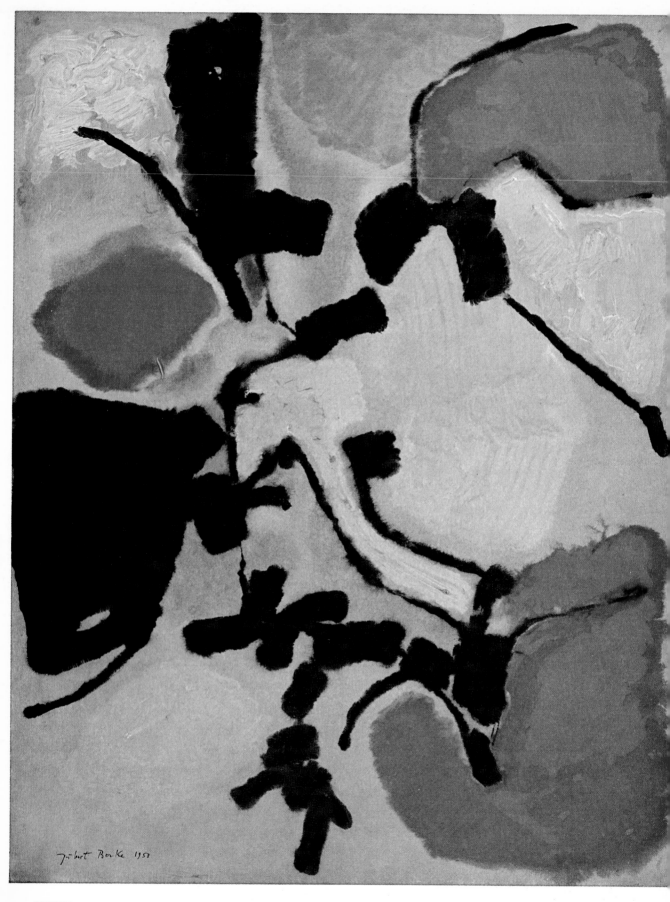

XXXII

Hubert Berke. Black-Red-Grey, 1953

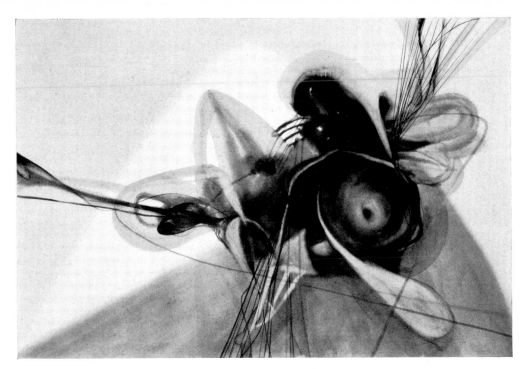

Rupert Stöckl
Vision, 1952

Rupert Stöckl (b. 1923) tries to immerse a multiple abstract play of form and color in illusory space. *Hans Platschek* (b. 1923), who also belongs to a younger generation, concentrates more irrationally on color in motion, letting it glow transparently or darken blackly, as if did not want to disturb its intrinsic life at any point. His braidlike forms swim away lyrically; scarcely born, they seem to want to vanish again, and it is hard to tell whether motion or quiet is intended. Every picture is based on a sustained color harmony of a subtle ochre, an atmospheric blue, an autumnal red or a sensitive gray. He lives in South America, but his *Dichtung Moderner Maler* was published in Germany.

Marion Bembé
Forms, 1956

From Berlin came Theodor Werner; we have already dealt with his contribution. *Hans Kuhn* (b. 1905) also painted first in a representational style. He lived for a long time in France and Italy, blending the color finesse of the French with imaginative content, as de Chirico had first done in the south, but Kuhn gave his forms a more flexible consonance. In his earlier paintings boats lie abandoned on deserted beaches, split columns rise up beside huge dream birds and mythical horses grazing. Fragmented forms are joined by ponderous, muted arches of color; walls are placed obliquely, indicating imaginary spaces beyond which the sea rustles monotonously. In a second phase, Kuhn assembled all objects in the foreground, forcing their conjunction. Spectral humans and vegetation were interwoven as objective recollection gradually disappeared. Soon after 1950, in a third phase, objects have been entirely eliminated; one finds only colored planes in a rather somber rhythm. Harmonious connections prevail; shrill colors are taboo. A dreamy phlegm is common to all phases of Kuhn's development. Lately he has turned to enamel painting; color is given a new luminous power and an extremely fluid mobility. This results in detailed, spongelike and trickly structures which invite the viewer to take a closer look. We

Hans Kuhn
Enamel Painting,
1957

270

Heinz Trökes. Dance in Autumn, 1947

must wait to see whether this technique, which could easily become frivolous, will produce deeper possibilities of expression.

Heinz Trökes (b. 1913) also developed his art in Berlin and turned to abstract painting from Surrealism. At first he created imaginary, yet identifiable, ironic monstrosities—a fishwife crawls across moon craters, an imaginary cannon fires into the cosmos, while in the distance there waits a shy balloon. These landscapes were first worked out with perspective, but then gradually flattened, so that the monsters were suspended in the picture in a relieflike fashion and took on an illusory existence somewhere between corporeality and mere symbol (for instance in *Barbaropa* or *Wunschbild für Geologen (Dream-Wish of Geologists)*. In a third phase these aspects also disappear. Now only gay color planes, stripes, drips and meshwork appear on the picture surface. Certain spectral elements have been preserved, but they no longer represent objective recollection (Plate XXXI).

With Trökes we see how the strongly fantastic style also may eliminate everything representational. This procedure would once have been considered impossible, although for a long time it has been customary to speak of "fantastic ornament" or "fantastic music." In this typical development Trökes both

271

Juro Kubicek
The Big Negress,
1948/1949

Rudolf Mauke. Rhön, 1947

Wilhelm Nay
Of Blue
Ascending,
1956

XXXIII

Fred
In M
1956

lost and gained. His tonality is sometimes sweet and therefore less convincing. At times his graphic fantasy (see his sketchbook) is greater than his imagination in color. Trökes described his working procedure in a way that is valid for most painters of the irrational: "I have no definite plan... I let myself be driven... begin in one corner or other... then I am often surprised. Involuntarily something attracts my attention... and from there I spin on. I interweave and connect, until it gives off a whole sound. Every drawing, every picture, is in its conception full of adventure... much of course doesn't come off and finds its way into the waste basket... It is the spontaneous ideas which astound me, not the dreams."

Juro Kubicek (b. 1906) paints with supple, freeflowing curves containing within their outlines vestigial elements of recognizable forms. In these he makes us think of the musical phase of Theodor Werner's art (see p. 248), although the identity of the forms lingers longer in Kubicek's work. Perceived, or sensed as in a dream, the sinuous curves of a female body emerge from the linear structure, endowing it with lyrical expression. Other pictures remind us of Max Ernst's late style. Kubicek gradually turned to total abstraction. He has experimented with rod-sculpture, using a veneer of synthetic resin to cover the rods, which reach out freely into the space around them like light-colored, tangible motion. When he feels a compulsion to express ideas he creates highly imaginative photomontages, intentionally unsettling and even frightening in their effect. But here also he preserves great elegance of form.

K. R. H. Sonderborg. 3. XI., 1954

Rudolf Mauke (b. 1924) introduces vibrant arches in his pictures. They give a symbolic effect, as do recollections of sailing boats or gliding skis in some of his other works. Color, drawing and indications of space are sparingly inserted so that little is stated but a secretive tensile rhythm, rendered with a minimum of means.

Much richer and more exciting is the work of *K. R. H. Sonderborg* (b. 1923), who is now living in Paris. A merciless linearity tears diagonally through his pictures as if it had no beginning or end but led out into the universe. These trajectories with astronomic effect, seemingly produced by meteors, suck up small particles as they whiz by. *Überschallgeschwindigkeit (Beyond the Speed of Sound)* is the title of

Ernst Wilhelm Nay
Parable, 1958

one of his pictures. Speed of motion here seems to correspond with the speed of work. *17:03 bis 18:34* is another title, indicating the exact time in which the work was painted–an hour and thirty-one minutes. Sonderborg says that he does not work regularly but stores up his dynamic impressions, which shoot out of him when the time is ripe. For the present he has eliminated color and compresses all decisive statements into black and white; at most red is sometimes added. He works into the black with knives, occasionally also with a cloth, as if it were necessary to stop the merciless tracks and provoke them. Sonderborg is a dramatizing agitator and has a completely different rhythm from the melodious K. O. Götz (see p. 285). In Sonderborg's pictures the agitating forces sometimes take on something of the compulsory character of machines. His father, a musician, composed hot jazz, and the individuality of the son broke through, indicatively, on the volcanic island of Stromboli.

Whereas the cultural climate of Berlin has not proved exceptionally attractive for abstract painters, this art form has developed exuberantly in the Rhineland, as if the proximity of Paris had a vitalizing effect. One of the strongest personalities is *Ernst Wilhelm Nay* (b. 1902), who came from Berlin and studied with Hofer. He is definitely a creator of rhythms in the new art form. In 1936 he painted his Lofoten pictures, pictures of fishermen and boats on these lively Norwegian shores, in which the influence of E. L. Kirchner is still effective. These were followed by freer but still representational work in a diagonally plunging, zigzag rhythm. Objective memories were still being interjected, but we also find rhomboid forms and atactical splinters and stops. Passionately glowing colors rub against muted colors. After 1946 the scaffoldings are independent and linearly taut, autonomous formations bordering occasionally on the decorative. But after 1950 Nay's colors become very light and spread out; all graphic outlines melt away. Now nothing but loose circular color areas flow through the picture, filling the surface atmospherically like blossoming globular clouds (Plate XXXIII). They give an effect of loosened, coloristic improvisations, yet they produce a rhythm in which the white, empty interstices can swing right along. Concerning the "relief" of his paintings, this painter says, "The picture is given depth and space not through its structure but in the change from cold to warm, from light to dark color." He gives color no value beside the structural one, and believes in excluding "other values, as for instance those of a symbolic, associative or psychic nature." In 1955 he published an indicative work: *Structural Value of Color.*

Georg Meistermann (b. 1911) stands alone in that he tries to bring the new art of abstraction into the church. Stubbornly he puts his faith in the fact that the transcendental should not employ any realistic pictorial means. Content which is not of this world can only be grasped through abstraction. At the same time he knows very well that whenever artistic expression has changed, the church has inevitably opened its doors in the end to a new *Zeitgeist*, from the rigidity of the Romanesque to the swinging rhythm of the Baroque. He hopes, therefore, that after the hiatus produced by the nineteenth century, the church will turn again to more fundamental pictorial methods. One senses his spiritual conflict in his paintings, in which highly ambitious overall planning is crossed with extremely individual motion (Plate XXX). "Earlier times," he said, "presented the observer with pictures of the values and ideals which bound him. Are we doing anything different? We are bound to freedom, but we don't say that it is easy to achieve." Since 1937 Meistermann has created innumerable glass windows, at first ecclesiastical, later also secular, in which he transformed the tradition of Thorn-Prikker. Between cool gray

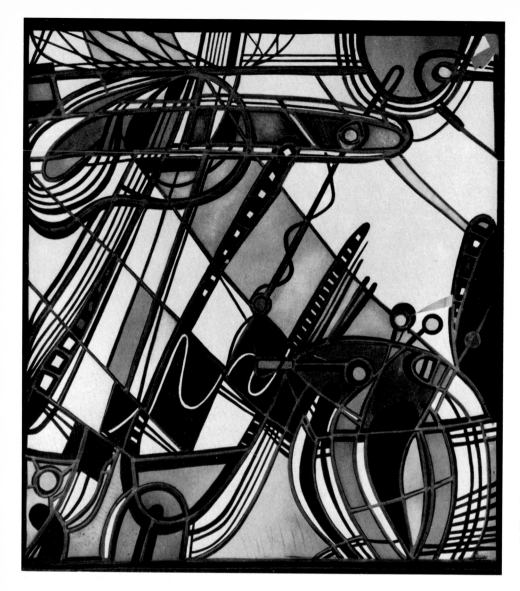

Georg Meistermann
From the Window of
the NWDR Building,
Cologne

glass and winding strips of lead lie glowing color areas. He started from the teachings of his masters, Nauen and Mataré, but then he tried, in freer articulation, to codify certain events of nature. In the 1940's most of his paintings looked like abstract, multiramate treetops or rich ribbon patterns. Processes of growth were symbolized and soaring formats therefore appear. From 1950 his color areas extend more to the sides and become larger; everything is more broadly and thoroughly rhythmicized, but diverging life forces come up constantly against cosmic enclosures. Lately he arranges his color areas more geometrically. He looks upon many of his pictures as experimental fields for the transparent glass compositions that are to follow.

For quite some time, *Hubert Berke* (b. 1908) painted both naturalistic illustration and nonobjective work. In the latter there are no luminous rhythms of the kind we find in Nay, but softly modulated, restful courses of color which seem to float side by side, separated now and then by black areas (Plate XXXII). A gentle melancholy is expressed. Sometimes we hear echoes of an autumnal day in blue, brown, yellow or green, then again of a winter night, in black, dark blue and white. With this painter the summers are not hot or the winters bitingly cold. When there is need for livelier tones, a rather noble gray, a white tone or a mild black satisfies it, so that nothing loud or uncultivated may arise.

Josef Fassbender (b. 1903) fills space in a more varied way. Wide stretches look as if they had been knitted with big stitches, rich colors alternate with flatter washes, quieter sections with others in a restlessly scribbled calligraphy. Interior planes alternate peculiarly between reminiscences of technical and floral forms. Everything serves to create a highly unexpected, extremely irregular ensemble, yet, strangely enough, the effect is balanced. One could not call his mood rebellious. The colors remain soft and close to each other. In certain pictures everything is based on various nuances of red, in others on green and black tones. From 1956 until he was called to Düsseldorf in 1958, Fassbender was in charge of the graphic arts department of the Werkkunstschule in Krefeld.

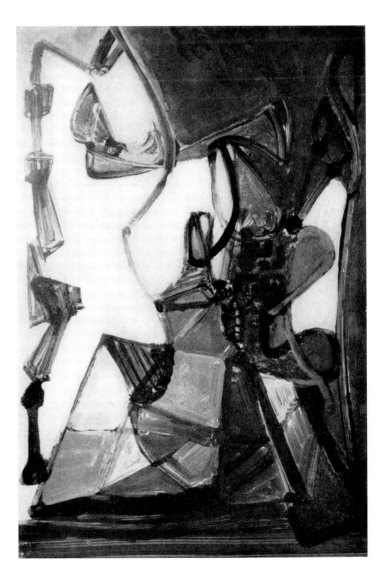

Hubert Berke. Motion

Hann Trier. Gordian Knot, 1957

The works of *Hann Trier* (b. 1915) were dominated at first by an energetic network of lines which seemed determined to destroy the abundance of color that shone between them. Sometimes wheel-like parts circle in an eccentric fashion with no consideration whatsoever for the overall organization. For a long time everything seemed permeated with rebellious forces, as if the painter wanted to make clear the perverse complexity of life. Thickly daubed black bars were placed against delicate linear radiations, heavy black spots against dissolving splashes. His choice of format was already proof of the energy of his statement. He did not choose the balanced square but preferred the rectangle, either rising up determinedly or lying radically on its side. Lately, though, his linear nets are spread out more stably and the color ground shimmers through more restfully.

Karl Buchheister (1891–1964) proceeded from subtly perforated, nervous compositions, transparent beneath a veil-like overlay. After the First World War, in Hannover, where he remained, he and Kurt Schwitters founded a group of abstract painters. Later he went over to the *Abstraction-Création* group. His experiments with "oil-reliefs" are unique. *Marie-Louise Rogister* (b. 1901) belongs to that northwest German circle whose members like to crowd the canvas as richly as possible with toothlike and crustaceous elements, in which the graphic effort is dominant.

Josef Fassbender. Mural in the Arndt Gymnasium, Bonn, 1954

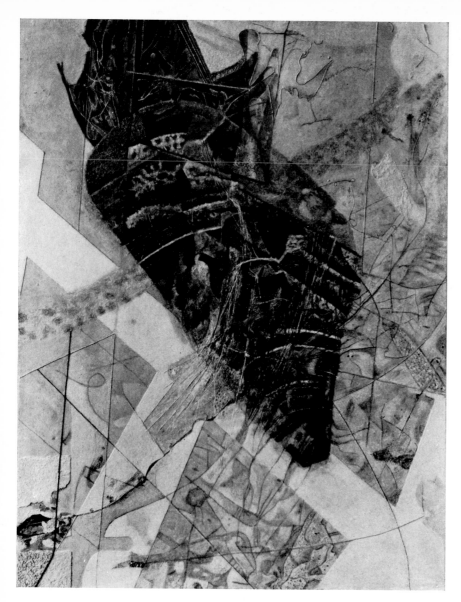

Karl Buchheister
Komposition Wu, 1956

For the Ruhr area we must mention the group *Junger Westen* (Young West) which was formed in 1953. Its premise is the working out of the inner tension resulting from the polarity between the modern technical world and irrational creation. The leader of the group is *Thomas Grochowiak* (b. 1914), son of a Recklinghausen miner, and self-taught. Today he mixes constructive and organic forms in his non-objective pictures. A versatile man, he has for years been in charge of the exhibition at the Recklinghausen Ruhr Festival and of the museums in that city, and has done much to further the visual education of the working man.

Marie-Louise Rogister
Jagged Rhythm, 1957

One of the most talented members of this group is *Hans Werdehausen* (b. 1910), a typical Westphalian. His development was slow. He began with firmly constructed figures, then turned to geometric abstractions. Finally he arrived at free, imaginatively mobile, nonobjective "Landscapes" made up of "suction and gravity, of whirlwind motion, of pressure from above and below"–all this on well-painted, sometimes transparent foundations which still allow certain suggestions of space. *Gustave Deppe* (b. 1913) overlays the surface with stringy bands of color that are held together in a paint-

Thomas Grochowiak
Planes and Scaffolding, 1958

Hans Werdehausen. Picture

erly style. Before that he concentrated for quite some time on the characteristic objects of industrial areas, on high tension cables, which he called *Ideale Mastenversammlungen* (ideal mast ensembles) integrating them like symbols. *Heinrich Siepmann* (b. 1904) favors more regular forms. In the beginning he placed geometric color planes side by side; later he used elongated bunches of lines in diffuse colors.

In Düsseldorf the situation of the young painter became increasingly lively. In 1952 a spark from the flame of French Tachism ignited a passion for subjective expression. "Group 53" was formed. Very few of its members were over thirty-five. *Gerhard Hoehme* (b. 1920), *Winfried Gaul* (b. 1928) and above all *Peter Brüning* (b. 1929) have achieved a

Gustav Deppe. Constant Rise and Fall, 1957

Reich an der Stolpe. Rhythm

Gerhard Hoehme. Painting, 1957

Heinrich Siepmann. Reaching Up

degree of fame. Among others who joined were Herbert Kaufmann, Heinz Mack, Rolf Sackenheim, Gerhard Wind, Otto Piene and Peter Royen. K. F. Dahmen and Hermann Dienz also deserve mention. Outside the circle, but bound in friendship to this young western-oriented group, we find the older painters Emil Schumacher and Wilhelm Wessel.

Emil Schumacher (b. 1912) has a special talent for extracting the essence of color and material by setting them against each other. He alternates surfaces cracked by twisting streams of color with the resulting ridges raised above these color beds. The possible threat of chaos is ruled out by his personality. The palette is composed of gray or various shades of

Winfried Gaul. Litho

brown, and all matter comes to life when a little sienna turns up beside cobalt blue, some white beside an earthy green, a dab of crimson lake beside a strip of ochre. Lately the many accents show a tendency to unite mysteriously, becoming "continents" which vanish into empty space as they approach the frame, rather like his *Tastobjekte* (Tactile Objects). Under this heading Schumacher creates compositions of fluid masses of paper, wire and color, resulting in something resembling a relief map with elevations, furrows and ominous craters where the shadows collect.

Peter Brüning
Picture, 1958

Rudi Baerwind. All in Red, 1957

times presses fragments of glass and porcelain which glow in these alien surroundings like something precious, archeological shards in an abandoned grave.

While anti-constructivist painting had one focal point in Westphalia (the Junger Westen group cited) and one in Düsseldorf (Group 53), another center developed in Frankfurt, around the painters Götz and Schultze in particular.

In his best pictures, *K. O. Götz* (b. 1914) confines himself mainly

Emil Schumacher. Tactile Object

Wilhelm Wessel (b. 1904) started off conventionally as a graphic artist and only in recent years has given himself up completely to painting. "Earth mould, the substance of my cigar ash, the patina of a stretch of asphalt, excite me today…" In these, he believes, there may be "more general metaphysical content than in the portrait of a person or in the material of our culture." Wessel feels a part of what was called in France *un art autre* (Dubuffet, Fautrier, Tapies). Substance demands form in its own right. Lately he has been using synthetic resin as a binding medium, a material which thickens to a barklike consistency. He covers it only very sparingly with color, achieving curious relief effects. Into this earthlike material he some-to black and white but succeeds nevertheless in unfolding broad, space-creating movements. These are painted with brushes of various widths, rubber erasers and cloth, spontaneously swelling and diminishing, yet always balanced. His spatial swirls sometimes achieve a melancholy expressiveness, almost balladlike in tone, and should not for a moment be categorized as Tachism. After most of Götz's work was destroyed in the bombing of Dresden, he published a highly stimulating journal, *Meta* (from 1948 to 1953), and subsequently worked on a similar publication, *Cobra*. He also edited *Das Bräutliche Antlitz* by René Char, and *Behaarte Herzen* by Hans Arp. He designed a *Fakturenfibel* (facture primer), but the manuscript was also destroyed.

Otto Greis (b. 1913) paints demonic fetishes based on silver-gray, black, white, red and ochre tones. His aim is to "give sensual values to the abstract picture and deliver it from its isolation." In Paris, where he spends some time every year, he is especially attracted to the Musée de l'Homme, "where the sculpture of primeval races still strongly radiates human values, even if we are no longer able to grasp the meaning."

Bernhard Schultze (b. 1915) was influenced by Wols, but transformed his ideas into a more colorful, romantic form of expression. In his pictures we find no active convolutions of form but painterly,

Wilhelm Wessel. Brick-red Field, 1956

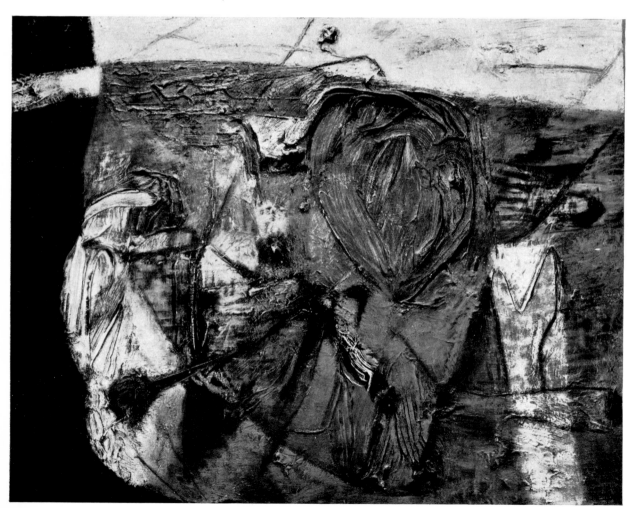

K. O. Götz
Gouache, 1956

muted colors. However, the "material process" demands expression: "Matter wants to stream, to flow back and forth." Some of his paintings look like topographical maps seen from the air. "The more technical the world around us becomes, the more vehement grows my desire to burst it asunder and seek the amorphous base of form."

287

As long as the painter sought to reproduce the visible, he often tried to hide the working procedure; now, however, the abstract painter delighted in revealing all his strokes, thickening, streaking and dissolving the color. The procedure itself had become expression and picture. Since Schultze works without any strong specific color contrasts but does employ priming and glaze, he strengthens the appearance of his work with relief effects. Cloth rags are laid on the surface and covered with so much paint that they look melted in, without the sharp play of contrasts seen in earlier work of this kind, such as that of Schwitters.

Heinz Kreutz (b. 1923) works with similar compositions, which tend, however, to become analagous to

Otto Greis. December, 1956

288

Right: Emil Schumacher. Picture, 1957

Bernhard Schultze
Irradiated, 1957

a real sky with clouds. *Reich an der Stolpe* (b. 1912), who lives in the Taunus Mountains, is an experimenter who has tried many techniques, also working with *objets trouvés et corrigés*.

In the extreme southwest, on Lake Constance, nonobjective painting was first represented by Ackermann and Bissier. The paintings of *Max Ackermann* (b. 1887) derived less from expressive precepts

Max Ackermann. Original Cell, 1952

Hölzel, Ackermann for years devoted himself to the theoretical question of a counterpoint system for line and color, and was
himself an inspiring teacher. "The dominating color always demands a good position
because it is the one that does the talking,
and a reading of the picture begins with it."
Julius Bissier (1893–1965) began with landscapes in the New Objectivity style; then,
through his friendship with Schlemmer and
Baumeister, he progressed farther afield. Of
his development he said, "In my youth I
thought I could best capture the essence of
things in the beliefs and forms of the old
masters... but many years of struggle with
nature led only to my defeat before the
schism existing between the power of the
object and the intrusive, unavoidable demands made by the law of the picture...
Since 1933 I have concentrated on a play of
entirely private symbols. I repeated these

Julius Bissier. Wash, 1953

than from Hölzel's system of color harmonics. For
a long time Ackermann was overshadowed by
Baumeister. His forms and colors were coarser and
less balanced, yet often sensously fresh. His pictures had a certain gaiety. But in recent years
they have grown more severe in composition; the
planes are larger and more even in color, and his
earlier, rather drastic expressiveness is being replaced by a luminous stillness. Like his teacher

290

Alo Altrip
G. 116

Fritz Landwehr. In Color between
Black and Brown, 1958

symbols over and over again in wash, in the style of the Oriental painters, clarifying and improving them with graphic calligraphy. In 1945 I decided to use color instead of wash... These objects have nothing to do with external nature, not with water, earth nor air; yet somehow they contain all these elements."

Georg Müller-Hufschmid (b. 1890), residing in Karlsruhe, paints weblike compositions in pallid colors. Their effect is existential and dreamlike. Related, quietly spun forms are repeated over and over again. *Rudolf Scharpf*, from

Gerhard Wind. Figuration H. IV

Wilhelm Imkamp. Moon-cat, 1952

292

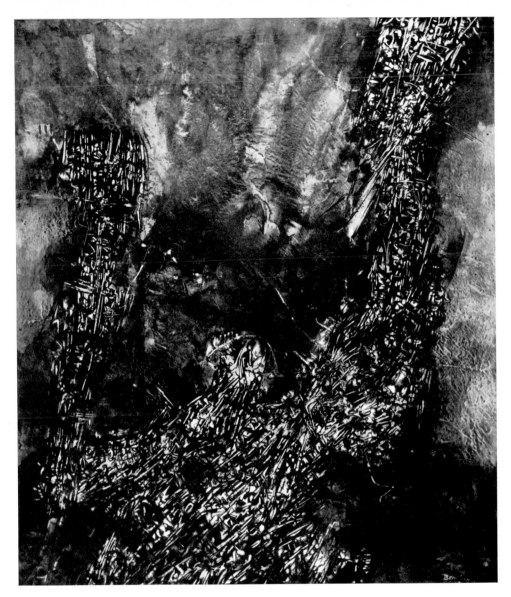

Klaus Bendixen
Transformation, 1960

a point of departure in the graphic arts, makes his strands swing in a more curvilinear fashion. *Alo Altrip* (b. 1906), who lives in Wiesbaden, came to nonobjective painting in 1939 and expresses himself today practically without color. Instead he has introduced a richer inner linearism in the wide sweep of his pictures. *Wilhelm Imkamp* (b. 1906) lives in Stuttgart. The clear construction of his paintings is sustained by a shell-like yet soft decorative tonality. *Boris Kleint* (b. 1903) began to paint under Itten's influence. He has taught at the School of Art and Handicrafts in Saarbrücken, and has worked on a systematic *Bildlehre* (Pictorial Science). Although he paints nonobjectively, he also explores new possibilities for objective presentation with his students. In these explorations he sometimes succeeds,

Claus
Jürgen-
Fischer
Towered, 1957

"but for the most part my efforts fail because the great interest of the young painter lies in abstract painting." Kleint creates in various ways–geometrically, with freely scattered forms, in small format or on large wall areas.

Several young painters in southwest Germany are directly or indirectly connected with the activity of Willi Baumeister as former teacher at the Stuttgart Academy. His inspiration radiates in many directions. *Klaus Bendixen* (b. 1924) came via Cubism to a division of his pictures into large planes which move back and forth in reaction to each other, thereby creating an effect of overlapping, but always preserving the picture surface. Dissociated textures lend irony to the composition. Forms, at first definite, then dissolved, confront us with mysterious symbolism. *Fritz Seitz* (b. 1926) favors heavy volumes and occasionally tries his hand at the human figure. *Claus Jürgen-Fischer* (b. 1930) seeks an intermediary path between organization and irrationality, between the specifically drawn and the painted parts of the picture. He became prominent as a result of an article he wrote attacking the philosopher Martin Heidegger, and, filling the triple role of artist, critic and philosopher, edits, together with Leopold Zahn, the journal *Das Kunstwerk*. The paintings of *G. K. Pfahler* (b. 1926) frequently remind one of densely filled geological formations, whereas in the work of *G. C. Kirchberger* (b. 1928) and *F. Sieber* (b. 1925) we are faced with magnetic fields of tension. *Heinrich Wildemann*, who teaches at the Stuttgart Academy, is trying to develop a style in which the paint itself will be expressive solely in terms of shifting color planes.

294

Emil Schumacher. Xerxes, 1960

Gottfried Wiegand
Pen drawing,
1957

Hugbert Brouwer
Forbidden Area,
1958

Gerhard Baumgärtel. Picture 20/65

Horst Antes. Interior IV (Geometrician)

Painting in Germany Since 1955 by Juliane Roh

Afterlife of the Art Informel

The continuation of *Art Informel* is clearly established in Germany. This was demonstrated in an exhibition of German painting arranged by Franz Roh for the Salon Comparaison in Paris in 1964, of which Restany said, "Recent German painting has not yet had its crisis of abstraction." In this representative exhibition every variety of abstract art was included, through every stage, culminating in what may be called Phantom Painting that juggled with fantastic recollections of reality. However, it completely overlooked the latest stylistic innovation that dealt with the consumer's world and life in a megalopolis, a development that has exploded *art informel* and left it looking like a mass of broken egg shells.

Collage and *décollage* were differently interpreted in Germany. In these the world of reality was not regarded as antagonistic to the *informel*, as, for instance, it was by the French *nouveaux réalistes*, but, on the contrary, as a part of it. What had been purely abstract structure now incorporated broken elements of the representational world. What had fallen into ruins could be assimilated, and that which had served formerly to symbolize the transitory by its construction alone was now given expressive implication through the injection of "the ruins of technology."

K. F. Dahmen (b. 1917) arranges rusty iron, rotted rope, torn canvas and old scraps of writing to form a poetry of ruin. Until 1965 he stressed the informal structure, but in his new 1966 montages, objects take control. Pieces of once functioning, practical apparatuses are here arranged like prehistoric fossils. The articles of civilization have, as it were, outlived man. Now they appear as diagrams, the signs of which can no longer be deciphered. An informal Nature-Romanticism has become a romanticism of the decayed artifact. A glimmer of immaterial color, no longer connected with any objects, asserts itself as the last existing force.

In Germany, Action Painting has developed along lines of its own, different from those of other countries. We find the grand gesture expressed freely only by K. O. Götz (see p. 287). With painters like *Gerhard Baumgärtel* (b. 1924), *Walter Raum* (b. 1923), *Ernst Wild* (b. 1924), *Dieter Stöver* (b. 1922), and *Hans Joachim Strauch* (b. 1930), all of whom live in Munich, a motor gesticulation becomes inhibited and is interrupted by elements of order that seek to arrest these motive energies. Raum confines all black-and-white contrasts in a powerful script, whereas Strauch tends to force symbols and gestures into a serial order Wild tames his *élan informel* with a geometric framework or a strong chromatic base. Baumgärtel reduces impulsive movement to primeval gesture in which "the buried mathematical core will reveal itself again." The spontaneity of the gesture is preserved but limited to a definite form. The struggle between pictorial antagonists takes place on the abstract white surface. The colors do not glow sensuously but with a cool fire. *Irma Hünerfauth*, also from Munich, belongs in this category. She proceeded from the creation of graphic scaffolding in space, which she has subjected to *informel* accents. In her latest works, "radiograms" of objects haunt this spatial tension as if held and drawn by invisible powers.

K. F. Dahmen. Object Picture, 1965

Walter Raum. Picture VII, 1967

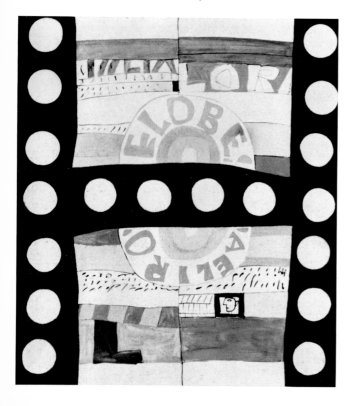

Beside this dramatic style we find a quieter wing of the *art informel*, which includes Schreiner, Schreiter and young Bernd Völkle. *Hans Schreiner* (b. 1930) modulates dark earth colors into suspended masses; compact layers float in a sluggish stream. *Johannes Schreiter* (b. 1930) has developed a process with which he achieves subtle color transitions. He ignites white paper at the edges and the smoke creates the finest color nuances, from dark brown to white. He arranges these scraps of color on black cardboard, in groups and rows, a process which results in a fascinating play of dark and light that could not be conjured up with any comparable method of painting. The strength of *Bernd Völkle* (b. 1938) lies in a completely varied color key which becomes unified in a single grandiose free formation.

Abstract Expressionism and Phantom Painting

In contrast to *art informel,* in so-called Abstract Expressionism a strong unbroken tonality and a form world somewhat akin to the painting of children play an important role. Here two German centers emerge–a Munich circle, formed by the group *Spur* (Track), which owes a great deal to the Dane, Asger Jorn, and a second group in Karlsruhe, less closely knit. Spur put quite a few of Jorn's esthetic theories into action, for instance the unconditional adherence to teamwork and the acceptance of experiment and play as necessary for the realization of a new art form that was to permeate all life. The results are basic esthetic experiences in the elementary use of form and color, which are intended to enable man to endure life in the city and consumer world. To this end Spur developed playful forms which deal with modern life more naively than Pop Art, at the same time also more artistically. Here the painters *Heimred Prem* (b. 1934), *Helmut Sturm* (b. 1932) and *H. P. Zimmer* (b. 1934) play leading roles. They have developed their individual styles yet are not averse to bringing their personal research back into the collective effort. Together, in 1963, they painted a huge hall in the Palazzo Grassi in Venice, and at the *Biennale* of Youth in Paris they showed their original *Spurbau* (Spur Structure). *Anja Decker* transforms stimuli of the Spur group into large-scale encounters of color. The group *Geflecht* (Interweave), which grew out of Spur, tries to combine sculpture and painting in an expressionistic fashion by dynamically intertwining strongly colored wood and metal strips.

Among the Karlsruhe Neo-Expressionists we find the former Grieshaber pupils *Walter Stöhrer* (b. 1937) and *Horst Antes* (b. 1936), and also *Herbert Kitzel* (b. 1928), who comes from East Germany, and his pupil *Hans Baschang* (b. 1937). Kitzel has let his figural motives become increasingly absorbed in a whirling maelstrom. For a while *Stürzende* (Falling Things) were intended, but soon nothing was left but the motion in the paint itself of falling and plunging. Baschang at first followed Kitzel with his frenzied diagonal brushstrokes, but he succeeded in arresting this motion and ordering it in fields of bright color. With powerful streams of color Stöhrer creates an extensive field of pictorial action. In the work of Horst Antes, a mythical figure slowly emerges out of a basically informal shifting of color. One-eyed monsters with powerful heads and long trunklike noses are perched on massive columnar legs, and on a close-up view threaten the observer. Later they appear as precise, plastic forms placed in front of abstract color signals. At present his development flows in the direction of an almost "classical" tranquility–the colors have always been radiant–and the monster becomes an emblem of burlesque.

Phantom Painting offers further varieties. *Piet Moog* (b. 1932) lets grotesque figurations issue from a dark world of color. *Jan Voss* (b. 1936), who spends most of his time in Paris, employs the scribbling style of children for a more narrative expression, and *Siegfried Kischko* (b. 1934) invented a fabulous creature with which he fills long narrative strips. *Herbert Schneider* (b. 1924) started off with a lavish language of informal signs, then connected them in strictly observed rows. Lately he has been enlivening these rows and compartments with a personal variation of Pop Art, inspired by the fresh colors and the naive script-and-picture language of peasant ex-votos, which he connects humorously with everyday events.

The works of *Reinhard Pfennig* (b. 1914) and *Peter Schubert* (b. 1929) border sometimes on Surrealism; this applies also to the ghostly world of signs of *Edgar Schmandt* (b. 1929) of Mannheim.

"Spur" Group
Spurbau, 1963

Surrealism has many faces. If one includes under the heading work which emphasizes the fantastic and suprareal, then Surrealism can "happen" in every style. In Abstract Expressionism, phantomlike formations sometimes crop up which are difficult to interpret. The open form of this style does not allow a more precise definition. For the true Surrealists, however, it remains characteristic that dreams and visions necessitate detailed reproduction. Most Surrealists are virtuoso draftsmen who transfer their anxieties to paper with great accuracy. Frequently perversities and cruelty are presented with so much esthetic charm that one feels the artist was bent on finding, via a detour through beauty, a *modus vivendi* that would make it possible to endure life in a world of demons. If one compares how voluptuously the Middle Ages depicted the terror of hell (Dante above all), then the only difference in contemporary versions is that the surrealist artists of today paint their own private hells.

Two older Surrealists should be included here. Both became well known to the broader public comparatively late–*Hans Bellmer* (b. 1902) because he has been living like a recluse in Paris since 1938, and *Richard Oelze* (b. 1900) because he lives in a painters' village near Bremen from which he only recently emerged. Both have in common a compulsive fixation on their themes. Bellmer expresses a witchlike pansexualism in his drawings; in Oelze's pallid-tone paintings, his fantasy circles around an ogling ground figure from whom issue cloud formations and entire landscapes. Herbert Pée wrote about Bellmer, "His drawings are labyrinths... everything flows. A hell of passions, as with Hieronymus Bosch, a worship of the body combined with lust and horror." And Wieland Schmied wrote of Oelze in 1964, "With Oelze the forest has gone through many metamorphoses... At twilight all appearances move so near to each other, the woods seem to come so pressingly close, there is no escape."

Hans Bellmer
La petite chaise Napoléon III, 1956

Richard Oelze. Montereggio, 1959

Bernhard Schultze. La grande Malone, 1962

The fantastic sculptured surfaces of *Bernhard Schultze*, discussed earlier (see p. 286), also seem somehow connected with a forest-experience. He calls them *Migof*. Sweetly decaying colors wind through space and are linked to form an impenetrable weave, conjuring up memories of spectral roots from the legendary woods of Nordic prehistory.

Most of the German Surrealists come from the north. *Horst Janssen* (b. 1929) and *Paul Wunderlich* (b. 1929) live in Hamburg. Janssen is exclusively a graphic artist. He began with large woodcuts in which space was transposed into a willful linking of planes. In his etchings (since 1958) his themes become more eerie, his invention more grotesque. Everything is first neatly skeletonized in thin strokes which are then drawn together into crinkly light-and-shade areas that are interwoven in a labyrinthine way. Wherever his form-dissolving luminosity does not penetrate, a gnawed face, an animal or human skull shimmers through.

Horst Janssen. Selbstbildnis

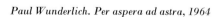

Paul Wunderlich. Per aspera ad astra, 1964

Wunderlich also celebrates a macabre world of death. Transparent bodies are laid on top of vials and retorts so that they seem to be suspended in space, transformed into homunculi and arranged in an almost heraldic fashion. Painting in precious irridescent colors on dark grounds, he achieves an overall effect of clear solemnity. If sometimes Janssen is in danger of a supra-sensibility that could lead to total disintegration, Wunderlich is threatened by an estheticized posture in his meticulously arranged *mementi mori*.

The borderline between Surrealism and a fantastic style of painting that uses signs and symbols is fluid. Whereas the true Surrealists exist to some extent under the dictatorship of their neurotic fantasies so that their creatures make themselves independent, rather like the sorcerer's apprentice, the symbolists among them connect their signs with a rich association of ideas. In *Rainer Küchenmeister* (b. 1926), who lives in Paris, ideas of root, seed-germ and shell are joined in a kind of *Keimgestalt* (germinal figure). In his watercolors it appears in delicate linear branches and precious blendings of color; in his oil paintings it is more powerfully abstract and raised to monumental proportions. In *Konrad Klapheck* (b. 1935) some of the discreet object-magicality of *arte metafisica* recurs, applied now mainly to technological subject matter. Apparatuses stand, big and still, in a close format. One senses the invisible powers emanating from them. Suddenly they are personalities with human attributes. The Portuguese, *Costa Pinheiro* (b. 1932), who lives in Munich, assembles abstract and objective signs in dreamlike pictorial riddles. Their color refinement is just as persuasive as their formal structure. *Dieter Krieg* (b. 1937) finds his symbols in the sterile perfection of today's hospitals. People, bundled and bound up in white mountains of cushions, surrounded by cold bars or hidden behind towels, die a hygienic, immaculate, clinical death.

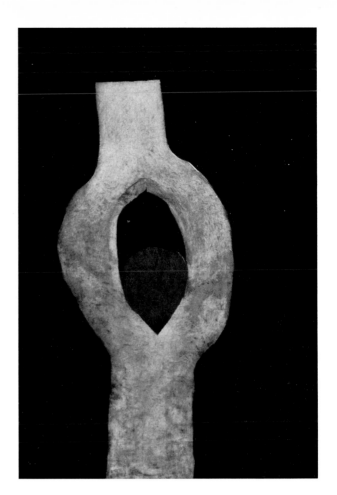

Rainer Küchenmeister. Body, 1964

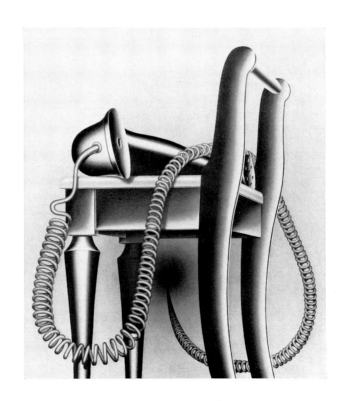

Konrad Klapheck. The Capitulation, 1966

Pop, Happenings and Collage

Pop Art came to Germany relatively late and remained an import for which there was not much demand. A group of artists, gathered around the Grossgörschen Gallery, adopted the "Consumer Style," with its advertising effects and emphasis on sex, often in a highly agressive, ironic form. The most outstanding of this group seem to be *Hans Jürgen Diehl* (b. 1940) and *Werner Berges* (b. 1941). *Lambert Wintersberger* (b. 1941) of Berlin goes beyond Pop, creating bizarre erotic scenes in which the shock is sweetened by the elegant softness of the color. Others confront Pop elements with Expressionist gestures, and create surprise by abrupt changes of style in the same picture. Here we might cite *Uwe Lausen* (b. 1939), who began with a vigorous Abstract Expressionism but was later influenced by the British painter Francis Bacon. A demonic, destructive streak, with convulsively entangled forms, gradually consumed the radiant gaiety of his colors. He subsequently clarified his pictures under the influence of the flat, poster style of Pop, but the new pictures, too, are dominated by an oppressive mood.

Sigmar Polke (b. 1941) uses a coarse dot-screen which causes the reality lying beneath to disappear. *Gerhard Richter* (b. 1932) paints fuzzy black-and-white photographs in gigantic formats. Here too a diffuse structure alienates reality in a very simple fashion. The simplicity of the procedure is somehow disarming–poetry "off the rack."

Frequently the aim of the Pop artist is to obliterate a reality that has already penetrated the picture, or at least to crowd it back, and this purpose is served by overpainting, tearing and pasting over.

Uwe Lausen
Geometer 66

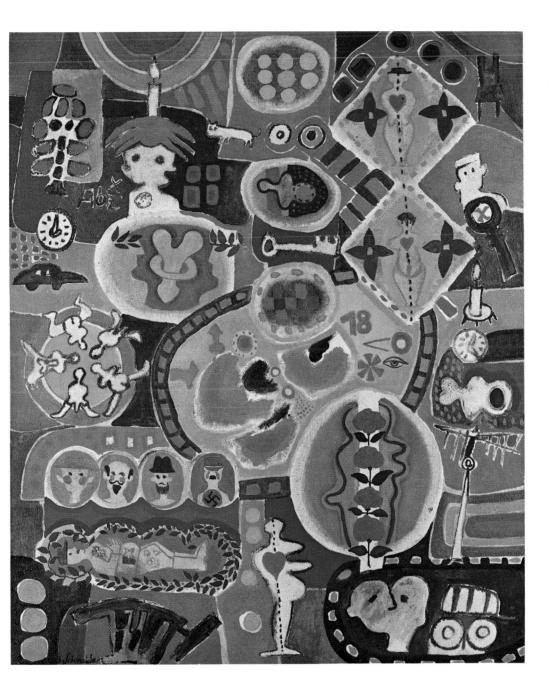

Herbert Schneider. Panopticon, 1967

Georg Pfahler. Spirit of Reality 50, 1964

Décollage, on the other hand, is supposed to lay
bare something that lies at the bottom. The veil
of abstract dreams is torn; behind it, the banality
of everyday life becomes visible.

In the case of *Herbert Kaufmann* (b. 1924) the
former tendency prevails. In his columnar drums
(Litfassäule), for example *Hommage à Litfass*, the
reality of old advertising kiosks is effective as a
dreamlike memory. The whole thing becomes the
kaleidoscope of a bygone world of enticement.
In his décollages *K. H. Hödicke* (b. 1938) strips off
advertisements, adding his own painted connecting
passages. In his warm colors, crass effects are
tranquilized, as if filtered to give esthetic pleasure.
Wolf Vostell (b. 1932) is quite different and his
approach is emphatically aggressive. His décollages reveal even when they delete. For the most
part we are dealing in his case with scores for
Happenings, with a quasi map of planned events
which are corrected by him as he goes along,
and also by the Happening itself. Vostell has
presented many Happenings in Germany, and
made a name for himself in New York with his
play, "For dogs and Chinese not allowed," which
was presented in the Something-else Gallery. The
sculptor *Joseph Beuys* became prominent in the
Rhineland as a producer of shocking Happenings.
That Pop and the Happening are more strongly

Karl Horst Hödicke. Passage II, 1964

represented in the Rhineland may be connected with the historic figure of Till Eulenspiegel, as well
as with the carnival traditions of that region. *H. P. Alvermann* (b. 1931), also a Rhinelander, combines
Pop with a moral involvement. Through shocking found objects which he builds into his pictures,
he speaks out against the inertia of the privileged groups.

In contrast, *Peter Klasen* (b. 1935), who lives in Paris, has no intention of shocking anyone with his
elegant and urbane collages. He is concerned with "the definition of the individual who has been reduced
to the level of a consumer." *Siegfried Neuenhausen* (b. 1931), again a Rhinelander, wants to master
artistically the sensational aspects of Pop, its obliteration of the borderlines between reality and illusion,
between fanciful and real life. He works with papier-maché, which permits him "to remain as amorphous
or to become as precise as the work at hand demands." Actually his effects rest for the most part on an
ironic substitution of values–a head may be perfectly flat, while a fall of hair is represented wholly
three-dimensionally in the foreground.

New Abstractions

Whereas Pop has become popular in Germany only since about 1963, everything related in the broadest sense to the "New Abstraction" has enjoyed a longer and more independent tradition. It may be recalled that *Rupprecht Geiger* (see p. 268) was constructing his quiet, colorful walls while the whole world around him was engaged with Tachism. His influence on some members of the young generation is revealed above all in their effort to make color's qualities of light an experience in themselves. Within this trend we can distinguish three different tendencies:

a) Work with unstructured color planes, more often than not in clear contrasts, in which symmetry and decorative harmony are again given an expressive function.

b) A tendency toward monochromy, toward the overevaluation of a single color, which develops a painterly or structural life of its own.

c) Manipulation of lines and the refraction of the surface to achieve instability of form; this may be extended to create a play of real light and motion (Op Art).

Among the painters who follow the first tendency, *Georg Pfahler* (b. 1926), who lives in Stuttgart, has made a name for himself. About 1960 he began to draw colors together to form coordinated blocks, spatially isolated, in an unstable equilibrium but related. Since about 1963 Pfahler has been painting smooth color planes, directly adjoining, across the entire surface. These color areas seem to control autonomously the degree of their expansion, and to keep their balance in suspension and thereby Pfah-

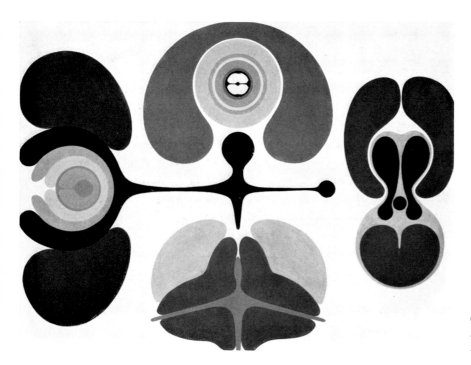

Gernot Bubenik
Natural History—Realization II,
1966

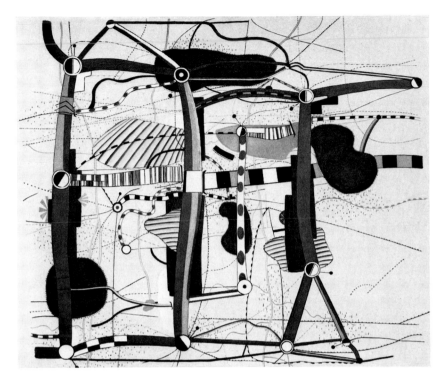

Peter Brüning
Légendes 14/64

ler avoids any oscillation of color at the edges. In his case color is not equal to light but an independent quantity. *Bernd Damke* (b. 1939) of Berlin works in a similar style, but his more luminous color areas, which sometimes swell chromatically, create more space. *Gernot Bubenik* (b. 1942) of Berlin connects the life of color planes with forms and formulas taken from seed-germ physiology. Genes and seed-buds are arranged to form burgeoning blossoms. A form-world never used before, culled from medical textbooks, is here given artistic importance. According to Bubenik, "Where the interest of the scientist stops, my work begins." *Winfried Gaul* (see pp. 283, 284) makes the most of the signaling function inherent in colors. He would like to carry over into the nonutilitarian world of art the accomplishments of our traffic signs. But the bare optic signal alone, with no secret behind it, is quickly exhausted, which is why these superficially sensational objects are closer to Pop Art than to the New Abstraction. *Peter Brüning* (see p. 283) proved that a master of abstract lyricism could also shift to harder colors and technological symbols without losing any of the enigmatic quality of his work. Roads and signs on maps become metaphors of a personal cartography, reformed into new ciphers for the ancient landscape of the soul.

Werner Schreib (see p. 241) has turned to using the husks of our consumer world and impresses them as ciphers on a plastic foundation. One might call the results *Tontafeln*, the "clay tablets" of our times–the "accidents" of breakage and rubble are delivered right along with the rest of the record.

Paul Uwe Dreyer (b. 1939) and *Heinz Kreutz* (see p. 288) have revived phases of Constructivism, the former by constructing scaffoldlike supports out of angular elements, the latter by assembling arcs and circles to form a delicate spherical architecture.

Rolf Gunter Dienst (b. 1939), *Jürgen Claus* (b. 1935) and *Arnold Leissler* (b. 1939) are trying to revive the use of ornament. Dienst pulls stripes, filled with so-called logograms, like a scroll across a monochrome surface. Leissler encloses his individual signs with parallel borders that look like neon lights, and Jürgen Claus fills sections of his magical sign world with symmetrically organized patterns. The ornamental accessory is always brought out of the frame to which it was traditionally confined into the picture where it is transformed into an independent expressive factor.

Monochrome Painting, the second direction followed by some of the younger painters of the New Abstraction, was seen first in an exhibition which Kultermann assembled in 1960 for the museum in Leverkusen. The older *Johannes Gecelli* (b. 1925) used monochromy for objective purposes—with delicate contours a figure took shape out of the independent life of the color. *Bernd Berner* (b. 1930) and *Klaus Jürgen-Fischer* (see p. 293) both began with a delicate color weave which created a spatial vibrato that either communicated directly with the color plane surrounding it or was stopped by painted-frame-motif. Here the problem of picture and frame is stated anew: a vibration area is the nucleus of an all-inclusive movement which the edge of the picture continues in augmented form, just as sound waves are amplified by the megaphone. *K. H. Graubner* was absorbed by similar problems. *Eduard Micus* (b. 1925) divides his canvases in two, as in an open book. The side he keeps empty is pure white, while the other is partially

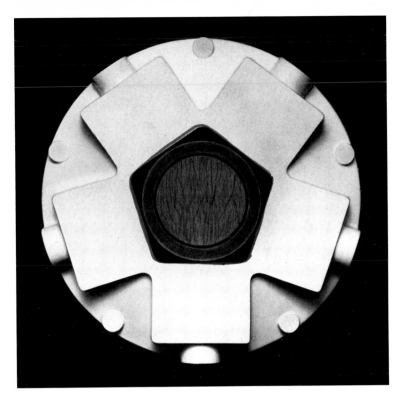

Klaus Jürgen-Fischer
Double-picture, 1967
Mannheim, Galerie Lauter

filled with colored stripes. Both sides are given a special stimulus by seams, soft plastic impulses resulting from the material itself.

Lothar Quinte (b. 1923) developed color out of the opposite, shadow. Glazed, painted black stripes become increasingly light toward the center and are suddenly pushed apart by a radiant red. *Reiner Jochims* (b. 1935) sees color as light in space. He too gathers light out of deepening shadows, which change softly but constantly, with many coats of glaze, so that his pictures are not much lighter than the cloudy sky in winter that borrows its light from the reflection of the snow. *Raimund Girke* (b. 1930) used to paint pure, delicately structured white areas. His latest works, however, toy more strongly with the mobile effects of optical illusion.

In our third group we are dealing with Op Art only in a limited sense. Almost all the artists under this heading start with the premise that light and color may change any given form without motion necessarily taking place. One might say that the triumph of light over static forms has been reached. In 1958, *ZERO* was founded, a periodical published in Düsseldorf by Otto Piene and Heinz Mack, who were joined in 1961 by Günther Uecker. The Frenchman Yves Klein was working in the Rhineland at the time. Together they dreamed of breathtaking Happenings, for instance of sculpture made of "air, water, ice and fire, that would be in a state of constant flux." In the ZERO program you could read, "ZERO is silence. ZERO is the beginning... the sky is above ZERO. The night–the eye–silently." Here a longing for quiet and contemplation is revealed which undoubtedly is linked to the tradition of German romanticism.

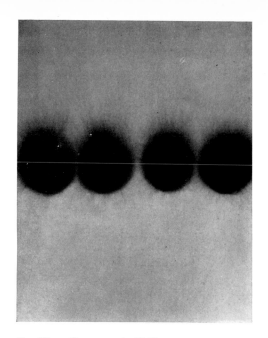

Otto Piene. Rouge et noir, 1961

fluctuation of light and shade is created which may be rhythmically manipulated. Mack dreams of gigantic reflector walls in the desert or on the sea that could magnify his play of light to cosmic proportions.

Günther Uecker (b. 1930) creates a play of light and shade through a forest of white nails on a white ground. At first he placed his columns of nails in strict, orderly rows, later he let them undulate slightly on a colored foundation. The white structures are made to oscillate by a change of lighting, without making a move of their own. *Hans Alber Walter* (b. 1925) transforms effects taken from Piene's Light Ballet into a skillful light-and-shade painting.

Heinz Mack. Light Peaks and Light Fields, 1963

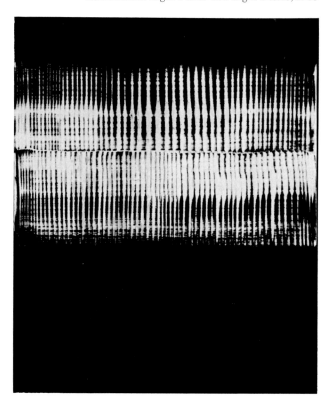

Otto Piene (b. 1928) lets the sensation of light and dark take place through light itself. In smoke pictures and fire-gouaches, something of the generative process of light actually is precipitated. In the finest gradations and dispersions, luminosity is created, to all appearances out of itself. To achieve this effect, Piene proceeds from a dark or light focus which radiates toward the edges, thus repeating in an artistic experiment something that takes place in the cosmos all the time. He has also created a "Light Ballet" in which he sends rays through perforated, rotating sheets of metal. *Heinz Mack* (b. 1931) works with aluminum and plexiglass which reflect the light like lightning. Through its own rotations, or through the motion of the observer, a constant

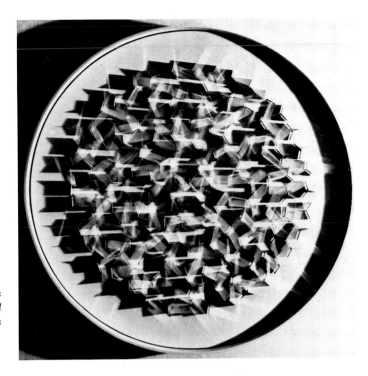

Gerhard von Graevenitz
Kinetic Object with Tri-winged
Elements

Another group, residing in south Germany, is working with related problems. They achieve kinetic effects primarily by interfering with a given order through black-and-white or colored elements. Symmetrical surface patterns force the eye to see dominant arrangements, which however, do not remain stable. This results in an illusory, jerky motion which may also be achieved with color. (The phenomenon of the after-image in the eye.) *Klaus Staudt* (b. 1932), *Rudolf Kämmer* (b. 1935) and *Roland Helmer* (b. 1940) are experimenting in this direction. *Ludwig Wilding* (b. 1927) creates net structures which artfully overlap, so that manifold perspective illusions are created. He carries these effects over into the third dimension by shifting a transparent, striped pattern in front of another lying behind (screen effect). *Gerhard von Graevenitz* transfers the principle of instability to mechanically mobile equipment. In contrast to other kineticists, his constructions are extremely simple; the almost magical effect is therefore all the more surprising. In this connection we must also mention *Uli Pohl* (b. 1935) who succeeded in creating the first actual light-sculpture. Whereas most other sculptors use reflected light to dematerialize form, Pohl hit upon the lens effect of cut glass to create illusory forms of light. He bores through a cube of glass, forming an arched hole. This creates, in effect, a lens that produces an image of an enlarged and changeable light form within the glass block.

This severe form of Op Art, which is not concerned primarily with sensations of movement but rather with silent, meditative effects, is very German. Here stimuli of Albers and Moholy have been revived in a different form.

Graphic Artists

Without regard for their stylistic affiliations, a few graphic artists are here listed separately. *Karl Bohrmann* (b. 1928) has attracted attention with his sensitive etchings, but his calligraphy, when compared for instance with that of Sonderborg (see p. 273), is weaker and more inhibited. Each stroke goes its own way. When two strokes move too close to each other, the result is a fragile explosion. *Gerhard Altenbourg* who lives in East Germany, may also be counted among the pure draftsmen. His minute, frail calligraphy is often used to create unusual landscapes. *Fritz Meckseper* (b. 1936) a North German, stands alone. He fills his subtle etchings with objects from the past—fire balloons, old maps and apparatuses, which he assembles to form mysterious, silent still lifes. A number of this group let loose their fantasy in letters and script—*Josua Reichert* (b. 1937) in powerful letter-woodcuts, *Carl Friedrich Claus* (b. 1930) in a minute script, *Gerhard Hoehme* (see p. 283) in big newspaper collages.

A unique case is the late work of *Alfred Kremer* (1895–1965) who painted conventional still lifes until he was stricken by a fatal illness. A year before his death he was possessed by a demonic urge to draw. He filled hundreds of sheets with *Gestaltzeichen* (figural signs) in a klexographic or ink-blot style. Skeletonized hands appear, symbolic birds and death-ships, the hanged, sun-wheels. A whole arsenal of archetypes rose up out of the depths of his subconscious, threatening the dying man with a shadowy power. These sheets are characterized by hallucinatory visions.

Karl Bohrmann. Etching, 1963

Bernd Berner. On Red

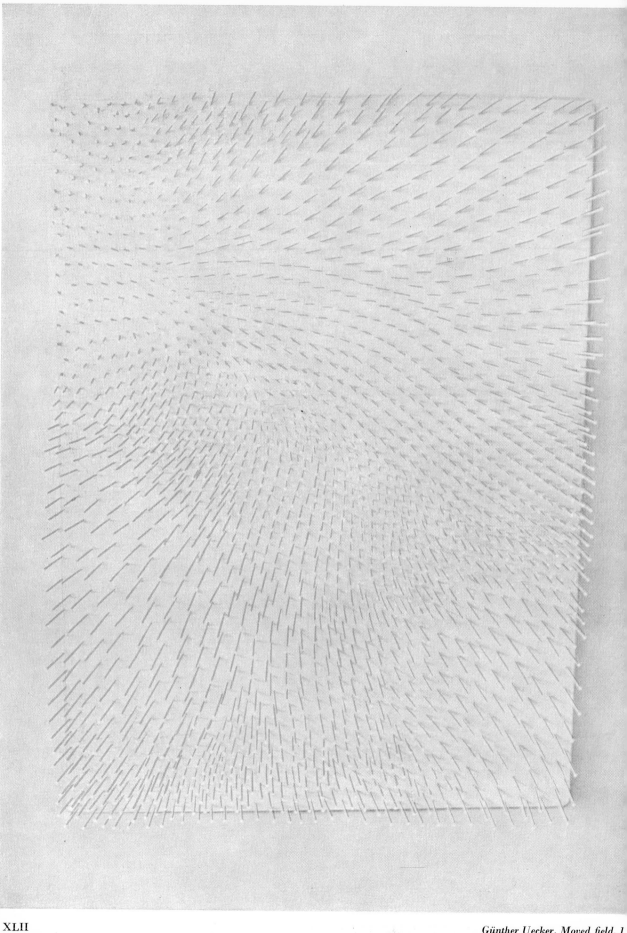

Günther Uecker. Moved field, 1

Fritz Meckseper. Philosopher's Stone, Etching, 1966

The reflections which summarize Franz Roh's review of painting in the twentieth century have lost none of their validity in the past decade. On the contrary, since the recent revival of a new representational style and a refreshed interest in kinetic art, they are more timely than ever. Therefore I would like to end with his conclusion from the earlier edition of this book.

"To sum up let it be said that it is not a sign of degeneration if today we find objective and nonobjective art existing side by side, since both satisfy different sectors of our being. The one will never be able to completely replace the other because point of departure and goal are so different. But hybridizations are possible, as is proved, for instance, by the late development of Max Ernst. In abstract painting we enjoy the fact that formal design or a construction in color has at last been freed of any specific relationship to a particular object. The result is that we experience a nonspecific pictorial organization without association or reference beyond itself, just as we experience it in music. In objective painting we are moved, contrarily, by constant reference to the representational world, and enjoy the interpretations and transformations undertaken by the painter. It should be possible for every richly endowed human

Alfred Kremer. As we live, so we strive, Drawing, 1964/65

being to be stimulated by both types of painting instead of bemoaning the fact, as many people do lately, that we are suffering from an impossible multiplicity of the arts.

"A comparative investigation should one day be undertaken into this plurality, which various epochs have experienced, for we are being deceived by misleading effects of the perspective of time. When we look down an avenue of poplars, the trees farthest away seem to be closer to each other. Similarly we tend to see the past as more cohesive, the present in which we live as more disintegrated.

"Because of the impetus toward motion which has also gripped the latest development of German painting, a big question looms on our horizon, one that was asked by Moholy as long as thirty years ago: Will this frenzy of motion, as captured in the single picture, perhaps be resolved in favor of the abstract film, in the actual motion of a colored play of lights, and like absolute music demand a passage of time? With such an eventuality painting need not entirely lose its specific meaning. The significance of the easel picture would still lie in its traditional ability to arrest and preserve dynamic form."

LINES OF DEVELOPMENT

The effect of the twentieth century revolution in sources, modes and media of expression was at first far stronger on painting than on sculpture. The latter, because of its three-dimensionality and the nature of its materials, is inherently more difficult to change. Nevertheless, Impressionism, Expressionism, Cubism, New Objectivity and Constructivism all influenced the outward forms of plastic creation, and ultimately both the traditional three-dimensionality and material solidity of sculpture were radically transformed... a development comparable to the transformation of the purpose of painting from realistic representation to nonobjective expression.

The relationship of sculpture to architecture also changed. After having become disassociated from other art forms in the course of the nineteenth century, repeated efforts were made in the twentieth to reunite sculpture with architecture. This endeavor, however, seems to succeed only in times of a unified *Weltanschauung*. Modern sculpture became isolated again because functionalist architecture, dictated by materials and modes of construction, rejected any additional embellishment.

In our technical age the materials of sculpture have undergone radical change. Marble and bronze, favored in the nineteenth century, are no longer the principal materials used; today's sculptor works with artificial stone, plastics, cement, iron, copper, brass, nickel, steel, aluminum, glass, wire, and with combinations of these materials. The urge has grown to explore their expressive possibilities. The traditional materials clay and wax were given a new meaning as the tendency toward abstraction gradually became dominant. And from the beginning of the century wood was used for a new, primitive form of utterance in the Expressionism of Barlach and the sculptural efforts of E. L. Kirchner and Heckel. But wood also served more traditional effects in the works of Mataré and Haizmann, who reveled in the polished texture of the veined material. Shortly after 1900 the group surrounding the then youthful Josef Wackerle favored clay for small-scale sculpture with richly colored glazes and neo-Baroque features; but Barlach's more expressive work in clay was done at the same time.

Gradually the growing tendency toward abstraction in painting became increasingly important for sculpture, and the sculptor began to turn away from the realistic human figures and animals emphasized by the nineteenth century. The torso became increasingly important. In the nineteenth century the conception prevailed that only the head as an independent fragment could function with expressive meaning for the whole body. Now, however, the sculptor no longer wanted to reproduce the body in its entirety

315

and turned to plastic configurations which played with the relationships between parts of the body. He began to leave out the head, the arms or the feet. Such a torso, he felt, reflected in its formal qualities the self-contained structure of life. Since all being was considered increasingly as a fragmentary manifestation, one could go so far as to say that the torso was a necessary symbolic form of a universal viewpoint.

Although the sculptor works with three-dimensional material and therefore with a displacement of space, a tendency crept in which was also to dominate painting: the sculptor wanted to perceive the body as something immaterial. The followers of Rodin had tried to dissolve the material core of sculpture by impressionistic means, through the absorption of light and air. This development was followed by the efforts of Lehmbruck, who made his figures increasingly thin so that what remained was hardly more than the expression of movement seeking loftier spheres. From this interpretation developed the abstractions which were to transform the play of human limbs into a system of rods, or–through Cubism–of juxtaposed concave and convex forms, for example in the works of Rudolf Belling. In some of his sculpture, Oscar Schlemmer reached a stage in which the human body, the quintessential theme of the nineteenth century, did not appear at all. As early as 1900 Hermann Obrist (see p. 397) had experimented in this direction. Today abstract sculpture is a secure and highly specialized field in which unspecified material and the individual artist's will to form have won out over nature.

In the field of abstract sculpture artists worked at first with solids that displaced space, but a few sculptors found this approach too material and massive. Therefore, the apparently paradoxical urge appeared –in Germany as elsewhere–to create "weightless" sculpture. Sticks, thin metal rods and discs were combined to embrace only an immaterial space and create a structure whose core was to be hollow space (as in the work of Hans Uhlmann). When such compositions were felt to be still too material and mechanical, experimentation began with a sculpture of wires (Norbert Kricke), in which nothing but thin lines moved through space. But in nonobjective sculpture these two possible ways of dealing with space do not exclude each other; they co-exist–the compact, space-denying, three-dimensional structure and the one that creates a *virtual* volume in the imagination.

The history of modern art is dominated by hidden references to earlier structural methods. In 1900, when Adolf Hildebrand was trying to free sculpture from the pursuit of a vague "message," such freedom was achieved by a more or less clandestine acceptance of Classicism, the Renaissance and modified Baroque influences. When the following generation of Lehmbruck, Barlach and Marcks found these traditions too sensual and earthy, and simultaneously tendencies toward simplification were growing, medieval art became covertly accepted and replaced the other sources. Out of this a leaning toward archaic Greek and Etruscan abstractions developed in various parts of Germany. But all these references to the past had to disappear as soon as nonobjective sculpture began to make its influence felt, for it created wholly new forms, without precedent in historic imagery.

Adolf Hildebrand (1847–1921) stood at the turning point between the nineteenth and twentieth centuries. He was related to the former in his sculpture and even more decidedly in his architectural designs, which resembled a repeater course in historic styles–as did all nineteenth-century architecture. Hildebrand's sculpture harks back to the themes and forms of Greco-Roman Classicism, the Renaissance or the Baroque period in its milder aspects. That such influences were scarcely noticeable at the turn of

Hildebrand
Archers,
1887–1888

the century is proof of how strongly the times were rooted in these traditions. But the efforts of Hildebrand, following those of Marées, to divert interest from the content to the fundamentals and essentials of vision, led toward the twentieth century. Hildebrand's *Problem der Form*, a very lucid piece of writing which appeared as early as 1893, was an auspicious opening for the many debates which still continue on the basic principles of artistic form. Altogether, the twentieth century to date may be understood as one continuous struggle over specific questions of visual creation, with ever changing efforts and results. Hildebrand, for example, declared that every piece of sculpture should be read in parallel planes from a single fixed, optimal viewpoint. With this unifying scheme he narrowed the whole nature of sculpture in the round by reducing it to a quasi bas-relief creation or wall sculpture. But three-dimensional sculpture should remain equally vivid from whatever side it is viewed; one should, so to speak, be driven around it.

Hermann Hahn. Eduard Wölfflin

Bernhard Bleeker. Portrait, circa 1908

318

Louis Tuaillon. Amazon, Berlin, 1895

In his own work Hildebrand succeeded for the most part in avoiding the hazard of decorative effects to which his theories might lead and which were so evident in his pupils. The best of his statues breathe life in spite of all theorizing and historicism, and avoid the rigidity that seems to cling to the classicists. Balance, rhythm and sensitivity were always present in his classical nudes, realistic portraits and harmonious reliefs. His most important achievement was the Wittelsbach Fountain, with which he bestowed a centralizing accent on a sprawling Munich square. In Munich also are his *Father Rhine* (c. 1900), the *Hubertus Fountain* (1903–1907) and the *Prinzregenten Monument* (1914). This last was modeled in the tradition of the Renaissance equestrian statue at the same moment (and in the same city) that Hermann Obrist was already struggling with abstract sculpture. For some time Hildebrand's monuments and memorials in Meiningen, Strasbourg, Worms, Bremen, Nuremberg, Berlin and Kiel were considered norms, mainly because of their excellent adaptation to the architectural environment.

319

Hugo Lederer
Bismarck Monument, Hamburg, 1901–1906

To this Italianate circle of Hildebrand and Marées, we must add *Artur Volkmann* (1851–1941), who today is underestimated. His themes were similar, realized in restful, heavier volumes, delicately polychromed. Hildebrand continued to be an influence, especially in Munich. *Hermann Hahn* (1868–1945), a generation younger, modeled portraits, but his main preoccupation was the design of monuments. He sought clarity of contour and proportion, but all his work, from medallions to large figures, savored of a more rigid, decorative classicism. In his sculpture, inner warmth and classical form were no longer united as they were in Hildebrand's. However, this union of qualities was occasionally revived in the work of *Bernhard Bleeker* (b. 1884). He also taught at this time in Munich, where he created his *Dead Soldier*, horse tamers and portrait busts. Representative of the same style in the north was *Louis Tuaillon* (1862–1919). He had astonished people with a work of his youth, an Amazon, a calm monument of great refinement and truly majestic proportions. However, in his later works, such as the *Charioteers* and the Kaiser Friedrich monument, both in Bremen, he was no longer able to sustain this nobility of form.

Max Klinger (1857–1920) occupies a unique place; this sculptor, painter and graphic artist (see p. 34) is today underestimated. His work combines neoclassical tendencies with psychological verism. Whereas Franz von Stuck's sculpture is superficial, Klinger created a genuinely original female type, charged with a strange expressiveness. It is indicative that his early etchings, before 1900, later inspired the Surrealists. His paintings include some rather theatrical scenes, but also a few figure compositions and landscapes that show a highly individualistic conception and tonality. In sculpture he experimented with simultaneous effects of different materials at a time when the pale marble statue was in vogue. In *Cassandra* and *Salome* he united different kinds of stone, and in his melodramatic *Beethoven* he went so far as to combine them with metal. The result might have been a vitalization of tension between the various materials had he not smothered them with virtuoso splendor. This exaggeration overshadows all Klinger's imaginative ideas and is a major reason for the lack of appreciation accorded him in the twentieth century.

Franz Metzner
War Memorial (detail), Leipzig, 1913

320

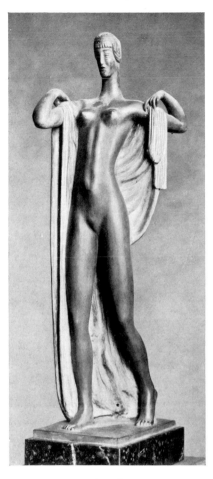

The sculptors Lederer and Metzner turned against such overly specific work, but they also rejected the dynamism of the Rodin school in order to concentrate on the creation of compact sculptural form—to a greater extent even than Hildebrand. In France Maillol had succeeded in achieving this goal because he was filled with a profound personal feeling of peace, but in Germany efforts at consolidation remained superficial. Lederer and Metzner, both born about 1870, faced this problem from different viewpoints.

Hugo Lederer (1871–1940) came from a region where German and Slavic elements meet. His objective was based on four values, but these were soon to be discredited because he realized them too superficially. As a result, the decorative, the heroic, the monumental, the symmetrical—concepts that had been judged valid at the turn of the century—were the object of a general and important re-evaluation. Lederer worked in a painterly, somewhat baroque style until about 1900, when the

Max Klinger. Cassandra, 1895

Wladimir von Bechtejeff
Striding Woman

achievement of his four-fold aim became almost an obsession—and a limitation. It is significant that he considered Franz von Stuck one of the greatest artists of his time. Lederer composed the large bronze fencer for the Breslau University fountain in a precise, cold monumentality. At almost the same time (1901–1906) he was working on his statue of Bismarck in Hamburg; the monument, fifteen meters high, towers rigidly above an abstractly designed socle. No expression of life was intended here, nothing but static force as it was understood at the time. All interior articulation had to be abandoned in order to bring out the blocklike quality of the form. Something important and new might have evolved if the sculp-

tor had not chosen to be so depersonalized, and to stylize for decorative effect. When Lederer later turned away from such architecturalizations–in *Mercury*, *The Miner* and in his statue of Heine–he did not go far beyond the ideals of the nineteenth century, yet confirmed them only superficially. His Berlin *Group of Runners* (1927) may still be counted as one of his best works. In it four athletic nudes move in a precise, angular rhythm.

Fritz Wrampe. Zebu, 1934

Franz Metzner (1870–1919) was driven even more radically by the urge to monumentalize and he indulged in some absolutely excruciating mannerisms. An immense, petrifying pathos is designed to intimidate the viewer. From the beginning Metzner stood on the borderline of sculpture and architecture, and there is no denying the fact that in his case sculpture derived from architecture. But in Metzner's sculpture, monumental bombast, a cult of the heroic, and megalomania become unbearable. On the facade of the Berlin Rheingold Building (1907) his decoratively designed figures are geometrically coordinated in an architectural framework that incorporated patterns based on the Jugendstil. Since 1903 he had been teaching in Vienna, which may account for this

Philipp Harth. Fountain Sculpture in Mannheim, 1950

Anatol Buchholtz. Polecat

Fritz Klimsch. Eos, 1904

influence. In his Leipzig War Memorial his heroes swell to a full sculptural volume with the proportions of mythical colossi, transfixed in eternal pathos.

Richard Engelmann (b. 1868) was a more subdued personality. Living in Florence, he was inspired by Italy and Latin traditions. He created several fine monuments, among them a reclining nude (which is truly reclining) in limestone, for a fountain in Görlitz for which he designed the whole structure (1910).

The gradual change in taste which has taken place may be illustrated by comparing five sculptors of animals. *August Gaul* (1869–1921) also lived for some time in Italy and might have succumbed to the restful style of nineteenth-century neo-classicism if he had not devoted himself entirely to the representation of animals, for which there were few norms. In the nineteenth century the sculpture of animals had developed coquettish aspects; Gaul's self-contained presentations were very different and were therefore greatly admired.

Philipp Harth (b. 1887) came to sculpture from architecture, and tried therefore to frame the expressive life of the animal within this context without erasing the animal's individual vitality. To a greater extent than Hildebrand he stressed the three-dimensional

324

element and a cautiously abstracted movement. Harth is one of those sculptors who work directly from the block, without a model. His theoretical writings were published in 1949 as *Aufsätze über bildhauerische Gesialtung (Essays on Form in Sculpture)*. He lived in Berlin until 1940 and then settled in Upper Bavaria.

Fritz Wrampe (1893–1933), who died prematurely, tried to overcome the classicism of his teacher, Hermann Hahn, with a free yet solidly shaped closeness to life. His animals were modeled to achieve a wholeness. Sometimes they look kneaded, the forms showing a tendency to overlap at the edges. He left many drawings which are striking in their rich perception of nature.

Renée Sintenis (1888–1965) found animals fascinating, but it was not their structure or natural volume which interested her above all; rather, she wanted to capture the motive power that drove the foal, the dog, the ram. Whereas others treated this motion as if its source were in the individual creature, Renée Sintenis interpreted it as an indeterminate life force that drove the bearer hither and yon. Instinctively she chose to portray the young animal, not yet full-fledged, who still gambols uncoordinated and unsure. For the most part she presents us with rough-surfaced, sketchily effective small animal figures whose windblown manes play an important role. But she also created some fine self-portraits and graphic works in which she again sketched motion in loose outlines.

The last in this group of animal sculptors is *Anatol*

Georg Kolbe. Torso, 1929

Buchholtz (b. 1927). His animal figures seem to have been modeled lyrically by powers which go beyond their individuality, and we therefore see less detail. A total form is set in motion, without particular or specific characterization. One senses that Buchholtz's work has been preceded by the symbolic and rhythmic animals of Franz Marc.

Returning to some transitional masters, we may first mention *Fritz Klimsch* (1870–1960), a popular eclectic who created nude figures, attractive monuments, statues of war heroes, fountains and some fine portraits—which neither offended any one nor contributed anything to the development of the art of sculpture. However, it was significant for the aesthetic standards of the period that in 1924 Wilhelm von

Karl Albiker
Relief for a
Variety Theater
in Basel,
circa 1915

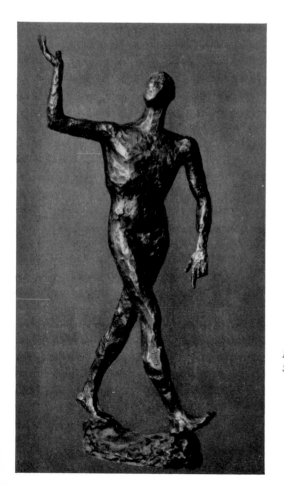

Josef Wackerle
Female Nude,
circa 1940

Ernesto de Fiori
Striding Man

Bernhard Hoetger
Relief in the Plane-Tree Grove,
Darmstadt, circa 1912

Bode compared Fritz Klimsch favorably with Rodin and Barlach, seeing in the "idolized Rodin" the acme of poor style and taste, and in the sculpture of Barlach "formless figures which stick to the ground like sacks of meal." Such a judgment, indicative of the middle class's taste for the mediocre at the time, meant simply that Klimsch did not have the power to go in either of the two ways that were to be decisive for the twentieth century–neither towards an enhanced feeling for life nor in the direction of a unified canon of form.

Georg Kolbe (1877–1949) roughened the surface of his sculpture so that light and air could penetrate, or he gave his figures a more relaxed, sweeping aspect. He worked very freely, yet his figures, modeled singly or in pairs, move without violence; life and form are integrated harmoniously. After Rodin's influence had been replaced everywhere by that of Maillol, Kolbe also concentrated on the more cohesive form. His expressive drawings are executed with a sure feeling for form. "I have Tuaillon and Gaul to thank for my apprenticeship... before that I struggled with painting." His main theme remained the female body in repose or in motion, with no support or drapery; at the most he would include some small, meaningful accessory.

The style of *Karl Albiker* (b. 1878), characterized by elegiac interweaving rhythms, is closely related to Kolbe's. In 1900 he studied under Rodin; subsequently, while living for several years in Munich and Rome, he absorbed other influences. From 1919 he taught at the Dresden Academy. *Richard Scheibe* (1879–1964), who vacillated between freedom and consolidation of form, also belongs in this intermediate generation.

The talented *Ernesto de Fiori* (1884–1946), a naturalized German, was a more important personality who stands close to Kolbe in his liveliness of form. He revived painted sculpture and was a popular

Bernhard Hoetger. Leopard, circa 1912

Käthe Kollwitz. Tower of Mothers, 1937

portraitist. *Josef Wackerle* (1880–1958) stood undecided between various possibilities of development. From 1917 he taught at the Munich School of Applied Arts and at the Academy. At first he concentrated on bland rococo designs for the Nymphenburg porcelain factory, but later he carried out commissions for monuments, such as the Munich Fountain of Neptune and the charioteer for the Berlin Reichssportfeld.

Bernhard Hoetger (1874–1949) was also a sculptor of some talent. He tried to combine all the antirealistic styles—including the older ones—but he was not always successful in blending them. When he arrived in Paris in 1900 he worked in the Rodin tradition (*Boatmen; Potato Eaters*, 1903). He was fascinated by the smooth surfaces and solid calm of Maillol, as is evident in his *Flight of Thought* and *Adoration* (1906). The Elberfeld Fountain of Justice and a fountain in Darmstadt followed. For Darmstadt's famous grove of plane trees he created reliefs that were influenced by the melodic line of Indian art. In 1914 he modeled the memorial for Paula Modersohn-Becker in Worpswede. This tranquil period made way for a phase in which he again experimented freely, still incorporating echoes from the past. From 1916 the firm of Bahlsen in Hannover employed him as architect; here he touched lightly on Egyptian

Ernst Barlach
Head from Memorial in the Gustrow Cathedral, 1927
New York, Museum of Modern Art

forms. Then, for the industrialist Roselius, he revived Gothic structural patterns, creating a building in essentially sculptural terms (Kaffee Hag, in the Böttcherstraße, Bremen). In his mighty head of Roselius he reached a peak of early-Asiatic strength. It was Hoetger's fate to be admired too much in his lifetime–by Tschudi, Meier-Graefe and Edschmid–only to be forgotten prematurely. Among his pupils and disciples was Emy Roeder.

Ernst Barlach (1870–1938), a sturdy Holsteiner, presents a contrast to Hoetger's smoothly flowing experimental style. His heavy blocklike forms may be described as cubic Expressionism, but he called himself a disciple of the medieval German sculptors. His aim was to combine closeness to the earth with inner tension. The attempt to achieve cohesive form, which made for an affected style in the work of Lederer and Metzner, achieved expressive results in the sculpture of Barlach.

The heaviness of sculpture is given correspondingly ponderous motion, the whole experienced through the overwhelming pressure of the mass itself rather than through the corporeal meaning of the figure, which becomes anonymous and symbolic. The elementary violence on which the Brücke painters had concentrated now penetrated sculpture. (Barlach's drawings, woodcuts and lithographs are closely related to the Brücke style.) We are not presented with individuals but with oppressive conditions of being–*Fugitive, Astrologer* (1909), *The Mad One* (1910), *Woman Sorrowing* (1911). Instead of the traditional classical nude we have coarse peasant creatures, heavily robed. After Barlach made a trip to Russia in 1906, these characteristics were exaggerated further. Powerful slabs of wood served as material;

Ernst Barlach. Avenger, 1923 · Hamburg, Barlach Museum

weathered, furrowed blocks were transformed into human beings. Barlach lived in north Germany, where Paula Modersohn-Becker and Nolde had found their way to similar styles. Sometimes, though, Barlach got caught in a superficial impetus toward monumentalism. "Somewhat hesitantly I began to leave out whatever could not contribute to the enforcement of a subconscious or intentional effect. I was no longer simply the tolerator or servant of the visible existence; I was impertinent enough to want to organize it. Naturally this course was often interrupted, and the planned structure deteriorated into overflowing ornamental effects."

Barlach was also a graphic artist and poet, and some consider him more versatile as writer than as sculptor. In his strange, somber dramas a rather stolid, grotesque humor sometimes breaks through which is not manifested in his sculpture, and his prose is dense with meaning. In his autobiography,

Alfred Lörcher. Terra Cotta

Selbsterzähltes Leben, his development is revealed. The National Socialists condemned Barlach and removed his war memorials in Magdeburg, Kiel and Güstrow; they confiscated 381 of his works and banished him into the loneliness in which he died. In 1937 he wrote, "A pimp or a murderer is better off. He at least gets a legal hearing and can defend himself. But we are simply repudiated, and whenever possible, purged."

His contemporary, *Alfred Lörcher* (1875–1963) of Stuttgart, worked in a milder style; one might almost call it feminine in contrast to Barlach's virile style. Lörcher modeled attractively rounded female figures in repose, figures which have the childlike innocence we find in Renoir's paintings. Form and limbs are blended harmoniously in a play of plastic unity. Later he also concentrated on the coordination of groups, especially in his reliefs. He wrote a book on medallion sculpture *(Plaketten, Medaillen, Siegel)* and another on tombstones *(Grabstein)*.

We now come to the experiments of Archipenko and Belling. *Alexander Archipenko* (1887–1964), from the Ukraine, belongs to our discussion because he worked in Berlin during the most important years of his life. Even before that he had received commissions from Germany and had sold much of his work there, and it was the Berlin *Sturm* which made him famous. In 1912 the Folkwangmuseum exhibited seventy-eight of his works, and the art of sculpture was presented with new problems. In the period after 1908 Archipenko's role may be compared to that of Picasso in painting.

Archipenko broke up his figures under the influence of Cubism. Certain spatial effects were achieved by the omission of mass–negative mass became expressive. "I want to make monumental music through mass and space." Beside stone and wood, he used metal and glass in the same work, and he partially painted it–not, of course, for the illustrative purpose of a sculptor like Klinger, but to make the tension created by the various materials resound. "There is nothing new in the painting of sculpture; I learned it from the Egyptians. My innovation is the conception

Alexander Archipenko. Silhouette, 1910
Darmstadt, Hessisches Landesmuseum

331

of form." The polished surface was to act as a light trap, and it is understandable that he later turned to transparent materials. "From 1946 I used transparent plastics, plexiglass, lucite, and modeled the light." In 1923 Archipenko moved to the United States and taught at the New Bauhaus in Chicago. In 1939 he opened his own school in New York and after 1946 concentrated on controlled light. He often illuminated his plexiglass sculpture from the inside, in a dark room. Beside his constructive pieces there are some naturalistic works, among them busts of the novelist Ernst Wichert (1923), and the conductor Wilhelm Furtwängler (1927). He described a machine he invented as "the actual connection between painting and time and space. Until now only music has used time as a creative element."

Rudolf Belling. Triad, 1919
Munich, Bayerische
Staatsgemäldesammlungen

Rudolf Belling (b. 1886), who was also working in Berlin, experimented with similar methods, and he too was influenced to a certain extent by Cubism. In his group sculpture, *Kampf* (1916), struggling human bodies are reduced to a canon of form. They press out into space in every direction, but the space between is also an active expressive element, contrapuntally related. In *Triad* (1919), the formal canon is even more systematic. This sculpture may be read as a completely nonobjective work, a bare power structure of anonymous forms straining toward each other and embracing the hollow space, which becomes active. What Hermann Obrist had been trying to achieve with a lyrical statement is now accomplished by dramatic tension. Belling was more drastic than his friend, Archipenko. At an early stage in his development he openly opposed Hildebrand's theories. He could not fathom why Hildebrand had defined the cube as a torment, nor why he demanded that one should view a sculpture in its totality from only one fixed point. Belling stated, "Just this three-dimensionality, which is the fundamental difference between painting and sculpture, must be stressed... so I began to create, at first using figures, and then so-called abstract forms, since the latter offered so many more possibilities." In Germany, therefore, the artist was working in a counterpoint of hollows and solid forms long before

Rudolf Belling. Sculpture 23, 1923
New York, Museum of Modern Art

Henry Moore made this possibility popular in the next stage. In 1932 Belling experimented with enclosing "aerial form" with wire contours. Unfortunately many of his compositions were overly stylized, especially his portraits. After the National Socialist ban on modern art, he accepted an offer from Istanbul and taught sculpture at the Art Academy in that city. In Germany he carried out commissions for Scala, the Berlin restaurant, and for the Buchdruckerhaus (Printers House), by the architect Max Taut. Belling's *Head of a Man* in mahogany and *Head of a Woman* in brass are his most famous works.

Otto Freundlich (1878–1943), a third innovator in sculpture working in Germany, has until recently been almost forgotten. He came from the province of Pomerania and studied art history under Wölfflin. In 1908 he moved to Paris where he associated with the painters Herbin, Gleizes and the Cubists. As early as 1909 he was painting abstractly. From 1919 to 1924 he lived in Germany again, and then returned to Paris. "The work of the artist is the sum of constructive action, but the culture of art, which has always existed, has remained the same–to prepare the future." He painted huge panels with lively color planes,

Hans Walther
Reclining Woman, 1920

Otto Freundlich. Sculpture, 1929

organized in layers and interlocking. In 1912
he showed his work at the famous Cologne
Sonderbund Exhibition; in 1918 he completed
a mosaic for the Feinhals Building in Cologne
and in 1928 he modeled his first large, completely abstract sculpture. This was followed
in 1932 by more monumental pieces. During
these years he participated in the shows of
the *Abstraction-Création* group. Freundlich
was also a victim of National Socialism. His
L'Homme nouveau was reproduced on the
cover of the catalogue of "degenerate art"
exhibition in 1937 and in the Nazi newspaper, *Der Stürmer*. In 1943, when Hitler's
armies occupied France, he was sent to a
concentration camp and deported to Poland.
There, like his friends, the painter Rudolf
Levy and the poet Max Jacob, he perished.
The work of *Hans Walther* (b. 1888), who has
been living in Erfurt since 1919, falls between
abstraction and representational art. In his

best works he aims at a calm monumentality, but even so, he too was attacked by the National Socialists.

The work of *Wilhelm Lehmbruck* (1881–1919) has been profoundly influential on all sculptors who have continued to respect the human body. In secret union with the Gothic, he stressed not so much volume as extension: the expressive elongation of the human figure which is born of idealistic feeling. Man was a perishable creature imbued with longing. Lehmbruck expressed himself entirely through the figure, but without the psychological affectation of many enthusiasts of the nineteenth century; the construction of the body itself seemed to belong to another world.

With his extremely spiritualized statuary, Lehmbruck set a standard which is valid today. Two female torsos, modeled in 1913 and 1918, are perfection in the symmetry of their formal transformation. His *Kneeling Woman* of 1911 is the quintessence of humility. His *Thinking Girl* (1913–1914) arises gently to meet an uncertain world. *Fallen Man* (1915–1916) is a poignant monument to man's surrender to the earth. At a later date it was considered a war memorial, and it would be hard to find a greater contrast to the blatantly triumphant war monuments produced by the nineteenth century. Lehmbruck's *Seated Youth* (1918) may be compared fruitfully with Rodin's *Thinker* and with a similar figure by the Austrian sculptor FritzWotruba, in order to evaluate Lehmbruck's success in bridging the gap between abstraction and empathy, spiritually and harmoniously, working from conventional forms very gradually toward purer solutions. Hypersensitive and broken by the horrors of the

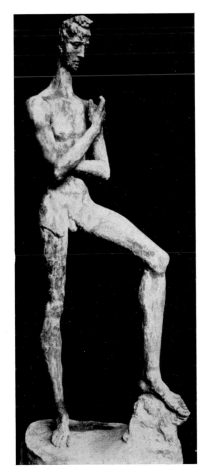

Wilhelm Lehmbruck
Ascending Youth, 1913
New York,
Museum of Modern Art

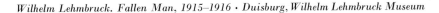

Wilhelm Lehmbruck. Fallen Man, 1915–1916 · Duisburg, Wilhelm Lehmbruck Museum

Gustav H. Wolff. Standing Woman, 1925

Wilhelm Lehmbruck. Kneeling Woman, 1911
Duisburg, Wilhelm Lehmbruck Museum

Gerhard Marcks
Prometheus Bound, 1948

First World War, Lehmbruck took his own life at the age of thirty-seven, at the height of his career. Beside his sculpture, his oeuvre included paintings, etchings and drawings.

Gustave H. Wolff (1886–1934) also died prematurely, and he has been unjustly forgotten. Self-taught, he painted and wrote, and in his sculpture he simplified forms in a specifically architectonic sense.

The sculpture of *Gerhard Marcks* (b. 1889) stands between the traditional and the new. He has created large sculptures, small static pieces, and works full of movement. The nonobjective sculptors call him a

Gerhard Marcks. Tyrolean Dance, 1951

realist and the realists point out his tendency to abstract. Mainly he is concerned with humans of tall stature or single animal figures, less often with groups. Marcks favors the lean, northern figure type, and in his sparse interpretations we find no trace of the swelling volumes common since Rodin and Maillol. He also avoided the melodramatic, expansive gesture found in the works of Barlach and the Expressionists. Volume is diminished by using angular forms. Some of his work recalls medieval sculpture, but his individuality always breaks through, even in later works which show an attraction to classical types. When Marcks had outgrown his teachers, Gaul, Kolbe and Scheibe, he took over the Dornburg pottery workshop at the Weimar Bauhaus, where Schlemmer was already working on abstract reliefs. In 1921 he began producing some unusual woodcuts in which everything was expressed in parallel shapes and lines. However, his desire to reproduce the human body more realistically grew increasingly strong, and he turned his back on the Bauhaus mode, though less drastically in his prints than in his sculpture. In addition to small works, Marcks created monuments in Hamburg and Cologne, completed Barlach's Bremen *Town Musicians* and the commission for the facade of St. Catherine's Church in Lübeck.

Joachim Karsch (1897–1945) was a contemplative man. He began to concentrate on sculpture in 1920, just as the paths of Expressionism and the New Objectivity crossed, as is evident in his work. In his *Harmonica Player* he succeeded in transforming into a work of art the genre motif of a musician in a

338

business suit. His aim was to capture the particular moment and give it permanent form. Karsch was closer to Marcks than to Barlach, whom he admired above all other sculptors. He pored over Dostojevsky and Knut Hamsun, wrote theological studies and some admirable poems, tales and novels. In 1933 he went to Rome for two years, but the city made little impression on him. He was inspired more by medieval German woodcuts, and worked often in wood. In the last war the greater part of his oeuvre was destroyed; some two hundred etchings, woodcuts and lithographs were preserved, but only in a few states.

Karsch too was considered degenerate by the National Socialists. In 1938 he wrote, "My heads were not racially pure... Everything I see going on around me only increases my utter hopelessness. The demand that art be comprehensible to everyone is grotesque. It has always been the duty of the artist to express that which is *not* yet comprehensible; only then can it gradually be understood." He fled from Berlin to the remote town of Gandern on the Oder River. When the Russians entered in 1945, he and his wife committed suicide. His very moving letters were published in 1948.

Joachim Karsch. Harmonica Player, 1934

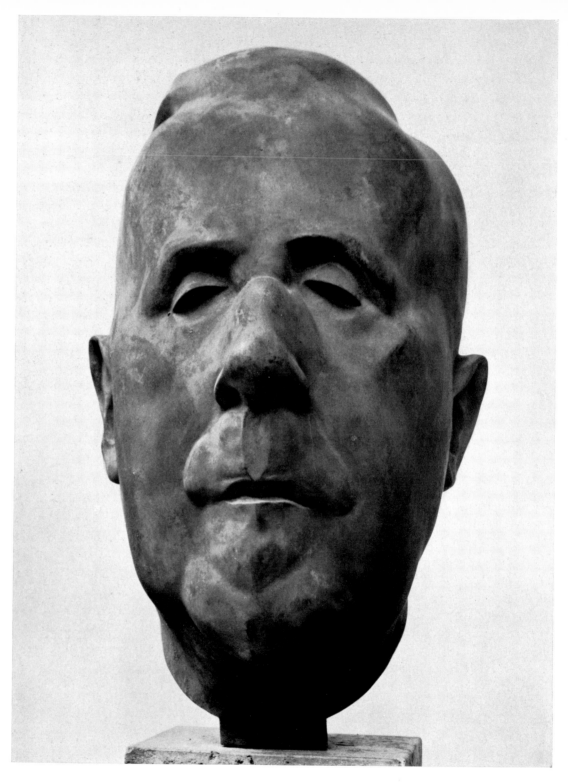

Edwin Scharff. Heinrich Mann, 1920

Edwin Scharff. Detail of the Marienthaler Church Portal, 1945–1949

Edwin Scharff (1887–1950), a contemporary of Marcks, tried to fuse the modern and the traditional, motion and repose. In his sensitivity to his material one senses that he came to sculpture from painting. In spite of some cutting and dissecting of form and a few cubist insertions, he remained devoted to the soft, stable surface. Sometimes his forms are cohesive, sometimes they seem to be blown by the wind. Riders, horse tamers, men in boats, are recurring themes, as well as women dancing, archers and horses jumping, in reliefs, and he also made single figures. Religious themes appear in his late works. His portraits will probably prove of lasting value, for in them he characterized with complete simplicity the outer and inner man—Wölfflin, Heinrich Mann, Liebermann, Corinth, Nolde, Cardinal Galen. Scharff also created melodic drawings and etchings for works of Shakespeare and Thomas Mann. His paintings were at first close to Maillol and Kolbe, who also painted before they became sculptors, but then Scharff adopted Cubism. In Paris, in 1912, under the influence of Rodin, he emerged as a sculptor. In 1923 he was called to the Berlin Academy; under the National Socialists he was dismissed from this post and forty-eight of his works were confiscated or destroyed. He was not able to resume his activities as teacher until 1946, when he was appointed to a post in Hamburg.

While Scharff favored the softly flowing effect that revealed the kneading and modeling which had produced it, the Rhinelander *Ewald Mataré* (1887–1965) concentrated on the precise capsuled form. After smoothing and polishing, procedures which were extremely important to him, his work achieved a

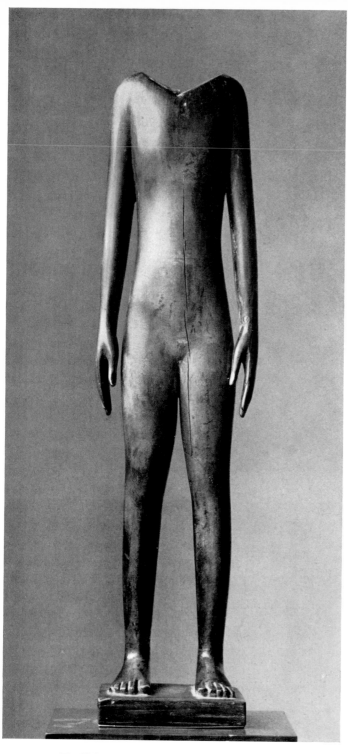

Ewald Mataré. Standing Figure, 1926–1927
Duisburg, Wilhelm Lehmbruck Museum

342

finish wholly divorced from any evidence of the process involved in its accomplishment. Sometimes he reached an attractive degree of perfection, at others not much more than a decorative effect. He sought a more pronounced abstraction, hence the omission of modeling from the stable surfaces of his woodcuts. The appearance was to be captured in an emblematic form language, with a minimum of tensile curves, which were limited to and produced by the contours. Instead of the momentary, Mataré sought definitive existence, which he succeeded in revealing mainly in his animal carvings. The human figure was a theme he used less frequently. In his sculpture in wood the beautiful grain must, above all, never be spoiled by incisions into its surface. In his metal work he enhanced the beauty of the material with the insertion of gems (*Mosaic in Bronze*). His urge to achieve a cohesive style sometimes resulted in an overly synoptic effect.

Mataré's colored woodcuts indicated that reliefs would be his forte, and he created charming examples in stone and clay. From 1948 to 1954 he worked on the four south doors of Cologne Cathedral, adapting his talents to older styles without becoming imitative, which was in fact, what was demanded of him by those who now criticized his noticeable asymmetry. Shortly after this he was commissioned to execute doors in Hiroshima and Salzburg. During the first half of his life, Mataré concentrated chiefly on worldly themes; then, with church commissions, he related his work to older prototypes. Under National Socialism he was dismissed as instructor at the Düsseldorf Academy and resumed teaching only in 1945.

Ludwig Gies (b. 1887), influenced by Expressionism, stylizes more powerfully than Mataré. He impresses his figures into crowded round forms, a method which occasionally results in an ornamental effect. Usually his themes are religious. He has executed much work for churches, liturgical objects, plaques and medallions. His crucifix for the Lübeck Cathedral (1920) caused a stir because of its crass style. In 1950 he began teaching at the Cologne Werkschule.

Emy Roeder (b. 1890) also struggled for a long time with form; in fact one might say that until about 1920 she was overpowered by it, and expression was neglected. But then her efforts began to show results. She does not round out her forms by modeling, but works with graduated planes, organized and articulated by long linear indentations which also unify by the repetition of pattern. Her better work has a distinctly stony, almost Egyptian character. Everything is clear, all surrounding space has been cut away, all exaggerated sentiment jettisoned. Her work is more virile than that of her first teacher, Bernhard Hoetger. In her portraits, for instance those of Erich Heckel and Hans Purrmann, she succeeds in reducing a highly individual head to a static structure. Her art, too, was banned as degenerate.

Joachim Utech (b. 1889) favors the majestic, decorative form and frequently works in granite.

Hermann Geibel (b. 1889) is a gentler personality. He lives in Munich, has traveled extensively in Greece, Dalmatia and Italy, and has taught at the Darmstadt Technische Hochschule. Geibel has been receptive to many possibilities and his style varies—he has modeled genre themes *(Bear with Foals)* and portraits and has also executed voluminous, surging abstractions, for example, his several versions

Ewald Mataré. Phoenix, 1949

343

Joachim Utech. Head, circa 1935

Hermann Geibel. Male Idol, circa 1950

Emy Roeder. The Painter Purrmann, 1950
Mannheim, Kunsthalle

Ludwig Gies. Pan, circa 1953

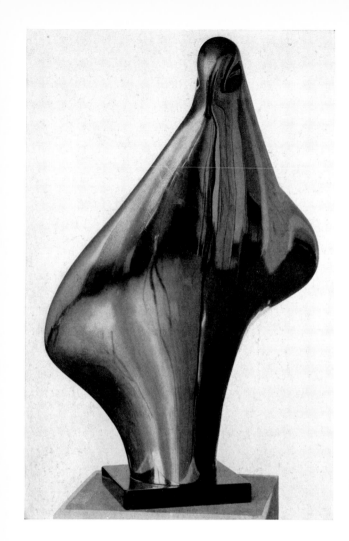

Richard Haizmann. Eagle, 1931

of *Europa*, his *Yoked Oxen* and *Idol*. The latter is exceptional in that the alabaster is polished. He has frequently expressed his views on sculpture. "I can see no sense in technological forms that have no technical function... but I do believe that one could go much farther in the deformation of natural proportions and in the transformation of the body surface... in this respect my assistant [Wilhelm] Loth has outstripped me."

Richard Haizmann (b. 1895), who is self-taught, strove for more vigorous abstractions. Like Mataré and Belling, he polished the surface and transformed some of his figures into symbolic forms, as his *Eagle* of 1931. In his early work he anticipated the later development of German sculpture, but as time passed he became bogged down in an occult sectarianism.

After studying stone masonry, *Hans Mettel* (1903–1966), under the tutelage of Edwin Scharff, arrived at a blocklike treatment of the human figure that is a definite departure from similar efforts at the time. His *Large Seated Figure* is consistently angular, resembling an architectural system. The irrational

Hans Mettel. Large Seated Figure, 1955

dynamics of life are overcome to such an extent that the body begins to look like a tool. When Mettel related a man and a horse, an overall reconstruction took place, and these unrelated creatures are experienced in harmony and kinship. In 1948 Mettel was made director of the Städel Art School in Frankfurt.

With similar tendencies but much greater vitality, *Hermann Blumenthal* (1905–1942), outpaced Mettel, who was almost his exact contemporary. Blumenthal, like Lehmbruck, belongs among those who reach perfection early. Both these sculptors died at the age of thirty-seven–Lehmbruck in the last year of the First World War, Blumenthal during the second. Whereas Lehmbruck's long thin figures tend toward self-containment and reserve, Blumenthal modeled sturdy youths who displayed their youthful vitality in energetic, angular motion. The figures seem to be hewn from trees; body, trunk and limbs are closely knit and we find no clear-cut differentiations, yet Blumenthal succeeded in creating a tense, burgeoning feeling for the life of the body as a whole. He presented man as a system of forces that

347

challenges the surrounding space. He was only twenty-four when he created his *Large Standing Man*, twenty-six when he modeled *Adam Crawling* and *Seated Man*, both in an archaic yet vigorous style. Only rarely did he soften the clear taut surface of his young bodies. His friend, the painter Werner Heldt, wrote of him, "He was big, strong and massively built, and his laughter was wonderful. He was forthright and courageous, yet often defenseless, incapable of any form of intrigue. His entire strength was dedicated to his work." The son of a factory foreman, he began to sculpt with nothing more than the knowledge of a stone mason. His talents earned him a grant from the German Academy in Rome, where he was impressed above all by Etruscan art. From 1937 to 1940 he shared a studio with his friend Heldt, Käthe Kollwitz, the sculptor Ludwig Kasper (a relative), and the painter Werner Gilles.

Hermann Blumenthal. Youth, 1936–1937

Kurt Lehmann. Reclining Woman, 1955

Gustav Seitz. The Chooser, 1956

Kurt Lehmann was born in 1905, the same year as Blumenthal. He too is interested solely in the typical aspects of the human body, either standing or seated. But he has had time to experiment with more controversial themes and methods, and he occasionally admits curves to the strictly angular scaffolding of his figures. He ranges from the tragic expression of *Man Breaking Down* (1946) to the humor of his puffy-cheeked, bosomy little *Reclining Woman*, who seems to swim on the surface like a seal. There are also solidly constructed figures–*Man Sleeping* (1949) and the *Woman Squatting* (1955). Only rarely does

349

Gustav Seitz. Odenwald Innkeeper, 1955

he turn from sculpture in the round to bas-relief, as in *Meleager* (1945). In 1949 he was called to the Technische Hochschule in Hannover. He has worked increasingly on commissions for applied sculpture, from door handles for the opera house to the monumental sandstone statue of St. Michael for the Frankfurt Paulskirche, and large stone figures for the firm of Bahlsen in Hannover and for the Chamber of Commerce in that city. He is concerned primarily with the young human body and rarely models

Karlheinz Goedtke. Rice Planter, 1952

Herbert Vollwahsen
Woman Watching, 1952

animals. Since 1954 fully rounded elements are less evident. He now seems to favor a flat, shifting angularity with which he produces abstractions.

Kurt Schwippert (b. 1903) creates paired figures in a calm, modest style, either as free-standing sculpture or in relief, mostly in Belgian granite. In addition he has also done draped single figures in wood, clay or bronze. In 1949 he was called to the Werkschule in Münster.

Gustav Seitz (b. 1906) was the son of a Mannheim worker in stucco, and learned his trade from the ground up. He works in a taut style, his figures falling between types and individualizations. He models healthy female bodies, occasionally with a dash of humor, as in *Woman Standing* and in *The Chooser*—a disguised *Judgment of Paris*. "I refuse to lose compactness through an exaggeration of motion. Besides, I love the health and power of nature, which remains my greatest inspiration." He was successful with compact sculpture in the round, and also with portraits and reliefs. At first he tended to be painterly, but he developed an increasing capacity for unified plastic expression. In 1939 he began to work independently and since 1946 has been teaching in Berlin. Of portrait sculpture he says that to be truthful

351

Erich F. Reuter. Conversation, 1952–1953

means more than to be faithful to nature, so that "a feature may be exaggerated or toned down in favor of expression... We shall see which type of realism and which form of portraiture evolves out of our time... we do not know."

Herbert Vollwahsen (b. 1906), like most members of his generation, has moved away from realism, although he kept close to nature in his earliest work done in a woodcarving school in Silesia. Later he studied under Karl Albiker in Dresden. In both architectural sculpture and in free-standing figures, he achieves absolute unity between the outlines of the figures and their sheathlike clothing.

Hans Ruwoldt. Striding Woman, 1956

Ludwig Kasper. Seated Woman, 1936

Erich F. Reuter (b. 1911) studied painting and stone masonry. In his figures he favors simplified gestures that reach out into space. In 1950 he attracted attention with a design for the memorial to the victims of the Berlin airlift, and in 1951 he was called to the Berlin Technische Universität to teach sculpture. His over-life-sized torsos, portraits and reliefs are for the most part clear and intense. Lately, he too has become preoccupied with the space between two figures, or parts of figures, endeavoring to make it an active part of the existing tension, as in his *Conversation* (1953).

In Munich the most important sculptors concentrated on the human or animal figure and

Toni Stadler
Kneeling Woman,
1956

354

turned away only gradually from the classical influence of Hildebrand and Hermann Hahn. Instead of accepting the forms of the High Renaissance, they showed a preference for the archaic style of classical antiquity. Only *Ludwig Kasper* (1893–1945) betrays the fact that he came from the school of Hermann Hahn. He modeled restful but specifically plastic figure types governed by Italian order and clarity, constructing his bodies without preparatory drawings or models, and always seeking to express the timeless, typical aspects of the human body. He went his way systematically, paying no attention to the Impressionism of Rodin, which was still influential, or to Barlach's Expressionism. In 1937 a visit to Greece confirmed him in his determination to preserve the natural volume of the human body in conjunction with the architectonic quality of its structure.

Toni Stadler (b. 1888), son of a Munich landscape painter, was stimulated by archaic form, although at first he seemed more dependent on Maillol. In Stadler the archaic tendency is sometimes expressed in very rigid forms, at others more freely–the result, in part, of his technique. For his bronze casts he uses *cire perdue*, the lost wax method. Wax is employed rather than clay. When the wax has melted away and been replaced by bronze, the casting retains all the vitality of the "lost form," including the

Toni Stadler. Dog, 1950 · Cologne, Wallraf-Richartz Museum

Priska von Martin. Young Stag, 1956

malleability of the material. If the touching up of the surface is limited, small runs and patches remain, and an immediate patina of sculptural quality is produced without the benefit of weathering. There is a danger that such superficial charms may distract from the work as a whole, or may be used to hide its faults.

Stadler was not striving for beautifully rounded forms but for closeness to nature with emphasis on its individuality. Similarly, the material, with its accidental effects, and the process involved in creating the form, must remain alive. His people appear to have been transfixed by the menace of outside forces, especially as they are virtually motionless and express primarily long-suffering endurance.

Heinrich Kirchner
Gravestone for
my parents, 1956

Many of the same observations apply to the work of Stadler's wife, *Priska von Martin* (b. 1912). If one compares her with contemporary German sculptresses–Sintenis or Roeder–one realizes how closely allied she is in her technique and feeling for life to Stadler, with whom she works harmoniously. Her forms also have an irregular surface which derives to some extent from an emotional feeling for nature, but also from the method just described.

Heinrich Kirchner (b. 1902), who teaches at the Munich Academy, is an experienced bronze founder. The archaic style of his forms is very rigid and primitive an he does not shrink from crude effects, such as spindly arms stuck into cylindrical trunks. Some of his figures are gigantic, but he also creates small dramatic scenes which seem to have been dug out of the surface. In his *Cowering Man*, an early work, he still aims at a fully rounded body, despite its elongation. Gradually, though, this solidity is pushed inward, as if the surface had been inverted. He arbitrarily reduces his figures–which are mostly religious and are covered with drapery–so that they look like flattened cylinders, on top of which perch equally flat round heads. Sometimes he scratches in alphabetical characters. Thus he produces very strange idols. In his Baptismal Font (1952) and in the doors of the Peterskirche in Munich (1955) he achieved impressive results in applying his style to the creation of decorative reliefs for an ecclesiastical building.

The work of *Anton Hiller* (b. 1893) derives still more rigorously from an archaic language of form; in fact the effect is almost monotonous. No trace remains of the influence of Hiller's teacher, Hermann Hahn. He preserves the aspect of his model above all in his standing figures, a subject he dealt with repeatedly, denying them movement and even surface mutability, in order to define a basic type of figure in repose, using a minimum of expressive means.

Anton Hiller. Youth, 1952

Georg Brenninger (b. 1909), who was once a building worker, studied sculpture with Hahn and architecture with Theodor Fischer, and then devoted himself to sculpture. Starting with a derivative style with changing surface effects, he subsequently showed a tendency toward ever more static forms. Finally all implication of change is cast aside and there remains only the simplest essence in capsule form. Since 1947 Brenninger has been teaching at the Technische Hochschule in Munich, and he has also been active in the rebuilding of the city.

Hiller, Heinrich Kirchner, Brenninger and other Munich sculptors seek only the expression of a clarified, quiescent volume and the elimination of superficial sensuous effects; above all they avoid motion as a

form of expression, with the result they may well have limited the possibilities of sculptural expression. If a dynamic personality such as Marino Marini in Italy or Armitage in England does not emerge soon, this Munich style may petrify into immutable schematism. One welcomes, therefore, the appearance of a man like *Alexander Fischer* (b. 1903), who also works in Munich. Fischer is absorbed by a form of sculpture that is close to nature and almost baroque in its mobility, an aspect he sometimes exaggerates dramatically. His spontaneous feeling for form may gain for him at least a temporary significance.

Hans Wimmer (b. 1907), from Lower Bavaria, also shows a tendency toward a subconscious reception of older forms. The existence of such influences is often recognized belatedly because evidence of their effect on truly creative artists is contained within the expression of new characteristics. Hildebrand was once considered original, an innovator, whereas

Georg Brenninger. Torso of a boy

Alexander Fischer. Rider, 1956

Hans Wimmer
The Conductor Wilhelm Furtwängler, 1953
Mannheim, Kunsthalle

today one realizes how dependent he was on older traditions—which led him instead to a renaissance. Wimmer's work is implicitly allied to medieval and kindred forms, in accordance with the change from empathy to abstraction which has taken place since Hildebrand. His bust of the archeologist Ernst Buschor, done in 1946, is related to Roman sculpture; his *Horse* of 1950 to old Chinese art; his dramatic crucifix in wood (Degerndorf, 1947) shows late Gothic influence, and the elongated, over-life-sized crucifix in Heiligenberg (on the Lake of Constance) is inspired by Romanesque sculpture. His mature works do not expand into the surrounding space; instead they tend to stand back aloofly. In 1952 Wimmer stated that he wished "the human figure and sculpture would remain allied with architecture." Although he had first studied with Bernhard Bleeker, his inclination to modesty and need for inner quiet remained dominant. "What is uninteresting," he says, "is always the most interesting." Even when he deals directly with life, as in his *Statuette of a Girl with Hat*, he shows no concern for psychological analysis, but presents the subject in a formal synthesis. Statuettes turn up frequently

359

Hans Wimmer. Crucifix in Heiligenberg, 1951
Fürstl. Fürstenbergische Schlosskapelle Heiligenberg, Bodensee

beside his larger figures, but above all he modeled portraits. Among the busts executed between 1930 and 1954 were portraits of Mussolini, Buschor, Furtwängler and Martin Heidegger. Since 1949 he has been teaching at the Nuremberg Academy.

The work of *Emil Krieger* (b. 1902) is also based on older traditions. He concentrates on full, rounded volumes. He received the Rome Prize in 1936, and he conducted life classes for sculpture students at the Munich Academy. In 1952 he carried out a commission for an over-life-sized female figure for the palace in Coblenz.

Josef Henselmann (b. 1898) is a rather isolated figure within the Munich environment. He favors wood sculpture and carves his work directly from the block, without a model. He created portraits, the huge crucifix that hangs high in the vaulting of Munich's Frauenkirche, and the Moses Fountain for the Maxburg, also in Munich. In 1947 he was commissioned to design a complete altarpiece for the Cathedral of Passau, *The Stoning of St. Stephen*, the most comprehensive assignment in the recent history of German church decoration. Whatever may be said about it—and there have been attacks from traditionalists as well as from progressive critics—the composition succeeds in commanding with dramatic pathos the large Baroque

Fritz Müller-Kamphausen. Thinker

Josef Henselmann
St. Stephen,
Passau Cathedral Altar,
1947–1953

Roland Friederichsen. Youth, 1953

Wilhelm Maly. Duo, 1926

space alloted to it. A blocklike form and theatrical (neo-Baroque) naturalism are integrated. A covering of silver leaf clinging to the figures relieves them of their inherent heaviness. For all their voluminousness, these figures, and the angel suspended above crowned by the Trinity, seem to be floating in the light-filled choir.

Also working in Munich, but with different orientation, was the painter *Wilhelm Maly* (1894–1943). (See p. 182.) He contributed to expressionist sculpture a unique work wholly different from the usual Munich type, a group carving in wood of a man and a woman, basic and monumental.

Fritz Müller-Kamphausen (1901–1955) of Munich worked with highly individual, very precise forms. He forced his figures into angular shapes, defining his subjects–towering women or impressive portraits –by their contours, within which he articulated the interior modeling in corresponding fashion. A more balanced, elegiac tone is conveyed in the sculpture of *Roland Friederichsen* (b. 1910), who produced both secular and ecclesiastical sculpture using a variety of materials.

In *Karl Knappe* (b. 1884) Munich has been provided with an experimenter of a kind missing since the demise of the Blaue Reiter. Knappe is not only a sculptor; he has produced mosaics and glass paintings entirely without preliminary drawings. He avoided imitation completely and sought only to express the intrinsic qualities of his pieces of stone and glass, a point of view leading to nonobjective art. In 1924 he introduced abstract formal rhythms in the reliefs of his Munich war memorial. He also created sharply characterized portraits, sometimes verging on caricature, as in his bust of Liebermann.

Marianne Lüdicke. Man Squatting

When he worked from a whole tree, he used a hollowing out process in which the negative form was actively complementary to the positive. Here, quite early, he developed a procedure which was later made increasingly famous by Henry Moore. Knappe's eigteen-feet high *St. Christopher*, carved out of one gigantic oak trunk, is an important example of this method. (Now in the Stuttgart Staatsgalerie.) None of the tree's force was to be sacrificed. Unfortunately, Knappe's curving forms are frequently given too much detail, especially when he indulges in the gentle swells and curvilinear motion of the Jugendstil. As a result his work has not received as much recognition as that accorded to Henry Moore, whose rhythms are more severe and more abstract. Knappe executed glass windows for churches in Hindelang, Weiden, and Gauting, for the Paulskirche in Frankfurt, and mosaics for Paul Beck in Stuttgart.

Knappe's *Gedanken zur Kunst unserer Zeit (Thoughts on Art Today)* was published in 1950. Amid a welter of vague ideas, he expresses some original thoughts. He hated all kneading in plaster or clay; in his opinion this was "like asking a true mountain climber to try to climb for years in a clay pit." He was skeptical of quite a few of his Munich colleagues. "In neo-archaism we have at best an artificial lung." "The true sculptor never knows ahead of time what the figure will be." He was also of the opinion that Rodin stood closer to the creative intellects of our day than Hildebrand or Maillol. For Knappe, wood or stone was "not material to be used merely to give form to an idea; its own intrinsic value must

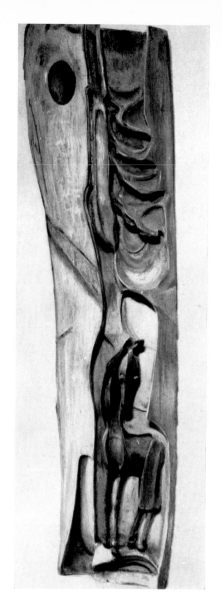

Karl Knappe
Christmas, 1945

Karl Knappe
Horse in the Forest, 1945

be preserved." Optimistically he believed that everything must turn out right if one just let the material take over. (I would like to stress this last point because it often has been applied to the most recent *painting*, with perilous results.)

Fritz Koenig (b. 1924), a much younger artist, also developed from this Munich school. At first he concentrated on clothed, elongated figures with small hands and slender limbs, which remind one of the work of Heinrich Kirchner. Subsequently he began to model groups in which the individual figures coalesce to form a solid unit, thereby contributing a new theme to German sculpture. In an extraordinary synthesis he was able to create the effect of whole herds of cattle, as he had seen them in the Camargue region of southern France, their backs and horns drawn together to form a highly expressive

364

Fritz Koenig
Quadriga, Bronze, 1957

plastic ornament. He also used this method of sculptural coalescing for crowded groups of human figures or troops of riders, and for the bronze, *Quadriga*. In a boldly symbolic crucifix only the blocklike figure of Christ stands out, at the top of a vague mass of shrouded human bodies "from which one arose to die for all."

Koenig has meanwhile become more abstract. He has produced a series of variations on the motif of the Venetian gondola. Since 1965 he has been absorbed by the theme of the caryatid and created huge, squared columns that support a heavy capital. The neck of the column becomes a zone of expression: laced together to form a knot, it acts as a joint supporting the weight, a fragile "human" center of force between heaven and earth.

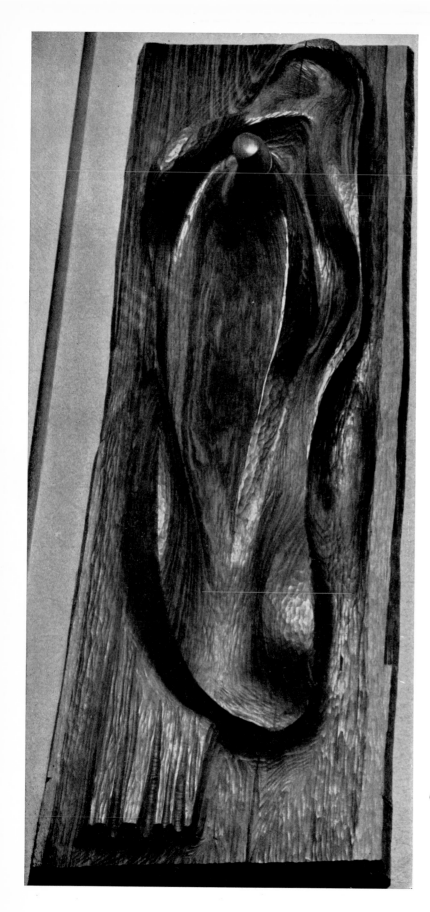

Otto Baum. Orchid, Wood, 1944–1945

The Way to Abstraction

Let us now consider a few sculptors who have not abandoned the human figure but have transformed it so radically that their work may almost be read as abstract. These sculptors continued to work in a manner related to that of Archipenko and Belling, but their specific problem with the Cubism of their day has meanwhile been worked out and does not concern us here. A sculptor such as the Swabian *Otto Baum* (b. 1900), for instance, concentrates entirely on the general underlying form in modeling a human or animal, articulating the body in as little detail as possible in order to preserve symbolically its suppressed animalism. In sculptures of humans realized in this fashion. Baum presents man as if his mighty limbs had been roused from their primordial sleep. In his *Primeval Mother* he is absorbed, like so many of his contemporaries, by the contrast between convex and concave, by the fascination of the positive value of hollow forms. In his portraits Baum proceeds from an expression of total volume. He once modeled a gigantic elephant, conceived as a mountain, and wanted to set it up on a hill in Stuttgart in all its monstrous dimensions. The fact that he admires Brancusi and Arp above all other sculptors is indicative, and occasionally he has tried nonfigurative sculpture.

Paul Dierkes (b. 1907), at one time a stone mason, has been teaching at the Berlin Hochschule since 1945. He too emphasizes the underlying block forms of his figures and animals. To prevent any interruption of this relationship to the material he removes only a very small amount from the block. As he comes ever closer to simplified abstract forms his figures are transformed into large plastic signs, symbolic forms of mythical themes, effective but occasionally oversimplified.

The primitive forms of *Wilhelm Loth* (b. 1920) have more vitality. He too wants to distort the object in an increasingly puzzling manner. A head is turned into a weird receptacle that looks as if it might burst, and is neither utensil nor portrait. When he

Paul Dierkes, Figure, 1951

models the whole body it stands in space like a heavy pottery jug; the handles are the arms. Man becomes mythical and is transformed into a primeval form which is neither human, animal nor vegetable, and this massive construction is then broken apart to give its swollen form an effect of fragility. No other sculptor today insists so radically on fragmentation. It seems as if Loth wants to point out the accidental quality of the threatening power of Being.

The sculpture of *Karl Hartung* (b. 1908) enjoys an immense reputation. When he came to Paris in 1929 he experienced the powerful, simple style of Brancusi. During the National Socialist era Hartung could only experiment secretly, but in 1945 he was able to come forward openly with mature works,

Karl Hartung
Reclining Woman, 1947

Karl Hartung. Composition VIII, 1948

and in 1951 he was called to the Berlin Hochschule. Hartung avoids placing the center of gravity beyond the axis of the figure and concentrates on a firm, virile beauty of form and material through whose structure everything is precisely defined. In his reclining nudes he brings the natural form and the form that he wants to reveal into an active relationship. He exploits only partially the juxtaposition of negative and positive forms since his purpose is to maintain the total volume as stably as possible. In this he is aspiring toward what one might call the self-containment of the statue in its original form. He emphasizes the smoothness of the surface, whether wood, stone, bronze or brass, which gives a final effect of noble power. Gradually all reminiscences of the human body have been abandoned, leaving only the expression of basic structures in a quasi-architectonic relationship of forces. Instead of swelling volumes, he sometimes erects parallel blocks, roughening the surfaces with rippling lines or shallow modeling to give them life, but these variations are never permitted to dissolve the structure as a whole. Sometimes his structures are too simple and rigid; it is therefore salutary that he returns occasionally to the human figure, as in his work for the Paracelsus Clinic in Marl. But his gigantic black-and white-drawings, with their rich interdelineation, also protect him from oversimplification. Some of these could perhaps be transformed into complex transparent reliefs. With their supports—each with its own interior rhythm—they could be read as mythical barriers, powerful stops against nothingness. *Bernhard Heiliger* (b. 1915), almost a decade younger than Hartung, also teaches in Berlin, and is as different from Hartung as empathy differs from abstraction. This contrast of Worringer's may be felt also within abstract art. Whereas in Hartung everything is stone and geometry, in Heiliger the accent is on organic life and irregular motion. Their opposing sensitivities are like those of male and female. Hartung favors the crystal, Heiliger the plant. The contrast is evident even when both exclude any imitation of nature. Hartung seeks a finished and unchanging condition; Heiliger wants motion to continue. Their drawings are also basically different, and betray the same contrast. Heiliger's forms are delicately blurred and in a state of mutation in which a melodic theme always remains perceptible.

Karl Hartung. Terra Cotta, 1948

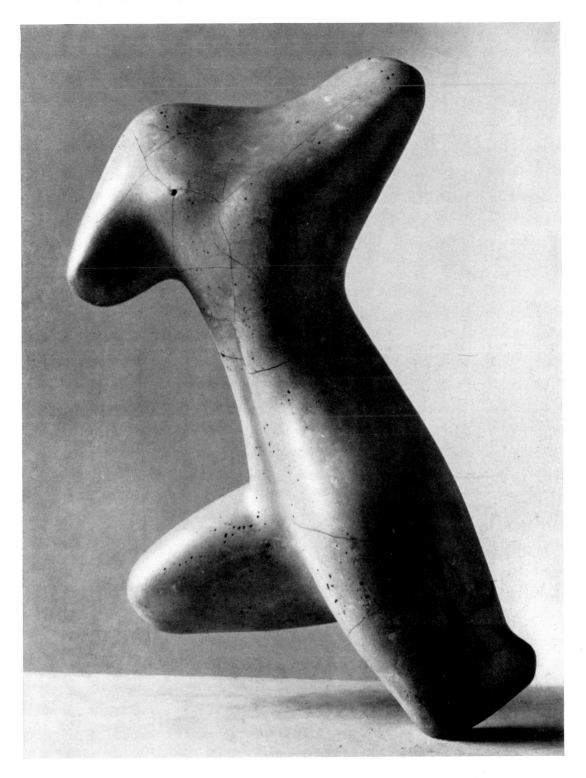

Bernhard Heiliger. Seraph, 1952

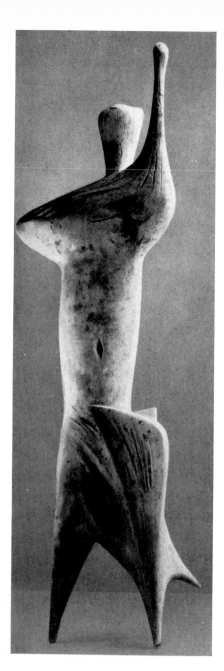

Sometimes Heiliger's sculptures of the human body are shot through with plantlike growth, as in his *Vegetative Sculpture* (1956), which he calls "Daphne in reverse... a tree that turns into a human being." He received a major award for his memorial, *To The Unknown Political Prisoner*, a kneeling torso trying to free itself from an entanglement of barbed wire. In 1954 he created *Two Figures in Relationship to Each Other*; although the bodies are placed far apart, contacts are established by distentions and gestures, mysteriously uniting them. Even his portrait heads (Carl Hofer, Ernst Reuter) are outlined in fluid curves, yet without loss of individual activity or expression.

In his portraits, it was important to him to "fuse likeness and image, the man and the symbol." His heads do not rest on a firm neck; they rise up out of an imaginary curve of the body or are entirely without a base. He transformed his *Nike* of 1956 into a towering plastic symbol proclaiming victory. Among his commissions are a large relief for the Berlin Schiller Theater and a smaller one for the city of Munich which is expressed only in abstract rhythms. What a long way this artist has traveled from Maillol, Despiau, and his beginnings at the Berlin Academy!

In Berlin there are other sculptors who are groping their way between the figurative and the abstract, without going quite as far as Heiliger or Hartung. *Alexander Gonda* (b. 1905) was a master

*Bernhard Heiliger. Nike, 1956
Munich, Bayerische
Staatsgemäldesammlungen*

*Bernhard Heiliger. Carl Hofer, 1951
Essen, Museum Folkwang*

372

pupil under Karl Albiker, and since 1945 has been teaching sculpture at the Berlin Hochschule. In *Daphne*, chiseled in limestone, meticulously rounded and polished, and in *Bird* and *Fish*, which he mounted on turntables, he maintains the compactness of the total volume and places it in space in all its precise solidity. In this emphasis on the compact volume he differs from Heiliger. Gonda also modeled portrait heads, poured in gray-blue concrete and polished, which evoke a sense of typical, timeless form, for all their individuality and respect for the personality of the sitter. In other works he tried to transform the volume of a figure into fantastic shapes. Recently he has been doing this using hollow space to contrast expressively with the swelling volumes.

Gerhard Schreiter (b. 1909), from the Erz mountains in Saxony, was taught by his father to use hammer and chisel at the age of twelve. He now teaches at the Bremen Art School. He is primarily concerned with the contrasts between hard and soft textures, and he draws space into the hollow areas of his forms. Using wax, he also models smaller works which nevertheless retain some degree of monumentality.

L. G. Schrieber (b. 1907), who was first a painter, is preoccupied with a very personal artistic problem. In

Alexander Gonda. Harlequins, 1956

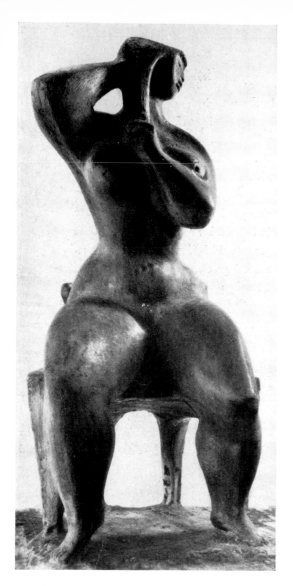

multiple-figure sculptures (his most successful works) he tries to go beyond the customary group treatment and he fuses the single bodies into one block. The figures in these free-standing sculptures are clothed in tight-fitting quasi-Egyptian robes under which their full cylindrical volume is revealed. Schrieber's figures are always based on reality. "We are not creators but creatures. Don't make a circle out of the sun, but a sun out of a circle!"

Seff Weidl (b. 1915), who has lived since 1945 in the Bavarian Alps, is more abstract. In free-standing sculptures, in reliefs and in graphic work, he preserves the appearance of objects in a simple rhythm of basic forms, bringing them close to architecture, but without obliterating the vitality of the structure.

Leo Smigay (b. 1900) works towards similar ends. He uses wood, stone and metal, his metal work being the most convincing. He too no longer wants to recount or describe, but to create a formal structure for which the

Gerhard Schreiter. Woman Combing her Hair, 1954

Ludwig Gabriel Schrieber. Passeo, 1957

374

Seff Weidl. Man Leaning Forward, 1954

human body is only a point of departure for a pure rhythmic expression. "My dream is a world as simple as possible, free of all complications."

The approach of all these sculptors seems to lie somewhere between the representation of complete human beings and the creation simply of their underlying structure. Let us now turn to a type of sculpture that is wholly free of objective reference and seeks a pure but original kind of three-dimensional form. This type has developed in the last years throughout the civilized world, just as it has in the field of painting. Karl Hartung, whose orientation has been abstract for some time, must be counted among its exponents. As in painting, within the field of abstract sculpture we find two possible ways of dealing with form. Some artists work with solid, space-limiting masses (the Brancusi type); others, the constructivists, define transparent virtual volumes by means of rods or other tangible linear media (the Pevsner and Gabo type).

Hans Uhlmann (b. 1900) has devoted himself to the second possibility. He grew up in Berlin and was first an engineer, but he became obsessed by irrational tensions which he tried to formulate. He was the first in Germany to concentrate on wholly nonobjective rod sculpture. Although he may have been influenced during his stay in Paris by Pevsner and Gabo, who had been working along these lines in the

375

twenties, he found his own point of departure. He began by containing imaginary space with steel bands, tubular and square-section rods and perforated metal sheets. Around an immaterial core he placed metal lines of force which encircled or bored through *virtual* volumes. What he had in mind was not only three-dimensional delineations but also an effect of symbols as similes of emotional powers. In the beginning Uhlmann included recollections of human heads or bodies, of bird or insect life, but gradually these constellations became an end in themselves, powered with high tension, sometimes displaying an almost Prussian energy. We are not supposed to decide between organic or a machine world; both are brought together into a secret unity. The construc-

Leo Smigay. Aggression, circa 1950

Hans Uhlmann
Steel Sculpture, 1954

Theodor Bechteler
House, 1958

Hans Uhlmann. Constellation, 1956

tive elements show a tendency to grow away from the control of the engineer and establish their own form fantasy. Uhlmann of course had to camouflage his proclivities in this direction during the years of National Socialism, but since 1950 he has been teaching in this mode at the Berlin Hochschule. His wash drawings also lie between expression and construction.

While Uhlmann was engaged in eliminating mass-volume, *Emil Cimiotti* (b. 1927), in Stuttgart, was developing abstractions of the other, space-constructing type. After studying with Paul Baum, Hartung and Ossip Zadkine, he sought to re-form the human figure in an abstract fashion whereby the limbs reach out into space like branches. The effect, however, remains an animalistic, distended form. He has since abandoned the human body as a medium of expression. Now lively masses protrude into space in every direction, always soft and voluminous, so that one feels their specific plastic quality. *Ernst Hermanns* (b. 1914), active in the Ruhr, works in a similar style. Emulating the processes of nature, he has created

377

Emil Cimiotti
Figures, 1956

works that are abstract but fully three-dimensional. In a relief of considerable proportions set up out-of-doors, he has succeeded in realizing his intention also on a large scale.

The work of *Herbert Hajek* (b. 1927) falls between constructivism and solid sculpture, and combines both. He makes treelike forms with cantilevered, perforated surfaces. A crusty veneer is left untouched, making the whole look like some unknown creature weathered by age. Technological and natural shapes are crossed without ever becoming imitative. In short, a process of nature is being reproduced, but the results are symbolic, since it would be difficult to find an analogy in nature. Hajek also works on religious themes in which he naturally must adhere to the given iconography.

Brigitte Meier-Denninghoff (b. 1923) belongs to the same generation. She studied with Henry Moore and Pevsner, and first worked in concrete. She then turned to smaller, perforated constructions in metal, consisting of closely woven sheaves and free rippling structures of tin, in which the process of soldering is stressed. This produces an effect comparable to that of the natural stalactites found in caves. The tin dries with irregularities; bumps and streaks appear and are connected by parallel rods. Clear, outstretched straight lines and unpredictable cross lines form a kind of symbol for the duality of our existence—its rational, technological element and its rampant tensions.

Herbert Hajek
Space-knot, 1957

379

Ernst Hermanns. Relief in Gelsenkirchen, 1957

Norbert Kricke (b. 1922) concentrates on only one of these forms of abstract sculpture, criss-crossing empty space with lines. All unbroken, massive material is rejected. His work differs in expression from that of Uhlmann in that it is more pliable and smooth. Uhlmann has turned more and more to a firm rod structure, whereas Kricke employs more sublimated means, as if his constructions were to be subordinated to universal space even as they curve energetically through it. Here we are dealing with something he calls "the change of tempo in suspension," and which he tries to achieve by coloring his rods and wires. A light line, in his opinion, appears to move faster than a dark one. His early works were more firmly constructed; later he favored loose sheaves which remind one of the stem-growth of plants, but any imitation of nature is far from his mind. From one root, many delicate lines of power travel out into

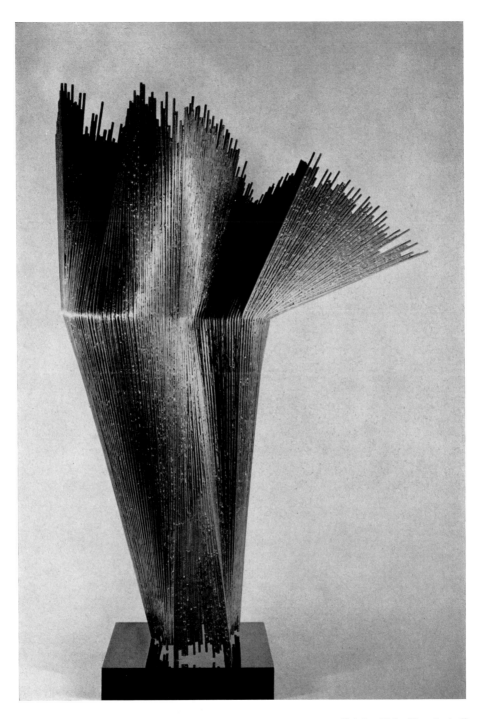

Brigitte Meier-Denninghoff
Dynamic Form, 1961

381

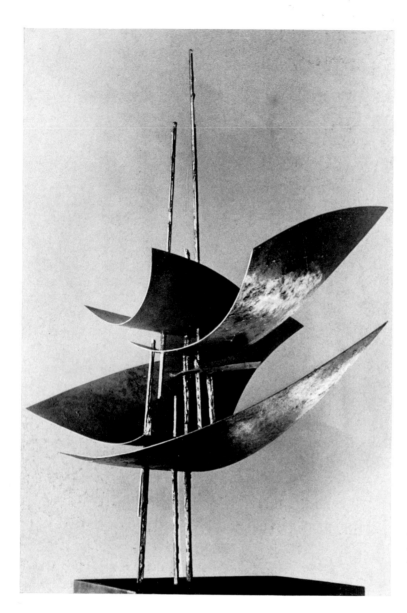

Brigitte Meier-Denninghoff
Movement upward,
1956

space, rising up or floating off, ever more distant from one another, only to find their way back to each other in the end. Recently he has been working with "vibrating surfaces," parallel wands of different lengths welded together. Kricke plans to include water in his art, and also fireworks, this ancient device making possible a colored space symphony.

382

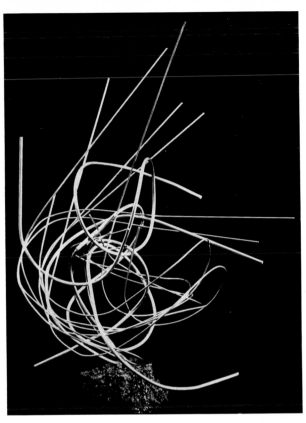

Norbert Kricke
Space Sculpture, Nickel, 1956

Norbert Kricke. Space Sculpture,
Steel, Copper, Brass, 1957

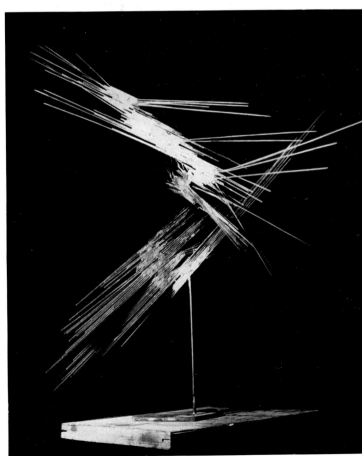

SCULPTURE IN GERMANY SINCE 1955, BY JULIANE ROH

Expression and Neo-Baroque

Sculpture, to a greater extent than painting, is a craft that must be learned. For this reason we find a concentration of fresh young talent wherever we have good teachers. Berlin, therefore, has become a center for a rising generation of sculptors because Hartung, Heiliger and Uhlmann are teaching there.

*Alois
Wünsche-Mitterecker
Falling Man*

E. R. Nele-Bode. Winged–Soloman, 1964

Though its young graduates frequently rebel against what they have been taught, one may nevertheless speak today of a Berlin School.

Lothar Fischer. The Gust of Wind, 1967

Friedrich Werthmann. Whirl, 1966

But before we turn our attention to these younger artists, one extraordinary, solitary figure of the preceding generation remains to be discussed. *Alois Wünsche-Mitterecker* (b. 1903) is an Austrian who today lives like a recluse in the Swabian town of Eichstätt. Hidden away here, a work of sculpture is taking shape, a work which is probably the largest of our century. In 1962 Wünsche-Mitterecker hit on the idea of a *Mahnmal,* or "exhortation monument" (in contrast to a *Denkmal,* which urges us only to think, *denken*). It was to illustrate the horror of human self-mutilation in war. Wünsche has conceived a battlefield with over one hundred life-sized figures, of which approximately fifty have been completed. It will not be possible to evaluate the quality and scope of this work until it has been installed in a lonely hollow in the Swabian Alps. Fighting each other here are creatures whom war has deformed into grotesque lemurs. Mysterious energy remains somehow alive in these hacked-off and mutilated figures. Grotesque stump-forms continue to fight: this is the pandemonium of war! As in all such comprehensive works of art, there will be experts who will find weak spots and probably see too much pathos in the effort. But one has the feeling that hereafter we may have done with triumphant war memorials and the false sentiment of veterans' cemeteries.

Although Wünsche chooses to remain outside the art world, he does not stand alone in his grotesque, demonic characterization of war. In the same period Nele-Bode and Lothar Fischer were modeling "Soldiers" who were no less grotesque, though certainly less melodramatic. In their case the game of war became a ludicrous joke. *Nele-Bode* (b. 1932) began to work with a lively structural fantasy. This was followed by a wildly exuberant phase which culminated in 1961 with *The Marchers.* Today her work is a shallow echo of those tempestuous figures—cell-shaped hollow forms with gigantic wings built up from many small units.

The work of *Lothar Fischer* (b. 1933) is of a comparable type of expressionism. Like Nele-Bode, Fisher lived in Munich in the early sixties; he was a member of the

Erich Hauser. Steel, 1965

Spur group and a disciple of their playful phantomism. He prefers to work with soft clay. His mutilated figures are bloated and bulbous, reminding us sometimes of the clumsy modeling of children. Here naivety intentionally becomes an artistic method.

Detlef Birgfeld. Small Composition, 1964

387

Ernst Hermanns. Sculpture, 1/66

Now to return to the generation of Berlin sculptors previously mentioned. *Rolf Szymanski* (b. 1928), *Gersom Fehrenbach* (b. 1932) and *Utz Kampmann* (b. 1935) create bulbous forms which derive from *art informel* but which, in their uninhibitedness, go far beyond their source. Szymanski and Fehrenbach especially may be distinguished by a vitality that can only be called baroque. *Guido Jendritzko* (b. 1925) was originally more severe in expression, but later his crumpled figures follow this expressive trend.

Kaspar Thomas Lenk
Stratification 31, 1966

Kampmann has meanwhile abandoned it and we shall return to him. *Ben Wargin* (b. 1930) and *Reinhold Hommes* (b. 1934), on the other hand, continue the Hartung tradition. In her iron sculpture, *Ursula Sax* (b. 1935) concentrates on compact symbols which she vitalizes in a strange fashion. Even landscape motifs, in some extraordinary way, may be found in them. There is no evidence of such a baroque trend among the young sculptors of South Germany, where Herbert Hajek (see p. 378 and below) and Fritz Koenig (see p. 364) are active. *Alfred Aschauer* (b.1931) and *Herbert Peters* (b. 1925) should be included in these profiles of the new generation. Both began to work with closed, stele-shaped forms, the surfaces broken by cracks and crevices. In later works

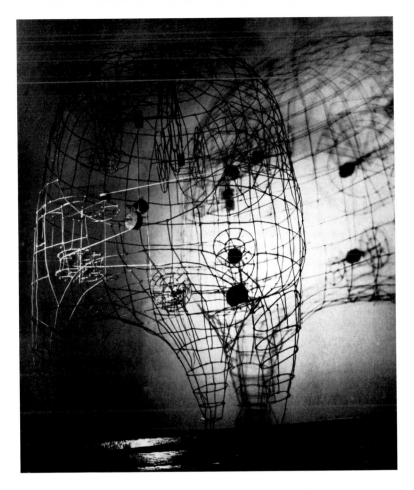

Harry Kramer
Three-footed

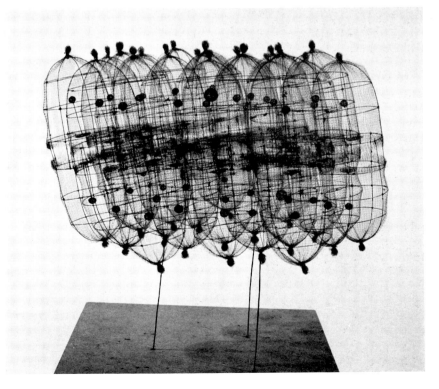

Günther Haese
Oasis, 1964

389

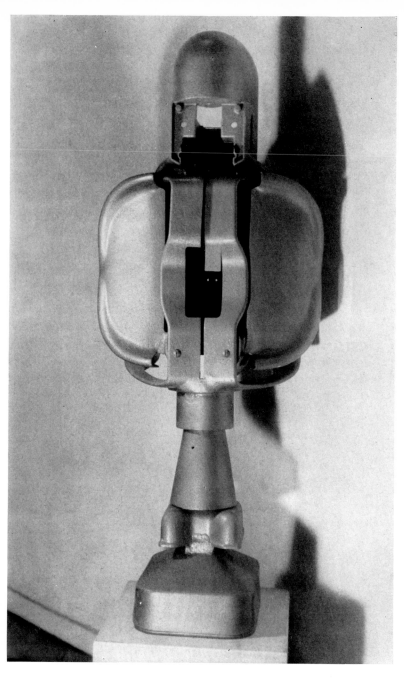

Hans Salentin. Sculpture VIII–IX– 65

by Peters, human forms peel off from an *informel* core.

Constructivist Tendencies

The expressive genre just described attracted attention mainly through its rich sculptural potentialities. In the meantime a more severe, more constructivist tendency has won acceptance, and a number of extremely varied personalities are working in this vein.

In Frankfurt both the brothers *Hans* (b. 1928) and *Klaus Steinbrenner* (b. 1935) work with heavy steles of wood or stone, articulated in cubist fashion, showing a feeling for proportion and discipline. Steles by *Franz Bucher* (b. 1928) are subordinated more to the individual pattern of growth in the wood itself, but Bucher gives them a polished form. At the Venice Biennale of 1966 the Rhinelander *Ferdinand Ris*, who has turned to sculpture from painting, attracted attention. To him the dialectics of volume and space are again important. He proceeds frequently from a round form which he breaks open like a bud. The different leaves thus formed are pressed back toward the center by the pressure of the space around them.

Sculptors in steel as different as Werthmann, Hauser, Nagel or Gerlinde Beck have a common goal. Iron has to be forged, but steel may be cut or welded. Steel is thin and elastic. In this material, forces may become apparent which activate space itself, making of it a field of tension.

390

The Rhinelander *Friedrich Werthmann* (b. 1927) uses steel bands which he welds into transparent, spherical forms. Going beyond their constructive purpose, they develop a life of their own and send long-stemmed tentacles out into space. Abstract steel compositions turn into semi-organic creatures, groping their way to possession of the space around them. With more advanced means, the Swabian *Erich Hauser* (b. 1930) achieves the body-space tension which Ferdinand Ris also has in mind. Here the resistance of steel–in contrast to bronze–turns the seams into supporting elements of the form. The surfaces of Hauser's steel sculptures are like stretched sails; spherical triangles find their way to each other in space, in constantly new configurations. Hauser leaves open cracks which catch the shadows, and the whole reveals itself as a concave form. The compositions which the Heidelberger *Hans Nagel* welds together from scrap iron and steel are less severe than Hauser's. Changes of surface structure and color are put in play, and the effect is more painterly. *Gerlinde Beck* uses steel to construct angular steles with a massive effect. Only the mirroring surface remains steel-like in appearance.

Hauser's steel sculptures have been compared to the work of old armorers. This applies even more strongly to the work of *Detlef Birgfeld* (b. 1937), who rivets steel plates together so that the whole looks like a robot in a coat of mail. *Ernst Hermanns* (see p. 377) combines steel cylinders, sheets and hemispheres in the simplest combinations. Only through the proximity of these basic forms is that fundamental tension between form and space again

Fritz Koenig. Caryatid, 1965

achieved. Kampmann, Lenk and Hajek have turned to polychrome sculpture, breaking decisively with their earlier styles. They are fully aware of the fact that autonomous colors form their own spatial effects and may therefore also work toward a sculptural reality, and they exploit those effects. *Herbert Hajek* (see p. 378) first introduced color into his work in 1964, as so-called *Farbwege* (color tracks). Strips of color are drawn, apparently aimlessly, over his bronzes. The object itself and these abstract signals are meant to challenge each other. In his latest works, the sculptor has accommodated the sculptured form to the

Horst Egon Kalinowski
Wine press of my Sorrow, 1963

requirements of the color. Now his basic form is white, divided optically by a shining band of color. With this method, blue or red, for instance, may rob a white object of all its gravity.

Utz Kampmann clamps together two symmetrical colored *volumina*, and the color brings out the plastic quality. *Kaspar Thomas Lenk* (b. 1933) has arrived at a curious form of sculpture-in-layers which he accentuates with color. His layer reliefs give an illusion of depth which may be fortified by one glowing signal color, or, on the other hand, it may be denied its spatial implication. Lenk toys with both possibilities. In every case the result is a composition that lies between painting and sculpture, in which the functions of both meet in a tense and original relationship.

Transparencies and Mobiles

Kramer and Haese have enriched wire sculpture with their playful innovations. *Harry Kramer* (b. 1925) constructs airy cages in which a simple gear moves, propelling nothing. As ironic automatons they are playfully busy, and may even pause at their own discretion. Since 1961, *Günther Haese* (b. 1924) has been composing thin, airy wire structures that shiver with every breath of air. Parts of watches are fitted into filigree nets where they do an elastic balancing act on thin wires. Haese's imagination has much in common with Klee's, even in the poetic titles he gives to his work.

Sculptured Surrealism

The classic Surrealism of the twenties did not produce a sculptor who may be considered specifically Surrealist, but in the meantime a genre which we could call Surrealism II has emerged, allied with Pop Art and prominent in sculpture particularly. The Americans George Segal and Marisol come to mind. In any case, much of Pop Art tends toward relief, toward panels plastered with objects, as for instance in the case of Alvermann, whom we have already mentioned. The mysterious caissons of *Horst Egon Kalinowski* (b. 1924), who lives in Paris, belong in the ambivalent realm of symbolism. Strange wood or iron parts, removed from their original function, lie or hang over leather upholstered boxes, assembled in an expressive plasticity and polished meticulously. A quiet fascination emanates from these objects, as though they were puzzling idols of an unknown culture. The artist gives them familiar mythological names. *Hans Salentin* also presents us with idols. He is attracted to the frequently physiognomic expressiveness of molds for machine parts and with them assembles imaginative figures, a machine-park of robots, partly uncanny, partly humorous.

392

ARCHITECTURE

Architecture in general, and modern architecture especially, differs from painting and sculpture in that it is always bound up with the practical functioning of life. Before it may serve to express the beauty that is the governing aim of painting and sculpture, the rational demands of the engineer have to be met. Therefore architecture offers a readier answer than painting or sculpture to a question that is frowned on today: Has this art only changed in the twentieth century, or has it also progressed? In the case of modern architecture no one can reasonably deny that there has been genuine progress.

In the nineteenth century architecture suffered from a profound dualism. New spatial concepts and construction were found only in buildings with practical functions. "Monumental architecture" remained the slave of styles that successively imitated the Gothic, the Renaissance and the Baroque. The efforts at reform made by Ruskin, Morris and Walter Crane were still essentially historic revivals. The competition for the construction of apartment houses sponsored by the Bavarian King Maximilian II in 1851 produced nothing but traditional style mixtures (even though some of them were quite good, as may still be seen today in Munich's Maximilianstraße). At the turn of the century, therefore, when Austrian and German architects began to seek new proportions and spatial concepts–with or without Jugendstil influence–it was common belief that a totally new architecture was about to evolve. But now that we have experienced the truly original and functional architecture of the 1920's, we realize that even after 1900 there were numerous relapses into the language of past traditions. These are evident even in the Amsterdam Stock Exchange (1898–1904) by Hendrik Berlage, although the architect said at the time, "We must find our way back to the truth... above all we must construct soundly... and in the simplest style possible."

German architecture underwent a purification process as this imitation of styles was gradually eliminated and the architect began to work more spontaneously in the spirit of his own time, as had been customary in nearly all earlier periods. Mere decoration and surface ostentation were overcome and the builder concentrated more and more on the function of the structure, that is to say, he began to plan from the inside out. New consideration was given to the development of domestic architecture from the standpoint of the sociological and spiritual requirements of present day society. Finally, the necessity for facing the greatest architectural problem of all–the planning of new communities–became increasingly

393

evident, and it was confronted. As early as the twenties, a period rich in new ideas, architects such as Gropius, Mies van der Rohe and Hilberseimer realized that modern materials, the traffic of the future, and the soul of man demanded new basic conceptions for city planning. Their ideas were hotly debated and modified at meetings of the CIAM, the International Congress for Modern Architecture. But for Germany much had to remain utopian concept because of the absence of building laws to permit the required reapportionment of property and to give the planners a free hand.

The architecture of the twentieth century could never have been realized without the new building materials. As early as 1851 the architect Joseph Paxton, who had begun his career as a simple nursery-man, was able to construct the gigantic London Crystal Palace out of prefabricated iron and glass. In 1855 it became possible to refine iron into steel that could be rolled in long bars; thus the unprecedented load-bearing steel scaffolding became feasible and the building was no longer dependent on the support of the masonry wall. During the 1860's the architect began to have reinforced concrete at his disposal. Concrete (cement mixed with sand, gravel and water) can withstand great pressure, but for purposes that require tensile strength it must be reinforced with steel. Before 1900 a process was developed with which supports, crossbeams and ceiling could be poured seamlessly to form a load-bearing unit, and with this, astounding possibilities were opened up to the imagination. Dimensions hitherto undreamed of could be spanned, making possible an entirely new concept of space. The architect, however, took advantage of this new freedom only very gradually.

In the architecture of our century, four stages may be defined. In the first we find neo-Baroque and neoclassical elements crossed with Jugendstil influences. Dualistic solutions resulted, some still rooted in the nineteenth century, others firmly established in the twentieth. Much was restyled superficially from a purely aesthetic point of view; the few innovations must be judged today as arbitrary or as decorative arts products. After all, the reforms of the Jugendstil were essentially ornamental. But we also find this ambivalence in other architectural trends, however varied, as in the work of Alfred Messel, German Bestelmeyer, Theodor Fischer, Paul Bonatz or Paul Schmitthenner.

In a second stage—as demonstrated by van de Velde and to some extent by Peter Behrens—pure form became more steadily visible, structural considerations were dominant, and the aim was to express the building as a whole. Monumentality was stressed, but for the most part still superficially and representationally.

In a third stage, buildings became more consistent and revealing of their techniques. They gave an impression of timelessness (Gropius, Mies van der Rohe, Bruno Taut). Construction and material fitted the requirements, and the architect reveled in new techniques whose intrinsic beauty was in itself a value worth expressing. The engineer became prototype of the architect as never before (although this could not be said of the professors of architecture at our technological institutes). Construction with iron, within a sheath of glass, dominated. The architect's attitude was unusually objective; he wanted only to design an impersonal shell, with expression provided by what lay within—the furnishings and their arrangement, the decor, the human beings moving around inside. The audacious years between 1920 and 1933 may be counted among the most exciting in architectural history. In this sometimes almost immaculate phase, German architecture achieved the desired purity by means of the most precise use of material and proportions, and set a standard which was to win worldwide acceptance.

A fourth stage, developed first in Brazil and Venezuela rather than in Europe by European architects, is only now emerging as an important direction in Germany. However, it was introduced in Germany in the twenties by Hugo Haering and Hans Scharoun. In this stage a greater fluidity of form is once more permissible. But this architecture differs from that of the Jugendstil-influenced first stage in that the entire building–in all dimensions, including its function–is to be ruled by motion. Instead of subjective characteristics, we now have a specifically architectonic individuality. The architect no longer seeks the simplest solution but the one with the most vitality, and speaks of the "organic" thing, rather than of construction. In modern painting a somewhat similar development is evident since the waning of Constructivism. It may be felt also in the change that has been imposed on furniture, if one compares certain shell- and kidney-shaped tables in today's market with the rectangular forms of the Dutch Stijl group around 1920, which in those days were influential also in Germany. Even the production of the great individual masters shows a similar trend. Le Corbusier's chapel in Ronchamp and Niemeyer's church in Belo Horizonte (Brazil) display irrational curves and a flowing style.

But one should not imagine that the division between stages three and four was very sharp. The "machine to live in" (Le Corbusier) of the third stage was not intended to despiritualize the inhabitant; on the contrary, its purpose was to lighten the housewife's task so that she might have more time for an inner life. In all these stages, the new direction did not abruptly displace the earlier one; as is always the case in the life of history, they overlapped.

The Jugendstil and How It Was Overcome

At the beginning of the twentieth century, the Belgian *Henry van de Velde* (1863–1957) was the first major architect to inaugurate a true reform of building styles. To Germany must go the credit for having attracted this master early in his career. In productive times of renewal, different cultural fields tend to stimulate each other. Van de Velde had been a painter, associated with the group around Seurat and Gauguin and the poetic Symbolists, but quite early in his career he felt compelled to work toward a change in man's way of life as a whole. "Actually my spirit found it immoral to produce a work of which there could be only one of its kind. This quality of the painting, the statue and the monument seemed to me an example of an exclusive egoism." He admired the electric light bulb "as a form that has never been seen before, as beautiful in itself as any form ever created by an artist." As early as 1894 he was designing chairs and tables whose structural detail was not obscured by decoration. Then he built his own house, Bloemenwerf, in Uccle (Brussels); it attracted a great deal of attention because of its extraordinary lines, although it derived in part from the older tradition of the English country house. Van de Velde belonged to the abstract, not to the floral wing of the Jugendstil. His form and ornamentation fell between two subconscious tendencies. On the one hand he was directed toward an affirmation of technology and industry, for unlike his predecessors Ruskin and Morris, he rejected a one-sided glorification of handicraft. "The same laws that rule the work of the engineer also rule all decoration." On the other, expression also motivated him. "The line is a force... it takes its strength from the energy

Henry van de Velde
Werkbund Theater
Cologne, 1914

of whoever drew it," a sentence that seems to foretell the abstract painting that was to be realized ten years later by Kandinsky. It is interesting to recall that Kandinsky was also affiliated in his beginnings with a vanishing Jugendstil.

In Paris, a first showing of Van de Velde's highly original work horrified people. Edmond de Goncourt spoke of "the tools of a dentist." In the twenties the steel tubular furniture of Marcel Breuer and Mies van der Rohe would meet a similar reception. But at the Arts and Crafts Exhibition in Dresden, Van de Velde finally gained recognition. He built the Folkwang Museum in Hagen for the collector Osthaus, and in 1911 was called to the Weimar Kunstschule.

Now the rooms of a house were to form a true organism. The distribution of rooms and the material were to determine each other, and everything was to be held together by lighter walls; closets were to be recessed or built in. But everything was still–at least partially–in a sweeping, richly curvilinear style; not until several years later did the Bauhaus, also in Weimar, oppose this rhythmic, linear style with its ideals of constructivism. But today the pendulum is swinging back, which explains a renewed appreciation of the Jugendstil.

In 1914 Van de Velde crowned his achievements in Germany with a theater for the Cologne Werkbund Exhibition, built consistently in a completely new style, without ornament or columns, and treated rather like an abstract sculpture. In its interior we find an entirely new distribution of space. If one compares this building with another at the same exhibition, the Austrian Pavilion by the Viennese architect Josef Hoffmann, also a reformer, one sees a contrast that is characteristic for the year 1914. However distinguished Hoffmann's buildings may have been, for the exterior he had nothing to contribute but an elegantly modified Greek temple. (Nevertheless, in other works, in Vienna, he proved himself a master of architectural reform.)

Van de Velde's further development did not take place in Germany, for during the First World War he was expelled as an alien. He went on to build for the Dutch maecenas Kröller-Müller, and was made director of the Brussels Institute for Architecture and Decorative Arts. At the Paris Worlds Fair of 1937

he made a great impression with his clearly defined, brick Belgian pavilion. Of his publications, his *Laienpredigt* (*Lay Sermon*, 1902), *Vom neuen Stil* (*Of a new style*, 1907), and *Les fondements d'un style moderne* (*Fundamentals of Modern Style*, 1933) are noteworthy.

Hermann Obrist (1863–1927), a Swiss, was born the same year as Van de Velde, and devoted himself exclusively to interior decoration, the decorative arts and sculpture. In Florence in 1892 he founded a workshop for embroidery which sought new types of design. He concentrated on the Jugendstil direction that favored plant forms; his elegantly rhythmicizing needlework piece, *Whiplash* (1895) demonstrates his style. Today Obrist is valued as a precursor, if not the initiator, of abstract sculpture, and in fact he was struggling with nonfigurative sculpture as early as 1900. From 1894 Obrist taught in Munich. His paper of 1903, *Neue Möglichkeiten der bildenden Künste* (*New Possibilities in the Fine Arts*), was an important publication.

The painter *Otto Eckmann* (1865–1902) designed decorative articles, some single chairs and colored wood-

Hermann Obrist. Fountain, Essen, 1913

cuts. Long-stemmed flowers and long-necked swans are Jugendstil themes, but with Eckmann they force their way out of the frame and trail across the walls in free, decorative rhythms. Before 1900, as a typographer, he created the flowing Eckmann type.

August Endell (1871–1925), from Berlin, was an imaginative, philosophically trained autodidact, a personality very typical of his day. In Munich he joined forces with Obrist and was active as an interior decorator. In 1896 he built his famous photographer's studio there, the Elvira House (destroyed in World War II). With its new, free arrangement of rooms and horizontal roof, and above all with its bold facade on which an abstract relief anticipated ideas of the early Kandinsky, the house was like a fanfare ushering in the modern age. This work was followed by the Neumann Ballrooms and the Wolzogen Theater, both in Berlin, and a sanatorium for the North Sea spa Wyk auf Föhr. He produced an exciting book on the beauties of the metropolis, and in 1918 he was made director of the Breslau Academy. As if foreseeing abstract painting and sculpture, he said, "We have to follow forms with our eyes, exactly and everywhere, every curve, every bend, every broadening, every contraction—in short we must experience every change. If we use our eyes like this, a whole new world of enormous wealth is created for us."

The Jugendstil influence could be felt everywhere. *Bernhard Pankok* (1872–1943) gave it expression mainly in his furniture. As a decorator he designed, among other things, interiors of steamers. He built the Lange House and the Rosenfeld Villa in Tübingen, and an Exhibition Hall in Stuttgart. His work fell somewhere between curvilinear form and classical ornamentation, without, however, always achieving a pure solution.

398

The satirical draftsman *Bruno Paul* (b. 1874) (see
p. 38) was typical for this period of upheaval in
which every kind of art was involved. He painted,
drew for the magazines *Simplizissimus* and *Jugend*,
changed from dabbler in the decorative arts to
architect, directed the Vereinigte Werkstätten (see
below), designed streetcars and the first ready-
made furniture in Germany. As architect, he favored a simplified classicism. *Richard Riemerschmid*
(1868–1957), from Munich, was also a painter who

Bernhard Pankok. Smoking room, Turin, 1902

Bernhard Hoetger. Bedroom in Worpswede

Bruno Paul. Dining room, Turin, 1902

turned to interior decoration and architecture. His
most enduring work was the interior of the Munich
Theater, the Schauspielhaus (1901). Here the
Jugendstil is effective in a harmoniously flowing,
simplified style; all the gilded plaster with muses
and masks, all the gathered draperies, have been
eliminated. The result is a feeling of intimacy.
Riemerschmid's influence was enhanced by his
activity for the Vereinigte Werkstätten (United
Workshops), a guild of designers–Riemerschmid,
Obrist, Endell, Pankok, Bertsch and Bruno Paul,

among others—who joined to form a craft shop for work and sale, similar to the one once formed around William Morris. Beside good furniture and accessories, sets of furniture were manufactured at modest prices. A workshop in Dresden was active along the same lines, and in 1907 the Deutsche Werkstätte was founded at Riemerschmid's instigation. In the same year he designed a highly original country house, and in 1909 the complete plan for the Gartenstadt Hellerau (Garden City Hellerau) which, for the first time in Germany, was intended to make low-cost housing possible outside city limits. In 1925 he built the Exhibition Hall for the Munich Verkehrsausstellung (Transportation Fair). For many years he was director of the Munich and Cologne Craft Schools. But his impressive plan for amalgamating the Munich Art Academy and School of Applied Arts was ignored. As educator he poured out a wealth of ideas; some were a little frivolous, but he knew how to hold the balance between the new view of regional art and modern styles.

In 1901 a decisive impetus for progressive architecture came from the Darmstadt Artists Colony, an exposition sponsored by Grand Duke Ernst Ludwig of Hessen. The buildings, erected on the Mathilden-

Richard Riemerschmid
Kammerspiele (renovated), Munich,
1901

Josef Maria Olbrich. Ernst Ludwig House,
Darmstadt, 1901

höhe, a hill near the city, were permanent structures. (They are now the home of the Bauhaus archives.) Here all the arts were to be brought together under the aegis of architecture. *Josef Maria Olbrich* (1867–1908) was a decisive influence in this undertaking. The proportions of his sprawling Exhibition Hall were something new for Germany and had probably been demonstrated before only by Frank Lloyd Wright in the United States. Olbrich's Wedding Tower of 1907, on the same site, was built in a style that was to become general only much later. Ribbon windows ran around the corner of the building, which was capped by a most unusual roof. Olbrich's own house in the same colony was highly original. And his distinguished but more traditional Feinhals Building in Cologne-Marienburg (1908) demonstrated that he could also work in a more conventional style. Olbrich, who died prematurely at forty-one, was a popular architect not only in Germany but also in Italy and Russia. Among other things he designed interiors for ocean liners.

Josef Maria Olbrich
The Architect's Residence, Artists Colony,
Darmstadt, 1901

Josef Maria Olbrich
Wedding Tower,
Darmstadt, 1907

The Austrian *Adolf Loos* (1870–1933) does not really belong to our study since his work—especially his important residential-house style—was developed outside Germany. However, he had a great influence on German architecture. Before 1900 he lived for some time in the United States; the utilitarian housing he saw there impressed him and this helped him to turn his back on the Jugendstil. With his loudly proclaimed dictum, "Ornament is a crime," he became a pioneer of the architectural "New Objectivity," although his ambitious plans for a Ministry of War and the Terrace Hotel Babylon were never carried out. *Peter Behrens* (1868–1940), from north Germany, also changed gradually to a more utilitarian style. One of his first efforts in this direction was his own house in the Darmstadt Artists Colony, which stands a little apart from the other buildings. It was often said that the house was not made up of forms but *was* one single form.

The decisive inspiration in the field of monumental buildings came not from Olbrich, but from Behrens. He had also worked in older traditions modified for practical use. In his crematorium in Delster (near Hagen), built in 1907, the influence of the Tuscan Romanesque church of San Miniato in Florence is evident; in his German embassy building in St. Petersburg (1912) one senses the influence of the simplified early nineteenth-century classicism of Friedrich Weinbrenner. But good taste and a sound

402

sense of proportion prevented Behrens from making any blunders for the sake of fashion. Any hazard of Behrens' taking this direction was eliminated by the commission from the Berlin Allgemeine Elektrizitätsgesellschaft, the AEG. In Behrens' appointment as architect for this mammoth electric company a giant step was taken toward raising the standards of German industrial building. Now Behrens could work in a field which had never been exploited by architecture before. His Turbine Plant for the AEG, built in 1909, was a revolutionary act which opened the way in Germany for an architecture that worked with materials as freely as possible, guided entirely by the requirements of the project as a whole. The steel supports of this structure are visible on the long walls, tapering toward the bottom as if to conduct the line of power down to the base. The glass front is tilted outward slightly to connect with the salient roof support. In this way the facade of the building was given the quality of relief without the ubiqui-

Peter Behrens. The Architect's Residence, Darmstadt, 1901

tous cornice. Some optical illusion is noticeable in the side view. Here Behrens achieved a solution from which Gropius could proceed. In 1912 Behrens designed the buildings for the Frankfurt Gas Company in the same precise style. His later work was neither as original nor as influential. He built a factory and office buildings in Düsseldorf, houses in Berlin and Hoechst, exhibition buildings in Cologne, Bern, Dresden and Munich.

Behrens found his way to architecture from painting, typography and the decorative arts, but as architect he was entirely self-taught—suggesting again that when the time comes for a change, the "outsider"

*Peter Behrens
Turbine Plant for the AEG,
Berlin, 1909*

Peter Behrens
Union Building, Bern

Peter Behrens
Crematorium in Delstern,
near Hagen, 1906–1907

is needed because he has preserved the freshness of vision required to see what changes are necessary, whereas the specialist may prove to be too inflexible. It is significant that Gropius, Mies van der Rohe and Le Corbusier began their work in Behrens' office. In his book *Feste des Lebens und der Kunst (Festivals of Life and Art)* Behrens revealed his humane side.

Hermann Muthesius (1861–1927) belongs with the prophets of functionalism, although his influence was chiefly theoretical. "Today we are no longer faced with a decorative movement," he declared, "but with a reconstruction of all human forms of expression." "From sofa pillows to city construction" was a much quoted slogan of his. In 1906 he played a decisive role in the Dresden Deutsche Kunstgewerbeausstellung (German Applied Arts Exhibition) which was planned to propagate industrial design. This fair was the prelude to the founding of the German Werkbund in 1907, a cooperative type of organization that was then nonexistent in other countries. It included architects, artists, artisans, entrepreneurs and industrialists, and its purpose was to ennoble the fruits of labor. This union contributed essentially to raising the standards of design in Germany. In 1933 it was dissolved by the National Socialists, and it was reactivated only in 1946.

BETWEEN ECLECTICISM AND FUNCTIONALISM

In this area, various personalities will be mentioned in a sequence based on the degree of their dependence on historical prototypes. *Friedrich von Thiersch* (1851–1921) was an imaginative builder but he remained eclectic. His astounding Ministry of Justice in Munich was built just before 1900–therefore not an early work–yet it derived from south German Baroque architecture. When Thiersch was asked to enlarge the building in a somewhat more functional style, he adopted still another tradition and completed it in north German brick Gothic. In his distinguished casino in Wiesbaden he also revived the past.

Such an acceptance of historical styles could, however, be developed more freely, as *Alfred Messel* (1853–1909) demonstrated in his Wertheim Department Store in Berlin. Following the trends of the new century, he unified the floors with unbroken vertical pilasters, eliminated the cornice, placed spans of glass between his pilasters, and for the interior designed large light rooms with a minimum of walls to ensure good visibility. But he could not resist giving the facade the effect of a Gothic church. *Theodor Fischer* (1862–1938) stood between the old and the new, seeking to reconcile them. His work was actually more traditional than it seemed to be at the time, for he remained devoted to small-town intimacy. Yet he attracted young progressive architects, such as Erich Mendelsohn (see p. 427). Around 1900 in Munich he was building schools that no longer looked like barracks, as well as bridges and a church, buildings in which he succeeded at times in breaking away from tradition and seemed no longer afraid of asymmetrical plans. Between 1906 and 1912 he designed the Pfullinger Hallen, the Jena University, the Heilbronn Theater, the Art Building in Stuttgart, the Garrison Church in Ulm and the Cassel Museum. In Munich he built housing developments, the police headquarters and a *Ledigenheim* (Home for Bachelors). He carried out these assignments in a variety of styles and was never rigid in his

Alfred Messel
Wertheim Department
Store, Berlin, 1896–1904

conceptions, yet he remained an eclectic, transitional
builder who rarely insisted on purity of form. His basic
character is revealed in his writings–*Stadterweiterungsfra-*
gen (*City Planning*, 1902), *Vorträge über Stadtbaukunst*
(*Lectures on City Architecture*, 1920), *Öffentliche Bauten*
(*Public Buildings*, 1922), and *Gegenwartsfragen der künst-*
lerischen Kultur (*Topical Problems of Art in Culture*, 1931).

Josef Maria Olbrich
Tietz Department Store, Düsseldorf, 1907–1909

406

Philipp Schaefer
Karstadt Department
Store, Berlin-Neukölln,
1928–1929

Theodor Fischer
School in Munich,
1901–1902

His friend and pupil from Lorraine, *Paul Bonatz* (1877–1956), favored the monumental, compact, sculptured mass. His Stuttgart railway station (1913–1927) is clearly articulated, but the effect is too colossal. This building has been greatly admired–especially since its tower became an impressive focal point for the city–but it must be admitted that a railway station really need not resemble a fortress, as suggested by its massive cut-stone exterior, nor does it require such a pompous entrance, nor such a high nave inside, reminiscent of a Romanesque cathedral. The building is simple and cohesive, for Bonatz avoided all ostentatious decoration of the facade and introduced a flat roof, but today one no longer looks for sacred halls when entering a railway station.

In a similarly exaggerated style Bonatz designed the City Hall in Hannover and the Exhibition Hall in Hamburg (1923), and in 1925 the first German skyscraper, for the firm of Stumm in Düsseldorf; he also designed banks and courthouses. His Basel Museum has some worthwhile elements. In 1950 he was in charge of the expansion of the Schiller Theater in Berlin. In his last years he worked on comprehensive assignments in Ankara, with Turkish architects. With his friend Paul Schmitthenner (b. 1884) he founded the Stuttgart School of Architecture with the purpose of combining the old and the new. Bonatz was uninterested in all theories; *Leben und Bauen (Live and Build)* is the title of his autobiography.

The work of *Max Littmann* (1862–1931) was more conservative. In 1901 he designed the Prinzregenten Theater in Munich, and in 1905 the Tietz and Oberpollinger department stores in that city. The Munich Anatomie was his most functional building. *German Bestelmeyer* (1874–1942), also active in Munich, built in a neoclassical tradition. In 1922 he replaced Thiersch as instructor at the Munich Technische Hochschule. He designed buildings for the expansion of the University (1906–1910), of the Technische

Paul Bonatz
Stuttgart Railway
Terminal, begun 1913

Wilhelm Kreis
Ehrenhof,
Düsseldorf,
1925–1926

Hochschule (1922), and of the Deutsches Museum in Munich and the Germanic Museum in Nuremberg (1917). In Munich he also built three churches and two office buildings, the Arminia and the Allianz. In the United States Bestelmeyer also designed the Busch-Reisinger (formerly Germanic) Museum for Harvard University.

All these architects concentrated on modifications of classicism, a style that continued to be used at the beginning of our century, at least for external effect, alongside the Jugendstil. *Wilhelm Kreis* (1873–1955) must be counted among these transitional builders. His brick buildings, with those of Peter Behrens, started a trend on the lower Rhine and in Westphalia. For a few years both men were in charge of the Düsseldorf School of Applied Arts. Kreis's first major assignment, the Bismarck Towers, was designed partly in a pseudo-Teutonic genre, and was sharply criticized by the art historian Adolph Lichtwark. After this his style became more severe, a development that may be followed from his Halle Museum and a department store in Karlsruhe to the Karl Marx Building in Düsseldorf. In 1925–1926 he designed buildings on a grand scale for the Gesolei, the Hygiene Exposition on the banks of the Rhine in Düsseldorf. The buildings exuded a serene monumentality and very little was left of historic influences, although it must be granted that they still looked a little too much like fortifications and their courtyards were enclosed too symmetrically. In later years an architect would have preserved the clear horizontality of the buildings, and he would have opened them up toward the Rhine so that the grandeur of the river view would have been part of the environmental design. Kreis also built the railway station in Meissen, the Dresden Hygiene Museum and a building of skyscraper type in Bochum. In 1927 he published *Kultur, Zivilisation und Kunst.*

Let us now consider some architects who concentrated on a simple, direct handling of forms in opposition to the continuing use of superficial, pompous effect or the subjectivity of the Jugendstil. First,

Paul Schultze-Naumburg (1869–1949), whose *Kulturarbeiten (Cultural Papers)* and volumes on residential housing were educational, including some good ideas on environment and architecture as well as practical suggestions for industrial design and clothing. In architecture he went back to the simple residential style of the 1800's, from which much could be learned. But this eclectic architect never developed new possibilities; on the contrary, during the National Socialist period he hindered progress with his demands for historic revivals. In his Saaleck Workshop, only simple old-fashioned Biedermeier furniture was copied or modified, a limitation which retarded the development of the United and the German Workshops.

The influence of the Mecklenburger *Heinrich Tessenow* (1876–1950) was more salutary, although tradition was dear to him too. But his conservative attitude did no harm since he remained open-minded to modern problems. He was a thorough teacher and stressed suitability, good craftsmanship and clean proportions. For the articulation of the building he favored uninterrupted lines, and for the room, simple, style-less, cubic furniture. He lacked the imagination necessary for new types of construction and devoted himself primarily to small private houses with their obligatory gardens. In 1910 he was active in Hellerau. For the Dalcroze School there, where city people were to be rejuvenated by dance and calisthenics, he designed a neat interior studio, but for the exterior he clung to a wholly unmotivated Greek-temple facade, albeit with a simplified profile. After the First World War he designed developments of small houses, a secondary school and plans for a sprawling palace in Hungary. He remained faithful to an almost timeless architectural style and was influential in Scandinavia. In 1930 he accepted a commission to redecorate the interior of the nineteenth-century guardhouse by Karl Friedrich Schinkel, Die Neue Wache, in Berlin. In 1936 he designed an open pavilion with a ceiling on thin supports which seemed almost to float. It was to be built on the shores of the North Sea Island of Rügen, and would have been in keeping with the architectural feeling of our day.

In north Germany the traditional brick edifice managed to withstand some of the disasters that befell architecture in the second half of the nineteenth century. In Hamburg the architects Schumacher and

Fritz Schumacher
School in Hamburg, 1914

Fritz Hoeger. Chile House, Hamburg, 1923

Hoeger tried to bring the brick building closer to a twentieth-century feeling via a greater simplicity of construction, but they too threw in ornamentally enlivening elements. They arranged the brick to form patterns, flat or in relief, or added terra cotta and shell-lime to clothe the wall surfaces.

Fritz Schumacher (1869–1947) was active mainly in Hamburg, where he was building commissioner, and he also occasionally acted as consultant in the expansion of the city of Cologne. In Hamburg he built the School of Applied Arts, the Johanneum, various schools, a professional building and an office building. In his larger structures he gradually tried to give his rather delicate-seeming brick walls more

Hermann Distel and August Grubitz
Montanhof, Hamburg, circa 1925

411

stability and he succeeded partially in 1923 with his Adult Education School. The walls are lightened by ribbon windows and the top story is drawn into the general plan of the facade by an unbroken mansard roof. Schumacher published his views on architecture, residential housing and modern brick buildings, but his principal theme was the development of Cologne and its problems, which concerned him not only as an architect but also as a comprehensive city planner.

Fritz Hoeger (1877–1949), from Holstein, built residences in Hamburg, but most notable were his romantic office buildings for the newspaper *Hamburger Fremdenblatt* and for the Hamburg-America Line; in these buildings he sought to introduce unifying style elements. In his Chile House (1923) one of the long sides was built to conform with the curve of the street, an innovation. Also new was the fact that the entire building rested on a low ground floor on plinths from which the remaining stories rose, held together visually by the vertical articulation; the top was spanned by three stories receding in step-like fashion, here emphasizing their horizontality.

The fact that such very different master builders as the American Frank Lloyd Wright, the Frenchman Tony Garnier, the Germans Hans Poelzig, Peter Behrens, Richard Riemerschmid, Fritz Schumacher, and the Austrians Josef Hoffmann and Adolf Loos, were born at approximately the same time is one reason why we have such an immense variety of architectural possibilities in the twentieth century. The Berliner *Hans Poelzig* (1869–1936) was a protean genius. He took a position between a neo-Gothic transitional style, such as Messel cultivated, and the constructivism that was to be realized later by Gropius. Gropius called him "a mighty stag who withdraws into a lonely thicket in order to remain true to himself." Poelzig, who painted and studied astrology, taught in Breslau, Dresden and Berlin. As Senator of the Prussian Art Academy and a director of the Werkbund, he had to cope with constant conflict over past and future. Between 1911 and 1917 he was active mainly in east Germany, where he

Hans Poelzig
The former Grosses
Schauspielhaus in Berlin, 1919

*Hans Poelzig. Foyer of the former
Grosses Schauspielhaus, Berlin, 1919*

designed and built in a constructive style. In his office building in Breslau (1911) he did not yet employ the vertical articulation he favored later, especially in his festival buildings. Here in Breslau, rather, he emphasized a horizontal stratification of the floors as Mendelsohn would do later, even more emphatically. Actually we have here already a concrete scaffolding with horizontally projecting floors. For the Breslau Centennial of 1913 Poelzig designed buildings that were still classical in style. But his truly characteristic constructions combined spaciousness with comparatively narrow exterior articulating elements, as in his designs for the Dresden Town Hall (1911), the House of Friendship in Istanbul (1916) and the Salzburg Festival Building (after 1920). These buildings never went beyond the planning stage, but the Berlin Grosses Schauspielhaus, Max Reinhardt's theatre for five thousand people, was realized in 1919. For the Schauspielhaus, Poelzig rebuilt the former Schumann Circus; thus everything had to be grouped around an arena with a tremendous dome. Since he was dependent on existing parts, he coated this whole vault, including the arched galleries in the dome, with concrete bands designed like stalactites to hide the architectural seams. With this "the sound waves shall be diverted and any echoing in the amphitheatre be prevented." The hall looked like a grotto. The dome rested on comparatively few thin pillars and "esthetically symbolizes the idea of suspension." Stage and proscenium could be raised or lowered; calyx-shaped bowls mounted on the supports of the foyer contained indirect lighting. For Germany these features were something new. In his design for a Salzburg Festival Theater,

*Hans Poelzig
Broadcasting Building,
Berlin-Charlottenburg,
1930*

Otto Bartning. Star Church, model, 1922

Poelzig suspended the balconies from an oval star-dome of closely serrated, reinforced concrete; the tiers overlapped, so that contrary to general usage the top gallery was closest to the stage.

Poelzig stressed over and over again how strongly he favored imaginative architecture and how little the suitability of material meant to him. His impressive designs for the skyscraper in the Friedrichstrasse, Berlin (1922) and the Hamburg Exhibition Hall (1925) were more functional, but again the plans were never carried out. However, his more prosaic design for the administration building of the I. G. Farbengesellschaft in Frankfurt was executed, and also his elegantly simplified design for the motion picture palace, the Capitol, Berlin (1925). In 1930 he saw his plans for the Berlin Broadcasting Building carried out in rather forbidding blue-black clinker brick. The structure is built in a compact style that is neither purely functional nor festive. Three studios are protected from the noise of traffic by the rest of the office building surrounding them, and the advantage of the design lies here in the screening aspect of the entire plan. Poelzig reached the peak of his achievements in his Congress Hall and the layout of the Berlin fairgrounds on which it stood, in his theatre for four thousand people in Charkov (USSR) in 1930, and in a Convention Hall in Moscow. Theodor Heuss, the President of the German Federated Republic who was an art historian and writer, has vividly described the development of this versatile architect in his monograph, *Hans Poelzig, Bauten und Entwürfe* (1939).

The Swabian *Martin Elsässer* (1884–1957) was building commissioner in Frankfurt from 1925, and after the Second World War taught in Munich. He started his career with the building of churches and schools, designed government buildings in Cologne and Mannheim, and the School of Applied Arts in Cologne. He frequently went beyond the styles of the transitional masters we are describing here. In Frankfurt he

Otto Bartning. Steel Church, Pressa, Cologne, 1928

Otto Bartning
Steel Church, Pressa, Cologne, 1928

built a huge market, an indoor swimming pool, a school and a church. Later, with E. M. Lange, he designed an excellent apartment building in Munich, eighty-two cooperative apartments with balconies facing south.

Side by side with this new functional direction, which is so precise as to virtually subordinate architectural expression to construction and material, there is a trend that may be called romantic or expressive. We shall mention here only two architects as prototypes and deal with other aspects of this approach in a later chapter.

Otto Bartning (1883–1959) devoted himself primarily to Protestant church art and at the end of his career could look back on the construction of one hundred churches. But he also designed hospitals, factories and private residences. When he expressed his own individuality, he rejected the cubic enclosed

Dominikus Böhm. St. Engelbert, Cologne-Riehl, 1928

Dominikus Böhm. St. Engelbert, interior

form and tended toward an expansive, crystalline style. The Wylerberg house, near Nijmegen (Netherlands), built from 1922 to 1924, looks like a crystalform thrusting angularly into the landscape in every direction; even the roof participates in this jagged motion, which results in a rather strange distribution of rooms. Such principles seem more practical for church architecture, as, for example, Bartning's design for his Star Church (1922), in which the congregation is arranged concentrically around the pulpit. Here a star-shaped vault of reinforced concrete is developed on a polygonal ground plan. In spite of a certain idiosyncrasy, Bartning succeeded in combining the requirements of a church with modern construction techniques. In the

Star Church, the ribs of the vault continue without interruption into the pillars, their curves gradually becoming the vertical pillars that create the aisles between the concentric pews. Bartning's very different, simplified Steel Church was built for the Pressa, the Cologne Fair of 1928. Using glass and steel almost exclusively he recreated a Gothic spirit without imitation of Gothic vocabulary.

At the beginning of the century Bartning had designed a small Diaspora Church, specifically a meeting house, a type he was to modify later in various ways. The Protestant Church, in contrast to the Catholic, is not directed exclusively toward the host and the reliquaries and it is primarily a meeting hall for sermon, prayer and song rather than a ritual edifice. Therefore the spatial order and architectonic relationship between altar, pulpit, pews and organ are of special importance. From 1929 to 1930 Bartning worked in Essen on a round church. This was followed by longitudinal buildings with the pulpit as axial focal point. In his Gustave Adolf Church in Charlottenburg (1932) he employed a fan-shaped ground plan which radiated from tower, pulpit and altar. He made a point of the fact that in a double nave church the side pulpit should be balanced by a unilateral choir loft. After the Second World War, with support from foreign countries assured, Bartning built forty-eight emergency churches with building material that had been requisitioned for the purpose, and with the cooperation of entire communities. Prefabricated parts were also put at his disposal, and this forced his romantic nature into a drastic simplification of forms which, in his opinion, could only stimulate the inner concentration of a religious person. Noteworthy among his publications are *Vom neuen Bauen* (*Of Modern Building*, 1918), *Neues Bauen* (*Modern Building*, 1919) and his autobiography of 1950.

Dominikus Böhm (1880–1955), father of architect Gottfried Böhm (pp. 481, 483), devoted himself largely to church architecture, but he also built residential houses, schools, hospitals and factories. As early as the 1920's he spoke a very characteristic language. Böhm was influenced by Romanesque architecture: large rectangular surfaces and low domes or barrel vaults were to be brought into balance. While the followers of the French architect Auguste Perret were dissolving walls into "nets," Böhm was concentrating on monumental mass effects. He built his churches in Hindenburg, Osnabrück-Schinkel and Nordhorn as powerfully as possible. Diaphanous walls were not his goal; the window was not to be a great opening to the outside world, but a circumscribed, mysterious inlet to the interior. He favored variously shaped vaults, as in his more delicate Abbot Chapel in Vaal, and, in a different way, in his churches in Frielingsdorf and Bischofsheim. Sometimes a subconscious expressionism breaks through, much of which is conditioned by the new materials. He was trained to be an ingenious artisan and therefore experimented at an early stage with the thin-walled, load-bearing shell, following the example of the nineteenth-century French architect Joseph Monier. In his Engelbert Church in Cologne-Riehl, Böhm omitted the "roof," since the vaulted dome rose from ground level, making a roof unnecessary. His quadrangular church in Birken has a tent-like roof which is supported by a light visible framework of girders on a broad concrete belt. In 1922 he indulged in exotic forms for his "christocentric rooms" in South America. In 1926, in a competition for the Frankfurt Peace Church, he coupled a long main hall with what one might call a circular church, and in 1953, he used a similar plan for his Catholic Church of San Salvador in El Salvador. In his Maria Königin Church in Cologne-Marienburg, the transverse wall and the baptistry dissolve into colored glass. Böhm also built churches in Bremen, Essen, Bocholt, Ringenberg, Offenbach and Frankfurt-Sachsenhausen.

Walter Gropius and Adolf Meyer. Factory buildings for Cologne Werkbund Fair, 1914

THE CONSTRUCTIVISTS

Before discussing the constructivists, let us first consider an extremely gifted transitional master, *Max Berg* (1870–1947). His Century Hall in Breslau was a centralized dome structure which, considering the early date, 1913, deserves admiration for the extraordinary spaciousness of the interior. This reinforced concrete building, with an exterior which still shows traces of classicism, spans colossal space.

Walter Gropius. Bauhaus, Dessau, 1926

Walter Gropius. Residence of a Bauhaus instructor, Dessau, 1926

Berg's Breslau Exhibition Hall (1925), a broad-based horizontal building which required an unconscionable amount of wood, was equally spacious. His hydraulic power plant and general plan for the city of Breslau also deserve mention.

The decisive figure for a purely functional architecture in Germany was *Walter Gropius* (b. 1883). Through the Bauhaus he led the way to the solution of almost every architectural problem. As a young architect he worked under Behrens from 1907 to 1909, and as early as 1910 he composed a memorandum on prefabricated houses. He envisaged a reasonably priced mass production of finished parts; various combinations of these parts were to guarantee the satisfaction of individual requirements. Gropius made architectural history with his Fagus Factory in Alfeld of 1911 (designed with the talented, short-lived Adolf Meyer). Whereas Behrens had retained cyclopean walls for his Turbine Plant, Gropius let all such blocking of stone elements disappear. "The role of the wall... stretched between the upright columns of the framework [is] to keep out rain, cold and noise." The supporting pillars on which his transparent walls were hung lay behind them. By letting the light glass "skin" continue without interruption around the corners, corner pillars were eliminated and the effect of floating achieved became a prototype for later buildings. Glass and iron, which Eiffel had combined as far back as the Paris World's Fair of 1878, no longer presented a duality. Architect and engineer had found their way to each other and above all to a unity of expression.

The Cologne Werkbund Fair of 1914 was the setting for a model factory in which Gropius and Meyer developed these new possibilities of construction further. Their factory office building presented a new degree of clarity and simplification of form: a windowless facade of yellow sandstone; a flat projecting roof with a terrace restaurant; to right and left two glass cylinders in each of which a spiral staircase seemed to float in space. Beyond a courtyard were the workshops, housed in a structure with three halls, a keel-shaped roof and curved surfaces–a building which proved that if he thought like an engineer, the imaginative architect could sometimes construct without great expense. There was also another innovation: the open garage, which Frank Lloyd Wright was later to call a carport. The transparent stairwell–not inspired by Wright–was received with astonishment and indignation.

Gropius's masterpiece was the Dessau Bauhaus (1925–1926), a group of connected buildings laid out like a compass card, projecting from a single center, the arms extended at right angles. The studio-houses of the masters were located not far from the main buildings, in the pine woods. The significance of this development was in the absence of enclosed courtyards which shut out the sun, such as we find at Oxford and Cambridge and on most university campuses or similar school grounds. Furthermore, there was no definite front view but a free distribution of the various functional buildings. However, these buildings were still connected physically, since the outmoded separation of the functions of private life and work was to be eliminated.

In the design of the large glass main building there was apparently no intention to separate even interior and exterior. The curtain wall was no longer made up of framed windows but was a glass skin behind which the supports disappeared. Students lived in a taller (six-story) building, each room with a balcony from which the occupant could enjoy the distant view of the countryside. A low transverse building contained the canteen, stage and auditorium, and it was possible to make these rooms into one large hall by rolling aside partitions. From a somewhat more elevated "command bridge" the whole area could be observed.

A great many masters and students were responsible for the interior decoration. The entire school was run on the old workshop system and sought as close a connection as possible with industry. The dualism of the nineteenth century—on the one hand a practical life without culture, on the other, esoteric art—was to disappear.

The Paris Trade Unions Fair of 1930 gave an overall view of what the Bauhaus had done toward the purification of architecture and building production. But Gropius also made a major contribution to private housing in his four-story row-houses in the Berlin suburb of Siemensstadt; and with his more complex multi-story apartment houses (designed with Marcel Breuer) he created a new type that was to be adopted later all over the world.

At first, however, nothing of this kind was carried out in Germany, and we shall deal with the eight-to-twelve story apartment house in a later chapter. These tall apartment houses made it possible to landscape great areas that would otherwise have been covered with single buildings, but Gropius was wise enough to see their disadvantages as well. "Our problem remains the lack of direct communication between the apartment and the earth," he said, but "the low house is not a cure-all." We should not forget that it was also Gropius who stressed constantly that "every rationalization makes sense only when it enriches life."

In spite of his very strong personality, Gropius was always ready to join forces with his colleagues. He worked with Adolf Meyer, Maxwell Fry, Marcel Breuer, and in 1945 founded the Architects Collaborative in Cambridge, Massachusetts. Thereafter, he executed all his buildings under its aegis, thus overcoming the usual separation of artist, technologist and entrepreneur. In 1936, during a short period of exile in England, he built Impington College in Cambridge, a group of buildings open on every side. Then came his professorship at Harvard University. In the United States, with Breuer, he has built private houses "as living organisms, as containers for the life going on inside them... New England's customary building materials—bricks or shingle siding on a wood frame—as well as the demands of the climate, have created local traditions." The Harvard Graduate Center provided him with a comprehensive assignment: a dining hall and seven dormitories, all steel constructions with attractive alternations of straight and curved facades, brick and limestone masonry and concrete slab roofs. The individual buildings are asymmetrically distributed in relation to each other. The dining hall is decorated boldly with works by Miró, Arp and Albers.

This was followed by his activities as adviser for the Boston Back Bay Center and the redevelopment undertaken by the city of Chicago, the crowning points in the career of this architect who had concentrated all his experience on city building ever since his move to Berlin in 1932.

Theory and words, when spoken by Gropius, had a different ring from the effusive and lyrical statements of Van de Velde, Wright or Le Corbusier. Gropius spoke to his fellow men more practically, more as an engineer. He wrote five Bauhaus books, and also *Internationale Architektur* (1925), *The New Architecture and the Bauhaus* (1935–1936), *Rebuilding our Communities* (1945) and *Architecture and Design in the Age of Science* (1952). In 1938, in collaboration with his wife and Herbert Bayer, he wrote a comprehensive work on the Bauhaus. If, in contrast to his pleasure in the experimental adventure, Gropius may be accused of harboring a certain cautious, doctrinaire attitude, it could be a streak of his old-Berlin heritage, an effect of the profound experimental character of the architectural development of his time, or perhaps a result of his many years as a teacher. In any case, all these elements seem to play a part in the lofty quality of his character and thought.

Hungarian-born *Marcel Breuer* (b. 1902), a longtime colleague of Gropius, is important both as designer and architect. He was the youngest of the instructors at the Bauhaus, where in 1925 he designed his famous and still popular tubular steel chair. In 1932, during a period of private practice in Berlin, he built the Harnischmacher House in Wiesbaden (destroyed during World War II). After leaving Germany, Breuer worked in London from 1935 to 1937 and then went to the United States, where he joined Gropius teaching at Harvard University. He was one of the recipients of the gigantic commission to design a new building for UNESCO in Paris, and he has built numerous private residences in the United States. A major recent work is the Whitney Museum of American Art in New York. Breuer published *Art in our Time* (1939), *The Modern House* (1940) and *Design of Modern Interiors* (1942).

The great constructivist architect *Ludwig Mies van der Rohe* (b. 1886), son of a stonemason of Aachen, is a contemporary of Gropius. Like many reformers, Mies was self-taught. He worked at first under Behrens, from whom Mies says he learned to think architecturally, in terms of monumental forms. Since 1912 he has been a very independent builder. In 1927 he was put in charge of the revolutionary Weissenhof Development, with which we shall deal separately since it introduced entirely new possi-

*M. Breuer
Harnischmacher
House,
Wiesbaden,
1932*

bilities in apartment-house construction. Mies was director of the Bauhaus during its final years, 1930 to 1933. In 1938 he emigrated to the United States where he became director of the Department of Architecture at the Armour Institute in Chicago (later called the Illinois Institute of Technology), remaining in this position until 1958.

One may say that Mies is the most impersonal and aloof of all the great architects active today. He admits a degree of dependence on the reserved style of the nineteenth-century architect Karl Friedrich Schinkel, but on the other hand declares, "It is hopeless to try to use the styles of the past in modern architecture. In any such effort, the strongest artistic talent must fail." He achieves his effects solely through balanced proportions, beauty of basic material, purity of execution in every aspect of the structure, and the exquisite clarity of the total conception. Actually he does not build from the inside out, in accordance with the well-known demand of his generation, but from a majestic overall plan into which the rooms are fitted and the walls, so-to-speak, are hung. They are intended to touch as little as possible, and are therefore like freestanding wings of a theatre, where life and the feeling for space may further unfold in unity. Compared with Le Corbusier, Mies is less inventive. Corresponding to the classic feeling in painting, sculpture, poetry and music, his work is based chiefly on the mature, clear, noble effect of the relatively inexpressive–one might almost say *un*original–features. Whereas Le Corbusier is constantly writing, making propaganda, painting and sculpturing, Mies, in an almost taciturn way, remains devoted to architectural perfection alone.

Two highly original projects of his are important. Both are designs for skyscraper office buildings in iron and steel (1919 to 1921), the first based on a prismatic, the second on a curved ground plan. Both carry through the construction of iron and steel logically and look like gigantic crystallizations of modern technology, all in the noblest proportions. These buildings are no longer surmounted with towers or any

Ludwig Mies van der Rohe. Lange Museum, Krefeld, 1928

of the other accessories which the architects who designed the early American skyscrapers felt were essential. Many rejected these constructions by Mies, although some of these very critics may well have been admirers of simple forms like the crystal or the ancient pyramids. They were indignant over the aesthetic of stereometrics which the constructivist painters were practicing at the same time. Mies spoke of a "skin-and-bone architecture," in which the upholstering flesh was to be provided by the human beings, furniture, materials and their functions. The nineteenth century had already put far too much "wealth of life" into its architecture. Now light, air and even the open space outside were to enter our dwelling places. Thanks to the new powers of technology they could do so without impairing the insulation against cold and noise.

A third project of that period was an office building with the supports set back and an overhanging roof. The outer walls were horizontal parallel bands of glass and concrete. When Mies designed a technical building of this sort, it never looked crude; it was a work of art. He frequently designed brick buildings, treating the material in broad surface areas yet just as neutrally and neatly. The Lange House Museum in Krefeld (1928) has an enduring nobility.

Two representative buildings brought Mies international fame—the German Pavilion for the International Exposi-

Ludwig Mies van der Rohe
Barcelona, Pavilion, 1929

Ludwig Mies van der Rohe. Tugendhat House, Brno, 1930

Ludwig Mies van der Rohe. Tugendhat House, Brno, 1930

Bruno Taut. Convention Hall in Magdeburg, 1922   *Bruno Taut. Schiller Park Apartment House, Berlin, 1924–1925*

tion in Barcelona (1929) and the Tugendhat House in Brno, Czechoslovakia (1930). Both demonstrate that the architect may be impressive–even create an effect of splendor–without ornamentation, through nothing but consummate basic form, separate yet unifying spatial concepts and materials. A deep, almost timeless feeling for beauty is evident here. Mies handles his designs for furniture in the same way. The simplest material tensions, steel curves, webbing and upholstered surfaces are always functional, yet at the same time elegant. Mies's designs for chairs in these two buildings have remained popular, and both the "Barcelona chair" and the tubular armchair for the Tugendhat House are still being made by Knoll Associates.

The Barcelona Pavilion was based on an open ground plan with steel supports. Its walls were free-standing partitions of travertine, onyx, bottle-green and black glass; above this a flat overhanging roof seemed to float. In his Tugendhat House, one comprehensive main space for the ground floor is divided only by an onyx partition and a semicircular wall of ebony. The exterior walls consist mainly of glass windows; alternating windows may be lowered into the basement to admit the magic of the garden outside. A house at the Berlin Architects Fair of 1931 was similarly effective.

In the United States, Mies has expanded the Illinois Institute of Technology on the basis of a gigantic master plan. Since 1940 auditoriums, professional and administrative buildings have been completed, with open and closed areas between them, almost everything brought into harmony by a twenty-four foot module.

In 1950 he built the elegant Farnsworth House in Plano, Illinois, and the Promontory Apartment Building in Chicago, with 160 apartments. From 1948 to 1950, two skyscraper apartment buildings designed by Mies were built on Chicago's Lake Shore Drive, with two hundred apartments each. The individual apartment could be reshaped by a shifting of its partitions. At last Mies was able to realize something he had envisioned in earlier models–the housing in one large building of a great many people who could enjoy an undivided park or lake in their surroundings. Most of his tenants were pleased and shared his viewpoint that if one could not live on the ground and walk out into one's own garden, the next best thing was to live close to the sky, with a wide view of land or water. Mies's best known recent work is the Seagram Building (1958) in New York City.

After the First World War, functional architecture developed rapidly. *Bruno Taut* (1880–1938), from Königsberg, was obsessed by the desire to synthesize Utopia and the New Objectivity. At first he

424

dreamed of "master builders of worlds," of designs for an Alpine architecture which was to reshape whole mountains, where valleys would be spanned by illuminated glass arches and domes, or by gigantic crystals hewn from the cliffs. In his book, *Stadtkrone (Crown of Cities)*, he included the sketch for a comprehensive *Volkshaus*, in which a new style of architecture and communal life were to be united. But Taut soon had to limit his fantasies and restrict himself to constructions that were within the realm of possibility, for he was appointed commissioner of building in Magdeburg. In his very original Municipal Building (1922) he found a new use for the flat, segmental rib, with which he economized on height without compressing the sense of space. His Berlin apartment house development of 1925 was consistent in the magnificence of its lines, and could still be built today. This is true also of his design for a publishing house. And his ideas for the revival of color in architecture could also be taken up in a modified form: he wanted to paint entire city blocks like ribbons to achieve an enlivening unity, and thus to transform the bad proportions of the nineteenth century and neutralize disturbing details. It is astonishing how many meretricious facades can be saved to some extent by a change of color.

His brother, *Max Taut* (b. 1884), was also a prominent German architect. In his Berlin Trade Union Building (1923) the reinforced concrete frame was no longer hidden but was made part of the architectural expression. His German Printers Building (1925) was constructed rather consistently of concrete, glazed tile and metal. His design for the Chicago Tribune skyscraper, a competition in which Gropius, Scharoun and others took part, showed a pure, tapered structure, devoid of the vices of early American skyscrapers. In 1947 he formulated important plans for the city of Berlin—which unfortunately could not be carried out—ideas for a reconstruction *Rund um den Zoo* (around the Zoological Gardens), an area which is a focal point and integral part of the city. It was to include a theatre and an office building and another office building on the nearby Tauentzienstraße. In 1951 Taut designed a housing development in Bonn and in 1953 one in Hamborn.

Now let us turn to that important enterprise which links the pre-World War II architect with the creators of contemporary residential housing. The controversial housing development of 1927 in Stuttgart, the aforementioned Weissenhofsiedlung, best demonstrates the innovations of twentieth century experimenters. Under the guidance of Mies van der Rohe, who was vice-president of the German Werkbund at the time, the following architects were involved: Behrens, Poelzig, Gropius, Bruno and Max

Bruno Taut. Britz Development near Berlin, 1926

Max Taut. German Printers Building, Berlin, 1925

Taut, Hilberseimer, Döcker, Scharoun, Rading, Schneck and van der Rohe himself, as well as the foreigners Oud, Stam, Bourgeois, Le Corbusier and Josef Frank. Mies imposed no stipulations except the use of a flat roof and let each man build whatever he liked. In spite of this freedom, the result was a surprisingly unified approach–if one wishes to avoid the word style. The apartment house by Mies himself was one of the first German examples of a steel skeleton construction in the field of residential housing. By exploitation of technical means, he aimed to rationalize material and make the building of the future cheaper. For the twenty-four apartments in the house, there were twenty-four different floor plans. The load-bearing exterior framework made it possible to arrange the nonbearing interior walls in any way desired; only stairs, bathrooms and kitchens were solidly installed. The skeleton included a wide opening toward the light. This building, although only three stories high, was a precursor of the slab tower that was to evolve later. Among the other buildings constructed in the development, Gropius contributed two prefabricated model houses; Rading, Scharoun, Hilberseimer and Taut designed new

Ludwig Mies van der Rohe. Weissenhof Development, Stuttgart, 1927

types of small houses. Le Corbusier designed a cube on slender steel posts, with an open space running beneath and a roof garden on top; the latter was a feature which did not become popular in Germany until much later. Another design by Le Corbusier, a home for a bachelor, was much criticized because of a room that ran undivided through the entire residence; the other architects had more respect for privacy.

It is perhaps possible to divide the German architects working in the period after the First World War into constructivists and organic planners (with due respect, of course, to those who fall between). The constructivists, who favored the New Objectivity and the cube, gathered mainly around Gropius and Mies van der Rohe; the "organicists" were grouped around Poelzig, Haering and Scharoun, however opposed these three architects may seem to be. The decades that followed were dominated by the constructivists, whereas today the organic approach is being revived. That is why some of the pioneers who were relegated to the background in the twenties as "romanticists" are more respected today. Expressing their view, Poelzig once said, rather emotionally, "If only we could take as a matter of course the technology that seems to absorb most people's interest and conceptions of art, we could once more free the arms of the soul." W. Luckhardt's *Auffassung von Entwerfen* (*Conception of Design*, 1920) is indicative: "Put aside the ruler, take clay or plasticine and just begin kneading it, without any influence from outside. You may notice, to your astonishment, how your shapes grow into the air around you, how they embrace and enclose it... and in the end the four-cornered box has turned into a loose, multiform mass... The ground plan is not the main thing, but the organism of the structure is." In a lecture in 1926, Hugo Haering also stressed the necessity of including the organic curve in the plan.

This "organic" creativity could of course be combined with elements of constructive functionalism. Erich Mendelsohn and Hans Scharoun are examples of architects who accomplished such a fusion. *Erich Mendelsohn* (1887–1953) sketched his Einstein Tower and the design for a skyscraper during the First World War, while he was in the trenches. These early designs are characterized by a rhythmic blending of broad curvilinear foundations with the mass rising above them to form an extraordinarily solid structure. The Einstein Tower of 1919 (completed 1924), in Potsdam, still betrays some of the curvilinear formulas of the Jugendstil and reminds us a little of Van de Velde's Werkbund Theatre. Here a mass of reinforced concrete seems to have been transformed into a kind of flamboyant sculpture. Mendelsohn continued to work dynamic features into a static solid style. In his building for the Mosse publishing house (1923), a boldly encompassing section consolidates single features that would otherwise fall apart. Mendelsohn said, "The building is not a passive observer of cars tearing by, nor of the movement to and fro of [pedestrian] traffic; it has become a receptive and participating mobile element." In his design for the reconstruction of the Herpich Building, a store in Berlin, he rejected Alfred Messel's use of vertical supports all in a row. (See Messel's Wertheim Department Store, p. 406.) Flowing horizontal ribbons of cream limestone and a continuous horizontal sequence of window-walls constituted the various stories, and provided, in his view, a balanced, harmonious adjustment to the course of the street. The ground floor was one unbroken glass front of shop windows, something quite unusual at the time and the reason for the bitter opposition of the municipal building department. This parterre zone was bridged by supporting girders on which the floors above seemed to float. These new constructions demanded of an astounded populace a complete reorientation of their feeling for proportion and weight.

Erich Mendelsohn
Hat Factory, Luckenwalde, 1921–1923

In his hat factory in Luckenwalde (1923), Mendelsohn shows us a different aspect of his imagination. Firm, three-segment arches of reinforced concrete form halls in which supports and cornice are joined to create a monolithic structure. The placing of the buildings and the articulation of their surfaces demonstrate that such an arrangement may give an effect of mobility even to an industrial building. His Schocken department stores in Stuttgart and Chemnitz, and his exemplary project for a textile factory in Leningrad, were equally majestic. In his designs of the twenties for residential houses he introduced new arrangements of interiors and new exterior effects. National Socialism drove Mendelsohn from Germany; he went to Palestine in 1934, where he designed the University Hospital in Jerusalem and the British Government Hospital in Haifa. He also formulated comprehensive plans for

Erich Mendelsohn
Schocken Department Store, Chemnitz, 1928

428

Ludwig Hilberseimer. Business District in a Metropolis, model, 1924

Haifa's business district, but these were never carried out. In 1941 he went, via England, to the United States, where he built hospitals and synagogues and taught at the University of California School of Architecture. While still in Germany, he published comparative studies on modern architecture in Europe, the United States and Russia.

Ludwig Hilberseimer (1885–1967) stood for the utmost functionalism and the most severe forms in large-scale building. Berlin was his main field of activity, but he also built an aerodrome in Staaken, just outside Berlin (1916), and an apartment house for the Weissenhof development in Stuttgart (1927). In Berlin he built a department store (1926–1927), an opera house, a flight school and a railway station. Above all, as city planner, he designed an entire skyscraper city (1924) with the gigantic problems of a fast-growing metropolis uppermost in mind. In the period before 1933 he created, with Martin Mächler, an astonishing plan for the core of the German capital, in which the north-south axis was centered on a railway station.

Some of Hilberseimer's big-city planning ideas have been widely accepted, such as "the elimination of all airless courtyards, sunshine for every room, adequate circulation of air throughout the entire apartment, widely separated buildings, and stricter zoning between residential and commercial streets." Some of his other ideas are less current: "to construct cities in layers–the business district with all street traffic below, and the residential area with pedestrian traffic above; all city and out-of-town communications to be underground." In the fruitful twenties he published works on city architecture, concrete as creative material, and on international modern architecture. With the advent of National Socialism

429

Ernst May and C. H. Rudloff.
Apartment House Development in Frankfurt-Niederrad, circa 1928

he emigrated to the United States where he taught at the Illinois Institute of Technology with Mies van der Rohe, and again did some comprehensive writing on city planning. In 1964 he published *Contemporary Architecture, Its Roots and Trends.*

Ernst May (b. 1886) was prominent among these "practical" modern architects. He was a bold entrepreneur and an active specialist in low-cost housing developments. In the twenties, as City Planning Commissioner of Frankfurt, he took charge of all housing in that city. Although today one would give the ground plans of such developments more variety and differentiate between heights, at the time they were a definite step forward. The Niederrad development, nicknamed "zig-zag houses," still adhered to some extent to the central courtyard plan. This was followed by a project at Höhenblick, near Frankfurt, in which the buildings stretched out in long rows, and by another in Praunheim with a livelier ground plan that included one-family houses with roof terraces. Then came the Frankfurt Römerstadt, with its many balconies and colorful interiors, and finally Riedhof-West, with rows of houses linked by horizontal galleries.

These social reforms developed through modern architecture were greatly admired. May received commissions from other countries and an invitation to visit the Kremlin which resulted in his appointment as director of city planning for the entire Soviet Union. In 1930 he moved to Russia with twenty faithful co-workers. Their first assignment was to build the city of Magnitogorsk in the Urals, for no less than 220,000 inhabitants. A gigantic iron works had been built by American engineers, and May's job was to arrange for the housing of the people involved in it. After Magnitogorsk, the construction of five cities in Siberia was anticipated, and Moscow was in need of an overall building plan which was to be based on a satellite system. However, due to a lack of material and the intransigence of the Russians, May was able to realize his plans only partially. In 1933 this adventurous innovator moved to Africa instead of

Arthur Korn. Sports Club (Haus der Turnerschaft), Berlin, 1924

Emil Fahrenkamp. Shell Building, Berlin, 1928

returning to Germany where the National Socialists rejected his ideas. Now he built in East Africa, under quite different climatic conditions. He planned the construction of Uganda's capital and of Jinja, on Lake Victoria at the mouth of the White Nile. He also built hotels, private homes and schools appropriate to the tropical climate, and created the African cultural center of Kilimanjaro. Since 1954 he has been active in Hamburg as architect for the city and in private practice.

Emil Fahrenkamp (1885–1966), from Aachen, worked at first in brick, which he continued to use occasionally throughout his career. The curved, vertically staggered facade was characteristic of his style. He carried out commissions for the Rhine Steel Works in Düsseldorf, Berlin, Stuttgart, Nuremberg, Frankfurt and Hamburg. For Essen he built a newspaper building and a café, and in Mülheim, in the Ruhr, a church and an office building. In Berlin he built the Rheniana and the curvilinear Shell Building; the latter, which has become famous, was the first skyscraper to be constructed in steel in Germany. In Ascona he built the spa-hotel Monte Verita.

The Berliner *Arthur Korn* (b. 1891) designed villas, residential buildings, shops, office and administrative buildings, preferably in concrete, metal and glass. He belonged to the strictly functional "November Group." His book *Glas* (1928) is characteristic.

431

Richard Döcker
Waiblinger Hospital, 1926

Otto Haesler. School, Celle, 1929

The Württemberger *Richard Döcker* (b. 1894) gained prominence with his residences in the Stuttgart Weissenhof development, with which he opened up some entirely new possibilities. He designed the Waiblinger Hospital, introducing the terrace-type structure which (in conjunction with his book on the subject) set a style for hospitals in Germany and in other countries. A harmonious graduated recession of the floors upward assured ample light and air, even though an economical ground plan was required. After World War II, Döcker was briefly in charge of building in Stuttgart and taught at the Technische Hochschule there. He also built schools, university buildings, factories, department stores, high-rise apartment buildings and individual houses. After completing work on the university of Saarbrücken, he built a university town for 10,000 students in Hyderabad (Pakistan).

During the twenties, *Otto Haesler* (b. 1880) designed exclusively in the modern constructivist style, exemplified by his school in Celle (1929), his administration building in Braunschweig (1930) and his Home for the Aged in Cassel (1930–1931). Above all, though, he was a specialist in low-cost housing, as may be seen in his developments in Karlsruhe, Celle, Rothenberg-Cassel, Misburg-Hannover and Haselhorst, and in his plans for Rathenow (Potsdam). Haesler favored the long, low building with little depth, on a north-south axis for the resulting even distribution of sunlight. Occasionally he let the stairwell jut out in front of the facade. In some respects the architect of today would proceed in a less rigid fashion. Haesler believed that city areas which had become obsolete should be ruthlessly torn down because "the scrap of one house built in the old, heavy, brick style could furnish the raw material for three built with modern technology." Furthermore, the constantly increasing cost of depreciation could also be avoided. Haesler's ideas are collected in his book, *Mein Lebenswerk als Architekt (My Lifework as Architect)*.

Wilhelm Riphahn (b. 1889) worked for the city of Cologne, where he built flat-roofed schools, a streetcar garage, housing developments and villas. In 1924 he designed the Bastei on the Rhine, an original little

Hans Luckhardt and Alfred Anker. Telschow Building, Berlin, 1926

restaurant with a view. His post-war work in Cologne includes the Concordia Life Insurance Building, built in collaboration with P. Doetsch. His new Cologne opera house (1957) remains a controversial work; not all seats command a good view of the stage, and the administrative buildings take up too much space.

The *Luckhardt* brothers, *Wassily* (b. 1889) and *Hans* (1890–1954), were active in Berlin. They were among the first architects to use the steel and concrete frame construction in dwellings. Against great

*Heinrich Lauterbach
Hasek House, Gablonz, 1930–1931*

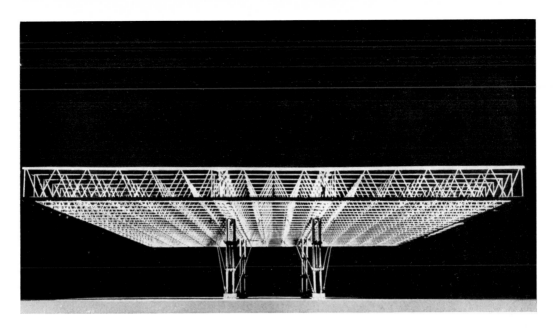

Konrad Wachsmann. Open Hall Roof, projection 17 meters

opposition they built an experimental housing development in the Berlin residential district of Dahlem (Schorlemer Allee, 1925–1926) and apartment houses in the suburb of Rupenhorn. Among their office buildings the Telschow Building on the Potsdamer Platz is the most famous. It was the first time that colored opaque glass was used for an entire facade of this kind. For the Berlin Exhibition of 1932 the brothers built one-family houses with new materials. Then National Socialism put an end to their planning. After the war, at the Constructa Exhibition in Hannover, they came to the fore again with their Berlin Pavilion. After the death of Hans Luckhardt, Wassily built a group of apartment houses on the Kottbusser Tor, and a four-story apartment house in the Hansaviertel, both again in Berlin, and then the impressive Ministry of Pensions in Munich (1958).

Heinrich Lauterbach (b. 1893) was active mainly in eastern Germany. He played a decisive role in the building of the Breslau Werkbund housing development (1928–1929) and opened up new constructive possibilities for the one-family house in Breslau and Gablonz.

Konrad Wachsmann (b. 1901) devoted himself almost exclusively to the development and combination of new constructive elements. From 1926 to 1929 he was architect for a wood construction firm, after which he worked in Rome. In 1941 he moved to the United States, where he worked with Gropius and founded the General Panel Corporation for the development of structural elements for skyscrapers, with emphasis on the support and spanning of wide areas. In 1950 he was called to the Illinois Institute of Technology in Chicago. Soon after that he became a peripatetic instructor in Europe, Asia Minor and the Far East, as well as in Ulm at the Hochschule für Gestaltung, and in Salzburg. According to his doctrine, the architectural planner was still not sufficiently familiar with modern synthetic materials, methods and procedures. The very tools needed by an industrial society that would have rapid growth in building requirements were frequently lacking.

435

Hugo Haering
Garkau Farm, plan, 1924

Hans Scharoun. Ledigenheim (Home for Bachelors), Werkbund Exposition, Breslau, 1929

Hans Scharoun
Schmincke House, Löbau,
1930–1931

Beside the architects who were following rational principles, a few should be mentioned who were determined that irrationality should not disappear entirely from architectural creation. Here we are faced with ideas that are becoming increasingly current today, in Germany as elsewhere. *Hugo Haering* (1882–1958) was a theoretical pioneer in this field, although it was Hans Scharoun above all who carried out these possibilities. Both architects abandoned plane geometry for the curve. Haering's theories were focused on the polarity of the geometric and organic. In painting, constructivism and expression represent a similar polarity. In architecture, naturally—because of its rationale—these poles can not be given their ultimate expression. Haering saw in them the difference between a classical and Germanic feeling for life. Actually it is a polarity that remains constant, and we come across it in every country. Haering saw in plane geometry the primitive element. From the straight line, the triangle and the square, a higher development led in architecture to the circle and the ellipse, both of which were vital

Hans Scharoun
Entrance to the Ministry
Gardens, Berlin, model,
1927

elements in all Baroque ground plans. And this was the "organic" at which we had to arrive once more, because it was the only system that could be correlated with human life. Otherwise the building was determined too much by exterior factors. On the Mediterranean, stone rules supreme, in the north, wood and the tree. Some of these rather exalted theories seem to be regaining popularity today.

In 1923 Haering built the Garkau Dairy Farm, near Lübeck, where every building had a different form. In 1929 he designed entire blocks for the city of Berlin, in Zehlendorf and Siemensstadt; in 1932 some houses in the Vienna Werkbund development; in 1950, a few rather insignificant residential houses in Biberach. Altogether, his anti-constructivist theories were more impressive than the actual results of his efforts.

Hans Scharoun (b. 1893) collaborated with Haering. He rejected all schematism and developed sweep-ing-form construction imaginatively. His work differs fundamentally from the classical norms of Mies van der Rohe. Scharoun built in East Prussia, took part in the Werkbund developments in Stuttgart-Weissenhof and in Breslau, and in the Siemensstadt development (Berlin); in 1930 he designed the rather odd Schminke House in Löbau. In 1950 he built a Home for the Aged, all on one floor, and a flamboyant balcony-house, privately commissioned. His plan for a Darmstadt elementary school (1951), never carried out, comprised many small buildings, like a village, for the various functions and phases of educational development through which the child would pass. His plans for the Cassel Theater were also never realized. We shall return to them later when we are dealing with theater architecture.

Through his theoretical writings, *Bernhard Reichow* (b. 1899) also fought against overly rational con-structive principles in favor of the vitality of organic structures. In his publications he sets forth some important fundamental rules for housing developments which he followed in organizing the new German cities of Wolfsburg and Sennestadt.

ARCHITECTURAL STYLES TODAY

As we approach the architecture of the immediate present, it becomes increasingly difficult to write history, for all is still in flux. The ultimate objectives of an overall development tend to get lost in uncertainty. To make a review possible, it seems advisable to divide the buildings into categories rather than to discuss them according to their designers. Since architecture always derives from practical problems and requirements, such an arrangement may prove to be instructive.

The One-Family House

The detached private residence seems to answer an enduring human need. It still plays a privileged role in the twentieth century, in spite of certain disintegrating forces which have appeared in family life within our modern industrial society. In the nineteenth century the one-family house played a more important role in England than in Germany, but in both countries it seemed a necessity–mainly because it led out into a garden in which one could from time to time change one's environment without the sense of leaving home. The advantage over the apartment house was of course decisive for families with children who had to be watched while playing outdoors.

Armin Schöning and Rudolf Lodders. One-family House, Bremen

Hermann Mäckler
One-family House
in Frankfurt am Main, 1953

Johannes Krahn
Krahn House, Frankfurt am Main, 1955

Heinz Rasch. Doctor's House in Hagen, 1956

Hans Broos
House in Gernsbach, Baden, 1952

The one-family home of the twentieth century has undergone specific changes because of the desire for more light and air. Gradually the wall facing garden and sun came to be made of glass, without interfering with the insulation of the house. A single large room became dominant, in which the function of parlor and dining room were united. In the villa of the nineteenth century, it was considered essential to have a drawing room, a dining room and a library; all these were separate rooms but were crammed into the ground floor, or ground floor and first, and were placed formally in the ground plan. Since that time people have become addicted to change: a bed may become a couch during the day, thereby saving space, altering the room's function, and making esthetic improvements possible.

Paul Schneider-Esleben. One-family House near Düsseldorf

Changes also came about gradually as a result of sociological developments; for example, the increasing scarcity of household help and the fact that the housewife often worked outside the home brought about a further technological development of the household that went far beyond the improved kitchen. Le Corbusier's description of a house as "a machine to live in" became current, and practical requirements produced this kind of house. There was no intention of despiritualizing the household with these innovations. On the contrary, their purpose was to give the housewife more time for an inner life. Today we have lost sight of how much practical relief has been brought into family life by the electrified kitchen, the telephone, heating systems, hot water, washing machines and refrigerators. And all these technological advantages we take for granted may be combined with a lively, even a romantic, formulation of space.

Rooms were made brighter not only by larger windows, but also by the use of plain light walls and by colorful furnishings. Above all, the new furniture was smaller–scaled–the sombre, ornate, mammoth furniture suites of the nineteenth century disappeared. The wardrobe, or "container" furniture, was transformed into the built-in hall closet, or the highly desirable walk-in closet. The room was once more experienced as a wide-open space, in contrast to the cluttered areas of the nineteenth-century home.

The twentieth century increasingly favored the one-family house all on one floor. It is more expensive to build than the two-story house, but sleeping and kitchen quarters can be isolated from the living area and one can step outdoors from any room.

The historical sequence was as follows. The tendency after 1900 was a gradual move away from eclecticism. Between 1910 and 1920 there was a reaction against the Jugendstil which was also considered

Sep Ruf. The Architect's House on the Tegernsee, 1953

Hans Maurer. The Architect's Residence, Munich, 1955

eclectic. In this period it was felt that the one-family house should be designed around a definite axis, to some extent still with neo-Classical approaches. After 1920, history was made by the radical reforms of Gropius, Hilberseimer, Otto Ernst Schweizer, Mies van der Rohe, and the Austrian Richard Neutra. But these great innovators did not prevail immediately because most architects would accept only the closed cube—or in some cases the flat roof as well—but they rejected all new arrangements of the interior. The traditional scheme that emphasized the parallel relationship to the street-front, and the so-called backyard, was still too closely adhered to. There should have been greater interest in movable, non-bearing interior walls which would permit changes in room size for a growing family. A further development of the low-cost prefabricated house was also of paramount importance. But at the end of the Second World War, when so much building space had been created by the devastations of bombing, no practicable law existed in Germany for a reorganization of real estate, and most building firms and savings and loan associations were stagnant. Wherever houses were built in groups, we rarely find a sensible ensemble which might have established some sort of feeling for livability. A solution is urgently needed to the problem of the extent to which individual small houses should be allowed to cover large areas, so that the land will not be cut up like a patchwork quilt. Schweizer demands a population density in city housing of at least two to four hundred people per two and one-half acres approximately, or the equivalent of a three-story apartment house on the legally required amount of surrounding land.

443

Hans Frieder Eychmüller
Split-level Living Room in the Architect's House, Ulm

Moreover, he considers row-houses, angled "wing" or chain houses just as important as the free-standing single building, especially where small land areas are concerned. Single houses become senseless if there is not sufficient distance between them.

If one wants a clear picture of the development and multiplicity of the German one-family house of the twentieth century, the following random examples may prove helpful: the Behrens House in Darmstadt (1901); Bartning's Wylerberg country house near Nijmegen (1923); the instructors' houses for the Dessau Bauhaus, by Gropius (1925); Ernst May's home in Frankfurt (1926); Mies van der Rohe's Tugendhat House (1930); one-family houses by Gropius in the United States; and Hans Maurer's home in Munich (1955).

Apartment Buildings and Row Houses

These have proved exceptionally profitable in Germany as elsewhere. In the nineteenth century they were constructed like barracks and frequently fell prey to real estate speculations. Crowded together, they presented the dismal, irregular exteriors encrusted with Renaissance or Baroque ornamentation that still mar some of the older streets in our big cities today. They were built with stress on a "representative" facade behind which lay dark, dank courtyards. Euphemistically these rear quarters were called "garden houses."

444

In the twentieth century we witness a gradual reform of the large apartment building. At first the aesthetic level was raised only for the well-to-do, through more practical ground plans, larger windows, balconies, more attractive entrances and staircases, and the use of better quality material. Very little was done, however, for the low-income group, except for a few developments of small one-family homes or two-story row houses on the model of a village community. This dependence on the village tradition was a mistake; the reform of the multi-story apartment house for the working-class tenant should have evolved out of the actualities of *city* life.

In a first stage of the reform of the apartment house, connected building blocks, all facing the street, were grouped around a large interior court. One disadvantage of this arrangement lay in the fact that construction was still aligned with arteries where traffic was growing increasingly heavy. True progress was made when the buildings were placed in parallel rows at right angles to the street, with adequate green space between. Now the apartments could be reached by driveways, assuring more peaceful living conditions. Most important, it was possible to achieve better lighting. In the old rectangular block, only residents on two sides of the building had enjoyed adequate light while the others starved for sun. The new type of row construction also permitted a variable orientation for all buildings; houses could face the street at different angles. If for some reason the architect was tied to a certain street direction, it was possible to organize the ground plans of the various apartments in zig-zag fashion, with the fenestration again planned to give the best possible light. Apartments with only a northern exposure were avoided. Green open spaces could be viewed from every side and the strong distinction between garden- and street-side was eliminated. Style-setting buildings of this type were designed as early as 1927 for the Stuttgart

Bruno Taut. Development in Berlin-Zehlendorf, 1927

Otto Salvisberg
Apartment House Development in Berlin-Lichterfelde, 1925

*W. and H. Luckhardt and Alfred Anker
Apartment Block, Berlin-Dahlem, 1925*

Erwin Gutkind. Apartment Block, Pankow, near Berlin, 1926

Weissenhof development already mentioned, and for the Berlin industrial suburb of Siemensstadt (1929–1931); some aspects of these developments could serve as models today. Scharoun considered a transverse living room with light on both sides obligatory wherever there was a density of apartments. It separated sleeping from living quarters, thus doing away with the necessity for a hall or foyer.

In spite of their diverse approaches and quality of execution, the following list of apartment-house developments gives a fair survey of the field: apartment blocks by Salvisberg in Berlin, 1921; Richard Döcker's group of apartment buildings in Stuttgart, 1923; the Berlin Britz development by Bruno Taut, 1925; buildings by Erwin Gutkind, also in Berlin, 1926; Conrad Rühl's Magdeburg development; developments by Ernst May in Frankfurt, Hamburg and Bremerhaven, and by Paul Seitz in Leverkusen; and Bernhard Reichow's mixed-development in Hamburg. The Hansaviertel, Berlin's bombed residential quarter, was rebuilt for Interbau, the International Building Exhibition held in Berlin in 1957. Architects from many countries contributed designs for a wide variety of housing types, from one-family houses and row houses to high-rise apartments. Among the buildings of special interest are those in which apartments of equal size may be organized quite differently by inserting or removing thin partition walls. The only constants are kitchen and bathroom, which form part of the installation block.

For the multi-storied row house, another possibility was introduced through Interbau (after Le Corbusier had realized it in his Marseilles Unité d'habitation). This was the "maisonette" or duplex apartment, in which the floor plans of neighboring apartments overlapped. The purpose of this arrangement was to create either a two-story space or an apartment with living and sleeping quarters on different levels. To minimize acoustic disturbances the bedroom floors were constructed to run as dividers between the living rooms.

446

Taut and Hiller
Karl-Legien Town, Berlin, 1929–1930

Paul Seitz
Apartment House
Development
in Leverkusen,
1952

Emil Freymuth
Siemens
Development,
Munich, 1955

447

Paul G. R. Baumgarten
Apartment houses in the
Berlin Hansaviertel, 1957

In Germany the low apartment house is more profitable than the high-rise apartment because the expense of an elevator, required in houses of more than four stories, is avoided. Another advantage of this type is intimacy—from the fourth floor one may still watch or call out to one's children in the play areas below.

Some of the new apartment developments are islands of peaceful living which have been removed from the mainstream of traffic; they therefore require their own shopping centers and schools if irritating trips to busy city centers are to be avoided. The large development may require its own church and auditorium. The number of such neighborhood units is increasing in Germany as elsewhere, thanks in some cases to social welfare building carried out with élan and a sense of responsibility. The Berlin Hansaviertel is the result of an effort to create a neighborhood unit in which varied types of apartments are developed and a community as autonomous as possible is the goal.

A great deal has been written about apartment house problems. A few among many German works on the subject are: *Probleme des Bauens (Building Problems)* by Alexander Klein; *Neuzeitliche Miethausgrundrisse (Modern Apartment House Ground Plans)* by Otto Völcker; *Vom richtigen Grundriss der Kleinwohnung (The Ground Plan for the Small Apartment)* by Hans Stolper.

A. von Branca
Apartment house, Munich, 1955

Ludwig Mies van der Rohe. Model for a skyscraper
at the Friedrichstrasse Railway Station, Berlin, 1919

Ludwig Mies van der Rohe
Skyscraper in steel and glass, model, 1920–1921

High-rise Buildings and Towers

These are closely related yet they may be distinguished as types. Today the *Hochhaus*, skyscraper or high-rise building is any structure with more than eight floors. Furthermore, a German building ordinance puts into this category all buildings in which the first floor lies more than seventy-two feet above the ground. This definition results in other requirements that complicate the entire project: the cost of interior arrangement and maintenance increases; specific regulations for window construction

W. Gropius and A. Meyer. Chicago Tribune Building, model, 1922

W. and H. Luckhardt. Chicago Tribune Building, model, 1922

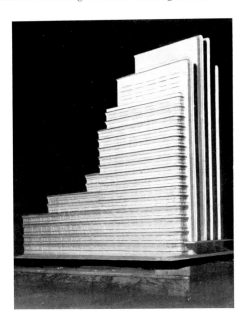

Ludwig Mies van der Rohe
Department Store in steel-concrete, design, 1922

Bruno Paul. Kathreiner Building, Berlin, 1928

must be observed to conform with fire laws; if the building exceeds four floors an elevator becomes compulsory. Fulfilling these requirements is economically practical only if the building has at least twelve floors.

The flat roof for the tall building seems here to stay. The gable roof has been jettisoned as alien form. The tower or spire-house differs from the *Hochhaus* in that it has no longitudinal extension but is concentrated around a central stairwell which usually faces north. Tall buildings and towers made headway in Germany only after the Second World War, whereas New York had its skyscrapers as early as 1883. Both types may now be found in Germany wherever land is exceptionally costly, new building methods have been sufficiently developed and the earth can bear the weight. (The last stipulation may be accommodated artificially by new construction techniques.)

All tall buildings were designed at first for industrial or business purposes since the costs could be recovered only by high rentals. Lately, however, this type has become common also in residential housing because construction has improved and grown cheaper; furthermore, immediate surroundings can remain untouched and serve as recreation areas which provide the big cities with breathing spaces. This type of building is impractical only when it rises up out of narrow streets, as it does in some sections of New York City, creating chasms that lie in eternal shade. Then every healthy relationship between built-up and free areas is destroyed.

The tower usually contains small apartments. The lower-floor tenants can enjoy their proximity to the landscaped areas, while those higher up have a grandiose view of land and sky. High winds may be disadvantageous to the upper floors and in very cold climates constitute a problem; yet quite a few contemporary architects feel that the five- and six-story house is on its way out. People want either to live close to the ground and be near their children at play, or to live high up and close to the sky, with a view. In the second instance, one lives "by elevator," and it becomes immaterial whether one is living in a five- or a ten-story house.

450

The designs for a tower office building which Gropius, Mies van der Rohe, the Luckhardt brothers, Scharoun and others submitted to the Chicago Tribune competition in 1922 constituted something entirely new in German architecture. In some respects they went far beyond any of the American designs because the means of construction had been put to work logically, and the historical styles customarily employed for the roofing of skyscrapers were discarded. These new buildings as planned by the German architects looked like towering crystals. Gropius designed a rectangular cell system, Mies van der Rohe a glass structure on a curvilinear ground plan. As early as 1922, therefore, we have two very different types of towers, both of which were to be developed further.

In the meantime, the tall buildings built in Germany fell at first between the old and the new. The Wilhelm-Marx House in Düsseldorf, built by Wilhelm Kreis in 1924, and the building by Koerfer (1925) on the Hansaring in Cologne, were still burdened with roof ornamentation and the force of the wall was overemphasized. The office building by Bonatz for the Stumm Steel Corporation in the Saar (1925) was more progressive, but Bruno Paul's Kathreinerhochhaus in Berlin (1928) was the first German office building to conform logically to the demands of the new era.

For a few examples of the progress made in high-rise apartment house architecture after the Second World War, we may refer to the early Grindel buildings in Hamburg, Ernst Winterstein's houses in

Johannes Krahn
Bienenkorb Building, Frankfurt am Main,
1955–1956

*Gerhard Weber
Administration
Building.
Frankfurt-
Hoechst,
1954–1955*

Theodor Kelter. Life Insurance Building, Karlsruhe, 1955

Braunschweig, and the high-rise buildings of the Bad Godesberg-Muffendorf development near Bonn; also buildings in Berlin-Lankwitz, Lübeck and Munich. The Berlin Hansaviertel mentioned above is one of the most advanced rebuilt city districts. Here at last it became evident that the giant honeycomb and cell systems are not going to lead to a totally despiritualizing uniformity of living—even if one sometimes gets this impression from the exterior. The Hansaviertel apartments have varied floor plans within the same building. Small rooms lie beside large ones in one-story, split-level or duplex apartments, with or without dividing corridors. Some are dominated by a large main room with an east-west alignment, therefore with light from both sides; this room may be connected with the kitchen or there may be a serving window. But most important, the kitchen and bathroom units may be moved into the interior, with artificial ventilation,

Hans Schwippert, Wilhelm Riphahn,
Eugen Blanck
Provincial Fire Insurance Building,
Düsseldorf, 1952–1953

Schwebes and Schoszberger
Office Building, Bahnhof Zoo, Berlin, 1956

453

Apel, Letocha, Rohrer, Herdt and S. Ruf. Apartment House Development, Bonn-Tannenbusch, 1951–1952

E. M. Lang and M. Elsässer. High-rise Apartment House, Munich, 1950–1951

Alvar Aalto. Apartment House, Berlin, 1957

leaving as much space as possible accessible to the light and air outside. And, as already mentioned, apartments are planned so that thin, non-bearing walls may be moved at little cost. In addition to the buildings of the Hansaviertel there are similar projects by Müller-Gottwald, Luckhardt and Hassenpflug. In some tall blocks, efforts have been made to allow for a community area—a floor for stores and recreation rooms—to be used by all tenants.

Apel, Letocha, Rohrer, Herdt, with Sep Ruf. Residential development in Bad Godesberg-Muffendorf, 1951–1952

Walter Gropius
Apartment House, Berlin, 1957

On any of these steel giants, adornment that is not an integral part of the construction would look like fashionable cosmetics. Monumentalization must also be avoided because it is contrary to today's desire for weightlessness and transparency, and such powerful buildings have enough monumentality in their own right.

The tower plan did not seem to give the architect much play for his imagination. Hans Scharoun, however, conceived of erecting two multi-story apartment houses standing close to and complementing each other–the buildings called "Romeo" and "Julia," in Stuttgart (1959). They are erected on a star-shaped ground plan. The difference in the heights of the buildings and angularly projecting balconies

P. Vago. Apartment House, Berlin, 1957

Emil Freymuth. Star Apartment House,
Siemens Development, Munich, 1953

guarantee "Julia" a maximum of sunshine. The apartments themselves, with their complicated and varied floor plans, make the tenant feel that in *these* large buildings he can maintain his identity.

But the architect is still wrestling with problems–for instance, insulation against drafts and waterproofing of the exterior. In the United Nations building in New York, for example, the window construction proved insufficient protection from high wind. On the upper floors a vacuum formed which sucked in rain water, and the air conditioning seemed only to add to the problem. An absolutely flawless wind resistance is a prerequisite; it is not considered desirable to count exclusively on the resilience of the skeleton to bear the entire burden, but rather it should be channeled along vertical and horizontal window panes.

In spite of these problems, it seems that the skyscraper, rising up isolated and lonely on a wide landscape, is to remain with us, along with other enduring residential types.

*Völker and Grosse
Schiller Theater,
Berlin, 1951*

Theaters, Concert Halls, Auditoriums

The construction of a theater poses its own specific problems. Its function has been important since the beginning–in ancient Greece it was ritual; in the Middle Ages, religious; since the Renaissance and Shakespeare it has been secular. And with the magnificent grand opera and ballet of the Baroque period, the place of performance became a center of entertainment–in the eighteenth century for the court and aristocracy; in the nineteenth, for the middle classes as well. Even in the twentieth century, the architectural formation of the German theater continues to be directed first at one, then another, of these varied purposes. It no longer seems important whether one should continue to build in a Baroque style with loges, or should turn to the balcony auditoriums. The latter had been demanded repeatedly ever since the nineteenth century, when Gottfried Semper and Wagner suggested the balcony auditorium would be more fitting for the new democratic class system. Yet such problems are, after all, concerned only with the grouping of the audience. Much more important today is the question of whether the stage should remain the focal point of a "peep-show" arrangement, a separate, raised and framed "picture" in front of the audience, or whether it should be designed so that audience and drama are joined. The second arrangement brings the twentieth century theater close to the ancient arena theater, in which the audience was grouped circularly around three-quarters of the stage or surrounded it completely.

On the whole the German theater architect has remained faithful to the axial plan, with the audience facing the stage from one viewpoint, regardless of whether the stage is designed "in relief" or given actual depth, with illusions of space and inclined platform. Whether wings are used as part of the stage or the action is to take place between curtains only is beside the point. For the architect, the primary desideratum is that everything on stage should be visible from every seat, to the last balcony row. His work stands or falls on this point: Is the stage practicable and capable of transformation?

458

In the Basel Theater, built in 1954 very close to Germany's borders, the architects Vischer and Weber seemed to have found the simplest solution in the design they submitted in competition. Slightly curved rows of seats rise on a sharply inclined floor; there are no balconies but visibility is excellent from every angle. The "stage" is actually only a large empty hall, waiting at our feet. The auditorium may function either as an arena or as a "peep-show" theater.

At the beginning of our century, Richard Riemerschmid reconstructed the Munich Kammerspiele, a comparatively small, self-contained theater with one balcony, in an unpretentious Jugendstil style. Nothing remained of the former sumptuously articulated, over-ornate auditorium with plaster decor. In 1901 the Munich Prinzregententheater was built, very disappointing from the exterior but equipped inside with all the technical stage innovations of Schinkel and Semper. The amphitheater, with no balconies, made a unified impression. The orchestra pit was sunken, invisible to the audience. In 1908 Max Littmann built the Munich Künstlertheater. Its reformed stage seemed to be a protest against the old courtly post-Baroque balcony theater and the illusionistic picture-frame stage. The players came on stage directly without concealing wings; the drama took place against a fixed backdrop of architectural decoration—a stage in relief, the full width of the auditorium. In 1912 Littmann built the so-called Big and Little Playhouse in Stuttgart, at the same time as Lossow and Kühne were designing the Dresden Schauspielhaus according to older traditions, with richly ornate balconies. Earlier, however, in 1909, Poelzig carried out his audacious plans for the Grosses Schauspielhaus in Berlin, with the seating in arena style. The actors did not have to confine their activities to the stage proper but, as in the circus, could step forward into the semicircle of the proscenium. Theaters built shortly after that by Oskar Kaufmann in Bremerhaven and Berlin, as well as his later Freie Volksbühne (1914) and Kroll Opera House (1924) in Berlin, were extremely impressive but quite traditional in style.

Deilmann, Hausen, Rave, Ruhnau. State Theater in Münster, 1956

Hans Scharoun. State Theater, Cassel, model, 1952

Paul Bode and E. Brundig
State Theater, Cassel, model, 1958

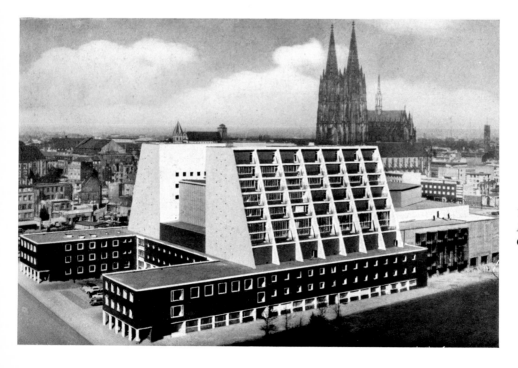

Wilhelm Riphahn
New Opera House,
Cologne, 1956–1957

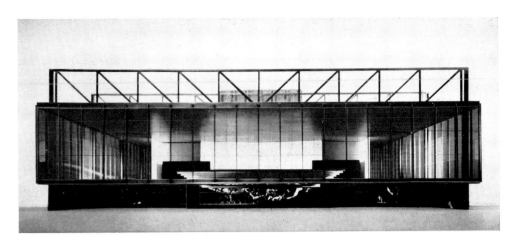

Ludwig Mies van der Rohe. Model for the National Theater, Mannheim, 1953

In 1914 Van de Velde had tried to find a new type, at least partially, for his Cologne Werkbund Theater; he introduced a bold division of the stage into three parts, but the innovation was not very successful. In 1923 Gropius transformed a barn of a building in Jena into a theater whose exterior, at least, was distinguished by a new utilitarian form. But Gropius's later designs for theaters never went beyond the planning stage, including his designs for the Soviet Palace (1931), which was to combine a huge assembly hall with a theater. His model for a "Total Theater" (1927) was more original. "With my Total Theater, which was intended for Erwin Piscator, I tried to create a theater instrument that with the help of simple and rational equipment could be transformed by the management into any type of theater desired–a picture stage in depth, a proscenium or arena. A complete transformation of the house was achieved by revolving the orchestra seat section 180 degrees on its axis. The proscenium, as part of the

Gerhard Weber. National Theater, Mannheim, 1957

orchestra section, was thereby automatically shifted abaxially and the stage transformed into a round arena, surrounded on all sides by rising rows of seats. This move could also be made during a performance."

After the Second World War, Apel, Letocha, Rohrer, Herdt and Lehberger reconstructed the Grosse Haus in Frankfurt. They gave it a mighty, sprawling auditorium but adhered to the traditional balconies and the old plan. In Berlin, Völker and Grosse built the Schiller Theater (1951), designed with only one balcony. A curved glass wall closes off the foyer on the outside. The National Theater, Mannheim, by Gerhard Weber (1957), incorporates a few aspects of a design submitted by Mies van der Rohe; some of the interior construction is visible from the outside. It is a theater only; all administrative buildings and workshops are housed nearby. Two stages confront each other: a large revolving stage for opera and a smaller one for plays, providing for the rather rare possibility of a modern arena stage. Mies, in his design, had joined auditorium, lobby, cloak room and entrance hall into one organism, and closed everything off toward the street with a transparent glass wall.

In 1952, Hans Scharoun, in collaboration with Hermann Mattern, designed a new State Theater for Cassel. It was to stand asymmetrically on a slope. Instead of the old traditional court theater, he developed a tense spatial organism. "The axial arrangement of a rational theater transforms the audience into a mass of single anonymous elements added together. But the irrational theater does not want this kind of mass for its partner: it seeks a community [of independent participating members]. All space designed for movement and sociability is optically joined, yet self-contained." However, instead of the Scharoun-Mattern design, a more traditional one by Paul Bode was chosen.

The new State Theater in Münster, built (1954–1956) by a team of Deilmann, Hausen, Rave and Ruhnau, is placed diagonally on the periphery of its grounds. The ruins of the old bombed theater have been left standing like a monumental sculpture in an inner court that is bordered by a restaurant on

Gerhard Weber. State Opera House, Hamburg, 1955

P. G. R. Baumgarten. Musikhochschule, Grand Concert Hall, Berlin, 1952–1954

supports and by the glass side wall of the lobby. The seats in the orchestra are so steeply inclined that the three balconies look like a continuation of the orchestra section. The auditorium itself is comparatively small and establishes intimate contact with the stage.

The Hannover Opera House was rebuilt according to plans that aimed at uniting old and modern forms. In his design for the new opera house in Hamburg, Gerhard Weber tried to express the old loge construction in a fresh, bold manner, probably influenced by the Royal Festival Hall in London. But his audacious stalls, jutting out into space like giant scoops, lack the congenial social ambiance of the court theater boxes from which they derive.

In Cologne, Wilhelm Riphahn built the controversial new opera house already mentioned. It looks like a gigantic cube and has been nicknamed "the Verdi Bunker" or "Memorial to the Unknown Director." Here the additional buildings for administration and utilities take up a conspicuously large area.

The motion picture houses and "palaces" which have shot up in the twentieth century face different problems. This visual drama is played out on a flat vertical surface, obviating the problem of depth that arises in the theater for live drama, where special attention must be given to the visibility from the seats at the side. In the motion picture house the acoustical problem is also different, because words and music are transmitted by an amplifier which can be regulated.

In Germany quite a number of handsome cinema theaters have been built. In later years the best of them increasingly renounced all distracting ornamentation. Johannes Krahn in Frankfurt, Störer in

Erich Mendelsohn
Universum Motion Picture House, Berlin-Wilmersdorf, 1927

Johannes Krahn
Motion Picture House, Frankfurt am Main, 1948

Paul Bode. Motion Picture House, Mannheim, circa 1950

Munich, and a few others, have designed fairly similar structures which are effective solely through the impressive sweep of their walls and ceilings. The result is an asymmetrical spatial style with but one purpose–to be effective as a fluid, hollow form. But the motion picture house is due to undergo further changes, not only because of the demand for ever-wider screens (cinemascope and cinerama) but also because of the possible advent of the plastic, three-dimensional film. Foyers are less necessary in the construction of movie theaters since the spectator comes and goes at all hours and remains anonymous. At the theater the chorus of applause and especially the social intercourse during intermissions, result in a more positive identity of the audience and consequently a need for "reception rooms." The exterior of the movie theater also plays only a minor role because it is frequently built–as profitably as possible–as a part of a business building, and the facade is used for giant advertising events.

In the development of the concert hall we must differentiate between two directions. First, there is the conservative way, followed by the architect who has continued to build in the slightly puritanical, decorative classicism which so many Europeans still seem to associate with festive productions. The result is usually a rectangular room with or without columns. The large concert hall in the Deutsches Museum in Munich is a good example of this style, as is the one in the Residenz also. Secondly, there is a new direction. The architect has no intention of offering the surfeited eyes of the city dweller any more visual pleasure, but wishes instead to force him to be all ears during the performance. Toward this end acoustic demands are constantly being studied and modified. For the hall itself, one possibility is the new shell design, built with consideration for sound only, with all expression in the totality of the hollow form, the material and the color.

The development of the concert hall has been advanced by some of the new broadcasting studios—Egon Eiermann's building in Stuttgart, Paul Bode's design in Nuremberg, and Gerhard Weber's structure in Frankfurt. But the finest concert hall is probably the one built by P. G. R. Baumgarten for the Berlin Musikhochschule. The strictly practical foyer is enhanced by Theodor Werner's enormous abstract wall painting; in front of it the visitor, who has been all ears a moment before, regains his eyesight. The main hall of the Stuttgart Liederhalle, by Abel and Gutbrod, renounces symmetry in order to serve a great many different purposes, and in spite of the size of the hall, the acoustics are splendid. The rest of this remarkably audacious structure is highly imaginative but unfortunately sometimes overelaborated. The exterior is disturbed by unduly stressed mosaic surfaces which overrun the architectural form.

As our concert halls develop increasingly into gigantic utilitarian stalls in which we are supposed to give ourselves up exclusively to aural delights, our painters and sculptors should be represented creatively in the foyers, which are festive meeting grounds during the intermission.

I should like to mention two more, very different, modern assembly halls, both of which serve a multiplicity of purposes. In 1951–1952 Walter Holtje built the Dortmund Westphalia Hall on an elliptical ground plan, to seat two thousand people. The steel-concrete skeleton is braced by stairs, roof and balcony construction. The projecting steel girders of the roof rest on twenty main supports which are held by steel tension rods that run down outside the glass wall. The entire building, especially when seen by night, looks like a peaceful colossus, yet the effect is one of transparency.

The concert hall built in 1957 in Berlin for Interbau is a quite different and most unusual building. The architect is an American, Hugh Stubbins, and with this hall he made a great impression on those German architects who are once more searching for the imaginativeness that lies beyond the new rationalism. Stubbins' Congress Hall rests on a gigantic, almost square foundation. The auditorium stands on an elevated platform and is tilted eastward. It is completely windowless, so that no sound may penetrate, and is topped by gigantic curved roofs of concrete which clamp everything together. With this building a completely new style was introduced in Germany. On both sides broad expanses of water mirror the structure, which also houses under its massive wings a two-story restaurant, a second conference hall and a studio theatre. Unfortunately the interior could not be completed in the style that might be expected from the exterior. The giant framework for the sail-like tension of the roof "skin" is not load-bearing, and as a result the exterior walls of the hall must carry the roof; the original plan to construct the walls to resist wind pressure only had to be abandoned. There is, therefore, a contradiction between exterior and interior. But the broad ramps leading from the docks on the Spree River to the assembly areas and plateau are beautiful, with their views of the Tiergarten and the ruins of the Reichstag. Between the old Parliament building and this exotic Congress Hall lie seventy years, but they could be a thousand. Both buildings are fantastic and must excite anyone who sees them—the Reichstag building representing the historicizing, ornate fantasy of the nineteenth century, the Congress

Abel and Gutbrod. Liederhalle (Concert Hall), Stuttgart, 1956

*Abel and Gutbrod
Liederhalle (Concert Hall),
Stuttgart, 1956*

Heinrich Rosskotten. Rhein-Main Hall, Wiesbaden, 1957

Hall the bold, sumptuous spirit of today's engineers. Thirty years ago architects were still experimenting with the simplest, most elementary possibilities, as if the field of architecture had first to be cleansed of impurities; now this Congress Hall may well be the signal for a new, audacious, perhaps even extravagantly imaginative architecture.

Walter Höltje. Westphalia Hall, Dortmund, 1951–1952

Hugh A. Stubbins with W. Düttmann and F. Mocken. Congress Hall, Berlin, 1957

In the last decade a series of remarkable assembly halls and theaters have been built. In his Berlin Philharmonic Hall, Hans Scharoun, who has won innumerable awards, was at last able to realize his original design for a concert hall with 2200 seats. He placed the orchestra off center in an oval hall. The seats are not canted, as in an amphitheater, but fan out and are assembled at different levels into small groups at divergent angles. The number of seats in each group comes close to the number of orchestra members. Thus the audience is divided up into so many "choruses" and seems to be participating in the proceedings. Orchestra and audience form a community.

For the theater in Ingolstadt, the problem of the architect, H. W. Hämer, was to fit the building into the oldworld silhouette of this city on the Danube. Hämer erected a polygonal structure of concrete and glass amid the historic surroundings. Since the proportions are good, the new goes well with the old, and the old buildings–which are of no great architectural value–are somehow enhanced artistically by the new. In the interior, the architectonic conception is stressed; the concrete walls have been left without a finishing coat. Günther Bock built a Cultural Hall for the small Hessian town of Sindlingen. In his sharply edged silhouette, he stresses the visible concrete structure more than Hämer.

Egon Eiermann and Sep Ruf. Section of the German Pavilion, World's Fair, Brussels, 1958

H. W. Hämer. Theater in Ingolstadt, 1966

Günther Bock. Cultural Hall, Sindlingen, 1960

Manfred Lehmbruck. Lehmbruck Museum, Duisburg, 1964

Gottfried Böhm, Tower Hall, Bensberg, 1966

Fritz Schumacher. School, Hamburg, 1914–1916

The building has the monumentality of a huge sculpture; the wavelike movement of the wall arrangement prepares us for what lies inside.

The city of Duisburg built the Wilhelm Lehmbruck Museum for its most famous son. Manfred L. Lehmbruck designed a congenial home for his father's works. Glass and concrete walls surround exquisitely balanced rooms in which the vitality of each separate sculpture may radiate fully.

The fortress character of a concrete building with no finishing coat was exploited by Gottfried Böhm in his new Town Hall in Bensberg on the Rhine in order to incorporate the new structure into the surviving walls of an old ruined castle. The old towers and walls once more have a function—a rare and highly successful achievement.

Schools

The schools of the nineteenth century looked like factories for learning, barracks devoted entirely to drilling—although in fact the pedagogues were at last beginning to take the nature of the child into account. But schools still loomed in the hearts of big cities, on streets with heavy traffic, or—like the town hall—stood on an elevation, designed to look impressive from the outside.

The schools built in Munich at the beginning of the twentieth century by City Building Commissioner Hofmann, and by the architects Hocheder and Theodor Fischer, were greatly admired, although the improvements made were for the most part decorative and had nothing to do with the educational requirements of the child. Not until several years after the First World War could "the century of the child" make an impression on school architecture. At this time the pedagogue Karssen, in collaboration with the architect Bruno Taut, developed a new type of school building in Berlin which was based entirely on educational requirements. Then Ernst May and his co-workers in Frankfurt designed the first pavilion school. Beside rooms for basic studies we now find classrooms for drawing and nature study, a workshop and a lunchroom.

471

Karl Otto and W. Ziegemeier
Leibniz School, Hannover, 1953

The Third Reich brought a temporary end to many such reforms because the National Socialists were anything but progressive in matters of education. When the question of improving the schools was taken up again after World War II, inspiration was first sought in England and the United States, where progress had not been so abruptly interrupted. Whereas at the turn of the century the design of schools

Adolf Bayer. Public School in Offenbach

*Günter Wilhelm. School on
the Gänsberg, Stuttgart, 1952–1953*

had been influenced by the architect, with the educators following somewhat hesitantly, now the latter took the problem into their own hands in an effort to meet the requirements of the child.

Beginning with the location, quite different demands were made. The school was to be situated away from traffic, in attractive surroundings which were to include grounds for play at recess and for sports. Whenever possible, square rooms with cross-ventilation were favored, without disturbing elements outside, and the whole should be of reasonable size to avoid bringing too many children together at one time. Instead of gloomy offices, administrative rooms should be gay and colorful. Wherever possible buildings should be on one level, providing easy access to the outside so that studies can be conducted outdoors in warm weather. Natural surroundings, style of room, and materials used should be esthetically pleasing and develop in the child a feeling for the beauties of his own period. A unified style should prevail, aimed at good lighting (in the corridors also) and avoidance of noise and crowding. In the classroom chalkboards should be green instead of black, and bulletin boards provided to display an exciting variety of reference material. But above all the fixed school bench and desk, with their cramped, intimidating austerity, should be replaced by familiar, small movable tables around which

*P. Seitz. Classroom
Leverkusen on the Rhine*

Max Bill. Hochschule für Gestaltung, Ulm, 1953–1955

the children can sit in groups. The teacher should no longer preside from a dais, like a stranger, but move freely within his "family." This seating arrangement around tables also requires that the classroom receive light from two sides; illumination of this kind is possible only through a unified arrangement for which various systems have been developed. Finally, there has recently been a demand for a covered hall for play in bad weather in addition to the free open space required for recess periods.

There have been complaints that such attractive schools will make the child's home seem poorer and shabbier to him. I fail to see any such danger. The more attractive the school, the more joyous the learning. Humanized school architecture is, after all, the result of a greater refinement in educational methods, which aim at making all learning an animated and pleasurable function of life.

The schools built by Fritz Schumacher in Hamburg between 1918 and 1933 still fall between older traditions and new concepts. In the fifties, Paul Seitz and Bernhard Hermkes, each in his own way, built schools for Hamburg in the new tradition. Günter Wilhelm was active in Stuttgart; Dieter Oesterlen in Afferde, near Hameln; H. Plarre in Berlin-Reinikendorf; F. W. Kraemer in Peine; W. Dierschke in Hannover. On the Bergstrasse, Odenwald, progressive schools were built by Vorlaender

Johannes Krahn. School in Saarburg, 1953–1954

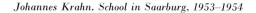

Alois Giefer and Hermann Mäckler.
Maria Hilf Church, Frankfurt am Main, 1950–1951

and Gerhard Weber; in Grötzingen by Alfred Fischer-Karlsruhe; in Mannheim by Richard Jörg, and in Saarburg by Johannes Krahn, who also did much toward the advancement of hospital architecture. However, it was the spatial imagination of Hans Scharoun that created for Germany its most original school, in Darmstadt. This ingeniously designed pavilion system provided outdoor space for every classroom. An extremely varied arrangement of rooms is achieved by a complicated, partly honeycomb ground plan which overcomes the usual monotony of classrooms in a row.

The design problems presented by university buildings are of course rather different from those inherent in schools for young children. In this category of buildings for universities, interesting work has been done at Frankfurt, Freiburg and Saarbrücken, by the architects Ferdinand Kraemer, Otto Ernst Schweizer, Horst Linde and Friedel Döcker, among others. The stadium problem was solved in a progressive fashion in Nuremberg and Vienna by Schweizer, a prominent city planner and instructor in cement construction.

Churches

A review of German ecclesiastical architecture from the Romanesque to the Rococo period reveals how radically the structure and expression of church building was altered while serving a ritual that remained, by comparison, unchanged. Each style served this cult in its own way. But the nineteenth century proved to be an embarrassing pause in church architecture as in other architectural fields. One after the other, the various historical styles were repeated. Not until the twentieth century was there a new search for a style which would be expressive of the times. In this respect secular architecture was able to progress faster. One frequently has the feeling that in the twentieth century the meaning of religion is no longer self-evident.

At first employer and architect—who, after all, must work together—seemed to approach the construction of religious buildings with inhibitions. The architect was more interested in the new problems presented to him by a worldly, industrialized society, whereas the ecclesiastical employer still clung to

Egon Eiermann
St. Matthew, Pforzheim, 1953

Dominikus Böhm. St. Maria-Königin, Cologne-Marienburg, 1954

476

Michael Kurz
St. Heinrich, Bamberg, 1928

Emil Steffann. St. Boniface, Lübeck, 1952

477

historic traditions. For him, a good church was an edifice that reflected some style out of the past. For such reasons the reformation of church architecture was delayed.

The reform, when it came, came from within. The liturgical movement itself demanded simplification. Instead of a building with several aisles, it seemed desirable to have one unified hall in which an unpretentious altar would once more serve as the simple free-standing communion table. And this was no longer to stand in the choir, far removed from the devotions of the congregation. A unified hall was desirable also for community gatherings. All this demanded new ground plans and spatial concepts, requirements which were welcomed by the architect.

New building materials and the potentialities of reinforced concrete for the framework were also conducive to a reformation. The first example of a transformation in style appeared in the churches of countries neighboring Germany. In 1923 the Perret brothers built a church near Paris which was erected logically from simple concrete structural elements to form a single integrated space with walls incrusted with glass. In 1927 this solution was modified by Karl Moser in a church in Basel where he used only industrial elements, left in their original state and without any addition of color. In spite of its austerity, this church set a stylistic precedent for many German architects.

Hans Herkommer
Church in Neuenburg, the Palatinate, 1929

Emil Fahrenkamp
Marienkirche, Mülheim on the Ruhr, 1928

A. von Branca. Herz-Jesu Cloister, Munich, 1954

Various directions now developed in German church architecture. One led to a tent style which could be built with any modern framework. The effect was a mixture of the utilitarian and the solemn. Space was contained by struts, as thin as possible, with great expanses of glass between them. Here we are no longer dealing with individual window units but with a diaphanous wall, as continuous and neutral as possible. In a few cases this strut-glass system was used also at the east end of the choir, which became a transparent or luminous laminated wall. The exterior walls were no longer boundaries against the outside world but windows to infinity. All in all, what the architect seems to have had in mind was a workshop for prayer. The congregation should be enveloped in light and assemble for its devotions in the simplest surroundings.

Of this type we have churches in Schweinfurt by Hans Schädel, in Frankfurt by Alois Giefer and Hermann Mäckler, and in Freiburg in Breisgau, by Linde, Heine and Diehme (the Ludwigskirche). In 1954 Dominikus Böhm built his luminous St. Maria Königin Church in Cologne. The year before Egon Eiermann had designed his somewhat similar Protestant Church of St. Matthew in Pforzheim. Here the walls are composed of perforated stone, assembled as in a mosaic in which varied glass discs gleam; the elements are left unfinished, yet structure and ornament are unified. But the diaphanous single-room

church was given its most complete expression outside Germany by Lloyd Wright, the son of Frank Lloyd Wright, in his Wayfarer's Chapel near Palos Verdes in California, a glass house borne by steel, into which the beauties of nature may enter from every side.

The direction followed by the second type of church architecture resulted in a building resembling a "sacred fortress." The severity of the church is fused with a compact massive form, shutting out the world beyond. It has a majestic facade inviting entrance within, and a bell tower standing guard, as it were, to one side. (The effect is, in some cases, very reminiscent of early medieval churches, with their formidable *Westwerke*, although the structural vocabulary is, of course, wholly modern.) For the exterior of his Frielingsdorf Church, Dominikus Böhm used traditional brick, and the effect is that of a fortification. He achieved a similar result at Cologne-Riehl. With its high soaring erection girders, Otto Bartning's "Emergency Church" in Cologne-Mülheim makes a similar impression with different means. So does a church built in Lübeck by Emil Steffann, although steel construction with hollow blocks is used, and the effect of the tent-style of structure previously described is also created. But Steffann, as an admirer of Le Corbusier's Pilgrimage Chapel in Ronchamp, wrote effectively against the luminous tent or "brightly lit church," in which the feeling of shelter is destroyed. The soul truly lost in meditation

Rudolf Schwarz
St. Anna, Düren,
1955–1956

does not desire illumination from without, nor the distractions provided by luxuriant color or stained glass; he would prefer to withdraw temporarily from the visual and acoustical disturbances of the outside world into a cave.

These two opposing tendencies were merged by Rudolf Schwarz and Gottfried Böhm, son of Dominikus, but other German architects also came close to a synthesis. Josef Lehmbrock constructed a powerful one-room church for a development of small houses in Düsseldorf. It has a transverse, reinforced concrete framework. The concrete side walls are slit, thus letting the light enter indirectly as through a louver. A monumental rose by G. Peltzer in heavy concrete and glass dominates the entire west wall. In 1955 the heavy-walled, totally enclosed type of church found its ultimate expression again outside Germany, in Le Corbusier's chapel in Ronchamp.

Dominikus Böhm
Catholic Church on the Island of Norderney,
1928–1929

Johannes Krahn
St. Wendel, Frankfurt am Main, 1957

The various possibilities of modern church architecture are by no means fully covered in our discussion of these contrasting directions—the luminous church and the fortress. Some conclusions about the state of architectural affairs at present may also be drawn from the tendency to place the altar as focal point in a variety of ground plans. In 1930 Rudolf Schwarz and Hans Schwippert built the Corpus Christi Church in Aachen, a single high room for the celebration of mass, to which they added, asymmetrically, only one aisle for a cloister and the confessionals. In 1956 Schwarz built the St. Anna Church in Düren on a similar ground plan. In his octagonal Heilig-Geist Church in Frankfurt, Martin Weber placed the altar so that the congregation surrounds it, and it seems to form an island; he did not, however, transform the building as a whole into a circular church. In Clemens Holzmeister's church in Merchingen, where the congregation faces the altar on three sides, the ground plan more nearly approximates a circle, as it does also in a church by Alfons Leitl in Mülheim-Ruhr. But as early as 1932, Dominikus Böhm had built a perfectly circular church in Cologne-Riehl; Martin Weber also built one in Frankfurt-

Bonames. For St. Albert, Saarbrücken (1955), Gottfried Böhm designed a round chancel surrounded by columns, with an oculus above the eccentrically placed altar. In Ringenberg, Hilberath, Munich and Frechen (North-Rhine Westphalia), churches were built with approaches to the altar from three sides, thus coming close to a central altar rotunda construction. In Essen-Rüttenscheid, Frankfurt and Cologne-Rath, several large halls or subsidiary rooms of various sizes lead up to the altar. On Sunday the largest hall may be used; on weekdays one of the smaller ones may serve as a chapel.

The possibility of bridging a vast amount of space with concrete gave exceptional impetus to the design of the church roof. Paul Baumgarten built a church in Berlin on a pentagonal ground plan covered with a roof of three triangular surfaces which support each other. The nave, with its open prow, thrusts out into space, in this case into a beautifully landscaped park on the Litzensee.

The south German architect Busso von Busse shows even greater originality in the wooden country church he designed in Klettham (Upper Bavaria). Ceiling rafters are extended under the canopy roof like the transverse framework of a ship and join with the supporting pillars to form curved triangles. Like the Gothic arch, this hall symbolizes a system of forces pointing the way to regions beyond.

Johannes Krahn
St. Wendel, interior, Frankfurt am Main,
1957

Paul Schneider-Esleben
The dome of St. Rochus,
Düsseldorf, 1954–1955

In the literature of sacred architecture, *Vom Bau der Kirchen (Of Building Churches)* by Rudolf Schwarz may be considered basic for the situation today. For the English translation. Mies van der Rohe wrote that it should be widely read, and not only by those concerned with the building of churches. But beyond the purely architectural question of how to construct a church for use and with meaning today, lies the theoretical problem of the suitability of abstract art *per se* for the building of a church.

484

Paul Baumgarten
Church on the Lietzensee, Berlin-Charlottenburg,
1959

Busso von Busse.
Erlöserkirche, Klettham (Upper Bavaria), 1962/63

Nonobjective art may be found in medieval churches–for example in the colored gradations of clustered pillars and connecting ribs which meet in the vaulting to form a polychrome heaven. Clearly expressive –and nondescriptive–ornament may be found also on the walls or in the series of stained glass windows. But in the twentieth century the question has arisen of whether a large window, or the painting of an apse can successfully formulate Christian content in the same way that wordless, absolute church music does. Since the entire pressure of our age seems to drive us increasingly toward the consideration of such eventualities, those modern artists who want to serve the church have become obsessed with this problem–among them, painters as different as the German Georg Meistermann and the Frenchman

Josef Lehmbrock
St. Reinhold, Düsseldorf.
Rose window by Günter Peltzer, 1957

486

Hans Schädel. St. Kilian, Schweinfurt, 1953. Stained glass by Georg Meistermann

Jean Bazaine. Here the limit of abstraction is drawn only where the church has given particular form to certain Christian symbols for centuries, for instance, symbolizing God the Father in a human image, and the Holy Ghost in a dove. An overall history of human symbolism would be necessary to establish how far and under what circumstances a transformation of the sacred symbol itself occurs through influences from the outside—that is to say, from the arts, or from their pressure.

Public and Industrial Buildings

In this area modern architecture has been exceptionally active and innumerable new spatial designs have been conceived and carried out. Within this category the nineteenth century had relatively few inhibiting prejudices—at any rate where the technological aspects of the construction were concerned. Furthermore, at the beginning of the twentieth century it was no longer a problem to jettison the sham facade; as a matter of fact, in some of the older functional buildings one could already see the beginnings

Hans Schwippert
Houses of Parliament, Bonn

of today's forms. Generally speaking though, new industrial buildings and styles were accepted more or less as a necessary evil; the notion still prevailed that only forms created by hand could be beautiful. However, after Van de Velde, and above all after the Bauhaus, a fundamental change took place. The industrial building was suddenly admired; in some cases the function as such and material in its original form were given an almost metaphysical value. In a movement contrary to the nineteenth-century idea, technology became a symbol of precision and perfection. Some of our finest examples of industrial architecture have arisen from this attitude.

Houses of Parliament, Bonn. Extension by Hans Schwippert added to the Pedagogic Academy built in 1930

Bernhard Pfau
Glass Industry
Building,
Düsseldorf, 1951

Sep Ruf
Office Building of
the Bavarian
Deputies, Bonn,
1955–1956

Emanuel Lindner. Röntgen Institute, Osnabrück, 1949–1950

E. van der Lippe and H. Maurer. Administrative Building, Siemens and Halske, Munich, 1955–1956

At the same time a strong feeling of responsibility developed toward the beauties of nature and their conservation. In many cases the factory has by no means marred them, but unsolved problems of a hygienic and social nature remain—noise and pollution. Fortunately the architect believes, in Germany too, that production and the buildings in which it takes place should never be ends in themselves but should always serve **mankind**, directly or indirectly.

In 1909 Peter Behrens pioneered factory construction with his Turbine Plant. This was followed in 1912 by both his assembly plant for the Berlin AEG and his gas works in Frankfurt. In 1914 we have the Fagus

Bruno Paul. Sinn Department Store, Gelsenkirchen, 1927–1929

Paul Schwebes. Office Building, Berlin, circa 1956

Egon Eiermann. Merkur Department Store, Heilbronn, 1951

Factory and the Cologne Werkbund Factory, both by Gropius. Mendelsohn's hat factory in Luckenwalde (1923) was followed by Max Taut's important design for the Machine Tool Works Norma. At the same time, but from a quite different approach, Bartning designed the Berlin-Tempelhof Ceramic Works, and two years later Arthur Korn built a shoe factory near Magdeburg. A wealth of ideas circulated in Germany, all concerned with the building of factories. Most of them were steel-frame constructions.

Friedrich Lindau. Branch Post Office on the Fair Grounds, Hannover, circa 1950

Günther Gottwald and Gerhard Weber. Small Market Hall in Frankfurt am Main, 1953–1954

Otto Apel. Department Store in Frankfurt am Main, 1954–1955

Hetzelt and Hennemann. Municipal Swimming Pool in Wuppertal, 1957–1958

Horst Döhnert
Transportation Exposition, Munich, 1953

In those days quite a number of bold and spacious assembly plants were built in Germany. Here one could fall back on the great tradition of the railway station which had already spanned enormous spaces in the nineteenth century. With the electrification of railroads, these huge stations have become obsolete and are being replaced rapidly by platforms with roofs of concrete sheets that seem to float in space, on either side of the short supports in the center. Filling stations and garages–those new transportation structures, with their sweeping lines and flowing concrete construction–frequently have their own intrinsic beauty and by no means desecrate the landscape. On the other hand, architecture has not yet found an esthetically satisfactory standardization for certain industrial motifs–the gas tank and the single chimney, for example. But air-conditioning shafts for mines as well as some large silos are frequently constructed in

Hans Haertlein
Siemens Steel Works, Berlin,
1927

Van der Lippe
and Maurer
Siemens
Administration
Building,
Munich, 1956

Egon Eiermann. Textile Factory in Blumberg, 1951

"natural" forms that are esthetically pleasing in their monumentality. Contrary to the implications of literature–from Schopenhauer's *Aesthetik* to Peter Meyer's *Kunstgeschichte*–monumentality is not to be associated exclusively with time-honored historical styles.

Werner Weidner. Württemberg Metal Works in Geislingen, 1951

Dieter Oesterlen. Gas Station, Hannover, 1952

Paul Schneider-Esleben. Garage, Düsseldorf, 1952–1953

Maize Silo in Barby an der Elbe, 1923

The effect of the Third Reich on industrial architecture was not as damaging as it was on types of architecture in which historic tradition or a rigid classicism were overemphasized. The factories remained neutral preserves which did not have to be adapted to ideologies.

Fritz Schupp. Mining Company, Zollverein 12, near Essen

498

Fritz Schupp. Germania Plant, Marten, near Dortmund, 1954

Fritz Leonhardt
Television Tower, Stuttgart,
1954–1956

Paul Schneider-Esleben. Administration building, ARAG Insurance Company, Düsseldorf, 1966

After the Second World War, German industrial buildings became lighter and more elegant, for instance the Hebmüller Body Plant by Heinz Rasch (1950), the machine shop in Oeynhausen by Emanuel Lindner (1951), and the textile factory built by Egon Eiermann in the same year in Blumberg. Buildings in Braunschweig by F. W. Kraemer (for Franke and Heidecke, and for Voets) and Eiermann's research laboratories for the Technische Hochschule in Karlsruhe (1955) deserve mention. Although in many cases the massive low building was favored, in Marten, near Dortmund, the towers and slanting transportation ramps of the Germania Works rise boldly into the sky, an astounding complex of huge buildings with clinker brick walls.

In the last decade the trend has been away from a totally utilitarian pattern for the office building. An interesting effort was made with the administrative buildings of an insurance company in Düsseldorf, the ARAG. Here Paul Schneider-Esleben designed a structure with the stories receding upward. The result is a slanting profile. A wide, free staircase on the narrow side leads from floor to floor. The total effect is that of a Mexican pyramid. Schneider-Esleben received his inspiration from the "hill house," about which there has been a great deal of controversy lately.

Another interesting example of recent industrial architecture is Curt Siegel's iron foundry in Lohr. Here the architect's problem was improvement of ventilation; his solution resulted in a concrete shell and imaginatively ballooning airshafts, reminiscent of Gaudi. Their expressive forms are due to recent research on air currents.

Curt Siegel. Foundry Lohr, 1962

Curt Siegel. Foundry Lohr, 1962

NEW DIRECTIONS

The Deutsche Werkbund was founded more than fifty years ago. Its influential propagation of a standard of good form (from spoons to city planning) has given the German public an insight, at the least, into expressions that do more than merely fill social requirements. We now believe that we can recognize a well designed cup; we now know that a radio is not just a piece of decorative furniture but a useful instrument; we now realize that decent housing is not the privilege of a few but a requisite for all. Schools and hospitals, railway stations and garages, factories and office buildings have been designed in accordance with their purpose and can be regarded without contempt. And in the case of theaters and festival halls, the designs have occasionally gone beyond these minimum requirements of aesthetic acceptability.

But in the total picture of the formation of our aesthetic environment there have been regrettable failures of achievement and development. The workers' housing projects represented the first great effort of many communities to overcome the gigantic housing shortage of the postwar era. It was necessary to build, quickly and cheaply, new living quarters outside the old bombed-out centers of the cities. Huge areas adjacent to these centers were filled with ugly, four-storied rows, separated by a communal green space, but open at their ends to the roar of traffic. Houses disappeared from the centers of towns, displaced by offices, stores, garages and administration buildings. The rapid industrial upsurge favored the automobile industry especially, to such an extent that traffic wholly transformed the appearance of our cities. Traffic streamed into them, destroying old squares, breaking up stylistically and functionally homogeneous districts, and spilling over with noise and stench into peaceful neighborhoods, despite all efforts to channel this eternal flow.

Medieval cities have frequently been turned into conveyer belts, thoroughfares for long distance traffic. Formerly beautiful street markets are now dumps for chrome and tin. It is no wonder that the pressure for country homes grows continuously. Laws protect the recreation areas of our countryside from private real estate operations but they do not prevent airfields from taking much of the remaining free land.

Not only the traffic but also rapid industrial development makes living in the cities a problem. Chemical plants poison the air, factories pollute the streams, and constructions for the disposal of sewage tower on the periphery of countless towns and villages. While city planners and traffic strategists remodel the metropolis and dream of new and better ones, the distress of its inhabitants increases, publicly expressed in pamphlets and articles. The psychologist Alexander Mitscherlich describes the "inhospitality of our cities"; the writer Gody Suter apostrophizes the big cities as "playgrounds for strategists of traffic chaos."

Meanwhile, the Deutsche Werkbund has designated itself pacemaker for this new universal criticism. "Good form" has been relegated to a minor position in its program; instead, "land destruction" is the term that crops up everywhere. Sometimes the protests break through the walls of the lobbyists and even reach the legislators.

An effort is being made to organize our space supra-regionally, to establish area-wide construction plans, and to promulgate laws which will arrest the further despoliation of our landscape. Sociologists, industrial experts and city planners meet to discuss the future structure of our cities. Such supra-regional planning is, however, difficult to bring to realization–especially as long as no law exists that would give public authorities the right to control the land and living areas, and that would also forbid private speculation with these public resources. Still, state-supported housing developments have at least achieved a status beyond that of "necessary evil." Such large-scale developments as the Northwest City in Frankfurt or the Mark quarter in Berlin are successful efforts to make the city human and habitable once again.

There is also a trend which makes it difficult to determine the future appearance of the city, for changes in the structure of industries are creating a situation which raises some doubt about the necessity for dense population centers. The factories of the future will no longer need an army of workers, whereas the so-called tertiary sector, namely the service industries, will need increasing numbers. The administration of factory or service industry is not, however, inevitably tied to the city; above all it should not be established in the city center. If such policies were followed, it is conceivable that living in the center of the city might again become possible.

Not only is the socio-economic industrial structure of the city changing, but also the utilization of its rural areas. Germany will most probably abandon a third of her land devoted to agriculture, for its further development would be uneconomic. What will happen to this land, what will become of the villages? Will not this development render re-possession of the cities for living of doubtful value if unused fields and empty villages are abundantly available? Possibly it will favor the emigration of the administrative services to the countryside.

In the face of these great problems of space organization and city planning, the question of aesthetically "absolute" or functional architectural types assumes secondary importance (although the new theater in Sydney revived this question, and aroused great excitement even in Germany).

The possibility of a "mobile" architecture, reinforced–practically speaking–by new building materials, is also much discussed. It would cease to be a theoretical problem the moment a Federated Europe came into being, for a federation would encourage a general mobility of its peoples.

Never before have *all* problems of future architectural practice been so open. They are becoming ever more complicated for a densely populated land like Germany, a nation which would like to preserve the appearance of its historic settlements, its smaller cities and its villages. The attainment of a balance between the preservation of historic monuments, the protection of the landscape and the realization of the necessary industrial changes appears to be the main task of the immediate future.

*

In closing I would like the reader to consider a question that was asked frequently at the turn of the nineteenth century and may be applied to all changes of style–when are we dealing with true progress and when has a style simply changed ? Twentieth century architecture as a utilitarian art form, in spite of its many failings, has definitely shown progress when compared with the hundred years that went before. When applied to painting and sculpture the question is more difficult to answer. Here the desire to be objective conflicts with the difficulties of theoretical cognition which confront all writers of intellectual history when faced with a scientific judgment of values.

Roman numerals refer to text, italics to figures.

Vowels modified by an umlaut are alphabetized as if spelled ae, oe and ue.

COLOR PLATES

(Reference to black and white illustrations appear in the Index under the artist's name; architecture is also listed by city.)

PHOTOGRAPH SOURCES

514

Stoedtner, Franz Dr., Düsseldorf 23 upper, 29, 42, 43, 67, 71 upper, center and lower, 132, 320 upper, 321 upper, 327, 335 upper, 399, 403, 411, 413 lower, 416 lower, 423, 424, 425, 426 upper, 428, 430, 433, 438, 445, 446, 447 upper, 449 upper and lower right, 450, 464 upper, 471, 479 left, 491 upper, 498 upper
Stock, H., Offenbach 472 lower
Strothjohann, Rita, Munich 354, 355
Studly, A., New York 81 upper
Sunami, Soichi 92
Sühwold, Cologne 460 lower
Thiemann, Elsa, Berlin-Neukölln 225 upper
Thomas, Galerie, Munich 306
Thudichum, Fritz, Munich 443, 490 lower
Troeger, Eberhard, Hamburg 441 upper, 468 lower, 492 upper, 496 upper

Ullstein-Bilderdienst, Berlin 462
Umbo, Hannover 134
Volkart, Stuttgart 294
Vondran, Elfriede, Munich 454 lower
Wagner, Hans, Hannover 472 upper
Warncke, Thea, Hamburg 218
Weber, Cologne 475
Weinhold, Kurt, Calw, Württemberg 207 upper
Werthern, Dietrich v., Munich 187 upper
Widmer, Dietrich, Basel 350 upper
Windstosser, Ludwig, Stuttgart 466 lower
Woelfle, Senta, Munich 187 lower
Wolff Tritschler, Frankfurt 344 right
Woscidlo, W., Frankfurt 452 upper
Wunderlich, Paul, Hamburg 302 lower

The reproductions of some of the illustrations were made from the magazine *Die Kunst und das schöne Heim.*

Permission to reproduce color plates IV–VII was granted by the Stuttgarter Kunstkabinett, Roman Norbert Ketterer. For some of the illustrations in color the blocks were kindly lent by the artists and by: Buchheim-Verlag, Feldafing/Obb., Plate V; Woldemar-Klein-Verlag, Baden-Baden, Plate XI; Dieter Keller, Stuttgart and Rembrandt-Verlag, Berlin, Plate XIV; *Das Herrenjournal*, Berlin, Plate XXIII; Gallery Müller, Stuttgart, Plate XL. All other plates were reproduced from the original in our own graphic arts shop.

The pictorial material for this book was assembled by the author and, for works executed within the last decade, by Juliane Roh.